GTG Kennedy – Yo one change
maker from another. Equality
is possible. Dixon

MISSION POSSIBLE

THE STORY OF REPEALING DON'T ASK, DON'T TELL

C. DIXON OSBURN

Printed and bound in the United States of America
Hardback ISBN: 978-1-7374824-0-6
Paperback ISBN: 978-1-7374824-1-3
eBook ISBN: 978-1-7374824-2-0

Book design by Stefan Merour

TO JEREMY

TABLE OF CONTENTS

ENDING MURDER AND HARASSMENT

GAME CHANGERS

ENDING DON'T ASK, DON'T TELL

EPILOGUE

PREFACE

M*ission Possible* is a behind-the-scenes account of how "Don't ask, don't tell" was repealed—from July 19, 1993, when President Bill Clinton announced the policy, to September 20, 2011, when President Barack Obama, Secretary of Defense Robert Gates, and Admiral Mike Mullen, chairman of the Joint Chiefs of Staff, certified to Congress that implementing repeal of the policy would have no effect on military readiness, military effectiveness, unit cohesion, or recruiting and retention.

I was a co-founder, with Michelle Benecke, of Servicemembers Legal Defense Network, the organization that led the effort to repeal "Don't ask, don't tell." This is the story of how we achieved repeal. It combines LGBT history, political strategy, and movement-building through the personal lens of a frontline advocate.

Mission Possible is extensively based on open-source materials. I also relied on my archives of SLDN's strategy blueprints, stakeholder reports, and other materials, as well as my copious notes. I conducted primary interviews with certain individuals to fill in gaps in my notes and knowledge. I use dialogue in the book to give the reader a fly-on-the-wall experience of our conversations with clients, Pentagon leaders, members of Congress, White House officials, and others. These sections are not from transcripts or recordings; they are reconstructed from memory and evoke the truth of the moment as I experienced it.

I wrote *Mission Possible* to provide a fuller account of the history and strategy behind the repeal of "Don't ask, don't tell." In his book *Conduct Unbecoming: Lesbians and Gays in the U.S. Military*, award-winning journalist Randy Shilts describes the experience of lesbian, gay, and bisexual service members from Vietnam to the Persian Gulf War. *Coming Out Under Fire*, by Alan Bérubé, looks at the lives of gay service members in World War II. *Mission Possible* explains not only the harrowing ordeals confronted by our clients under "Don't ask, don't tell," but how we, against all odds, convinced a nation that the law should be repealed.

C. Dixon Osburn
September 2021

THE
BEGINNING

CHAPTER 1

MY BIRTHDAY

I sat on a brown leather sofa in the living room of our brick rowhouse in Georgetown, watching C-SPAN, tears streaming down my face. That's not a typical reaction when watching C-SPAN. On a Saturday. The week before Christmas. But this day was different.

It was December 18, 2010—my birthday. Majority Leader Harry Reid had called the Senate in on a Saturday (a rare occurrence, especially in a lame-duck session) to vote on the repeal of "Don't ask, don't tell"—my life's mission.

I had co-founded the Servicemembers Legal Defense Network (SLDN) with Michelle Benecke in August 1993 to overturn what was, at its core, the ban on gay[1] service members that President Bill Clinton had so disastrously wrought the previous month. Seventeen years later, as the votes were being cast, I thought, "Congress, you cannot fail me on my birthday."

The outcome was far from certain. While a majority of law-makers in both houses of Congress supported repeal, Republican Senator John McCain, who was probably the best-known military veteran on Capitol Hill, had already successfully filibustered a vote on "Don't ask, don't tell" repeal—twice. On this day, he tried again.

"We're in two wars, and I believe that right now would not be the right time to repeal it," he said. "That's my position, and I will hold it."[2]

His concerns were supported in part by the chiefs of the Army, the Air Force, and the Marine Corps, all of whom had testified two weeks before that now was not the time to change. The Marine Corps' commandant, General James Amos, had said, "If you go up to Bethesda [Naval] hospital ... Marines are up there with no legs, none. We've got Marines at Walter Reed [Army Medical Center] with no limbs. ... I've got Marines that came back to me as their commandant and said, 'We have concerns.' So if they have concerns, I do too. It's as simple as that."[3] Gay service members were an improvised explosive device, hidden and deadly to straight service members who stepped on them.

On the other side, in support of repeal, were the chairman of the Joint Chiefs of Staff, Admiral Mike Mullen; the chief of naval operations, Admiral Gary Roughead; the commandant of the Coast Guard, Admiral Bob Papp; Secretary of Defense Robert Gates; and the commander in chief, President Barack Obama.

The first vote was to determine if at least 60 senators would vote for cloture, thereby ending McCain's filibuster. The Democrats held the majority in the Senate with 56 votes, but breaking a filibuster required 60 votes. The chamber's two independents—Joseph Lieberman of Connecticut and Bernie Sanders of Vermont—caucused with the Democrats, bringing the tally to 58 senators for repeal if the Democratic side held firm. But if the vote stuck to party lines, the 42 Republicans were more than enough to block consideration of the bill.

Moreover, the Democrats couldn't count on all 58 votes. West Virginia's Joseph Manchin, winner of a special election the month before to fill the seat left vacant by the death of Robert Byrd, was waffling. He had voted no on an earlier vote to invoke cloture, but he also signaled that "Don't ask, don't tell" should be repealed at some point. James Webb of Virginia, a former secretary of the Navy, raised a possible deal-breaker in an eleventh-hour letter to Gates on December 17.[4] Ron Wyden, a staunch supporter of repeal, was in Oregon for prostate cancer treatment, and it was unknown whether he could return to Washington for the vote.[5] To defeat the filibuster, the Democrats might need five Republicans to break ranks.

Republican Susan Collins was a co-sponsor of the Don't Ask, Don't Tell Repeal Act, but she had sided with McCain in September on the first vote to block consideration of the bill.[6] Lisa Murkowski, Olympia Snowe, Mark Kirk,[7] and Scott Brown[8] had signaled support for repeal after the Pentagon published a study on November 30 concluding that it could implement "Don't ask, don't tell" repeal without harming military readiness, but they weren't co-sponsors of the bill. Murkowski and Brown had voted against cloture during a second filibuster on the repeal legislation just nine days before,[9] calling their votes today into doubt. Kirk, like Manchin, was new to the Senate, having also won a special election in November.

7

I shifted nervously on the sofa. I glanced down and back up to the television screen like a nervous parent watching their child at a piano recital, hoping they wouldn't mess up.

During breaks in the action, I rushed upstairs to cook—the only reason that I wasn't in the Senate gallery to watch the vote live. I was making dinner for 75 friends who were coming over that evening to celebrate my birthday. I had developed this crazy habit of catering my own birthdays for way too many people—a tradition that left me exhilarated for days before in the planning and exhausted for days after from the execution. I was roasting a 10-pound salmon topped with a homemade pesto, serving it with a pan-fried corn and tomato salad and a Roman dish of sliced fennel, white mushroom, parmesan, extra virgin olive oil, and lemon juice. We had three cases of cava chilling. My apron was stained with pesto and tears.

This was it. If the Senate didn't repeal "Don't ask, don't tell" in 2010, it would still be the law of the land today. As we now know, the Republicans controlled one or both chambers of Congress from 2011 to 2020, and the Republican majority did not support repeal.

Stacy Vasquez—a 12-year Army veteran, one of the Army's top recruiters before she was discharged under "Don't ask, don't tell," a former SLDN client, SLDN staff member, and plaintiff in an unsuccessful lawsuit challenging the law—captured what was at stake:

"I'm nervous about what's going to happen tomorrow," she told *The Washington Post* the day before the vote.[10] "I'm personally nervous because this isn't process and procedure to me. It's not just a vote. This is my life. ... This is what I was called to do; it's what I want to do; it's what I'm inspired to do."

8

The Don't Ask, Don't Tell Repeal Act did not automatically repeal "Don't ask, don't tell." It put into place a process to repeal the law once the president, the secretary of defense, and the chairman of the Joint Chiefs certified to the Senate and House Armed Services Committees that they had reviewed a Pentagon study on how to repeal the law and could assure those panels that repeal would not degrade military readiness. Despite the precatory language, everyone understood that a vote for the bill was a vote to end "Don't ask, don't tell."

I listened for key Republicans. Brown and Collins voted to invoke cloture and defeat the filibuster. John Ensign, a possible swing vote, voted no; earlier that day he had said, "We've got a lot of stuff to do. We've got to be focusing on jobs right now."[11]

The knot in my stomach grew tighter. Lindsey Graham, a Republican, voted no. (One always hopes that he will display greater moral courage than he does.) Manchin voted no, meaning that we lost a key Democratic vote. Then Kirk, Murkowski, and Snowe voted yes, as did another Republican, George Voinovich—which was a surprise to some. Despite his cancer, Wyden flew in from Oregon to vote yes.

The motion to invoke cloture passed, 63-33.

My shoulders shook. I sobbed with joy and relief. We had won.

The Senate moved from the procedural vote to the substantive vote on the Don't Ask, Don't Tell Repeal Act. Only a simple majority was needed to pass the bill, so victory was 99.9% guaranteed, but three senators changed their votes from the way they had voted on cloture.

Manchin chose not to vote. (Later, at the Atlantic Ideas Festival, he would admit to MSNBC's Rachel Maddow and *The*

Atlantic's Steve Clemons that his decision not to vote for repeal was a mistake.)

Significantly, two Republicans who had voted no on cloture voted yes on repeal—Ensign, whom we had hoped for,[12] and Richard Burr, whose support we did not expect.

"Given the generational transition that has taken place in our nation, I feel that this policy is outdated," Burr said in a statement released after the vote.[13] He questioned the timing, but added that "repealing Don't Ask Don't Tell is the right thing to do."

Voinovich, who had voted in favor of cloture and voted for repeal, said, "[I]f we know that they are qualified, then we ought not to have them lying [about] who they are [under] 'Don't ask, don't tell.' It just is inconsistent with common sense."[14]

In the end, eight Republicans joined all but one Democrat in voting for gays to serve openly in the armed forces.

I turned to my partner and future husband, Jeremy, and said, with tears in my eyes, "I think we are going to have a few more people here tonight for the party." Sure enough, hundreds arrived, overflowing the narrow halls and stairs of our home. As I stood on a catwalk that separated the kitchen and dining room and over-looked the living area on the ground floor, I was asked to make a few remarks.

"Senator McCain said today that there will be high-fives in the salons of Georgetown if 'Don't ask, don't tell' is repealed," I said. "Yes, sir. On that you are correct!" The crowd cheered.

"Tonight, we celebrate. Michelle and I started SLDN in 1993. I remember the calls at all hours of the day, from every base and installation around the world. The calls from young men and women who were scared and frightened. Who were hounded and harassed. Who only wanted to serve our country, but were denied that opportunity because of 'Don't ask, don't tell.' Today, no more. Today, we are free."

The cheers again rang out. The three cases of cava disappeared, and friends replenished the bubbles with several more cases that night.

The repeal of "Don't ask, don't tell" in December 2010 marks one of the most significant civil rights achievements of our generation. It was the first time that Congress had passed legislation embracing equality for lesbian, gay, and bisexual Americans. It stands as a stunning reversal of the legislative ban on gays in the military implemented just 17 years before.

How did our country and our military move from opposing gays in the military in 1993 to overwhelming support in 2010? What convinced senior leaders like General Colin Powell, Admiral Mike Mullen, General David Petraeus, General Wesley Clark, and General John Shalikashvili to support gay troops? What galvanized two retired generals and a retired admiral to come out as gay? How did my small, scrappy, entrepreneurial organization, the Servicemembers Legal Defense Network, manage to win on an issue that had been abandoned by other leading civil rights organizations and was declared dead in 1993?

This book examines the arc of justice from 1993 to 2010 from the front lines of the battle. It takes us deep into the history of those 17 years. It tells the stories of those caught in the crosshairs of the gay ban—how their lives were ripped apart, and how their stories changed public opinion. It reveals what was said in the Pentagon meetings that paved the way, and how we won allies. It discusses our victories and setbacks that took us from the arms of grieving parents in Kansas City to clandestine meetings at a nail salon. It all leads to a heart-stopping endgame in the final months of 2010—in the courts, on the streets, and in Congress—that led to the final repeal of "Don't ask, don't tell" on my birthday.

One of my most cherished tributes came from Ben Dillingham, a Vietnam veteran from San Diego: "This Marine would willingly follow you in attacking any hill." Repealing "Don't ask, don't tell" wasn't just a hill; it was a mountain, and SLDN's co-founder, Michelle Benecke, and I, with deep humility, could not have done it without the support of many battalions. Here is how it started.

CHAPTER 2

IF THESE WALLS COULD WEEP

On July 19, 1993, I sat on a hard-edged folding chair in a wood-paneled conference room at the storied Religious Action Center for Reform Judaism to watch President Bill Clinton announce on television his new policy on gays in the military. The location begged for history to be made again: The Civil Rights Act of 1964 and the Voting Rights Act of 1965 had been drafted in that same room.

Gay Americans had voted overwhelmingly for Clinton the previous November; he had actively courted our votes and our money. At the center of the circle was David Mixner, a charismatic, preacher-voiced activist who had introduced Clinton, then the governor of Arkansas, to an influential group of LGBT donors in Los Angeles and pledged to raise millions for his campaign.[15] Clinton asked how he could help. David's reply: He could get rid of the ban on gays in the military with the stroke of a pen, by executive order.

Clinton agreed. Gay Americans were part of the American family, he said—the first such comment from a major-party presidential candidate, and a balm for deep wounds long suffered. Jimmy Carter's administration had drafted the ban we were now trying to revoke. Ronald Reagan had ignored us and the AIDS epidemic that ravaged the nation. George H.W. Bush vigorously courted the burgeoning social conservative movement that sought to enshrine anti-gay discrimination into law through ballot initiatives.

Clinton, by contrast, pledged to end the discharges, courts-martial, and harassment of patriotic gay Americans serving in our armed forces. His pledge was a concrete step for equality that he could deliver. We had never had an advocate-in-chief. Our hopes were high as he took office in January. Our hopes were dashed six months later.

Watching with me in the Religious Action Center conference room were staff and volunteers of the Campaign for Military Service,[16] a civil rights coalition hastily formed in February by David and other leading advocates to support Clinton's pledge to end the ban on gays in the military. The effort was necessary because Republican Bob Dole, the Senate minority leader, and Democrat Sam Nunn, the powerful chairman of the Senate Armed Services Committee (whose name had been floated, but passed over, for secretary of defense), had begun an immediate counteroffensive to squash repeal, even before Clinton had made a move to issue an executive order.

LGBT and civil rights leaders agreed to form the coalition to coordinate efforts and launch an unprecedented fundraising effort to secure victory. Among the members were the Human Rights

Campaign, the National Gay & Lesbian Task Force, the Lambda Legal Defense and Education Fund, People For the American Way, and the American Civil Liberties Union. It raised over $1 million in less than six months—a record effort for the LGBT community. The Religious Action Center for Reform Judaism, headquartered in a stately red brick house with mahogany floors and paneling on Massachusetts Avenue, was our home—and an integral partner.

Sitting in the room were many of the best and brightest civil rights leaders of the day. Tom Stoddard led the Campaign for Military Service. He had previously transformed Lambda Legal Defense and Education Fund into a vital impact litigation organization that won the first HIV discrimination case in 1982 and ended anti-gay discrimination in housing, employment, and public accommodations in New York City in 1986.[17] His life was cut tragically short by AIDS years later, at age 48.

One of my favorite memories of Tom was his story on debate preparation. He said that when he debated Moral Majority founder Jerry Falwell on *Nightline* in the late 1980s, he reached over and touched Falwell's arm. "You know that's not true," he said. Simply touching Falwell's arm so discombobulated the anti-gay minister that he fumbled through the rest of the interview.

Fred Hochberg, a brusque yet affable New Yorker, helped lead fundraising and strategy. He later became head of the Small Business Administration in the Clinton administration, dean of The New School's Milano School of Management and Urban Policy, and president and chairman of the Export-Import Bank under President Obama.

Chai Feldblum, a wise-cracking intellectual, was chief legal counsel. She was a leading architect of the Americans with

Disabilities Act and a former professor of mine at Georgetown University's law school. She taught me how to pound the facts when the law was not on our side, and even in the 1990s, the law was not on the side of LGBT equality. We had to craft the statutes in Congress and develop the jurisprudence in the courts to chart the course for equality. Chai was later appointed by President Obama as a member of the Equal Employment Opportunity Commission and was a chief strategist that led to a Supreme Court decision ending employment discrimination against LGBT Americans in 2020.[18]

I was just a lowly volunteer at the Campaign for Military Service, recently graduated from Georgetown with a law degree and an MBA, but my life was about to change dramatically.

The television networks carried President Clinton's afternoon address, the culmination of a six-month firefight. The House and the Senate had held multiple hearings on gays in the military. Norman Schwarzkopf, the Army general who had led coalition forces in the Gulf War and was popularly known as "Stormin' Norman," warned about the threat gay Americans posed to unit cohesion. Colonel Margarethe Cammermeyer, a decorated Army nurse who had served in Vietnam, was asked by Republican senator John Warner, a former Navy secretary, if she couldn't just be quiet about being a lesbian as part of her patriotic duty to country. General Colin Powell, chairman of the Joint Chiefs of Staff, stood on the steps of the Pentagon, recounting the number of calls the Pentagon had received countenancing against any change to the ban. Senator Nunn visited Norfolk, Virginia, and, as the cameras rolled, asked a hapless sailor whether he would *really* want to share bunks with a homosexual. General Carl E. Mundy Jr., the

Marine Corps commandant, circulated a video titled "The Gay Agenda" to the Joint Chiefs and his fellow marines.[19] Politicking in fear makes bad policy.

Every day for six months, newspapers, radio, and television carried stories about the great debate gripping the nation. Never before had gay Americans been featured so prominently during dinner table conversations, and that was a great thing. The policy that resulted from the debate was not.

Flanked by the Joint Chiefs of Staff, Clinton addressed the nation from National Defense University, at Fort McNair, before an audience of military officers. Not a single representative from the LGBT community was invited. The absence of the very people whose lives were at stake should have been a red flag that what the president was about to announce was not a new era of civil rights, but the press didn't notice.

We watched as Clinton announced that gay Americans could serve in the armed forces so long as they did not engage in "homosexual conduct." He asserted that the new directive on gays in the military "represents a real step forward," "a sensible balance," "a substantial advance," and "an honorable compromise."[20] If you had known nothing about the issue, you might have come away from the speech thinking that the long-standing ban on gays in the military had been lifted. It had not.

♦ ♦ ♦

"Don't ask, don't tell" contained the same prohibitions on gay service as the prior bans, which dated to World War II. A gay service member faced discharge if they stated that they were lesbian, gay or bisexual; engaged in physical contact with someone of the same sex for the purposes of sexual gratification; or married, or attempted to marry, someone of the same sex[21]—an act of foresight, since marriage equality would not be legal in some states for years to come, and would not be legal nationally until the Supreme Court so ruled in 2015, four and a half years after the Senate joined the House in repealing "Don't ask, don't tell."

"Don't ask, don't tell" allowed someone to be fired for being gay and punished someone for coming out. Service members could be separated from the military for coming out to anyone, anywhere, anytime, including their parents, friends, colleagues, clergy, or doctor. A "homosexual act" was so broadly defined that it included sex, holding hands, and hugging—unless you were straight.

A heterosexual service member could have sex with someone of the same gender and claim he was drunk and would never do it again, and he could be retained. Under what was called the "queen for a day" exception, he could even say he was gay, then say he was just kidding, and he could be retained. Only those who truly identified as gay faced discharge—even if they promised abstinence.

One of SLDN's early clients called and spoke with staff member Jean Podrasky. He asked, panicked: "I just had sex for the first time with another guy. Am I in trouble?"

"Don't tell your commander," Jean said. She wasn't a lawyer, and told him so, but it was sound advice.

He called Jean the next day. "I did it again. Am I in trouble now?"

"Oy," Jean later said to me, with a nervous chuckle.

What was supposed to make "Don't ask, don't tell" an improvement over prior bans were guidelines that provided some freedom for gay service members and reined in investigative abuses of the past. The new rules allowed gay service members to go to gay bars, read *The Advocate* and other gay-oriented publications, join a gay sports league or chorus, or march in a gay pride parade, and those activities in and of themselves were not evidence that could be used to discharge someone. (During the Senate Armed Services Committee hearing, Jamie Gorelick, the Defense Department's general counsel, answered "yes" when asked if this might be considered "a small measure of privacy.")[22] But if someone asked you if you were gay, having seen you drinking, reading, or marching, and you said you were, that act of coming out was a basis for discharge. The books and posters could be used as corroborating evidence.

The "Don't ask, don't tell" guidelines also contained a multitude of investigative limits—what came to be known as "don't pursue." We called the law at the outset "Don't ask, don't tell, don't pursue" to emphasize the promise to not witch-hunt.

Powell told the Senate Armed Services Committee: "We will not ask, we will not witch-hunt, we will not seek to learn orientation,"[23] adding that there would "be due respect for the privacy rights of all service members." Nunn said that the policy would not condone "sex squads,"[24] confirming that new rules discouraged charging service members with violating Article 125 of the Uniform Code of Military Justice, which made it a crime for any service member, straight or gay, to engage in oral or anal sex.

The primary concession to gays serving our nation was "don't ask"—the promise that gay service members would not be asked to disclose their sexual orientation—but it was a myth that few people understood at the time. We are asked about our sexual orientation every day, in questions about our families, whom we're dating, our plans for the weekend. People want to know about the people in our photos, and our favorite musicians and films.

Under "Don't ask, don't tell," gays had to change the pronouns of their partners and invent heterosexual lives, or face discharge for being honest about who they are. As Diane H. Mazur, a law professor and a former Air Force officer, wrote in 2000, the "Don't ask, don't tell" policy "requires service members to continually conceal everyday information about what they do, where they go, and whom they see, far exceeding the scope of information more directly associated with intimate behavior. To keep secret the latter is difficult enough; to keep secret the former is to change the catch phrase of the policy to 'Don't Ask, Don't Tell, Lie Consistently.'"[25]

At a conference in Virginia several years later, Chai Feldblum called "Don't ask, don't tell" the "you can be gay, but I have a headache forever" policy. Actually, you couldn't even tell someone why you had a headache ... forever. Gays in the military required a lifetime supply of Advil.

The "Don't ask, don't tell" guidelines also contained one gaping loophole: Evidence that the military had violated the letter or spirit of "Don't ask, don't tell"—that it had asked, pursued, or harassed service members who were or were perceived to be gay—could not be used to suppress evidence, because the guidelines created "no substantive or procedural rights" upon which a service member could challenge his or her discharge. It was the wink-and-a-nod provision, the "business as usual"/"lack of accountability" clause.

There was one other aspect to "Don't ask, don't tell" that ultimately made it a worse policy than before, despite the promises to not ask, pursue, or harass lesbian, gay, or bisexual service members. In November 1993, Congress passed, and President Clinton signed, legislation that codified "don't ask, don't tell" into law, but the statute contained none of the promised protections, other than ending the practice of asking recruits at accession whether they were gay—a promise that the Pentagon would uphold only spottily. By making "Don't ask, don't tell" a law, Congress removed the authority from future presidents to issue an executive order to repeal the ban or amend the regulations. The law went into effect in February 1994.

◆ ◆ ◆

After we heard Clinton's announcement, David Saperstein, the esteemed rabbi who led the Religious Action Center, offered a prayer, or lament, before those of us assembled in the conference room. Summoning the memories of the Civil Rights Act and the Voting Rights Act that were given life in that same room, he said, "If these walls had eyes and ears, they would weep for what they have heard."

We didn't have time to cry. The phones started ringing off the hook. Michelle Benecke and I answered the calls.

Michelle was a freshly minted Harvard-educated lawyer and former Army captain who electrifies any room she walks into. Her intellect, wit, and charm create an unmistakable magnetism that draws people to her. She was the lead military advisor for the Campaign for Military Service and legal counsel to the countless service members who had contacted the organization. An Army brat who loved to talk about walking the halls of the Pentagon with her dad, Michelle understood the military.

"This is great! We can come out!" said one excited soldier in a call to us.

"No, you can't," we said.

"Other sailors are calling me part of 'Clinton's Navy' and calling me 'faggot.' How do I get them to stop?" asked another.

"Tell your commander," we advised.

"But he's the one telling the sailors that fags shouldn't be in the Navy."

Another caller asked, "What do I do now? I have come out to several of my friends in the service because the president had said he would lift the ban. I wanted to support my commander in chief by showing guys that gays like me are serving with them. I feel so betrayed."

"Pray that your friends do not turn you in," I said. "If they do, though, we're here for you."

After I gave this reassurance to one service member, I felt a serious pang of misgiving. Were we promising something we could deliver?

The Campaign for Military Service had agreed to disband once a policy, for better or worse, was announced. If we stopped, where would these patriots turn for help? The president they had relied on to make them safer just dug them deeper into the trenches of discrimination.

CHAPTER 3

THE PHOENIX RISES

The Campaign for Military Service was no more. The coalition disbanded. I was surprised at how quickly it all ended. Michelle and I kept asking the campaign leaders: What was going to happen next? What was the after-action plan?

Some went on vacation. Others had to immediately pivot to fighting the anti-gay civil rights initiatives popping up in cities and states around the country. We asked whether any organization was going to continue the work with service members. We heard crickets.

Michelle and I were the last folks darkening the halls of the Religious Action Center as the phones kept ringing. Soon, we were told that the Religious Action Center needed the desks and rooms back. Late one night, she asked, "What are we going to do?"

We were faced with a stark reality. Neither the public nor Congress nor the Pentagon supported gays serving openly. No one, including the leading LGBT organizations, wanted to revisit the issue any time soon. We drafted and distributed a lengthy memo analyzing the contradictions and infirmities of "Don't ask, don't tell," but members of Congress, and the press, had moved on.

"It will take us 20 years to repeal 'Don't ask, don't tell,'" I said.

"That long?" she asked.

"Congress won't touch this again under Clinton."

"Mmmm." Michelle's brow furrowed.

"Assume he is reelected," I hypothesized. "That's eight years. Who knows who will succeed him? Assume it's an anti-gay Republican or that we haven't yet turned the momentum. That's another eight years. It will take a third president to do this."

That president was Barack Obama. It took 17 years, beating my prediction by three years. It didn't occur to me at the time that 20 years was light speed for civil rights.

We faced a daunting task, but my view was that once you get your foot in the door, don't pull out; push harder. Michelle and I crossed the street to the Jockey Club for a glass of chardonnay—a common occurrence during those years. Sinking into the leather club chairs, we discussed how we could help LGBT troops and pave the way for ultimate repeal of "Don't ask, don't tell."

Michelle had a vision. I went home and drafted our business plan.

The next morning, I presented it to Michelle. "Holy crap!" she said, laughing heartily. "I'm glad you went to business school." The fight for gays in the military would continue.

◆ ◆ ◆

We called ourselves the Servicemembers Legal Defense Network. It was a mouthful. Bob Hattoy, an irrepressibly ebullient guy and the first openly gay man with HIV to address the Democratic National Convention, called us "SLDN. Celine Dion." Like Tom Stoddard, he left our world too soon.

We decided that we could not use the words "lesbian," "gay," or "bisexual" in our name because we didn't want the fact that a service member had called us to be used against them as a basis for discharge. We explicitly said that we helped everyone hurt by "Don't ask, don't tell," including straight service members who were perceived to be gay or were accused of being gay as a means of retaliation. "Don't ask, don't tell" was frequently used as a tool of vengeance. Hence, in the years that followed, we insisted in call after call with commanders that no one should infer a person's sexual orientation or gender identity simply because that person had contacted us.

Out of respect for all services, we also couldn't limit our name to one branch. We couldn't call ourselves the Soldiers Defense Network, because it could offend—or worse, discourage—sailors, airmen, marines, and coastguardsmen from calling. If you thought SLDN was a mouthful, how about "Soldiers, Sailors, Airmen, Marines, and Coastguardsmen Legal Defense Network"?

We also decided to call ourselves a "network," as Michelle and I would have to rely on our networks of law school friends to find pro bono counsel—lawyers who would assist us at no charge—in those early days. It was a good thing that she and I had attended the two largest law schools in the country—Harvard and Georgetown, respectively—and that we had friends who were so generously willing to assist. Despite our youth, our positions as executive directors of an organization gave us access to the top partners at law firms, and we gladly provided the bridge between those partners and our friends at their firms who wanted to help us.

Audrey Denson designed our logo: a white eagle's head in profile against a blue background. Five stars, the highest rank in the armed forces, and a rank given only during a time of war, haloed the eagle. We proudly wore the logo as a pin on our coat collars, and it turned heads as we walked the halls of the Pentagon.

SLDN's vision, formally adopted in 2001, was "Freedom to Serve." It spoke to the freedom to be one's true self, the freedom to serve our nation, and the constitutional freedoms our men and women in uniform take an oath to defend. Freedom to serve was our inspirational call to action.

Our mission was to repeal "Don't ask, don't tell," though it was much more than that. Our earliest quarterly reports described SLDN as "the sole legal aid and watchdog organization for men and women harmed by the 'Don't ask, don't tell, don't pursue' policy and the HIV ban." By our 1996 annual report, we had clarified our mission as "ending witch hunts, death threats, imprisonment, lesbian-baiting, and other discriminatory actions against men and women in the military harmed by 'Don't ask, don't tell, don't pursue' and related policies through direct legal assistance, watchdog activities, policy work, and litigation support." With a new strategic plan in 2001, we defined our mission as a "legal services, watchdog, and policy organization dedicated to ending discrimination against and harassment of military personnel affected by 'Don't ask, don't tell' and related forms of discrimination."

Our goals made clear what we meant by ending discrimination and harassment. Our first and primary goal was to "lift the ban" preventing gays, lesbians, and bisexuals from serving openly and honestly in the military. The second goal was to protect service members from harassment based on perceived sexual orientation or gender identity. Third, we advocated for policies and practices that improved the lives of service members, short of full repeal. Last, we pledged to support service member and veteran pride as lesbian, gay, and bisexual persons by building community and grass roots.

SLDN employed three main tools to achieve our mission—legal, political, and educational. There were only two avenues to repeal "Don't ask, don't tell": through the courts or through congressional action. We pursued both.

In the courts, we developed our own litigation and supported other cases through amicus (friend of the court) briefs that provided judges with information about the implementation of the law, based on our clients' experiences. In 1993, there was some optimism that the Supreme Court might find "Don't ask, don't tell" unconstitutional, since lower courts had found the prior ban unconstitutional or impractical in application. The current ban was, in all material respects, the same. My gut, however, told me that we would have to ultimately convince Congress to repeal "Don't ask, don't tell" because the courts too frequently deferred to the military, allowing them to punt on the constitutional questions raised by the federal government's discrimination against lesbian, gay, and bisexual service members.

To convince Congress to repeal "Don't ask, don't tell," we needed to lay the groundwork. Few who joined the repeal fight in the final years of the policy truly understood what had been done to make it possible. As SLDN launched in 1993, we couldn't argue that Congress should repeal the law in 1994. The ban was the law for now. We had to build our case against "Don't ask, don't tell" with stories and data from the field demonstrating how the law—and not gay Americans—undermined unit cohesion and military readiness.

Providing pro bono legal aid to service members caught in the crosshairs of "Don't ask, don't tell" assisted both in the litigation and in advancing repeal by identifying stellar plaintiffs and amassing the needed data and stories. Pursuing political strategies, even those short of full repeal, provided educational moments that laid the foundation for repeal. Our education campaign ultimately galvanized public, military, and political opinion to support gays serving openly in the armed forces.

SLDN's battle plans were clear and straightforward. Implementing them wasn't. How do you start an organization with no money and no staff on a losing issue and engage in battle against the Pentagon, Congress, and public? Someone once asked me how I started SLDN. "Very naively," I replied.

◆◆◆

As Michelle and I stayed behind answering the frantic calls for help in the upstairs cubicles, the Religious Action Center again, but very politely, said that it would need to reclaim its offices. The only lifeline for gay service members was being cut. We needed a new home, and fast.

With no money and no paid staff, we found one at the National Veterans Legal Services Program (NVLSP) on S Street, above the

Townhouse Safeway in Washington's Dupont Circle neighborhood. NVLSP represented Vietnam veterans seeking recompense for exposure to Agent Orange. Ruth Eisenberg, who served on the board of the National Gay & Lesbian Task Force and worked at NVLSP, helped us get in the door. NVLSP generously donated space, computers, metal desks, and phones for our first four months to see if we could make a go of it. We cleared space in the library amid stacks of file boxes.

NVLSP's leader, David Addlestone, had defended one of the most famous gays in the military in the 1970s, Air Force Staff Sergeant Leonard Matlovich. Matlovich was the first openly gay American to appear on the cover of *Time* and be interviewed on *60 Minutes*. He is buried at Washington's Congressional Cemetery with an epitaph, "When I was in the military, they gave me a medal for killing two men and a discharge for loving one."[26] It was his court challenge that prompted the Carter administration to revise the gay ban to require discharge for patriots who engaged in statements, acts, or marriage that confirmed that they were gay—the same basis for discharge as "Don't ask, don't tell."

We incorporated SLDN in August 1993. At its inception, it was barebones-basement-entrepreneurial. We secured donated desks, chairs, and file cabinets from law firms. TechSoup donated software. Whenever we traveled in the first years, we slept on friends' sofas to save a dime.

We built almost everything from scratch. Michelle developed a legal intake process and a system for legal filing. We crafted organizational policies and protocols. We gratefully inherited a donor database from the Campaign for Military Service that provided the heart of our initial funding outreach.

We started with no money and two volunteers. I drafted a first-year budget of $200,000, out of which Michelle and I received $36,000 each in initial salary, singlehandedly dropping the average salary of first-year graduates that our alma maters love to boast about. I was amazed that I could write a fundraising letter to strangers and that they would send us checks.

Our budget doubled to $390,000 the next year. By 2000, just seven years into our existence (and the year Michelle moved on), our budget grew to $1.5 million, and we led a staff of 12. By the time I left SLDN in 2007, the budget had reached nearly $3 million, and 17 people were on staff.

I didn't think about the daunting nature of what Michelle and I were undertaking. I didn't think about the movement we would have to build and the growth we would have to cultivate. We just did it. And we had some fun along the way.

We threw "End the Witch Hunts" fundraisers at Halloween and auctioned off carved pumpkins, hoisted by service members. John Bowab, a theatrical and television director and producer whose credits included such diverse productions as *Mame* and *Ellen*, hosted an annual pool party at his home in the Hollywood hills. Sailors and marines drove up from San Diego and took turns flipping burgers. One year, *Out Magazine* listed it as one of the top 10 A-list parties in the country. We held dance parties on the USS *Midway* in San Diego and picnics on Treasure Island in San Francisco that coincided with the Blue Angels flyovers. In the Hamptons one year, celebrity chef Daniel Boulud made his famous foie gras burgers—gratis.

We never lost sight of our mission. To preserve the privacy of service members at our events, we required photographers to ask permission before taking any pictures, warning them that they had to be sure no one in the background was snapped inadvertently. We didn't want attending an SLDN event to be used as a basis for discharge.

One night, at a small event at an art gallery in Philadelphia, I approached a guy standing alone in the corner. I could tell he was nervous.

"Welcome," I said. "I run SLDN. What brought you here tonight?"

"I'm in the Air Force," he said.

"Thank you for your service. What do you do?"

"I'm an Air Force pilot," he said. "In fact, I just got back from Baghdad a couple of hours ago."

I said, "Wow! How are you still awake?"

He got quiet. He looked down to the floor, and then back up at me. "You know, I walked around the block three times before deciding to walk through the door tonight. I fly into Baghdad using night vision goggles because we fly in the dark to avoid enemy fire. I was more scared coming here tonight."

"We are here to support you."

As is typical with many entrepreneurs, hours and circumstances were never the issue. Michelle and I worked long and hard. Late afternoons, we would often go for runs in Rock Creek Park to let off steam. The daffodil runs in early spring were the best. We got stuck in our office elevator once and demanded that the elevator company patch us through to our scheduled meeting with pro bono lawyers working on a case.

Sometimes I would emerge from our office to get an iced mocha or agua fresca and wonder why there were so many people on the streets, only to realize it was already evening rush hour—and I would head back into the office for another three or four hours. One time I answered the phone and Trent Norris, a Harvard classmate of Michelle's who lived in San Francisco, stuttered, "Um, you're there?" I had lost track of time. It was midnight on a Sunday.

When working long hours, against all odds, a wry sense of humor helps. One time I was in San Diego, having Friday cocktails at a bar overlooking Balboa Park soon after "Don't ask, don't tell" had become law, and a sailor told me that guys on his ship had a name for me: "That fag."

"That's great," I said, laughing, imagining myself running down the beach like Marlo Thomas, flying a kite with my face on it, the new version of *That Girl.* I was also amazed to learn that I had become a topic of conversation at a military installation 3,000 miles away from Washington, among people who didn't know me, within months of starting SLDN. That meant we had touched a nerve—and that was a good thing.

◆ ◆ ◆

It is easy to understand why Michelle co-founded Servicemembers Legal Defense Network. She had attended the University of Virginia on a ROTC scholarship, then distinguished herself in the Army as one of the few women in a Patriot air defense artillery battery.[27] She faced possible discharge herself: She passed up a full scholarship to Harvard Law School, courtesy of the Army, because she couldn't return to military service with the sword of Damocles—the gay ban—hanging over her head.[28] She pledged then and there that she would take care of her troops. For her, it was deeply personal.

It took a decade for me to truly come to understand why I co-founded SLDN. Dr. Paul Boskind, an eminent psychiatrist, asked me once why I had made "Don't ask, don't tell" repeal a life mission. I am not a veteran. My dad had served in Korea. Several lines of my ancestors fought in the American Revolution.

Military service, though, was not a deeply embedded value in our family, as it was in Michelle's. Nor had I been a gay leader in college or graduate school when I volunteered at the Campaign for Military Service.

I met Paul in San Antonio, Texas, at an SLDN fundraiser. It was a warm fall evening under the live oaks. I told him what Michelle and I often told potential donors: that repeal of "Don't ask, don't tell" was essential to our liberty because "Don't ask, don't tell" was a federal law of discrimination, and how the federal government treats us sets the stage for all of our rights.

"That's not it," Paul said.

I told him that "Don't ask, don't tell" was the only law in the land that demanded that gay persons be fired from their jobs because of who we are and whom we love.

"That's not it," he said.

I persisted: "Denying military service to an entire class of Americans struck at the heart of what it means to be an American and to be a citizen."[29] In the infamous *Dred Scott* decision upholding segregation, the Supreme Court held that the denial of military service to African Americans buttressed the notion that they were not full citizens of the United States and were not deserving of equality.

"That's not it," he said. "Why are *you* doing this?"

I thought a moment and said something I had never said before. "Because I was beat up as a gay kid?"

He raised his finger in triumph. "Aha!"

Paul's intervention taught me to look inward, examine my life's experiences, and share them. I tend to be a very private person about my own challenges, upsets, and setbacks. It is those moments of adversity that can also serve as a great well of inspiration.

I believe in fairness, but I believe in it because I have been denied it. I grew up in Fort Worth, Texas, at a time when being gay was not a dinner table conversation. *The Fort Worth Star-Telegram* did not feature stories on gay rights, only the occasional item about a gay man being entrapped and arrested by the police. There was no mention of LGBT history in the textbooks, or classroom discussion of gay rights as human rights. To confirm what I was feeling, I had to ride my bike to the downtown public library and look up "homosexuality" on microfiche. It directed me to the psychiatry section. Being gay was classified as a mental illness.

I've been called "fag" many times. In the sixth grade, I was told not to stand like a girl. In the eighth grade, I was beaten up by a kid who hit me repeatedly with his gym bag while calling me names. The lock in the bag hurt. A guy threatened to attack Jeremy and me while we were holding hands in Rehoboth Beach, Delaware, a summer mecca for gays. I have been denied employment at a major law firm because I am gay. More recently, I was told that a senior colleague of mine at another organization had criticized a speech in which I came out, arguing that I should not conflate gay rights with human rights. My mother-in-law and my stepmother refused to come to my wedding.

After leaving SLDN, I was interviewing for a position with a major civil rights organization. The name partner of the search firm told me that while the organization was looking for diversity, being gay was, in his words, "no longer a big deal." It was a big deal for me.

Working on behalf of civil and human rights is one of the most incredible and humbling privileges one can have. Michelle and I took the nascent SLDN and settled in. We had our strategy. People were starting to donate. We were slowly hiring staff. The question now was whether we could prove our mettle.

BATTLE PLANS

CHAPTER 4

911 FOR SERVICE MEMBERS

How were service members going to find us? And what would we do if they did?

Scared, confused, shaken, and wary, the men and women trapped in the snares of "Don't ask, don't tell" came to us in droves. Some believed that we might be a front for a service's criminal investigative agency. One caller grilled me at the beginning of our call: "Who are you? What is your mission? Can you send me your incorporation documents? Who funds you? How can I trust you?" After I answered the questions, she said, "Okay. You're good. Can you help?"

Between the two of us, Michelle and I conducted 1,000 intakes from August 1993 to the end of 1995. In 2004 alone, we processed 1,025 intakes, but by then I had four staff attorneys assisting. On any given day, we had anywhere from 118 to 219 matters open. With stacks of folders piled high on our desks, we processed them as fast as we could. We acted with the lightning speed of a public defense attorney—ascertaining what had happened, procuring investigative reports, reviewing evidence, developing leads, interviewing witnesses, consulting with military lawyers if any had been tasked, intervening with commanders, seeking help of pro bono lawyers as needed, galvanizing members of Congress on behalf of their constituents, pushing and pressing any lever we could to get a good outcome for our client, and disrupting business as usual in the military's quest to oust gay service members. Michelle and I bounced case files off each other to make sure that the facts lined up and that we weren't missing something crucial.

We described our earliest legal strategy as "a fighting chance." We wanted to give service members a chance to live their lives with dignity and respect despite the new law as well as protect them from the worst outcomes pursued by overzealous or misguided commanders. Michelle described our aim as "us[ing] guerilla lawyering to problematize the implementation of DADT."[30] Maureen Keenan, an SLDN supporter, once told us, "As a lawyer and former Army officer, I am inspired by your innovative approach to individual cases." As Michelle and I sought to disrupt business as usual, we had a number of early successes.

In 1994, SLDN stopped a witch hunt at Pope Air Force Base, North Carolina, where a commander had reportedly asked for a list of all personnel who had contributed to gay and AIDS organizations through the Combined Federal Campaign. He was looking to unmask the lesbian, gay, and bisexual members at his base as the gay ban went into effect. He dropped his demand after our intervention.

In 1995, SLDN had a Navy discharge recommendation over-turned when we demonstrated that the evidence relied upon wasn't true.[31] In another case, I asked Hilary Rosen, the president of the Recording Industry Association of America, to convince George Stephanopoulos, a senior advisor to President Clinton, to stop the discharge of a lesbian soldier who had applied to become a White House Fellow.[32] The soldier had been outed by an admiral who sat on the review committee.

"Are you 100% sure of the facts and that you want me to call Stephanopoulos?" she asked. I was. She did. And he stopped it.

SLDN also successfully defended a client at court-martial, where he was being tried on the incredible allegation that he had solicited another service member for sex in front of 200 other service members.[33]

The Navy forced the retirement of a captain who had threat-ened not only discharge, but our client's life.[34] Accountability was a rare feat.

In 1996, we persuaded an Air Force commander to drop action against a client who told his psychologist that when he was a child, a man had abused him.[35] Air Force investigators, offen-sively, maintained that the psychologist's notes were evidence that the service member was gay and had engaged in gay sex.

In 1997, the Marine Corps disciplined a gunnery sergeant who had made repeated death threats against suspected gay service members on the internet.[36] At one base, a commander dropped all proceedings against one of our clients after concluding that allegations made by a prostitute/drug dealer were not credible.[37] The same person had made false allegations against other service members, but the service only pursued our client because of the allegation that he was gay. In another case, an Air Force commander dropped a case against our client based solely on information that he had visited a gay-related website.[38]

In 1998, we stopped the Army from discharging women who were seen hugging—alleged evidence of a "homosexual act," rather than the truth (one soldier was consoling the other).[39] The Marine Corps prosecuted four marines for lobbing a tear gas canister into Remingtons, a gay country-and-western nightclub in Washington.[40] We thwarted a witch hunt in the Coast Guard when an unnamed person reported seeing women hanging out at a private party and speculated that they were lesbians.[41] We secured a hardship discharge for a gay sailor so that he could take care of his partner.[42] We successfully defended before a discharge board a service member who was falsely accused of sodomy.[43]

In 1999, SLDN protected four women from a witch hunt in the Air Force.[44] A sergeant had asked them about their personal lives and questioned one of them in detail about her friendships with other women in her unit. The questioning started after an airman turned in a list of people whom he accused of being gay. We contacted the military defense attorney immediately; after quick and aggressive intervention, the matter was dropped. We stopped another fishing expedition against an Air Force staff sergeant.[45] Investigators had asked him to describe "where, when and with whom" he had had sex. In another case, we persuaded the Air Force to grant partial clemency to an airman after he was sentenced to seven months in prison for going AWOL from Moody Air Force Base in response to unbearable anti-gay harassment.[46]

The breadth of our reach and power of our outcomes reinforced our belief that SLDN was needed and could make a difference. One client, Jake Engert, told us, "[T]he thought that I ... had the power to alter my position was the furthest thing from my mind. But after my first talk with an SLDN representative, I began to understand that I wasn't without hope, and I was still allowed to keep my dream alive."

One service member said that SLDN "made me feel as though everything was going to be all right, at a time when I felt like my world was collapsing around me."[47]

Another told us, "My aunt, who was 6,000 miles away, found SLDN on the internet, and I called immediately. Within one minute of talking to an SLDN representative, I knew I had an advocate, and I was not alone."[48]

In addressing our national gala in 2004, Lieutenant (junior grade) Jen Kopfstein said, "Many of you in the room ... know just how irreplaceable SLDN is when you're alone, afraid and tired of living a lie."[49]

The testimonies made clear the effect that "Don't ask, don't tell" had on our brave men and women—those who were unafraid in the face of enemy fire. These case snippets represent only a smattering of the deluge of cases Michelle and I handled in our first six years. They highlight that the services were regularly violating the spirit of "Don't ask, don't tell"—and that in some instances, commanders and discharge boards were willing to uphold the rules when SLDN intervened.

Bridget Wilson, a military lawyer based in San Diego and one of the pioneers in the fight for lesbian, gay, and bisexual service members, captured the core of our strategy this way: "This is a realm where moral victories count. Change happens one person at a time. Make it impossible for [the Pentagon] to enforce this policy. Fight back at every level. Make sure that no case goes quietly. Rub their noses in it when we win. Shame them with how despicable this policy is when we lose. Don't give up."[50]

In one case, the area defense counsel at the Space and Missile Systems Center in Los Angeles forbade further investigation into our client "based on Servicemembers Legal Defense Network involvement."[51]

Another military defense attorney told us, "I think you win more cases being feared than loved, and your organization certainly causes fear among promotion-obsessed officers."[52]

A gay marine told SLDN's board chairman, Tom Carpenter, that I was a "pinko commie civilian, but watch out, because he knows what he is doing!" I counted that as high praise from a marine, even if my politics were decidedly progressive center.

Commanders feared that SLDN would call them out publicly, and that is, in part, how we disrupted business as usual. Our first legal director, Stacey Sobel, said, "They feared us because they knew we were right, and we had the evidence to prove it." For us, storytelling was essential to our advocacy—and to convincing the public and decision-makers that "Don't ask, don't tell" was not the benign policy sold to the American people in 1993.

◆ ◆ ◆

Our primary vehicle to tell the stories of those targeted under "Don't ask, don't tell" in the first decade was our annual report, detailing the findings from the field. We titled our reports *Conduct Unbecoming* after Randy Shilts's landmark book of the same name—and after the catch-all criminal offense in the Uniform

Code of Military Justice that punishes "actions that dishonor or disgrace the uniform."

These reports were brutal to produce. While we were juggling hundreds of open cases each day, we also spent six weeks each year, working late into the night, every night, and on weekends, to review every case file and extract from our notes on violations of the promises made under "Don't ask, don't tell."

We assessed the types of violations, where they were occurring, and by whom. We discerned where there were patterns of command misconduct and tried our best to place what we gleaned from our cases into a context that was useful. By our seventh annual report, we even broke down our analysis by service, so that each branch could assess its own actions independently of, and concurrently with, other services. We named names, and in our last volumes we reproduced hundreds of pages of documents we had obtained from the field that corroborated our conclusions.

We released these reports in press conferences at the National Press Club. Michelle and I both spoke, as did one or more of our clients. We were surprised that reporters were keen to learn about our findings, though they never accepted what we said freely. They challenged us to prove our findings and claims, and we met the task.

After these events, Michelle and I would leave the club, do an afternoon of follow-up calls with reporters, and then head to a local bar to see if our stories actually made the network news. One time, the bartender looked at me, then at the television, then back at me, and said, "Hey! That's you!"

Michelle and I felt a tingle of excitement when we were on television, but it was always about our clients, not us. Did we get the message out? Did we serve them well? Did the reporter tell the story accurately? The day we published our annual reports was the first evening we allowed ourselves to go home by seven o'clock, exhausted, but satisfied with our delivery of the findings.

The data from our cases was the indispensable source of information for the public and the Pentagon. As *Boston Globe* columnist Tom Oliphant wrote, "Every year since President Clinton tried and failed to meet a campaign pledge to join the rest of the advanced world and ban discrimination, ... there has been a detailed report of what's really going on. Naturally, it doesn't come from the Pentagon. Instead, it comes from a private organization, Servicemembers Legal Defense Network, which combines actual legal representation with expertise and advocacy."[53]

Andrew Sullivan took the Pentagon to task for claiming that the reasons for the surge in gay discharges "are not known. And would be difficult to ascertain. Compare this with the documentation of the Servicemembers Legal Defense Network."[54]

Even the Pentagon ultimately conceded that it relied on our annual reports to know what was happening with its own policy.[55] The credibility and trust we developed through our advocacy were essential to our effectiveness in Congress, at the Pentagon, and in the White House.

After our second annual report, Democratic congressman Marty Meehan contacted us: "I just finished reading [your report]. ... I am troubled that the DOD has apparently failed to follow its own 'Don't ask, don't tell, don't pursue' policy." After our third annual report, in a letter dated February 12, 1997, 36 House members led by Democrat Lynn Woolsey urged Secretary of Defense William Cohen to take steps to end abuses under "Don't ask, don't tell, don't pursue."[56]

On May 30, 1997, Meehan again sent a letter to the Pentagon, pushing officials to exercise leadership in enforcing the limits on gay investigations. That December, after meeting with SLDN and other gay-rights leaders, Democrat Richard Gephardt, the House minority leader, wrote the Pentagon, calling for compliance with the limits on gay investigations.

With each letter, Michelle and I knew we were getting the attention of congressional and Pentagon leaders. We were laying the groundwork for the day when we could persuade a member of Congress to introduce legislation to repeal "Don't ask, don't tell."

Every year, the Pentagon responded to our findings. Michelle and I met with the under secretary of defense for personnel and readiness, Edwin Dorn, and the Pentagon's general counsel, Jamie Gorelick, shortly after we started SLDN in 1993. We briefed Dorn each year through 1997. We briefed Deputy Secretary of Defense John White in 1996; after George W. Bush became president in 2001, we briefed his under secretary of defense for personnel and readiness, David Chu, multiple times. Carolyn Becraft, assistant secretary of the Navy for manpower and Reserve affairs from 1998 to 2001, once told a panel discussing military personnel issues advocated by outside groups that SLDN was one of the most effective because our name appeared on the distributed daily schedules of senior leaders in the Pentagon more than any other group.

The Clinton White House also responded. On May 31, 1995, we met with Abner Mikva, the White House counsel, and Elena Kagan, an associate White House counsel (and, later, a Supreme Court justice). In between those jobs, when she was dean of Harvard Law School, she called the military's gay ban "a profound wrong" and "a moral injustice of the first order."[57]

On June 12, 1995, at a White House reception for lesbian and gay elected officials sponsored by the Gay & Lesbian Victory Fund, Vice President Al Gore acknowledged to Michelle and me that he was concerned by the reports of continuing witch hunts. (By 1999, he would call for repeal.) Around the same time, White House Chief of Staff Leon Panetta told Susan Leal, an out lesbian and a member of the San Francisco Board of Supervisors, and James Hormel, an LGBT activist who two years later would be named, through a recess appointment, the first openly gay ambassador (to Luxembourg), that he would look into violations of "Don't ask, don't tell."

On July 21, 1997, White House press secretary Mike McCurry publicly walked back a statement he had made on July 3 that the "don't ask, don't tell" policy "is a good one [and] it is being implemented effectively by the Department of Defense."[58]

We had written McCurry a week after he uttered those words, saying that the president should not support ongoing violations of "Don't ask, don't tell," and we mobilized our supporters to send their concerns to McCurry. He invited us to the White House and walked into his office holding a stack of faxes.

"I have clearly got something wrong based on the letters I am getting," he said. "Tell me what I did." After our meeting, he walked into the briefing room.[59]

We were amazed that he issued a retraction of his statement, which called increased attention to his misstatement. McCurry then told reporters that the Pentagon was reviewing the policy's implementation due to the violations documented by SLDN.

◆ ◆ ◆

With the Pentagon's failure to lead, Michelle and I took it upon ourselves to get the word out to the field. We purchased ads in the classified sections of the *Army Times,* the *Air Force Times* and the *Navy Times* alerting anyone being investigated under "Don't ask, don't tell" to "Say Nothing. Sign Nothing. Get Legal Help." The ads included our phone number.

Under Article 31 of the Uniform Code of Military Justice, service members had the right to speak with an attorney before making any statements. More than once, we learned that a local JAG—a member of the Judge Advocate General's Corps, the military's legal branch—had clipped the ad and given it to a service member saying, "I can't help you, but they can."

We printed the same advice on business cards that we distributed by the thousands. They weren't fancy, but they served their purpose. Gay rights pioneer Frank Kameny had first used the "Say Nothing, Sign Nothing" mantra in 1973 in response to a witch hunt of women at the Women's Air Corps barracks in Washington. According to Bridget Wilson, he produced flyers informing soldiers of their rights and papered the entire barracks. Bridget and Gary Rees, a founder of the San Diego Gay and Lesbian Center, used the same tactic to disrupt a witch hunt of female marines at Camp Pendleton. They added "Get Help" to their advisory.

We also launched what we called our "Eyes and Ears" tour to reach out to LGBT service members at military installations in or near Atlanta, Charlotte, Colorado Springs, Fayetteville, Norfolk, Pensacola, San Antonio, and San Diego. We set up SLDN booths at Pride Days. Gay service members and veterans frequently attended Pride Days in New York City, San Francisco, and Los

Angeles, far from their bases. But many also attended Pride Days in areas with significant military populations, such as Washington and San Diego. Our outreach helped build a movement, and soon veterans volunteered to staff our booths—support we needed, given our small staff size.

In 1998, we published 4,000 copies of what we called a "survival guide" that provided detailed information about what "Don't ask, don't tell" actually said. We wanted service members to know the perils of the law, but we also wanted to highlight the promises made in the regulations that could possibly salvage someone's career. We hoped that military lawyers could use the tools we provided, and that commanders who wanted to protect their troops could have a peg or two to hang their hats on and defend their decision to drop an investigation. The "Don't ask, don't tell" regulations contained specific limits on investigations that, if enforced, could have made life less intolerable.

We sent copies of the guide to every top commander, military defense attorney, and military library. In 2000, *The Nation* wrote that our guide "is the only document that tells military gays how to cope with the current policy and what their rights are (the DoD provides no such material)."[60]

♦♦♦

In 1995, a West Point professor asked Michelle and me if we would speak to a political science class about the "Don't ask, don't tell" policy. "I like to start fires," he told us.

Michelle and I strategized on how to approach the class and agreed that we should teach them a lesson in leadership through the

Socratic method. We knew that the Army was not training soldiers on the nuances of "Don't ask, don't tell," so we did. I started.

"You will soon take up leadership positions in the Army. You will lead your soldiers. You will have to make decisions. But sometimes those decisions may not be easy. Let's take an example. What would you do if your soldier came to you and said, 'Sir/Ma'am, I am being harassed for being gay'? What would you do?"

The first cadet answered, "I would investigate the harassment and hold the harassing soldier accountable."

A second cadet responded, "Well, he said he's gay, so I also would have to investigate him. He violated 'don't tell.'"

The third cadet offered, "Isn't the harassment bad enough? Shouldn't we help the soldier?"

A fourth cadet proclaimed, a bit too shrilly, "The 'Don't ask, don't tell' is a policy of discrimination, and I won't enforce it."

The professors attending the class quickly scribbled down that cadet's name. "Oh, dear," I thought. "That guy's in trouble."

Michelle and I asked several questions along the same lines that generated active discussion. She wrapped up the discussion with these words: "We didn't come here today to debate the wisdom of 'Don't ask, don't tell.' We wanted to highlight that the regulations as written, and as you now sense, have a lot of gray areas. You as a commander are going to have to decide how you want to interpret that gray area. In the Army, we know and understand how to follow orders. We expect those orders to be clear. But as a leader, you will find that at times the rules are not clear, and you will have to use your best judgment on how to act."

The superintendent at West Point dropped by the class and asked two questions of us: "Does Israel allow gays and lesbians to serve openly?"

"Yes, sir," I responded.

"And what evidence is there that their armed forces have faced any disruption to unit cohesion?"

"There is no evidence of that, sir," Michelle said. "In fact, the evidence is that openly gay troops are welcomed."

"That's what I thought."

He pivoted and left the classroom. Without stating his position, the superintendent had just taught his cadets that the rationale behind "Don't ask, don't tell" was wrong.

Two years later, Michelle and I were invited to train Navy JAGs at Norfolk. We stayed with two gay World War II veterans, John Cook and Waverly Cole, and their dog, CoCo. We were also asked to train Army JAGs at the JAG School in Charlottesville, Virginia.

The requests to speak, train, and testify would continue, and with each acceptance, we won friends and allies who would become essential to repeal. It is not surprising that our intakes surged to more than a thousand per year by 2004. By the time I left SLDN, we had provided free legal counsel to more than 8,000 service members; by the time "Don't ask, don't tell" was repealed, SLDN had assisted more than 12,000 service members and built a significant grassroots community ready to fight.

CHAPTER 5

REPORTING FOR DUTY

The only way to repeal "Don't ask, don't tell" was through the courts or Congress. Given that Congress was preparing to put the policy into law in 1993, many eyes turned to the courts to uphold their dignity.

On an autumn afternoon in 1993, a few months after President Clinton had announced the new policy, Navy Lieutenant Paul Thomasson arrived at the SLDN office, deep in the maze of the National Veterans Legal Services Program. He was dressed smartly in uniform, hat under his arm. As I greeted him, he saluted and, with a wry grin on his face, announced, "Reporting for duty." He wanted to be "the guinea pig" to constitutionally challenge "Don't ask, don't tell."

Thomasson's credentials were remarkable. A 32-year-old anti-submarine plane pilot, he "consistently received the highest possible performance ratings, he was one of a few junior officers selected for a Joint Chiefs of Staff Internship, and his supervisors, including senior Naval officers, praised his work." Rear Admiral Lee F. Gunn stated in an evaluation that Thomasson was "a true 'front runner' who should be groomed for the most senior leadership in tomorrow's Navy."[61]

In an annual evaluation of the young officer, prepared after Thomasson had informed him that he was gay, his boss, Rear Admiral Albert Konetzni, wrote: "Lieutenant Thomasson is one of the finest junior officers I have ever had the pleasure to serve with. ... Continue to challenge him with the most difficult assignments, he will excel."[62]

I was told by a mutual colleague that Konetzni, then the Navy's head of military personnel policy and career progression, faced blowback for his evaluation. "Why did you do that?" he was reportedly asked. The admiral's response: "Did you want me to lie?"

It wasn't just his commanders who were confident in Thomasson, even after he came out.

"Sailors serving under the lieutenant lined up to support him," Eric Schmitt wrote in *The New York Times*. "'Of course it was a shock at first,' said Petty Officer Jack Trumbull. 'But it was really no big deal. What a person does in his own time doesn't make any difference. He was a top performer.'"[63]

There was some optimism that the courts would find "Don't ask, don't tell" unconstitutional or inoperable in some ways, as precedent was mounting. On November 16, 1993, two weeks before Clinton signed "Don't ask, don't tell" into law, a three-judge panel of the U.S. Court of Appeals for the District of Columbia

Circuit ruled that disenrolling Naval Academy Midshipman Joe Steffan for coming out was unconstitutional.[64] One of the top students in his class, Steffan was expelled from the Academy after coming out in 1987, just six weeks shy of graduation.

On June 1, 1994, a judge on the U.S. District Court for the Western District of Washington state ruled that the Pentagon had violated the equal protection clause by discharging Colonel Margarethe Cammermeyer in 1992.[65]

Cammermeyer had earned a Bronze Star in Vietnam and served as chief nurse in the Washington State National Guard. She had been married for many years, and had four sons, before coming to terms with her sexual orientation. A leader with integrity, she never considered lying to a security clearance investigator when he asked the standard question about whether she was a lesbian. The court ruled that the armed forces could not discharge her under the regulations that were in place prior to "Don't ask, don't tell."

On August 31, 1994, the U.S. Court of Appeals for the Ninth Circuit held that Petty Officer Keith Meinhold could not be discharged from the Navy for coming out in an interview on ABC's *World News Tonight*. Rather than basing its decision on freedom of speech or equal protection grounds, though, the court ruled that a mere statement of sexual orientation without "a concrete, expressed desire to engage" in sex did not violate the statutory language of the ban.[66] Advocates hoped that the courts would now find "Don't ask, don't tell" unconstitutional or inoperable in some way, because it was the same wolf in sheep's clothing.

Despite the successes in *Cammermeyer v. Aspin* and *Meinhold v. United States Department of Defense*, storm clouds gathered around *Steffan v. Perry*. The U.S. Court of Appeals for the District of Columbia Circuit granted a rehearing before all nine judges and reversed the prior judgment, 5-4, on November 22, 1994, one year after "Don't ask, don't tell" became law. Judge Laurence Silberman, writing for the majority, held that the military was within its rights to discharge those who say "I am gay" based on the presumption that they would engage in sex in violation of the Uniform Code of Military Justice, because the "human sexual drive is enormously powerful and ... an open declaration that one is homosexual is a rather reliable indication as to the direction of one's drive."[67]

Michelle called me when the decision came down, putting a reporter on hold. "What is our response?" she asked.

"Did we win or lose?" I asked.

"We lost."

"Tell the reporter that this is one inning in a long ball game," I replied. Michelle's quote appeared the next day.

Paul Thomasson was another step up to the plate. The courts were divided on how to rule on the constitutionality of the pre-1993 gay ban. We hoped that the cases brought under "Don't ask, don't tell" would join the chorus of those finding a ban on gay Americans problematic.

We discussed the process with Thomasson, advising him that litigation was not for the faint of heart. His entire life would go on trial, both in court and in the media. There was no guarantee of victory and every possibility of failure. I deeply admire and am humbled by those willing to undergo the rigors of litigation.

Convinced that the case was a perfect opportunity to challenge "Don't ask, don't tell," Michelle and I turned to our legal networks to determine who and what firm would be willing to represent him. Covington & Burling, a top Washington law firm, answered the call.

We helped Thomasson draft the statement to his commanders that would set into motion the discharge process that would trigger the legal action. President Clinton announced the "Don't ask, don't tell" policy on July 19, 1993, and signed legislation that turned the policy into law on November 30. The Defense Department enacted final directives pursuant to the statute on February 28, 1994. Each branch of the military then issued service-specific regulations.

On March 2, the day after the Navy implemented its new regulations, Thomasson delivered a letter to four admirals at the Bureau of Naval Personnel, where he then worked as an admiral's aide, informing them that he was gay. (Ironically, the Bureau of Naval Personnel is the agency charged with discharging gays.)

Thomasson wrote that being gay was "more deeply rooted than all societal, religious, parental or peer pressures can effect [sic]."[68] The Navy immediately initiated separation proceedings, resulting in a discharge decision six months later. The U.S. District Court for the Eastern District of Virginia granted an injunction to stay the discharge pending a consideration of the underlying merits.

In a preview of what would become the standard judicial opinion in cases challenging "Don't ask, don't tell," that same court in June 1995 echoed the *Steffan* line of reasoning, rather than the *Cammermeyer* or *Meinhold* line of reasoning. It ruled that "don't tell" did not violate Thomasson's First Amendment right to free speech because the declaration "I am gay" was evidence of a proclivity to engage in criminal conduct proscribed by the Uniform Code of Military Justice.[69]

The court further held that the law did not violate Thomasson's equal protection rights because the government had articulated a reasonable basis for its discrimination—namely, that the presence of openly gay service members would undermine unit cohesion and military readiness, citing the July 1993 testimony of General Colin Powell, the chairman of the Joint Chiefs of Staff, before the Senate Armed Services Committee as authoritative on the matter. The government was not required to provide any other evidence other than the unsubstantiated opinions asserted during congressional hearings. The court accepted the argument that gays serving openly in the military created "sexual tension" and violated the "privacy" rights of other service members.

The court declined the invitation to conduct a more probing analysis, holding that "rational-basis review in equal protection analysis is not a license for courts to judge the wisdom, fairness, or logic of legislative choices." And, the court added, "it is difficult to conceive of an area of governmental activity in which the courts have less competence. The complex, subtle and professional decisions as to the composition, training, equipping, and control of a military force are essentially professional military judgments."[70]

In sum, the court accepted, without question, the prejudice underlying "Don't ask, don't tell" and declined to second-guess or challenge the government's contentions.

Thomasson appealed the decision. The Fourth Circuit Court of Appeals, sitting *en banc*, affirmed the lower court's decision, 9-4, in April 1996. Underscoring why "Don't ask, don't tell" was in many ways worse than the prior regulatory gay ban, the court noted that what "Thomasson seeks to upset here is a carefully crafted national political compromise, one that was the product of sustained and delicate negotiations involving both the Executive and Legislative branches of our government. ...

"Thomasson requests that we simply set aside these lengthy labors of the legislative process and supplant with our own judicial judgment the product of a serious and prolonged debate on a subject of paramount national importance. This would, however, be a step of substantial gravity. The courts were not created to award by judicial decree what was not achievable by political consensus."[71]

The courts, I thought, were supposed to check unconstitutional actions by other branches of government, not give them wide leeway to run roughshod over those rights.

In early 1993, George Stephanopoulos had asked leaders at the Campaign for Military Service whether they would prefer President Clinton to issue an executive order to repeal the gay ban and lose as Congress passed legislation, or sign into law a compromise that eked out some gains to end witch hunts. The answer was unequivocal: Issue the executive order and lose. Do not be on the same side as Congress, or the courts will use that as evidence that the ban is constitutional. Stephanopoulos was reportedly surprised by the recommendation. The court decisions would validate what the Campaign for Military Service had feared.

The question for Thomasson was whether to petition the Supreme Court to hear his case. On the one hand, his record was exemplary, the questions presented were clear, and the Supreme Court had not adjudicated the constitutionality of the gay ban in its current or prior forms. On the other hand, the early promise of decisions reinstating Colonel Cammermeyer and Petty Officer Meinhold were challenged by the adverse rulings in Thomasson's case, as well as the one just decided against Steffan.

Would other cases challenging "Don't ask, don't tell" that were pending provide a better opportunity? Would it be better to go to the Supreme Court with a favorable ruling that presented a clear split among the appellate courts? Michelle and I both wanted Thomasson to succeed. We were deeply invested in a good outcome. But we both urged him not to petition the Supreme Court.

It was his choice to make, and that July he chose to go ahead. We told him that we would not file an amicus brief in support of the petition, but we also would not oppose it. We stood ready to help if the Court granted his petition.

The hurt in his voice left an indelible imprint on my heart. I felt that we had let him down.

The Supreme Court denied his petition.[72]

CHAPTER 6

JUST GOOD FOLK

n May 1993, while Congress debated gays in the military, Air
Force Captain Rich Richenberg came out to his commander.[73]

Richenberg was an electronic warfare officer, stationed at Offutt
Air Force Base in Nebraska. During Operation Desert Storm, the
aerial bombardment that preceded the invasion of Iraq in 1991,
he commanded the control center aboard an AWACS aircraft.[74]
He was rated in the top 10 percent of all Air Force officers.

Once Richenberg told his commander that he was gay, he was
assigned to desk duty, processing awards and commendations—
an act that could only be seen as punitive. As he told the press,
"Despite a manning shortage in my unit, I was taken off flying
status."[75] His discharge hearing was held in abeyance, pending the
final outcome of the debate on gays in the military.

I met Richenberg in Dallas in the autumn of 1993, shortly after SLDN started, through William Waybourn of the Gay & Lesbian Victory Fund. "You two should talk," Waybourn said in his understated Texas drawl.

Richenberg and I became good friends. As he drove to be with his family in San Antonio that Christmas, he stopped to see me and my mom in Fort Worth. He is what Texans would call "good folk."

Richenberg had come to terms with his sexual orientation later in life, at 35. Once he did that, he felt he had a moral duty to do the same to the Air Force. "My whole military career ... they have taught us the proper values that go along with being an officer," he said in an interview with the *Omaha World-Herald*. "They include honesty, integrity and leadership. I had no choice but to come forward with my commander so I could continue to serve with honor and integrity."[76]

On December 3, 1993, a board of officers recommended that Richenberg be discharged. Despite his stellar service record, he received a general discharge, not an honorable discharge. Michelle, who attended the hearing, told the *Omaha World-Herald*, "The only reasonable conclusion is Captain Richenberg is being punished because he has chosen to fight back in an attempt to save his career."[77]

The actions of Richenberg's command—relegating him to desk duty and recommending a derogatory discharge characterization—contrasted sharply with those of Paul Thomasson's Navy command. Richenberg's command was hostile, but his fellow Air Force officers were cool. They even threw him a birthday party, complete with chocolate cake.[78]

It was not unusual before "Don't ask, don't tell" for gay service members to receive derogatory discharge characterizations. In World War II, service members who had been identified as gay or as having engaged in sex with someone of the same gender received "blue discharges"—so named because they were on blue paper, intended as a mark of shame.[79] Less than fully honorable discharges raise red flags for civilian employers that can impact hiring decisions, and derogatory characterizations can result in denial of some (or all) veterans benefits.

The rules governing discharge characterizations under "Don't ask, don't tell" required that they reflect a service member's complete service record. Michelle and I pushed hard during the 1990s to ensure that service members who were discharged for being gay and who had no derogatory information in their service record received fully honorable discharges. We ultimately succeeded in convincing the secretary of the Air Force to upgrade Richenberg's discharge to fully honorable. We were mostly successful in reversing the trend of retaliatory characterizations—one of the early demonstrations that we could deliver change.

The Pentagon ordered the Air Force to redo Richenberg's discharge hearing, since the one in December had taken place under the regulations in place prior to "Don't ask, don't tell." He called me and asked whether he should submit a statement that he would abide by the rules requiring celibacy of those who affirm that they are gay.

"Rich," I said, "you are a person of integrity. You need to decide how you want to live your life. I don't think anybody should have to take a vow of celibacy in order to serve our country. I can also tell you that there are plenty of gay service members living open and full lives despite the law. It all depends on your command, and on you."

Richenberg concluded that he wanted to serve and would abide by the military's rules. He told his discharge board in April 1994 that he would not have sex.[80] Under "Don't ask, don't tell," coming out created a "rebuttable presumption" that one would have sex in line with the statement. Richenberg chose to rebut the presumption. Despite his promise, fully consistent with the rules, the second board of officers again recommended discharge.[81]

Now it was up to the courts. Michelle and I lined up counsel at a Minneapolis firm, Robins, Kaplan, Miller & Ciresi, to represent Richenberg. Tom Kayser was a retired Air Force colonel and a partner in the firm.

While Richenberg's journey through the military and federal judicial systems started 10 months before Thomasson's, the initial decision in his case came six months after Thomasson's. Similar to the ruling in *Thomasson*, Judge Lyle Strom of the U.S. District Court in the Eastern District of Nebraska held that the deference courts owe to congressional judgments is "perhaps never more pronounced than when the 'case arises in the context of Congress' authority over national defense and military affairs.'"[82]

"It is difficult to conceive of a more legitimate governmental concern than matters of national security and the safety and security of American military personnel," he wrote. "A policy designed to protect these interests by eliminating a potential threat to them is certainly aimed at a legitimate governmental purpose." He implied that gay service members were a "potential threat" to national security and the safety of fellow service members; there was not even an ounce of self-reflection by Strom over his bias.

The wrinkle in the case, though, was how the judge would address Richenberg's attempt to meet the "rebuttable presumption" standard. With a metaphorical wave of his hand, Strom simply declared, "It is of no constitutional consequence that plaintiff may in fact have no propensity to engage in homosexual conduct."

When courts are unwilling to pierce the veil of prejudice, it leads to wrong outcomes. Bad law begets bad law. The courts upheld "Don't ask, don't tell." A three-judge panel of the Eighth U.S. Circuit Court of Appeals affirmed the district court decision on October 3, 1996, and a hearing *en banc* was denied the following January.[83]

Other cases challenging "Don't ask, don't tell" all met the same fate, including *Able v. United States,* a smart case filed by two preeminent civil liberties groups, the American Civil Liberties Union and the Lambda Legal Defense and Education Fund, and a pair of cases before the Ninth U.S. Circuit Court of Appeals. For *Able,* Michelle and I identified one of the plaintiffs and three experts to testify at the trial—SLDN Military Advisory Council members Major General Vance Coleman and Brigadier General Evelyn Foote, along with a future member, Captain Mike Rankin, a Navy doctor. We wanted experts to testify at our cases, but judges often didn't—a decision that deprived them of the wide-ranging expertise we thought crucial to counter the problematic legislative record in support of "Don't ask, don't tell."

The district court in *Able* decided in favor of the plaintiffs, the only one to do so. Judge Eugene Nickerson ruled that "The Constitution does not grant the military special license to act on prejudices or cater to them."[84] The appellate court reversed that decision, ending the first tranche of litigation challenging "Don't ask, don't tell."

It was increasingly clear to me that the courts were not going to be our salvation unless there was a change in Supreme Court precedent and/or a change in the American ethos. My instinct when Michelle and I founded SLDN that we would have to win "Don't ask, don't tell" repeal in Congress was, unfortunately, proving true.

Richenberg called me after the court's final judgment. "So what should I do now?"

"We could sure use an electronic warfare officer to help with our computers and database," I teased.

"Well, I might just do that."

In 1998, he packed his bags in Omaha and moved to Washington, where he worked in our office for a year. He then fell in love and moved to San Diego.

Richenberg developed deep friendships with others facing the consequences of "Don't ask, don't tell," including mentoring a young marine, Corporal Kevin Blaesing. We'll meet him later.

CHAPTER 7

POLICY CHOPS

Our success defending our clients inside the military and our failure to convince the federal courts that "Don't ask, don't tell" was unconstitutional meant that we had to focus on tearing down the pillars upholding the policy and laying the foundation for repeal.

The question was whether, as a prelude to repeal, we could change certain laws, regulations, systems, and practices that discriminated against our clients. To our great surprise, we found that we could. It started in late 1993, when Michelle and I convinced the Pentagon's general counsel, Jamie Gorelick, and the under secretary for personnel and readiness, Edwin Dorn, to require that service members suspected of being gay be read their Article 31 right to remain silent—the military's equivalent of a Miranda warning.

Our second policy success, in May 1994, was ending the practice of recoupment against the men and women who were discharged for being gay and had attended or were attending the services' military academies, Reserve Officers Training Corps programs (which pays college tuition), or graduate school on the military's dime. Under this practice, service members were required to repay the full cost of those scholarships if they were disenrolled or discharged for cause—which included "Don't ask, don't tell." We fielded dozens of calls from service members who were caught in the crosshairs.

Many who join our armed forces do so because it is a way up and out of their hometowns. Education provides advancement that they might not otherwise be able to afford without the military's financial support.

We argued that gay service members should not have to repay those scholarships. Each was willing to serve and fulfill their contractual obligations; it was military policy that was preventing them from doing so. We argued that college and graduate school are often the times when young men and women come to terms with their sexual orientation and where they are first able to be free and open about who they are. Had they known that they were lesbian, gay, or bisexual prior to attending the military academies or ROTC programs, or accepting a fully funded graduate school education, they might have made different choices. Also, some who knew they were gay prior to accepting a military scholarship might have believed that they could abide by the regulations, but the reality of serving in the closet was too difficult.

Our arguments resonated with Deputy Secretary of Defense John Deutch. While provost of the Massachusetts Institute of

Technology in 1990, he had defended two ROTC students, Robert Bettiker and David Carney, who were facing recoupment after being disenrolled for being gay. In a letter to Secretary of Defense Richard Cheney, he argued that it was "wrong and short-sighted" both to prevent gays from joining the ROTC program and to "require avowed homosexuals to disenroll and pay back their scholarship funds."[85]

Cheney agreed. He dropped recoupment actions against a number of individuals whose cases had been featured in the press, including Bettiker and Carney.[86] In his book *Conduct Unbecoming: Lesbians and Gays in the U.S. Military*, Randy Shilts wrote that when Cheney was traveling to Asia and had a layover in San Francisco, he read about the Navy attempting to recoup the tuition of a Naval Academy graduate, Orlando Gotay, and erupted, "Goddamn it. I've told the military departments not to hit people up for back tuition."

But when Bill Clinton was inaugurated in January 1993, Cheney was replaced by Les Aspin, and the services returned to their aggressive recoupment actions. This battle was an early warning in our efforts to repeal "Don't ask, don't tell" that unless politicians are fully committed to a new policy, the services will outlast them.

We asked Deutch to follow Cheney's precedent and end the practice of recoupment against gays. On May 14, 1994, he issued a memorandum directing that coming out, in and of itself, was not a basis for recouping educational benefits.[87]

Deutch's right-hand man was Eric Fanning, a graduate of Dartmouth College, who in a meteoric and pathbreaking career would later become the first openly gay secretary of the Army.

Michelle and I met with Fanning on several occasions in a tiny office deep in the trenches of the Pentagon. We presented the stories of the men and women from whom the Pentagon was seeking recoupment. He spent weeks tracking down who exactly had the power to overturn recoupment actions consistent with the Deutch memo.

As a result of our intervention, the Army dropped its case against Clayce Rodamer, a West Point graduate who was serving at Fort Bliss, Texas, when he finally acknowledged his sexual orientation.[88] When he came out to his superiors in 1988, he was told that he could resign or face court-martial. Even after he came out, his commander recommended him for promotion to platoon leader, but that support didn't prevent his discharge.

Two years later, the Army sent him a bill for $76,000—the cost of his West Point tuition, payable to the United States Department of the Treasury. By the time he contacted SLDN, the Army had added penalties and interest, so the recoupment sought was now in excess of $175,000. I joked that the Pentagon was "happy to take check, cash, or credit card."

In addition, the Army had referred the charges to a collection agency, damaging Rodamer's credit and preventing him from securing a loan.[89] He had retained a private attorney in Dallas, where he lived, but we worked his case at the Pentagon.

We also helped to raise public awareness of the Pentagon's punitive recoupment actions. Just before Rodamer was to appear on *Nightline* to tell his story, Army officials called the program to say they were recommending that the Defense Department drop the collection action.[90]

Rodamer captured what SLDN had argued to the Pentagon: "I never broke a contract with the military. They broke it with me."[91]

Despite Deutch's memo and Fanning's interventions, the Air Force was determined to pursue recoupment. We were determined to pursue all avenues to resist. With the assistance of pro bono counsel Kate Kenealy from Akin, Gump, Hauer & Strauss, we persuaded the Board of Corrections for Military Records to overturn recoupment actions against two former Air Force Academy cadets, Lisa Giddings and Dana Teagarden.[92] Each had been disenrolled for more than seven years when the Air Force notified them of its intent to recoup back tuition of $52,000 and $70,000, respectively.

In the end, SLDN assisted more than a dozen clients who faced recoupment—just one of many ways the services tried to punish gay service members beyond firing them for being who they are.

◆ ◆ ◆

A significant policy victory in 1995, due to the leadership of Representative Barney Frank, was ending discrimination in the issuance of security clearances.

The ban on granting security clearances to gay Americans arose after World War II during the so-called Lavender Scare, when politicians equated being gay with communism.[93] President Harry S. Truman established an informal loyalty program. His successor, Dwight D. Eisenhower, formalized the ban in an executive order making "sexual perversion" a basis for exclusion from federal service. The restrictions continued even as the Crittenden Report[94]—named for the officer who headed a Navy panel that studied the issue—concluded in 1957 that there was "no sound basis for the belief that homosexuals posed a security risk."[95] (The Navy immediately classified the report.[96])

Frank, the openly gay Democratic firebrand from Massachusetts, called us wanting data and analysis regarding service members kicked out of the military because of the security clearance process. Given the "Don't ask, don't tell" debacle, he wanted to exact from President Clinton an executive order banning security clearance discrimination. Three years previously, Frank had stopped an anti-gay witch hunt by executive branch officials who had used the security clearance process to root out suspected gay employees.[97]

We provided the data from our burgeoning caseload. We argued that what the government wanted during security clearance investigations was information regarding risks to our national security, not information about a person's sexual orientation. We argued that "Don't ask, don't tell" was, in fact, an impediment to the security clearance process because gay service members were, by law, forced to keep their mouths shut about their private lives. As a result, the government wouldn't know if gay service members were in relationships with foreign nationals that might pose security risks or subject them to blackmail. By ending sexual orientation discrimination in the security clearance process, and encouraging full disclosure, the investigators could better assess actual security risks.

Clinton agreed, signing Executive Order 12968 in 1995.[98] It helped gays in the military by carving out an area where lesbian, gay, and bisexual service members could be open and honest about their sexual orientation without fear of reprisal. The permission to speak openly about one's sexual orientation to security clearance investigators was consistent with the view of both the president and General Powell that "Don't ask, don't tell" created a zone of privacy where discreet disclosures were fully appropriate. We were able to counsel clients, investigators, and JAGs that sexual orientation disclosures during the security clearance process were no longer grounds for discharge, saving careers in the process.

The executive order also helpfully undermined a central tenet of the statutory ban on openly gay service members: that disclosure of being gay to anyone, anywhere, anytime would disrupt unit cohesion. It also provided an opening for us to argue for more situations where gays and lesbians should be able to speak openly about themselves and to contend even more forcefully that "Don't ask, don't tell" ultimately should be repealed because, in fact, honesty did not disrupt unit cohesion.

In addition, it provided protection against discrimination to the tens of thousands of lesbian, gay, and bisexual civilian personnel and federal contractors, not to just those serving in uniform. The policy success reflected the vision shared by Michelle and me—that our work should benefit not just our clients, but the larger universe of those impacted by discriminatory laws.

Word about the change in law was slow to filter down through the chains of command, but we helped that happen. Shortly after the executive order went into effect, we persuaded a commander that he shouldn't convene a discharge board based on information obtained during a security clearance investigation.

This wasn't the only time the military still tried to discharge someone based on coming out during their security clearance process, but those occasions became rare—and when we intervened, we managed to stop each one.

Gay rights pioneer Frank Kameny had been fighting since 1962 to have his security clearance reinstated, and had also been fighting on behalf of others who had had their security clearances denied or revoked because they were lesbian, gay, or bisexual.[99] He said that Clinton's announcement of the executive order "represents a change as from night unto day and would have been beyond the wildest expectations of anyone years back."[100]

◆ ◆ ◆

Our next policy success in those early days was overturning the prohibition on military service by people who had tested positive for the human immunodeficiency virus (HIV)—the virus that causes AIDS.

After the Republicans, led by Newt Gingrich, took control of the House of Representatives in 1995, Representative Bob Dornan (known to some as "B-1 Bob" for his "relentless crusade" in support of the bomber manufactured in his Southern California district[101]) attached an amendment to the National Defense Authorization Act for fiscal year 1996. The NDAA, which is introduced annually and authorizes the appropriation of billions of dollars in military spending for the next fiscal year, is considered must-pass legislation and typically is festooned with amendments that might not get passed if they were stand-alone bills.[102]

Dornan's amendment banned HIV-positive personnel from serving in the military, ordered the discharge of those who had been diagnosed with the virus, and cut off all medical benefits and care to them and their families. The final version of the legislation included that provision.

Although he objected to the HIV ban, calling it "blatantly discriminatory," President Clinton signed the defense authorization bill into law on February 10, 1996,[103] imperiling the careers of

1,049 HIV+ military personnel.[104] The largest political group for the LGBT community, the Human Rights Campaign, was caught flat-footed, even though we had warned them about it.

We rolled up our sleeves to see if we could undo the damage. The Human Rights Campaign formed a coalition of allies to develop a strategy to repeal the HIV ban. SLDN was part of that coalition, along with the AIDS Action Council, the National Association of People With AIDS, the Lambda Legal Defense and Education Fund, the ACLU, the National Gay & Lesbian Task Force, People For the American Way, the National Lawyers Guild, and others.

We reached out through our growing networks of veterans and service members to let them know that we would represent HIV+ service members affected by the ban. We were prepared to litigate and built a network of sympathetic health care providers. Through them, we discovered that Dornan's office was trying to intimidate local hospital commands into releasing medical records of HIV+ service members—and halted it.

One of SLDN's clients was Petty Officer Carl Brown.[105] He had served for 16 years, earning four Good Conduct medals and a Navy Achievement medal. He had been HIV+ for 10 of his 16 years of service, and his fellow crew members were aware of his status. We stood ready to defend him against any discharge action.

SLDN met with White House Counsel Jack Quinn and representatives from the Department of Justice. Through our and our allies' efforts, on the day before he signed the defense authorization bill into law, the president ordered the Department of Justice not to defend the HIV ban in federal court.

The Human Rights Campaign persuaded Magic Johnson, the NBA superstar who had been recently diagnosed with HIV, to write a letter demanding repeal of the ban. Magic Johnson pulled on the heartstrings, but not the policy strings.

We insisted that the primary voice had to be the Pentagon's, and successfully lobbied for a statement. The Pentagon opposed the HIV ban; Dornan had introduced his amendment without consulting military leaders or obtaining military or medical opinion about the ban.

The statement was issued by Defense Secretary William J. Perry and Army Gen. John Shalikashvili, the chairman of the Joint Chiefs of Staff. "Discharging service members deemed fit for duty would waste the Government's investment in the training of these individuals and be disruptive to the military programs in which they play an integral role," they said.[106]

Shalikashvili called the ban "unwarranted and unwise."[107] He would later play a pivotal role in the debate on repealing "Don't ask, don't tell."

SLDN also brought to light a letter, written by the Joint Staff surgeon during the debate on gays in the military, that said that the risk of HIV posed no threat to members of the armed forces and should not form a basis to discharge gay service members. The words of the secretary of defense, the chairman of the Joint Chiefs, and the Joint Staff surgeon mobilized members of Congress to immediately support a bill repealing the HIV ban only two months after it was signed into law—an incredible about-face.[108]

We would have to step up again in 2000 to persuade the Department of Veterans Affairs from removing HIV+ veterans from the military disability system.[109] Several had already been forced from the program, and 152 veterans were in imminent jeopardy of losing their critical benefits. Our quick intervention, led by SLDN staff attorney Jeff Cleghorn, a former Army major, helped reverse that decision.

HIV-related policies affecting service members and veterans were not explicitly part of SLDN's mission. Their pros and cons did not directly affect the debate on gays in the military, though critics of gays serving openly raised the threat of HIV, even in 2008. The two were separate issues.

The Pentagon itself had acknowledged, as medical experts had already concluded, that HIV was an equal opportunity virus. There were many heterosexual service members who had contracted it, and the Pentagon had developed best practices for prevention and treatment. Michelle and I knew, however, that some of our clients would benefit from repeal of the HIV ban, and someone needed to step up to assist.

BACKLASH

CHAPTER 8

"LIEUTENANT STUNNING"

The case of Navy Lieutenant Zoe Dunning highlighted both our early successes in fighting the ban on lesbian, gay, and bisexual service members and the backlash that would grow during the 1990s.

Dunning graduated from the U.S. Naval Academy and spent six years on active duty, then joined the Navy Reserve so she could attend business school at Stanford University. In 1993, three days before Bill Clinton was inaugurated, she came out in support of his pledge as a presidential candidate to lift the gay ban.[110] She wanted to provide a face to the issue.[111] A freckled, funny-as-hell spitfire, she combined a Wisconsin-born wholesomeness with a Bay Area edge.

The Navy moved to discharge her, but Clinton had ordered that all discharges be held in abeyance pending the outcome of the "Don't ask, don't tell" debate. No one noticed that the armed forces didn't implode between January and June despite the ban on discharges, just as the military hadn't crumbled during the first Gulf War when President George H.W. Bush ordered a "stop loss" to prevent discharges of gay service members until the war was over. Politicians hate it when a good theory is trumped by an ugly fact, but they are also wildly adept at cognitive dissonance.

Later that year, a military tribunal ordered her discharge. She appealed that decision in one of the first cases to test Clinton's offer that lesbians could serve if they did not have sex with women. They could have sex with men as long as they didn't say that they were lesbian. Straight men could have sex with gay men under the "queen for a day" exemption. It was so complicated.

At her appeal, Dunning's defense team argued that her statement about her sexual orientation did not provide evidence of any intent to engage in criminal sexual misconduct. They also said that she agreed to abide by the new regulations. In December 1994, the board of officers hearing her case agreed, and she continued to serve as a Navy officer.[112]

It didn't hurt that one member of the board was resigning in two weeks and perhaps didn't fear ramifications; another said that he opposed discrimination; and a third said he had a gay sibling. Nor did it hurt that Dunning lived in San Francisco; the discharge board was convened nearby; and the prosecutor slipped by calling her "Lieutenant Stunning." (When the *Oakland Tribune* called me for a reaction, I was stunned.)

Dunning's precedent was short-lived. At the urging of the Family Research Council, an anti-gay activist organization, Pentagon general counsel Judith Miller, the successor to Jamie

Gorelick, and three senators—Democrat Sam Nunn and Republicans Phil Gramm and Dan Coats[113]—immediately put together new guidelines that clarified how boards should rule. From now on, the new guidance said, a promise to abide by "Don't ask, don't tell" did not suffice to rebut the presumption that a gay service member intended to have sex. (Captain Rich Richenberg found the same result in the Air Force.)

The "Dunning memo," as we called it, foreclosed what could have made "Don't ask, don't tell" an awkward step forward. It would have been a step forward because gay service members could be open and agree to abide by the law—not that such a burden should have ever been imposed. In addition, the presence of openly gay service members would have helped accelerate acceptance.

But such a compromise also would have been awkward. It could have forced many service members to make an abstinence pledge that they would not want to keep. The sexual part of their lives would have had to remain compartmentalized.

The irony of "Don't ask, don't tell" and prior restrictions is that many lesbian, gay, and bisexual service members did serve openly. The catch was that if someone turned you in and your commander wanted to enforce the rules, you could lose your career and livelihood. "Don't ask, don't tell" meant a life on tenterhooks.

The benefits of Dunning's case were twofold. First, the "Dunning memo" showed that the government had no intent of providing a mechanism by which others who came out could retain their jobs—proving that "Don't ask, don't tell" was, in fact, not a compromise, as the public had been led to believe.

Bruce Lehman, the commissioner of the U.S. Patent and Trademark Office and the first openly gay man confirmed by the

Senate,[114] arranged for us to meet with Miller. Michelle and I were all business, trying to convince her that she should rescind the memo or follow through on our recommendation that the Pentagon publish guidelines that clarified the investigative limits under "Don't ask, don't tell." Lehman provided the fire, telling Miller she "should be ashamed" of herself for supporting the Family Research Council over the president. I kept a poker face, but internally I raised my eyebrow. Miller did not implement any of our recommendations.

The second benefit of Dunning's case is that she continued to serve in the Navy Reserve, as an openly lesbian officer, until 2007, undercutting the main argument of critics that her presence would undermine unit cohesion. She retired with the rank of commander, receiving stellar performance evaluations throughout her career.

Zoe Dunning was not the only exception to the rule, though each was due to legal intervention. After being reinstated by court order, Army nurse Margarethe Cammermeyer, a colonel in the Washington state National Guard, served openly for several years. Marine Sergeant Justin Elzie retired on February 18, 1997, after serving for four years as an openly gay man at Camp Lejeune, North Carolina. During that time, he was named NCO (noncommissioned officer) of the Quarter and a top marksman on the base. His final fitness report stated that Elzie possessed "the leadership abilities to lead the Marine Corps into the twenty-first century."[115]

Prior to his retirement in 1996, and having won his court case under the old ban, Petty Officer Keith Meinhold served as an openly gay sailor for three and a half years, during which time his crew was named the most combat-ready in the Pacific Fleet. In

Meinhold's final evaluation, his commander said that "his inspirational leadership has significantly contributed to the efficiency, training, and readiness of my squadron."[116] One of Meinhold's co-workers, a self-described "bigot from hell," told National Public Radio that he had changed his views about gays in the military because of Meinhold.[117]

As Michelle and I noted in SLDN's first annual report, "These service members are only a handful of those who have been serving openly ... and who, as clear documentation shows, have had a positive impact on their unit's good order, discipline and morale."

◆ ◆ ◆

Meinhold agreed to a speaking tour with SLDN after his retirement, and he got more than he bargained for at a stop in Chicago. The morning we left, he caught a taxi and picked me up at my hotel. We were headed to Minneapolis, where the law firm Robins, Kaplan, Miller & Ciresi was hosting a fundraiser for us.

The cab arrived. I put my bag in the trunk and got into the taxi. I immediately noticed two things that were odd: First, there was a woman, a friend of the driver, slumped down in the front passenger seat, flicking a Bic lighter. Second, the driver said he wanted to stop for gas, and he would restart the meter at zero. Meinhold was chatting happily, and I was trying to not look concerned.

At the next light, a car swerved in front of our taxi. The occupants jumped out and ordered us out. The woman in the passenger seat blurted out, "Freddy, don't use your gun."

Meinhold and I figured that we were being robbed, and that our lives could soon end in a flurry of bullets. We ran as fast as we could.

It turned out that one of the guys who jumped the taxi was the owner of the cab, which Freddy and his female friend had stolen. The owner grabbed the keys and opened the trunk. We took our bags and ran to the Loop, by Lake Michigan, where we caught another taxi to O'Hare. I doubt that the hazards of nonprofit life compare to Navy service, but our adrenaline was sky-high that morning.

◆ ◆ ◆

The fact that Colonel Cammermeyer, Lieutenant Dunning, Sergeant Elzie, and Petty Officer Meinhold could serve openly with the support of their commanders and peers stood in sharp contrast to the zealous efforts to oust others. Miller's "Dunning memo" was not an aberration. Instead, the government's mean-spiritedness was just getting started as other draconian policies emerged.

CHAPTER 9

THE DOCTOR IS IN

The case of Marine Corporal Kevin Blaesing[118] showed that under "Don't ask, don't tell," an individual could not have private conversations with military physicians or psychotherapists.

Blaesing was assigned to the Marine Corps Security Force in Charleston, South Carolina, and had been named Marine of the Quarter. He was a sweet, wide-eyed kid from Muscatine, Iowa, just twenty-two years old. In May 1994 he sought counseling from a base psychologist because he was having questions about his sexual identity.

Many young adults who join the military have not yet come out to themselves. Military service is the worst crucible in which to figure it out. Yet Blaesing asked questions in a way that was quite savvy. He never said, "I am gay." Instead, he asked the psychologist: "What does it mean to be gay?" "How do you know if you're gay?" "What's the difference between hanging out with guys and being attracted to guys?"

The psychologist concluded the session saying, "By the way, you know I have to tell the commander about our conversation."

"I wish you had told me that first," Blaesing replied.

He got in touch with Michelle, who immediately contacted Blaesing's commander and convinced him to back down. After all, Blaesing did not "tell."

Several weeks later, there was a change of command—and a change of tune. Blaesing's new commander, Lieutenant Colonel M.J. Martinson, revived the case and ordered discharge proceedings. We contacted the military defense attorney's office, who intervened again. The base legal office urged Martinson to drop the case because Blaesing did not "tell." The psychologist confirmed that Blaesing had not actually come out to her. Martinson would not be dissuaded. In his view, just thinking about being gay was enough to warrant discharge.

We assisted the military defense lawyer who argued the case before the administrative discharge board, and won. The board ruled that Blaesing had not violated "Don't ask, don't tell."

Martinson was furious, and he retaliated. He downgraded Blaesing's performance evaluations against the advice of the corporal's direct supervisors, who thought highly of the marine. The new performance report, with its poor ratings, effectively killed Blaesing's chances for reenlistment.

Blaesing's case was not the only instance in which medical and mental health professionals sabotaged the careers of service members under "Don't ask, don't tell."

An Air Force civilian psychotherapist at Keesler Air Force Base in Mississippi told her client, Captain Ruth Ross-Powell, that she was "required" to turn Ross-Powell in to her command because she had told the therapist that she was bisexual. The captain soon found herself the target of a command-directed inquiry into her private life. Ross-Powell, a 29-year-old dentist, told us that she had sought help for dealing with her sexuality and never conceived that a fellow member of the health professions would ever violate patient confidentiality. Despite our intervention, Ross-Powell was discharged.

Captain Joseph Berger, an Air Force physician at Goodfellow Air Force Base in Texas, outed a patient of his, an airman first class, after surmising the patient's sexual orientation. The airman had sought assistance for a medical condition resulting from a sexual assault.

Berger wrote to the airman's commander, essentially telling them he believed that the airman was gay: "I am required to notify you ... so further actions can be taken." As a result of Berger's violation of the airman's medical privacy, the airman became the target of an Air Force investigation into his private life that resulted in his discharge.

The discharge was insult to injury. The airman had sought medical treatment because he had been sexually assaulted. The doctor revictimized the patient, abandoning the Hippocratic Oath and the privacy rules under "Don't ask, don't tell." The Air Force never responded to an inspector general's complaint we filed on the airman's behalf.

A military physician described the dilemma this way: "The medical necessity for inquiring about sexuality is not even debatable. That the military compromises the physical and mental health of gay service members by denying them candor with their military physicians is reprehensible."

Gay service members were caught amid competing norms. Most physicians and mental health professionals adhered to doctor/patient confidentiality. The Pentagon's position was that they should report medical information to the command that might require a command action, including discharge. "Don't ask, don't tell" tried to carve out an exception to that principle by creating a zone of privacy, but the Pentagon never distributed the guidelines.

The question was why some medical and mental health providers felt *compelled* to turn in gay service members, rather than adhere to the professional norm of confidentiality. Our cases started to provide the answer.

We found that the Navy's General Medical Officer Manual included these instructions: "Homosexuals should not be referred to psychiatry. This is not a medical matter, but a legal matter. The referral should be made to the command legal officer or the judge advocate general. ... [T]hose who seek out [a mental health provider] to disclose homosexual conduct ... are *asking* [emphasis added] to be discharged."[119]

Guidance in the Virtual Naval Hospital, a digital library for Navy physicians, stated this about privacy: "Your patients basically have none with you. If the Captain wants to know anything that a patient told you, you must reveal it. Also, if your patient tells you something illegal or dangerous, e.g., ... homosexuality..., you are *required* [emphasis added] to report it."[120]

Lieutenant Dennis Townsend, a Navy physician, told us that it was his understanding, based on the training he had received as part of the military's Health Professions Scholarship Program, that "as a physician, I am required to inform a sailor's command of his/her homosexual orientation if they reveal that information to me."[121]

By definition, the General Medical Officer Manual asserted that gay sailors were not people who were seeking medical advice; instead, they were walking, talking legal problems who *asked for* adverse personnel action simply by going to a mental health provider. The pervading ethos was to "blame the gay," something we would see in case after case.

While the Virtual Naval Hospital guidance acknowledged the latitude that a limited privilege offered for counseling, it did not allow for any latitude in "gay" cases, where counselors were *obligated* to report gay sailors to the command for discharge. The guidance inflamed matters further by calling gay Americans "dangerous."

Whenever we reported the language that undercut the privacy rights contained in the "Don't ask, don't tell" guidelines, the Pentagon repeatedly excused it as a minor oversight. At our request, the Pentagon removed the sections on gay service members from the General Medical Officer Manual and the Virtual Naval Hospital after SLDN exposed them. In 1998, the Pentagon stated that mental health providers were no longer "required" to turn in gay service members.[122] It's the old "don't do it, but if you do, no foul" rule: The Pentagon refused to make confidentiality a bright-line rule and failed to distribute guidance through the medical chain of command.

In 2000, President Clinton signed an executive order providing for a limited psychotherapist privilege, another of our growing number of policy successes. This privilege ensured, for the first time, that certain conversations between military patients and their mental health providers could not be used as evidence of criminal activity in a court-martial, absent treason, threats to national security, or other limited circumstances. It meant that lesbians, gays, and bisexuals who talked about consensual sexual activity could not have those disclosures used at court-martial for criminal conviction for sodomy or indecent acts under the Uniform Code of Military Justice. It did not, however, prevent commanders from using as evidence those same conversations as a basis for administrative discharge, which is what had happened in the 1990s to Corporal Blaesing and other clients.

That executive order resulted from several years of work. The Joint Services Committee, an inter-service group of lawyers that reviews the criminal code and makes recommendations to align the code with emerging federal law, first made its recommendation in 1997.[123] Often these recommendations do not see the light of day, absent political or public interest.

The proposed regulation was published in the Federal Register for public comment. SLDN submitted comments regarding the limited psychotherapist privilege and encouraged its adoption, aligning the military criminal code with the Supreme Court's 1996 decision in *Jaffee v. Redmond*, which recognized that a psychotherapist-patient privilege existed under the Federal Rules of Evidence. The Joint Services Committee included some of our recommendations to limit the number of exceptions to the rule. The final language was sent to the secretary of defense for approval before being sent to the White House for consideration as an executive order.

I called Richard Socarides, a special assistant and senior advisor to President Clinton, to discuss the proposed executive order. He was the first White House liaison to the gay and lesbian communities, and the son of a notoriously anti-gay New York psychiatrist who believed that being gay was a mental illness.[124]

"Are you sure you want this?" he asked.

"Absolutely," I said, though I did have some doubts.

I had approached Clinton Anderson, director of the American Psychological Association's LGBT Concerns Office. The APA took the position that it would not support the limited privilege unless the exceptions to the rule were even narrower and the privilege applied to the administrative context.

It was understandable that the APA sought a broader privilege. So did we. The language in the proposed executive order fell far short. The question was whether we would rupture relations with the APA if we advocated for the executive order—and, even more importantly, whether we would actually harm efforts to secure greater legal protections for patients in the military.

Anderson was silent on those matters, and I took his silence, and the lack of lobbying by the APA, as a sign that the executive order was not a priority for the organization and that SLDN was free to lobby for it. My view in 2000 was that the executive order created an opening, and I marched through it.

The limited psychotherapist privilege didn't solve the full problem, or even the main problem. We didn't know of a single case in which a gay service member had been criminally prosecuted based on comments made to a mental health provider. But it did serve as a building block for future action, providing a point of entry for a more comprehensive privilege that extended to administrative discharges.

The military had extended confidentiality between military attorneys and their clients, and between a clergy member and a penitent, from the criminal context to the administrative one.

There was precedent to conclude that the military could do the same with the psychotherapist privilege. In March 2010, the Pentagon issued new rules making explicit that the psychotherapist privilege also applied in the administrative context. Laying the groundwork leads to bigger changes.

Two years earlier, in 2008, I was honored by the gay and lesbian section of the American Psychiatric Association. I had been invited by a former client, Dr. Martin Chin. An Air Force physician, he had been stationed in Japan, where he served as a psychiatrist, an internist, and a flight surgeon. Despite Chin's medical expertise, his commander approached him and said he would never be promoted because if it became known that he was gay, it would "expose him as a liar" and "bring embarrassment to the Air Force."[125] Dr. Chin had never "told," but he could not, as a matter of integrity, remain in the Air Force after that.

Addressing the guests, I quoted Carl Jung, who once said that those who discriminate may be able to "deceive [themselves] in the belief of [their] obvious righteousness. But deep down, below the surface of the average man's conscience, he hears a voice whispering, 'There is something not right,' no matter how much his rightness is supported by public opinion or by the moral code."

"I find great optimism in Jung's words," I said. "We know that we are right about ourselves and the equality and dignity that is ours. And, we know, deep down, our opponents must eventually agree."

Corporal Blaesing had faced the indignant righteousness of Lieutenant Colonel Martinson in 1994. Dr. Chin had experienced blowback in the medical corps in 2004. In 2008, despite the significant progress we had made in our efforts to repeal "Don't ask, don't tell," we clearly still had a fierce battle ahead.

CHAPTER 10

YOU'VE GOT MAIL

Timothy McVeigh discovered the perils of personal online communications under "Don't ask, don't tell."

This wasn't Timothy McVeigh, the Oklahoma City bomber. This was Timothy McVeigh, senior chief petty officer on the nuclear submarine USS *Chicago*.[126] He was a tall, lanky, bottle-blond, by-the-numbers thirtysomething who had enlisted in the Navy when he was 18 and knew no other life.

McVeigh's crime was participating in a toy drive for his shipmates' children. He sent an email about it to the wife of a fellow noncommissioned officer on the *Chicago*, but he mistakenly sent it from his AOL (America Online) personal account, not his military account. The wife, a civilian Navy volunteer, said that she didn't recognize the email address, which didn't include McVeigh's name, though the subject matter was clear and the email was signed "Tim." She looked up the AOL profile associated with the account and found that "Tim," who used only his first name and city in his profile (and did not say that he was in the Navy), had listed his marital status as "gay."[127]

She gay-panicked. She turned the email over to her husband, and he gay-panicked. An investigation ensued. We have all sent emails that we regret, but this one—not because of the message's content, but because of the sexual orientation of the person sending it—would cost McVeigh his career.

A Navy paralegal called AOL to collect corroborating evidence from a technical support representative. The paralegal lied to tech support, saying that he was a friend of McVeigh's and was "in receipt of a fax sheet and wanted to confirm the profile sheet, who it belonged to."[128] The technical support representative confirmed McVeigh's identity, and the Navy moved to discharge him.[129]

Americans have always been concerned about privacy. We are leery about troll farms harvesting our online profiles, surveillance drones overhead, phone companies aggregating our metadata, and the spread of facial recognition technology. In polls, Americans agree that they are willing to give up some liberty for security— but we are concerned when those intrusions hit close to home, and many do not trust the government to stay within bounds.

This gross intrusion into McVeigh's privacy became the crux of our defense. The question was not whether he was, in fact, gay, but that there are, or should be, some restrictions on ferreting out sexual orientation. This idea was at the heart of the investigative limits that were supposed to rein in the gay ban.

With the expert assistance of Christopher Wolf at Proskauer Rose, we sought an injunction in federal court against McVeigh's discharge. Chris subsequently became one of the foremost experts on electronic privacy law—inspired, he says, by his work on the McVeigh case.

In January 1998, Judge Stanley Sporkin, a Republican appointee on the U.S. District Court for the District of Columbia, agreed with us. He ruled that "the Navy has gone too far," and that it "violated the very essence of the 'Don't Ask, Don't Pursue' by launching a search and destroy mission"[130] against McVeigh, ignoring the military regulations that attempted to restrict exactly those types of pursuits.

While we had not succeeded in having the courts overturn "Don't ask, don't tell" on constitutional grounds, we hoped to build precedent that would strengthen the guidelines' investigative limits. McVeigh's case was the first to affirm our position. Unfortunately, it was the only time that a federal court attempted to rein in the government's excesses under "Don't ask, don't tell."

The Navy sought to appeal the McVeigh decision. We were concerned that the district court ruling would be overturned, given the lack of "substantive and procedural rights" that the government had successfully argued elsewhere. But we knew that the privacy concerns raised in this particular context gave us additional leverage.

Chris and SLDN told the Department of Justice and the White House that settling the case would end what could become a long, publicly embarrassing story of government overreach. We also noted that the Navy had a face-saving way out: It could end the case by extending the Navy's Temporary Retirement Program to McVeigh as part of its efforts to downsize. The Navy would drop the case. McVeigh would retire. The government agreed.

McVeigh didn't want to leave the Navy—but he also agreed, albeit reluctantly.

Under the agreement, the Navy promoted McVeigh to master chief petty officer, one of the highest ranks available to enlisted personnel, and he was given his prorated pension benefits under the Temporary Retirement Program. Those benefits amounted to more than a million dollars, payable for the rest of McVeigh's life. But he had to cut short a military career that he had loved, and the only career he had ever known.

"What am I going to do now?" he asked me.

"What do you want to do?" I replied.

"Do you know anyone with a private nuclear sub they need someone to run?"

McVeigh was genuine and sweet. He accompanied me to New York City one time to share his story with SLDN supporters. His case highlighted the absurdity of "Don't ask, don't tell," the self-inflicted wound to military readiness by losing such a highly trained and accomplished sailor, and SLDN's effectiveness at getting results.

It might have been McVeigh's first time in the Big Apple. That night, as we walked back to our hotel rooms, a fabulous glittered drag queen clicked her heels across the cobblestones of the Meatpacking District. McVeigh's wide-eyed stare was refreshing for the jaded. He had truly never seen a drag queen before, except, perhaps, when crossing the equator—an oddly homoerotic, cross-dressing celebration on some Navy ships.

Sometimes you will find unlikely allies to join your cause. This case provided one of those opportunities. I approached the Electronic Privacy Information Center to join us in fighting McVeigh's discharge. They agreed.

EPIC's mission is to protect the privacy rights of Americans, both on the internet and from other forms of government and corporate intrusion. Having EPIC join SLDN helped to broaden the appeal of the McVeigh case, placing "Don't ask, don't tell" in the context of a national privacy debate. Enlisting unusual allies, as we did with the American Psychological Association in the context of psychotherapist privilege, strengthens advocacy.

In addition to the litigation, SLDN and EPIC lobbied AOL to change its privacy policy. The online service should not have provided information about its subscriber to the Navy without a lawful search warrant or court order.

AOL was facing a potential public relations nightmare, and it acted quickly. The company apologized to McVeigh. It also published the results of an internal investigation, concluding that the Navy "deliberately ignored both federal law and well-established procedures for handling government inquiries about AOL members."

In addition, AOL adopted a new, industry-leading privacy policy to protect its consumers. Had that policy been in place earlier, McVeigh may have continued his career on nuclear submarines, protecting our nation. While SLDN's mission was clearly focused on repeal of "Don't ask, don't tell," Michelle and I always looked at the larger context of our work, and secured policies—governmental and corporate—that benefited society.

CHAPTER 11

A WALKING TALKING CONTRADICTION

S teve May found that even his position as an elected official didn't protect him from the poison of "Don't ask, don't tell."

His conservative constituents in a wealthy Phoenix district knew that May—a lower-my-taxes Log Cabin Republican Mormon— was gay when they elected him to a seat in the Arizona legislature in 1998.[131] He also was an officer in the inactive Army Reserve, and had thought it unlikely that he would be recalled to active duty. Then the Kosovo war erupted in 1999, and the Army recalled him to the active Reserve as a first lieutenant.

As quickly as the Army recalled May, it moved to discharge him.[132] At issue were statements he had made to an Arizona House committee, prior to being recalled, about pending legislation that would prevent any Arizona city from providing domestic partner benefits to city employees.

"When you attack my family and you steal my freedoms, I will not sit quietly in my office," he said. "And that's exactly what this is. It's an attack on my family, an attack on my freedom. This legislature takes my gay tax dollars, and my gay tax dollars spend the same as your straight tax dollars. If you're not going to treat me fairly, stop taking my tax dollars."

May's comments were printed in the *Phoenix New Times*,[133] an alternative weekly, under the headline "Gay Right-Wing Mormon Steve May Is a Walking Talking Contradiction." A member of May's unit handed a copy of the paper to his commander, and the Army initiated discharge proceedings.

I asked Steve to speak at our national gala in 2004, along with Barney Frank, the liberal firebrand congressman, at Sequoia, a glorious restaurant along Georgetown's riverfront. Michelle and I actively cultivated bipartisanship, and I asked each to focus their comments on why "Don't ask, don't tell" should be repealed.

One never tells Barney Frank what to do, however, and he started talking about why elections matter and why it was important to elect Democrats. He was building to a fever pitch as I stood on stage with him, wondering how best to introduce May. I decided if Frank made the partisan pitch, I would dispense with any elaborate introduction and just say, "And now for the other point of view." Fortunately, he concluded his remarks by urging voters to ask political candidates their positions on issues like "Don't ask, don't tell" and vote accordingly.

May's sentiment that night was exactly what he had expressed to *The New York Times*, and it was the heart of the narrative that Michelle and I were building.

"This isn't about gay rights," he told the *Times*. "It's about the security of the nation. The issue for me as a policy-maker is I want to make sure the nation is aware of the dangers this policy creates for our military preparedness."[134]

May's case was ultimately resolved by our pro bono lawyer extraordinaire, Christopher Wolf, when the Army halted its discharge process and the Department of Justice agreed to drop administrative action against him, allowing him to return to the inactive Reserve when his active Reserve commitment expired. The government had in fact been so slow about the process that his two-year Reserve duty was ending.

The government was justifiably concerned that May might prevail in a lawsuit because it had sought to punish an elected official for comments made carrying out his official legislative duties. In the public mind, this case was yet another example of extreme government overreach—and SLDN's effectiveness.

It also was another example of an openly gay service member serving well and with the support of his or her unit, like Margarethe Cammermeyer, Zoe Dunning, and Keith Meinhold. May's direct commander said that May's performance "has been nothing less than outstanding."[135] The unit knew he was gay and, according to the commander, was performing better than it ever had. Thus, contrary to the stated rationale for "Don't ask, don't tell," the presence of an openly gay man was enhancing military readiness, and the Army's attempts to discharge him were undermining unit cohesion.

CHAPTER 12

PAPA DON'T PREACH

The public expects a certain level of privacy when it comes to matters of family and faith. Under "Don't ask, don't tell," service members repeatedly found that there was no sacred place.

In February 1996, during her junior year at West Point, Cadet Nikki Galvan found that out the hard way.[136] Her commander, Lieutenant Colonel Abraham Turner, asked her, in front of four cadets, to define her relationship with another cadet. "Are you friends, pen pals, or lovers?" he said—a blatant violation of "Don't ask, don't tell."

Galvan held firm and refused to answer his questions. At the suggestion of faculty members, she filed a harassment complaint against him.[137] Turner retaliated, ordering that her diary and hundreds of emails be confiscated. The Army had ordered Galvan to keep a diary to process her grief over the recent death of her mother. It then used it against her.

At an SLDN event, Galvan described how her fellow cadets responded. "When the news spread around West Point, my female friends became afraid to talk to me for fear of being labeled a 'lesbian.' My cadet life became unbearable. Walking to class, male cadets would shout ... 'Dyke.' My roommates forced me to move into a different room because they were uncomfortable. There was no one I could talk to. I felt alone, confused, and afraid." That, she said, is when she got in touch with SLDN.

In a letter notifying Galvan of a hearing to determine her continued enrollment at West Point, a hearing officer stated that she had violated regulations "by making various statements in her diary indicating a propensity or intent to engage in homosexual acts or conduct."[138]

Turner tried to expand his investigation against Galvan into a witch hunt that targeted as many as 30 women at West Point.[139] Three resigned as a result. One cadet's mother wrote to Army Secretary Togo D. West Jr., agonizing over the fact that her daughter felt she had no choice but to resign just before graduation because the Army threatened to criminally prosecute her and recoup her tuition.

While these cadets lost their opportunity to serve, SLDN's intervention stopped further pursuits. West Point never investigated Galvan's complaint against Turner. She was disenrolled, but because of our intervention she received an honorable discharge and was not required to repay her tuition.

◆ ◆ ◆

In another case, a service member came out to her parents and told them she was living with her partner. Incensed at the big reveal, our client's father showed up at her unit. He reportedly fulminated, gesticulated, and screamed. He outed her to her unit and her commander. He demanded that she repent or go to hell. Clearly, he was not happy.

The entire unit got quiet in that "bow your head, turn your eyes downward, this is really awkward" sort of way. Our client remained calm and stone-faced.

Her father was screaming in Korean, so no one in the unit understood him—and our client wisely did not translate. She apologized to her unit about her "crazy" dad.

Other children who came out to their parents and friends did not fare so well; they were turned in to their commands and discharged.

◆ ◆ ◆

An airman at Offutt Air Force Base in Nebraska called me in despair. His roommate had just turned him in to his command through the base chaplain.[140] He said that they had been talking about their families and the roommate mentioned that he had a lesbian sister. The airman thought he could confide in his friend that he too was gay, but the roommate freaked and outed him. There was nothing we could do to stop the discharge because under "Don't ask, don't tell," the Pentagon took the position that saying you were gay to anyone, anywhere, anytime constituted telling.

◆ ◆ ◆

Divorces can turn ugly, but "Don't ask, don't tell" provided an aggrieved spouse with a new weapon. Lieutenant Commander Karen Soria, a well-respected Navy chaplain, found herself on the blunt end of the "Don't ask, don't tell" stick.

Newly divorced, she had developed a friendship with a woman who was also in the midst of a divorce. The friend's husband was jealous of their friendship and wanted to hurt his wife, so he told Soria's command that Soria and his wife were in a sexual relationship, producing as evidence a friendship card in which Soria expressed her caring and gratitude for their friendship during a difficult time. He also ripped out of Soria's personal journal an entry about an erotic dream she had had about his wife.

There was no evidence that the two were romantically involved. There was strong evidence that the husband was being vindictive. Nevertheless, the Navy initiated discharge proceedings against Soria. Disgusted by the Navy's actions, she resigned her commission and continued to minister as a civilian.

◆ ◆ ◆

Senior Airman Brandi Grijalva discovered that even conversations with clergy and their assistants could—and would—be used against her. While stationed at Tyndall Air Force Base in Florida, she sought help from a chaplain's assistant about problems she was having at home.[141] The chaplain's assistant assured her that their conversations were safe and confidential, but when she came out as a lesbian, the chaplain's assistant broke his promise. Grijalva was investigated and discharged.

◆ ◆ ◆

In Heidelberg, Germany, Sergeant Gidonny Ramos came out to her civilian husband, who told her command. She was instructed by her superior, a sergeant first class, to see an Army chaplain.[142]

The chaplain berated Ramos for being a lesbian and ordered her into compulsory marriage counseling. He told her that while some Christian chaplains accepted gays, he was not one of them. He said that she was "going to hell," that "homosexuality is a curable disease," and that she did not belong in the Army and was "an embarrassment to the uniform." He urged her to seek information from the "ex-gay" ministry movement, a so-called therapy discredited by the American Psychological Association.

Ramos, realizing she was trapped in an untenable situation, confirmed to her commander that she was a lesbian and was honorably discharged.

◆ ◆ ◆

Captain Monica Hill, an Air Force physician, had just finished her residency and was due to report for active duty when her partner of 14 years, Terri, was diagnosed with terminal brain cancer. Hill sought a deferment from reporting to active duty to care for her partner and be with her during her final months.[143]

The Air Force demanded to know the reason for the request, and Hill was honest. Rather than granting the deferment or offering family support services, as it would for a heterosexual officer in a similar position, the Air Force suspended her orders and launched an investigation into her statement, assuming that she had lied to avoid active duty and questioning her about her sexual orientation and sexual conduct. Time and again, those enforcing

"Don't ask, don't tell" assumed that LGBT service members were lying, causing trouble, or avoiding commitments, rather than just being humans living truthfully.

Hill was with Terri in the hospital when she died on the same day that hijacked jetliners struck the World Trade Center and the Pentagon and crashed in a Pennsylvania field. Though Hill was now available to report to active duty, the Air Force discharged her shortly thereafter. Hill, like Lieutenant (junior grade) Jen Kopfstein, soon would play an important role in challenging "Don't ask, don't tell."

◆ ◆ ◆

Another soldier avoided discharge, but at great personal sacrifice. He was stationed in Afghanistan after the Sept. 11 attacks when he received word that his partner had been hit and killed by a car while walking across the street in San Diego. The soldier asked his commander for permission to return to San Diego for the funeral.

"Whose funeral is it?" the commander asked.

"A very close friend, sir."

"I'm sorry, soldier, but I cannot grant leave for a friend's funeral."

"He is a *very* close friend, sir."

"I can only grant leave if it is an immediate family member."

He chanced speaking in code. "Sir, I can't *tell* you how close of a friend he was, and you can't *ask* me. But, *please*, sir, let me go home just for a few days."

The commander understood the predicament and showed some compassion. "I can't do that. I need to report that the decedent is a family member, and I can't lie. But, son, take the day off to gather yourself."

The soldier went to his tent and sobbed deeply. He had been robbed of his lover and best friend, and he was denied the ability to pay his last respects in person.

◆◆◆

While "Don't ask, don't tell" specifically allowed service members to march in gay rights rallies, they could not acknowledge their sexual orientation through words or acts. Marching is a fundamental freedom of association protected under the First Amendment of the U.S. Constitution, unless you are in the armed forces and run afoul of "Don't ask, don't tell." This was the predicament that Navy Petty Officer First Class Rhonda Davis faced.

In June 2006, Davis attended a marriage equality rally on the Brooklyn Bridge in New York City. During a radio interview, she said that she was in the Navy and that she hoped that one day she would be able to marry her partner.[144] While the military deploys troops abroad to protect the freedoms enshrined in the Constitution, including the right to protest government policy, the Navy discharged Davis for exercising that right.

Story after story laid bare the awful truth of "Don't ask, don't tell."

CHAPTER 13

LACKLAND

ackland Air Force Base in San Antonio, Texas, became an early symbol of how President Clinton's "honorable compromise" had failed. If you believed that "Don't ask, don't tell" truly allowed gay service members to serve as promised, with due respect for privacy rights, it would have been reasonable to expect that gay discharges would diminish. The opposite occurred. The worst offender in the first years was Lackland, the Air Force's basic training command.

◆ ◆ ◆

According to the Pentagon's own statistics, gay discharges across all services surged from 617 in 1994, the year "Don't ask, don't tell" was implemented, to 1,227 in 2001. The 2001 discharge figure was the highest since 1987, when the armed forces discharged 1,380 gay troops.[145] As they did in every conflict from Korea to Vietnam to the Gulf War,[146] gay discharges declined after the United States went to war in Afghanistan in 2001 and Iraq in 2003—from 906 in 2002 to 261 in the final year of the ban. A total of 13,650 service members ultimately were kicked out under "Don't ask, don't tell."[147]

The Pentagon hated to provide this discharge data; it was a no-win public relations situation. If discharges increased, the Pentagon was removing service members vital to our national security; the downward trends after 9/11 demonstrated that the Pentagon increasingly, though not fully, valued all service members.

For the first couple of years, the Pentagon provided the discharge data directly to SLDN upon our request. Then the Pentagon hemmed and hawed, so we asked members of Congress to request the data, and the Pentagon complied. Then the Pentagon slow-walked release of the discharge data even to elected officials, so we drafted an amendment, to be attached to the National Defense Authorization Act for fiscal year 2005, requiring the Pentagon to provide an annual breakdown of all discharges—total discharges, reason for discharge, and from what military installation or ship the person was discharged.

So that it wouldn't be dismissed as a "gay bill" (which it wasn't), we made sure it wasn't publicized that we had prepared the amendment's language. We asked Marty Meehan, who would later be a leader in the fight for repeal, to introduce it in the House. Duncan Hunter, a notoriously anti-gay Republican and chair of the House Armed Services Committee, reportedly called it a smart amendment. Government data remained the gift that kept on giving.

◆ ◆ ◆

The question remained: Why were gay discharges skyrocketing at Lackland? "Of the Air Force's 414 homosexual discharges last year—a record high number—271 were at Lackland," Eric Rosenberg, a national correspondent for Hearst Newspapers, reported in January 1999.[148] The Pentagon blamed the gays for the increase in discharges through 2001, calling the departures "voluntary," but there was nothing voluntary about the forcible removal of service members from their units.

On January 22, 1999, we wrote to Brigadier General Barry W. Barksdale, the base's commander, to register our concern, request a meeting, and suggest that "an independent and impartial panel be established to investigate the matter." Apparently, he was amenable.

Air Force Under Secretary Whit Peters asked Michelle and me to meet with him, and he proposed that we investigate why the gay discharge rate was so high there.[149] He arranged for lodging on the base, meetings with the command and with drill instructors, and focus groups with airmen. Because we wanted to use a methodology that was familiar and acceptable to Pentagon leaders, Michelle and I asked a retired colonel who specialized in conducting focus groups of military personnel to accompany us.

We arrived at Lackland late in the evening. Peters had arranged for us to stay in the visiting officers' quarters. The clerk peered up from the computer reservation and looked at me with surprise. "General Osburn?"

"Don't give me lip, son. Is the room ready?" I'm not sure why I said that. I can be flip, but I also didn't want to give the clerk any reason to doubt the reservation.

"Yes, sir!" And he handed me my key.

Michelle, the retired colonel, and I had a six o'clock start the next morning, the beginning of two days of intensive meetings. We tried to determine how much the men and women at Lackland knew about the "Don't ask, don't tell" policy, what the training was like, how and when they trained new recruits, at what point during the basic training recruits supposedly came out as gay, and what insights they could offer on why recruits were coming out.

Michelle and I insisted on a session with airmen that was closed to superiors. We were amazed when one of the airmen came out to us. That was brave.

"I knew I was gay coming into the Air Force, and I knew that there was 'Don't ask, don't tell,'" he said. "I wasn't prepared for the level of harassment, the constant name-calling."

Airmen confirmed that superiors frequently used words like "faggot" in training. Some saw it as a form of hazing; others thought it was inappropriate. The failure to curb harassment and hold accountable those who harassed foretold something dire later that year in the Army, but it just as easily could have happened here.

In a conversation with drill instructors, a female drill instructor observed that gays were "just trouble." We asked what she meant by that.

"Well, I don't want to kick anyone out of the military," she replied. "It makes me look bad. If an airman comes out, I have no choice, even if they're good."

Another drill instructor said, "I think they are just making it up because they can't hack it. I don't like it. They should have to gut it out like everyone else. They shouldn't get an easy way out."

"What if there is a different way to look at this?" I asked. "What if they aren't trying to get out, but they don't know the rules yet? Basic training is hard and new for these airmen, and it should be hard, because you're building the best Air Force. But what if these eighteen-year-olds are just bonding with their fellow recruits and coming out as gay like they did in high school, not knowing that there's this law that forces your hand. They haven't been trained on 'Don't ask, don't tell' yet."

"Oh," the first drill instructor said. "So they aren't trying to make my life difficult, then. The law makes their life difficult. I hadn't looked at it like that."

I continued: "We also know for some service members who call us, it's an issue of integrity. Some of these young men and women probably didn't understand what 'Don't ask, don't tell' requires of them. It requires them to stay in the closet and tell absolutely no one who they are. They can't do that as a matter of their personal honor.

"Perhaps some arriving here thought they could, but boot camp is a reality check they hadn't understood. So, for some, even though they had dreamed of joining the Air Force, they aren't willing to do it if they can't be true to themselves, and 'Don't ask, don't tell' forces your hand."

"I get that," the other drill instructor said.

Our October 11 report to the base command and to Under Secretary Peters synthesized what we had learned from our interviews, as well as from the cases we had handled in recent years.

We noted four factors contributing to the disproportionate discharge rate at Lackland: confusion about "Don't ask, don't tell," anti-gay harassment among trainees, lack of recourse when targeted, and a reflexive response to immediately discharge airmen, regardless of the facts.

We offered a pragmatic solution—and while it wasn't fully consistent with the draconian gay ban that had been enacted, it, as I would say as a Texan, "might could" solve the high rate of gay discharges at the base. We suggested a two-strike policy: that when an airman came out as gay during basic training but prior to their receiving the "Don't ask, don't tell" training that would follow later, they pull the airman aside, in private, and tell them what the law required. They had to shut up or they would be discharged. We also asked that they train that harassment of any kind, including using anti-gay epithets, would not be tolerated.

Those changes were made, and gay discharges at Lackland Air Force Base plummeted 600 percent from 1998 to 1999.[150]

Whit Peters later became acting secretary of the Air Force. I have always appreciated how he entrusted Michelle and me to conduct an investigation at Lackland Air Force Base. Leaders do not run away from controversy. They try to understand it and address it. If only other leaders had done the same.

CHAPTER 14

THE HOMOSEXUAL QUESTIONNAIRES

n the years after Congress passed "Don't ask, don't tell," Michelle and I discovered through our casework that not only had the Pentagon not distributed the "Don't ask, don't tell" guidelines or a simpler memo of command guidance that emphasized the promises under the policy, it—and the Air Force and the Navy—had done the opposite. The backlash against service members included a veritable "how to" guide for asking, pursuing, and harassing.

One of the clearest mistakes was the failure to replace recruiting forms. The statute governing "Don't ask, don't tell" required that recruits not be asked about their sexual orientation when they were enlisting. Yet as early as 1994[151] and as late as July 2002, SLDN obtained recruiting forms, dated 1989,[152] that asked enlistees "Are you a homosexual?"

In 1998, thanks to our constant pressure[153] (which included a terse letter from Patrick Kennedy, a Democratic member of the House Armed Services Committee), Defense Secretary William Cohen ordered that the old forms be replaced. In 2002, three recruiting offices, as well as the Air Force Reserve Publications Command, told SLDN that the enlistment application containing the question was the only form available to recruitment offices. Mike West, forms manager for the Air Force Reserve Command, told us, "I can assure you [the form in question] is the latest version officially released for use."[154]

The Pentagon dismissed our concern, just as they dismissed the aberrant medical directives that required doctors to turn in gays, explaining that recruiting stations were just using up old stock before implementing the new forms, eight years after "Don't ask, don't tell" was implemented.

◆◆◆

On November 3, 1994, nine months after the "Don't ask, don't tell" law went into effect, the Air Force Judge Advocate General headquarters published a memo that authorized witch hunts.[155] The memo directed investigators to launch investigations into "other military members" who were "discovered" to be gay during an investigation against another airman.[156]

Rather than limiting an investigation to the person who said he or she was gay, the memo authorized going after others. That is a witch hunt. In addition, it authorized interrogating a wide range of potential witnesses—including parents, siblings, school counselors, roommates, and close friends—to dig up derogatory information that might lead the Air Force to consider other discriminatory action.[157]

The memo was written in reaction to the May 14, 1994, memo from Deputy Secretary of Defense John Deutch that prohibited recoupment against gays unless they were lying to avoid their military obligation.

The Air Force set out to prove that gays were lying about their sexual orientation, thus allowing it to recoup those scholarship funds, and authorized a dragnet in case other gays would be discovered in the process. The guidance flouted the "Don't ask, don't harass, don't pursue" guidelines, and it bled from anti-Deutch sentiments into all investigations.

Judith Miller, the Pentagon general counsel who was responsible for the Dunning memo, published another memo echoing the Air Force guidance.[158]

◆ ◆ ◆

In November 1994, the Navy's appellate litigation group issued a memo suggesting that joining a gay organization, or even supporting such organizations and the sailors who join them, may be "inconsistent with good military character."[159] The memo was issued in response to the discovery that a sailor sang in a gay men's chorus, an activity specifically allowed in the "Don't ask, don't tell" guidelines.

The memo suggested that military character, impugned by permitted associational activities, could serve as an additional basis for downgrading a performance evaluation or for discharge. It chillingly suggested that friends of gay service members might be subject to derogatory action simply for their associations.

In addition, the litigation group offered increased legal support to commanders, inquiry officers, and prosecutors in any case where a service member accused under the new policy was seeking assistance from outside organizations, civilian lawyers, the press, or members of Congress.[160] That provision was a direct response to SLDN's legal aid; we were, of course, delighted to discover that we had become such a threat in one year's time.

◆ ◆ ◆

Under "Don't ask, don't tell," the military promised to no longer ask service members about their sexual orientation and to respect a certain zone of privacy. If there was credible information that a service member was gay, such as coming out and declaring "I am gay," there was no need for an inquiry.

But in the vacuum of leadership, the services developed elaborate inquiry protocols. The Navy's "Homosexual/Bisexual Questionnaire" for investigators[161] asked the following: "Do you engage in homosexual/bisexual activity?" "Have you attempted to engage in homosexual/bisexual activity?" "Do you have a propensity to engage in homosexual/bisexual activity?" "Do you intend to engage in homosexual/bisexual acts?" "Are you engaged in a homosexual/bisexual marriage?"

An Army questionnaire went even further. It asked soldiers if they had engaged in a homosexual/bisexual act because they were "drunk" or "as an experiment" or "because you were influenced by another."[162] Affirmative answers might become a basis either for retention under the "queen for a day" exception or for criminal charges, depending on a commander's mood, since drunkenness, experimentation, and manipulation might qualify as indecent acts or conduct unbecoming.

The Army questionnaire was also worse than the Navy's because it required soldiers to answer the questions as part of a sworn statement. If the soldier lied, or made a "false official statement," he or she could be prosecuted under the Uniform Code of Military Justice. This meant that a soldier could go to jail for not being truthful about being gay when asked.

Affirmative answers to the Navy and Army questions led to additional questions of where, when, and with whom. The questions were routine. Some of the "evidence" of being gay bordered on the absurd, such as attending the Dinah Shore women's professional golf tournament in Palm Springs;[163] reading Anne Rice gay vampire novels;[164] listening to k.d. lang; having a Melissa Etheridge poster;[165] holding a CD whose sale had supported breast cancer research;[166] reading Randy Shilts's *Conduct Unbecoming*, a book detailing the military's discrimination against gays; and, ironically, reading *Exclusion: Homosexuals and the Right to Serve*, a book by Army JAG officer Melissa Wells-Petry that supported the military's ban on gays.

We even caught the Naval Criminal Investigative Service admitting in court that it was entrapping gay men at Washington-area gay bars from at least 1998 to 2000, even though the "Don't ask, don't tell" guidelines specifically permitted visits to such establishments.[167] In response to an inquiry by Representative Barney Frank, NCIS denied that it was making "random" notations of license plate numbers outside gay bars, but agents had "walked through the parking lot and in a precise and purposeful manner ... wrote down the license plates of 20 cars that appeared to be military ... then [ran them] through the computer identification system."

SLDN's legal director, Stacey Sobel, who probably finds as much humor in the surreal as I do, wrote the perfect memo in response, demanding that "you halt all Navy surveillance operations targeting gay-friendly establishments, and any adverse actions being taken against those ensnarled in these operations."[168] The Navy complied.

None of the services, or the Pentagon general counsel, rescinded any of the "guidance" we uncovered. The hard evidence helped to shift public opinion and sway journalists covering "Don't ask, don't tell," They saw that the efforts to root out lesbian, gay, and bisexual Americans serving our nation were overzealous, cruel, absurd, mean, and counterproductive. The backlash was severe.

ENDING WITCH HUNTS AND CRIMINAL PROSECUTION

CHAPTER 15

PLATFORM SHOES

One of SLDN's first cases after we opened up shop at the National Veterans Legal Services Program was a witch hunt involving 21 marines at Camp Hansen in Okinawa, Japan. One of those marines was Craig Haack.

Haack was a 21-year-old corporal, far from his home in Portland, Oregon. He had survived boot camp. He was making something of himself. He was independent. He was serving our nation. Then, in a blink, his new life came crashing down around him.

Late one night, criminal investigators, led by Special Agent Jose Abrante, pounded on his barracks room door and barged in. They ransacked his room. They turned his bed upside down, throwing sheets and pillows aside. They seized his computer, his address book, magazines, and even a pair of platform shoes, claiming that they were all possible evidence of homosexual conduct. (Later, I teased him, saying, "Platform shoes may be evidence of bad taste, but not homosexual conduct.")

Abrante asked Haack point-blank: "Are you gay?" Haack, stunned, did not answer.

From March to June 1994, investigators asked 21 marines about their sexual orientation, their sexual conduct, and the orientation and conduct of other service members. The Marine Corps was doing exactly what Clinton and the chairman of the Joint Chiefs of Staff, Colin Powell, had promised would not happen—a witch hunt.

Before "Don't ask, don't tell," these efforts to purge mass numbers of lesbian, gay, or bisexual soldiers, sailors, airmen, and marines from the ranks were not uncommon, and included hundreds of detailed questions about their sex life, including who, where, how, and how often. As long ago as 1919, the Navy enlisted operatives at the Newport Naval Station in Rhode Island to solicit sailors for oral sex, then court-martialed those who said yes.[169] It was more than a tad ironic when one of the government's operatives was questioned on the stand and said that he had eagerly volunteered for the job.

Randy Shilts's groundbreaking book *Conduct Unbecoming,* published in the last days of the 1993 debate on gays in the military, detailed dozens of gay and lesbian purges from the armed forces. Perhaps the most infamous was at Parris Island, South Carolina, the home of the Marine Corps Recruit Depot. From 1986 to 1988, the Marine Corps interrogated 246 women, discharging at least 27 and jailing three for being lesbian.

The Navy conducted purges of lesbians on the USS *Norton Sound* in 1980 and on the USS *Dixon* in 1981. In 1986, the Army ousted eight women from West Point for being lesbian. In 1988, the Navy investigated 30 women, including every African American, on the USS *Yellowstone* and discharged eight. That same year, it investigated five of the 13 female crew members on the USS *Grapple*.

Gay activists estimated that as many as 40 airmen were discharged during a purge in December 1989 and January 1990 at Carswell Air Force Base, in Texas. The Air Force acknowledged that a dozen were discharged and six other investigations were ongoing[170] In 1992, during an interview on ABC's *World News Tonight,* Petty Officer Keith Meinhold told of witch hunts on the USS *Blue Ridge* and USS *Independence* that had resulted in the discharge of 42 sailors.[171]

In Haack's case, the question, in our opinion, was not whether he was gay, but whether the Marine Corps had violated any regulations under "Don't ask, don't tell" by questioning him and 20 other marines about their sexual orientation and that of others. And if it had, what could be done about it?

The regulations promulgated by the Pentagon and the services after "Don't ask, don't tell" became law contained some important language that would support the "don't ask" rhetoric, limiting inquiries in very specific ways. Commanders were asked to exercise "sound discretion" in investigating allegations where "credible information" existed. Credible information could not rest on rumor, hearsay, protected associational activities, going to gay bars, or reading gay publications. The rules warned commanders not to ask a service member if he or she was lesbian, gay, or bisexual, or to expand any inquiry beyond the specific allegation made. They expressed a strong preference that agents of the services' criminal investigation units no longer lead the investigation, thus de-escalating the possibility of criminal charges and courts-martial as opposed to administrative discharge.

But Michelle and I knew that, in the end, "Don't ask, don't tell" would not live up to its rhetoric because neither the statutory language—the fine print in the law, as it were—nor the regulations promised to end wide-ranging investigations.

The regulations "provided no procedural or substantive rights," thereby eviscerating any of the averred protections. Thus, under "Don't ask, don't tell," if a service member got caught in a witch hunt, or was assaulted, or was asked if he or she was gay, or was hounded with hundreds of questions, or was threatened with court-martial by a criminal investigator, he or she had no "substantive or procedural rights" to challenge a discharge from the military based on those actions. There was a clear disconnect between President Clinton's promised "step forward" and the plain letter of the statute. Where we had the best chance of success was in early direct intervention with the command.

We persuaded Jon Bowie, a partner in the San Diego office of Skadden, Arps, Slate, Meagher & Flom, to take Haack's case. In 1989, he had been the first openly gay partner at Skadden to bring his same-sex partner to a retreat for lawyers and their spouses. He had previously worked for another top firm, Sullivan & Cromwell, where he was passed over for partnership because he was gay.

I say this to provide some context of the world in which we were living not all that long ago. Even in the most progressive law firms, being openly gay in the late 1980s and early 1990s was neither common nor accepted.

In 1991, when I was a student at Georgetown Law, the school warned us against listing any LGBT clubs or classes on our résumés or academic records. Chai Feldblum, who was the chief legal counsel for the Campaign for Military Service, a leading legal scholar on LGBT rights, and my professor, advised us to consider whether to list her class on sexual orientation and the law on our official transcripts. I was a summer associate at a San Francisco law firm that, according to an associate at the firm, chose not to extend an employment offer after my second year because I was gay.

Jon was a man of gentle demeanor and fierce intellect, an early legal mentor to Michelle and me. His writing was spare, elegant, precise, and damning. We called it the "Bowie memo" and aspired to replicate his style.

I recall one letter that he shot off to Okinawa. Having duly notified the Marine Corps that he was representing Haack and that any communications regarding the investigation should be directed to him, he learned that the Marine Corps had violated the attorney-client relationship and hauled Haack in for additional questioning. The spare letter of one paragraph to the base commander said, "Imagine my surprise when I received a call at 3:00 a.m. from my client who informed me that he had been called in for questioning. Please desist, or you will be in court in California this week."

We loved it. That the admonishment came on Skadden Arps letterhead, rather than SLDN letterhead (a pitiful set of computer-generated stars at the top of a piece of copy paper), gave it even more zing.

Jon then prepared, with our input, a longer memo outlining the ways in which the Marine Corps had violated the regulations implementing "Don't ask, don't tell." We were at his house in Rancho Santa Fe, a San Diego suburb, watching from his poolside as hot-air balloons in hues of red, orange, and yellow came to life. He reviewed the memo one last time and said sardonically, "If I read this letter, I would be persuaded, unless I knew the law." That indeed was the dilemma.

The Marine Corps discharged Haack. The good result was that he didn't face criminal charges for any alleged sexual conduct. Another marine, who had not called us, was convicted of sodomy and served 35 days in prison.

Before Congress repealed the crime of consensual sodomy as part of the National Defense Authorization Act for fiscal year 2014, service members faced five years in prison for every act of sodomy or "indecent acts" for which they were convicted under the Uniform Code of Military Justice. If they did it twice in one night, they could get 10 years.

In theory, the UCMJ provisions applied equally to men and women, gay and straight. They even made oral sex between a husband and wife illegal. Gay service members, though, had often found themselves disproportionately targeted when allegations involved consensual adult behavior. That is why one of the key provisions of the "Don't ask, don't tell" regulations was aimed at removing criminal investigators from the process.

The Marine Corps did not own up to its mistakes in violating "Don't ask, don't tell" in Okinawa. It should not have launched a criminal investigation. It should not have launched a witch hunt. It should not have asked 21 marines if they were gay.

Despite ample documentation of the violations of the "Don't ask, don't tell" regulations, Special Agent Abrante faced no discipline. His actions were excused as a failure of training, not execution. Meanwhile, Corporal Haack lost his budding career in the Marine Corps.

The witch hunt and the dismal response to fix it exposed the difficult fight Michelle and I were undertaking. One Pentagon official told me that as the new rules were better implemented, a situation like Okinawa shouldn't happen again. But it was just the beginning.

CHAPTER 16

CIAO

The first major witch hunt we confronted was in Okinawa; the next one, 14 months later, was in Italy.

Reminiscent of the lesbian purges in the 1980s on the USS *Norton Sound,* the USS *Dixon,* and the USS *Grapple,* we documented how the Navy targeted up to 60 women on the submarine tender USS *Simon Lake* in Sardinia in November and December of 1995. Seaman Amy Barnes believes that her refusal of a male sailor's overtures prompted the rumors. She said, "If you're a woman and single and don't want to sleep around with every guy, they think you must be gay."[172]

The command's investigator questioned numerous shipmates about Barnes and others, employing high-pressure tactics to try to extract information. Two sailors filed sworn affidavits that they had been threatened with prison unless they accused Barnes of being a lesbian. In an affidavit dated March 26, 1996, Heather Hilbun stated that an investigator had threatened her, saying, "If you do not tell the truth, you will go to jail for 10 to 15 years."[173]

The investigator then allegedly questioned Hilbun about her own sexual orientation and that "of at least six other women by name."

The second sailor said that "[c]ommand investigators threatened and intimidated me into giving involuntary statements [about Seaman Barnes] by telling me that I would be violating Article 78 of the Uniform Code of Military Justice [accessory after the fact] and would go to jail if I did not answer their questions and cooperate."[174] They asked her dozens of questions about Barnes's sexual orientation and that of other women on the ship.

Barnes called us, asking if we could help. We lined up attorneys from Arnold & Porter. We documented what had happened and secured the witness statements that proved the witch hunt, threats, intimidation, and ham-handedness of the investigation. We were in direct contact with Barnes's commander, trying to secure a satisfactory resolution to the case—without success.

Barnes's commander transferred her to Norfolk, Virginia, to initiate discharge. She refused to sign discharge paperwork and leave quietly.[175] When she demanded an administrative discharge hearing, Navy officials moved quickly.

On Friday, March 29, in the middle of the afternoon, Barnes's military lawyer called us to let us know that the command was moving to discharge her the following Monday. If she wanted to stay in the Navy, she needed an injunction—immediately.

We rushed to federal court to get a temporary restraining order, which would prevent her discharge while we sought more permanent relief. I pushed Michelle out the door and into a cab to get to the court in time for the hearing. Michelle was always the attorney you wanted on your side—sharp and tough, never giving an inch. She joined our pro bono counsel in court, while

I helped finish the written filing with other lawyers at Arnold & Porter. I arrived at the U.S. District Court for the District of Columbia soon thereafter.

"Your honor," said one of the Arnold & Porter lawyers, "our client has been denied her right to an attorney during her administrative discharge."

Judge Emmet Sullivan looked at the assistant U.S. attorney who, it appeared, had just been given the case. "You denied her an attorney?"

Rifling through her papers, trying to understand what was going on in the case, she answered, "Your honor, she was on an island." (She was actually in Norfolk.)

The judge, with glasses half-cocked: "You deny attorneys to people on islands?"

Michelle and our attorneys from Arnold & Porter won the day. We got our client a temporary restraining order.

As we moved for a preliminary injunction, we introduced evidence of the witch hunt. We were hopeful that given Judge Sullivan's incredulity at the TRO hearing, he would rule favorably on our request for an injunction. The witch hunt was clear.

Rather than admit its mistake, though, the Pentagon dug in, defending the very conduct it had promised not to do. Before a district court, the government argued for the first time that "regardless of whether the record contains evidence showing the Navy's reason for commencement of the investigation, or the manner in which the investigation was conducted [i.e., a witch hunt], plaintiff has no legal basis upon which to challenge those events here."[176] The government further argued that the "Don't ask, don't tell" regulations "create no enforceable rights"[177] for service members targeted in a witch hunt or by other improper command actions.

We knew that this was the exception that made any promised protections meaningless. Earlier, we had tried to fix it. On May 4, 1994, Michelle persuaded the Advisory Board on the Investigative Capability of the Department of Defense, a panel created by Congress to look into the "current state of affairs" regarding military investigations,[178] to recommend a rule excluding illegally obtained evidence as "fruit of the poisonous tree,"[179] but the Pentagon didn't adopt the recommendation.

Neither did Judge Sullivan. He denied our request for a preliminary injunction, and Barnes was discharged.

She sued the Navy for reinstatement. Rather than litigate the matter and further publicize its noncompliance with the promises under "Don't ask, don't tell," the government opted to settle the case for a modest sum that gave Barnes the means to attend college.[180]

While the Barnes investigation and discharge unfolded, Michelle contacted Steven Honigman, the Navy's general counsel, demanding an end to the witch hunt. Besides Barnes, one other sailor caught in the witch hunt was discharged but did not fight it.[181] The other sailors caught in its snare survived. As Michelle noted, "While we have no official confirmation, we know that officials called the ship's command; circumstances suggest it was these calls that stopped the witch hunt."[182]

Barnes was denied a Navy career. We couldn't establish a legal precedent that witch hunts are wrong, but we proved something important in the court of public opinion. Despite all the promises that "Don't ask, don't tell" was a step forward, the government in Barnes's case confirmed in writing what we already knew—that it was a lie. A sailor couldn't even challenge a witch hunt. The public was beginning to see that "Don't ask, don't tell" was a lie, too.

CHAPTER 17

COME TO JESUS

In 1996, the same year as the witch hunt in Italy, we documented another witch hunt at Hickam Air Force Base in Honolulu, Hawaii, that targeted 17 men from all branches of service.

I received a call from Senior Airman Andre Taylor. He called from his barracks room, with his bedcovers pulled over his head to muffle the sound of his voice. He told me later that he found Servicemembers Legal Defense Network by going to the base library with friends who were also implicated in the witch hunt and looking up "gay organizations" in the Washington, D.C., Yellow Pages. They went after hours so that no one could see them look up the word "gay."

Taylor spoke to me in barely a whisper. He was scared. He didn't know if I was the real deal or a front for the military's criminal investigation services. He held a flashlight under the covers so he could see the phone.

"I don't know what to do," he said. "I don't know who to trust. ... Could I go to jail? ... What do I tell my mom?"

"We're here to help you," I told him. "We'll get through this."

He told me years later that just knowing someone was in his corner helped, regardless of the legal outcome. Though gay service members often felt shunned and were living in the shadows, SLDN accorded them dignity.

The Hickam witch hunt started with Bryan Harris, a senior airman who was facing court-martial for sodomy and sexual assault. The prosecutor promised in a pre-trial agreement that the Air Force would reduce his sentence from life to 20 months if he gave the names of all the men with whom he had had sex. He decided the only way to save his hide was to comply, so he provided 17 names, some incomplete. The Air Force, Army, Navy, and Marine Corps discharged the ones they could identify.

I know of no other case in the military where prosecutors reduced the sentence of a heterosexual male service member accused of sexual assault if he gave the names of female service members with whom he had had consensual oral sex—an illegal act under the Uniform Code of Military Justice. Nor do I know of any case where the military agreed to leniency in the case of a service member accused of adultery if he or she identified fellow officers or enlisted personnel who were engaged in extramarital affairs—also forbidden by the UCMJ.

I flew to Honolulu—paid for out of my own pocket, as I often did because our budget was so limited—to meet with Captain Bob Saragosa. He was one of the 17 men named by Harris. Because he was an officer and Harris was an enlisted man, the Air Force was threatening Saragosa with court-martial for both sodomy and fraternization. Under the UCMJ, the military has the authority to prosecute fraternization between officers and enlisted members as a separate offense.

I asked him to meet me under the large banyan tree at Hula's, a local gay bar. (The bar has since moved and, alas, there is no banyan tree.) This was a "come to Jesus" meeting.

Saragosa was stoic and reserved, or maybe he was in shock and denial. His words were measured. He lowered his eyes, as if looking inward, as he tried to decide on his next steps—and the implications of any action.

I advised him that the Air Force planned to charge him criminally and that he needed to do everything he could to get the service to back down. We had already lined up a pro bono criminal defense attorney in Honolulu because we were so short-staffed and were located almost 5,000 miles away. A JAG officer once called me and asked for the phone number of our "local Honolulu office." Here I was.

I told Saragosa that he should go public. If people knew that the Air Force was conducting a witch hunt—something the Pentagon had promised would not occur—the service stood to receive significant bad press, and that could generate the leverage needed to get it to back down. The one thing the Pentagon hates more than losing a fight is negative attention.

"I can't," he said. "I'm not out to my family."

This was the bind in which "Don't ask, don't tell" placed many service members. The law's goal was to get gays to shut up. The archaic view was that gay Americans would be so ashamed of themselves that they would not be open and honest about who they are. They would not even speak up to defend themselves, to demand equality, to decry injustice, to highlight hypocrisy. The closet is a powerful silencer. "Don't ask, don't tell" was a federally imposed closet.

"Don't tell" was the most insidious aspect of "Don't ask, don't tell" because it was a federal gag order. It prevented the very people impacted by federal law from speaking up to protest it. A gay soldier could not tell his or her member of Congress about his or her valor, sacrifice, or hardship as a *gay* soldier, because that proclamation was grounds for dismissal from the Army. Policy-makers could not gather reliable data about gay service members because official policy rendered those service members invisible.

Laurence Tribe, who taught constitutional law at Harvard Law School for five decades, once noted that there perhaps was no other law in the country that targeted a population group and then prevented them from actively speaking up or contributing to the political dialogue in response to that regulation.[183] Michelle and I had to figure out how to give voice to the voiceless, and to give those voices timbre and meaning—a way to be heard. One way to overcome invisibility was through storytelling.

"Bob," I said, "there is a very real possibility that by the end of this week you will be in jail. Do you want to call your mom now, or when you are in jail?"

I had never told someone that they *had* to come out. I respect the journeys we all take in coming to terms with who we are. I knew when I was four, but I didn't come out until my early twenties. I was uneasy making him do something he did not want to do. He clearly did not want to do it. But he did.

He called me the next day to report that he had spoken with his mother.

"I told her I was in trouble," he said. Her reply: "Honey, does this have to do with 'Don't ask, don't tell'?"

We both laughed. "Moms always know," I told him.

Now that Saragosa had come out to his family, he was willing to speak publicly. I usually wouldn't recommend going from the closet to "ta-da!" overnight, but this was a legal necessity. Fortunately, the mere threat of bad publicity convinced the Air Force at the eleventh hour to back down from the court-martial.[184] However, Saragosa was discharged under "Don't ask, don't tell," ending yet another promising career.

The witch hunt also ensnared Technical Sergeant Daryl Gandy.

An Air Force inspector general's report concluded that the service had not specifically "asked" Gandy or his colleagues about his sexual orientation in violation of "Don't ask, don't tell." Clearly, the Air Force had its own "homosexual/bisexual questionnaire." These are the questions his co-workers and friends were asked:[185] "Do you have any reason to believe that TSgt Gandy doesn't like girls?" "Have you ever had the feeling TSgt Gandy is interested in men?" "Have you ever seen TSgt Gandy hug, kiss, or hold hands with another man in a way that was more than just a means of saying hello?" "Would you be surprised to find out that TSgt Gandy is gay?" "What is it like to work in a unit with so many homosexuals?" "Has TSgt Gandy ever talked about women to you, you know, the way men talk about women?" "Where does TSgt Gandy hang out? With whom?" "Has TSgt Gandy ever had a girlfriend?" "Does anyone in your office know that TSgt Gandy is gay?"

"I did not 'tell,'" Gandy told the *Honolulu Star-Bulletin* in February 1997, "but was, nevertheless, the victim of a very real witch hunt. The Air Force 'asked' and pursued."[186]

A week later, I wrote this to the *Honolulu Star-Bulletin*: "The Air Force cannot be allowed to violate its own regulations if order, discipline, and military readiness are to mean anything."[187] When I told Neil Abercrombie, a Democratic member of Congress from Hawaii, about the witch hunt, he replied, "But that isn't the aloha spirit."

In April 1998, the Department of Defense finally admitted that the witch hunt at Hickam Air Force Base had been improper, and that criminal prosecutors should not have used a pre-trial agreement to solicit names of suspected gays to root them out.[188] The bell, however, could not be un-rung. Every service member who had been identified by investigators, including Andre Taylor, Bob Saragosa and Daryl Gandy, had lost their careers. However, no other pre-trial agreements were used to purge gays after that time.

In 1996, *Nightline* became the first television program to assess "Don't ask, don't tell" implementation in depth, using the Hickam witch hunt as an example of the law's failure. What the story didn't mention was that "B-1 Bob" Dornan, the conservative California congressman who strongly opposed gays in the military, was at it again. He introduced amendments to the National Defense Authorization Act for fiscal year 1997 that would reinstate the strict Defense Department policy on gays that had been in place before "Don't ask, don't tell"—meaning that witch hunts would once again be allowed by law—and would require that recruits be asked if they were gay. The amendments made it into the final House version of the legislation.[189]

It was not a negligible question whether we should fight this language. We would never support laws that required witch hunts, but we had a law where witch hunts were still conducted despite the promises to the contrary.

On the other hand, the fact that one chamber in the legislative branch actually supported the services "asking" and "pursuing" meant that legislators believed those provisions to have substantive meaning. So, while the question was not incidental, we dismissed it and publicly opposed the latest House subterfuge. We, along with the Human Rights Campaign, successfully lobbied Senate allies to oppose similar legislation in that chamber and strip the Dornan amendments in conference.

In 2000, the Pentagon published new guidelines that essentially regulated the end to witch hunts, based on our years of input and advocacy. It announced that investigators should conduct only the minimally necessary investigations in discharge actions, imposing a requirement on commanders to refer any gay discharge action up the chain of command to the secretary of their service if they were seeking the authority for anything more than an insubstantial inquiry. Before the new guidelines were published in 2000, however, there was one more witch hunt at the military's premiere language program—the Defense Language Institute in Monterey, California.

CHAPTER 18

DLI

In 1999, SLDN documented a witch hunt at the Defense Language Institute in Monterey, California. Fourteen airmen had contacted SLDN,[190] many finding their way to us because someone had scratched the name and phone number of our legal director, Stacey Sobel, on a bathroom wall at an off-base coffee house frequented by LGBT service members.

DLI permitted a culture where rampant asking, pursuing, and harassing flourished. The primary instigators were Air Force enlisted leaders, inquiry officers, and civilian language instructors. The base would epitomize the failure of "Don't ask, don't tell" when, after 9/11, it dismissed sorely needed Arabic linguists who happened to be gay. This is how that failure began.

In March and April 1999, Air Force Master Sergeant Rodney Hamlet and Senior Airman David Vigil conducted a witch hunt to determine the sexual orientation of student leaders under their charge. By their own admission, it was based on nothing more than rumors.[191]

Vigil threatened two female airmen first class with the criminal charge of "conduct unbecoming" and proceeded to ask them whether they were in a relationship, which they denied.[192] He and Hamlet then asked Airman First Class Deanna Grossi and others to confirm that the two were lesbians. When Grossi said she didn't know, Hamlet asked her if she too was part of the "nasty rumors ... flying around DLI."[193]

Grossi reported that she became a target of harassment. When she told an airman that his comment about a female student leader being "queen dyke" was inappropriate, he replied, "Oh no. Not you too."[194]

From that moment, others started harassing her as well. When one student asked for a Serbian translation for "rainbow," a symbol of gay pride, a classmate said, "Oh, Grossi [who was studying Serbian] would know."[195] An airman whom Grossi had turned down for a date reportedly made repeated sexually explicit gestures and comments to her, such as holding his fingers up to his nose and saying, "Let me smell your hand so I can see if you did the same thing I did last night."[196] After she had traveled to San Francisco for the weekend, a civilian language instructor asked her in front of the class if she had had "fun ... with her girlfriend."[197]

Vigil also reportedly asked a male airman to keep an eye on a male student, saying he didn't want any "fags" in his Air Force.[198]

Another DLI student reported overhearing a military training leader say, "You can tell the student leaders on dyke flight because of their short hair."[199]

The pervasive anti-gay climate and threat of investigation led Airman First Class Katrina Bandle to come out in April. She was discharged—but not until the command completed an over-reaching investigation that forced her classmates to testify about her sexual orientation.[200]

In May, Airman First Class Bill Johnson came out as a direct response to DLI's anti-gay climate and the knowledge of the witch hunt. Johnson wrote to Hamlet, "The only means by which I can avoid becoming a target of harassment or witch hunt in the future is by [coming out] to you."[201]

When he met with an inquiry officer, she asked him: "Who are the airmen at the post who you know are gay?"[202]—a clear attempt at a witch hunt. She also improperly asked him and his friends about any sexual conduct that could have resulted in criminal charges. The inquiry officer allegedly hounded one friend about whether Airman Johnson was dating someone until the friend finally caved and identified the person.

In June, Airman First Class Antonio Milani said he saw another airman first class, John Petrozino, "making out with a guy" in the parking lot.[203] When Petrozino heard about the rumor, he explained that he had been with a female friend wearing a baseball cap over her short hair and had hugged her and kissed her good night—and she confirmed it to Milani, who apologized. But having heard what Milani was saying, Petrozino's roommate, identified only as Airman First Class Shell, reported it, saying that he felt compelled to do so—a mistaken belief.

147

In fact, Petrozino was gay, and he felt he had no choice but to come out to escape ongoing harassment. Notably, his inquiry officer found that the evidence "suggests that a hostile and intolerant environment existed in [Petrozino's] flight and the squadron. Both A1C Milani and A1C Shell admit to spreading rumors that the subject was gay and making derogatory comments about homosexuals in general."[204] Petrozino was discharged. Milani and Shell suffered no consequences.

Over the summer, rumors began circulating that a female airman was a lesbian. In the fall, at least 20 students asked one of her friends, Airman Erin Hollenshead, if she was dating the female airman and called the two women "lipstick lesbians."[205] They reported that classmates made anti-gay comments, such as "If I ever found out someone is a faggot, I would kill him" and "Gay people shouldn't have joined in the first place. They don't deserve to serve our country."[206] Both women were discharged after feeling that the only way they could stop the harassment was to come out.

The next year, Airman First Class Robert Firpo was harassed by the civilian language instructors as well as by fellow students. One said, "Fag, you don't belong here." His roommate posted a sign in their barracks room reading "Fag free zone." He received 100 anti-gay comments on the note board outside the door of his room.[207] Despondent over the pervasive anti-gay climate, he turned to the unit chaplain for counsel. The chaplain chided Firpo, telling him to "grow up and figure out which sex is the correct one to be attracted to."[208]

A physician at the DLI medical clinic asked an airman who was being tested for mononucleosis whether he had "been swapping spit with [his] roommate."[209] That airman, like others, felt compelled to come out to his commander, explaining, "The point is that things that aren't supposed to be said by anyone in the military are being said. And the people taking offense to these comments are too fearful for their own personal safety to say something."[210]

In an effort to stop the witch hunt and curb the harassment, SLDN contacted DLI's commanding officer; the staff judge advocate at Goodfellow Air Force Base, who was also the staff judge advocate for DLI; and the secretary of the Air Force. In a sign that change was happening, however slowly, the staff judge advocate, Lieutenant Colonel David Wesley, cooperated. He sent Air Force personnel to Monterey to educate airmen on "Don't ask, don't tell."

Airmen reported to SLDN that one of those responsible for the witch hunt was forced to retire from the service. The Air Force also offered Grossi a verbal apology, though it was too late to save her career. "They told me they realized there is a problem at DLI, and they were sorry about what happened to me," she said.[211]

The anti-gay climate, however, would continue to fester. After al-Qaeda attacked the United States, the targeting of linguists with Arabic and other critical language skills just because they were lesbian, gay, or bisexual came to symbolize the height of stupidity.

CHAPTER 19

MUSTANG

The threat of prosecution under the Uniform Code of Military Justice was real. Whether the charge was sodomy (Article 125), indecent acts (Article 134), conduct unbecoming (Article 133), making a false official statement (Article 107), or accessory after the fact (Article 78), commanders and criminal investigators had punitive tools to use against lesbian, gay, and bisexual service members.

On September 16, 1994, we wrote to David Ogden, the Pentagon's deputy general counsel, informing him that we were "disturbed to learn from Air Force attorneys that they had been recently instructed to court-martial service members for consensual gay acts, contrary to the clear guidance of the February regulations to handle such cases administratively." We described how the Air Force had prevented a sergeant at Nellis Air Force Base in

Nevada from going on terminal leave (paid accrued leave taken immediately prior to separation or retirement) so he could be prosecuted for consensual sodomy with another man. Commanders at Hurlburt Field in Florida had prevented the retirement of a captain accused of consensual sodomy.

Two years later we intervened on behalf of a top Russian linguist at Kelly Air Force Base in Texas. He had 19 years of service—one year short of retirement with a military pension—and was being prosecuted for consensual sex.

All these men had stellar service records.

As Captain Saragosa, Seaman Barnes's colleagues, Corporal Haack's fellow marine, and these airmen discovered, they were not alone in facing the threat of imprisonment. In 1993, just weeks after launching SLDN, we had alerted the Pentagon's general counsel, Jamie Gorelick, to our concern that commanders and investigators could use the UCMJ to threaten service members who came out. "The suggestion that the criminal process could be invoked against someone who makes a statement is preposterous," she replied."[212]

Our concern was real.

In the summer of 1996, the captain of the USCGS *Coutwell* reportedly asked Petty Officer Third Class Kelli Sprague, "Have you ever told anyone on the ship you are gay? Have you ever been confused about the way you are? Have you ever acted on the confusion?" He then reportedly threatened her with criminal prosecution for making a false official statement if she did not answer his questions truthfully. She told him the truth—that she was a lesbian. In a memo she wrote after the incident, she asked, "When your commanding officer asks you a question and informs you that lying is against the UCMJ, what choice do you have but to tell the truth?"[213]

When Navy cryptologist David Compton came out to his commander at Fort Meade, Maryland, that same year, the inquiry officer defined his task: to "prove that the service member was lying," at which point he would charge Compton with making a false official statement.[214]

In 1997, the commander of the USS *Eisenhower* ignored a series of anti-gay threats, including death threats, against four sailors within a two-month period. Instead, he threatened the sailors with criminal prosecution for making false official statements.[215]

One sailor from the *Eisenhower* called SLDN to report that someone had tacked the warning "Leave or Die Fag" to his bunk. A second sailor, Airman Barry Waldrop, also found this dire warning—"You're a dead faggot"—scrawled in permanent marker on his bunk. A third sailor contacted SLDN after being knocked unconscious in an off-base assault by an unknown assailant who called him "faggot." A few days before, the tires of his car had been slashed while the car was parked on base. A fourth sailor found "Leave Fag" written in ketchup (perhaps an attempt to imitate blood) on his bunk.

Rather than investigate these threats seriously, the command demanded that the sailors "prove" they were gay and threatened them with making "false official statements" if they could not. All four sailors were discharged.[216]

In 1996, an employee of a photo-developing franchise made copies of photos belonging to Air Force Major Terry Nilson and turned them over to the Air Force's criminal investigation unit. The photos simply showed Nilson with his arm around another man—nothing else. Still, the Air Force investigated Nilson for sodomy, and he was discharged.[217]

We discovered that the Air Force, more than any other service, was pursuing criminal charges against suspected gay service members. Michelle and I met with Air Force general counsel Sheila Cheston in the first quarter of 1996 to press the service to end prosecutions of gay men for consensual sex. No action was taken.

A highly decorated Air Force officer discovered that criminal prosecution was not an idle threat. Major Debra Meeks was a "mustang," one of a handful of officers who were commissioned after working their way up through the enlisted ranks. She was set to retire on February 28, 1996, when the Air Force charged her with consensual sodomy, based on an allegation made by a civilian roommate. (Sodomy under the UCMJ included both oral and anal sex between members of the opposite or same sex.) Criminal investigators at Lackland Air Force Base had solicited the allegations in the course of a witch hunt against Meeks and 11 other women.

Under "Don't ask, don't tell," commanders were supposed to handle allegations of "acts" in the administrative discharge system, not the criminal system.[218] Allegations that could lead to charges under the UCMJ were supposed to be handled in an evenhanded manner, meaning that a commander should treat straight and gay service members similarly if what they were alleged to have done was basically the same thing.

"When Meeks contacted SLDN, she had already concluded that staying quiet was a sure road to prison," Michelle recalled. "She wanted to fight the charges, publicly if needed, to hold the Air Force accountable. All she needed was a crack legal defense team."[219]

Michelle secured the pro bono services of Michael Tigar, a professor at the University of Texas Law School, and Peter Held, a San Antonio lawyer who had spent 18 years in the Air Force as a JAG officer. Meeks was acquitted by a seven-member jury[220] six months after her planned retirement date. After the verdict, she put her head in her hands and slumped in her chair, her ordeal over, as Tigar put his arms around her. Had she been convicted, she could have been sentenced to as many as eight years in prison and lost her pension.

Asked why he chose to represent Meeks, Tigar said, "I was offended by what had happened to her and how she had been treated. It seemed to me that having a pajama police force was a waste of money."[221]

By 2000, the threat of criminal prosecution of gay service members for consensual acts had all but ended, even though Article 125 remained on the books until 2013.[222] Witch hunts, too, had abated. Bridget Wilson, a military lawyer and gay rights activist, said that SLDN's signature achievement prior to the repeal of "Don't ask, don't tell" was ending the witch hunts and criminal investigations that had been commonplace before our founding.

As we noted in our fifth annual report, "Mass investigations have waned. Criminal prosecutions of homosexual service members have decreased."[223] That was progress.

ENDING MURDER
AND HARASSMENT

CHAPTER 20

BULLSEYE

"When you have a federal law that treats you as a second-class citizen, it gives others permission to treat you that way," I said in April 2000. *Newsweek* picked it up as one of its quotes of the week.[224]

Michelle and I considered it one of our most solemn duties to protect service members who were or were thought to be lesbian, gay, bisexual, or transgender, and to ensure that our legal interventions made a difference.

The Pentagon repeatedly denied that harassment was an issue. Eventually, it would confirm everything we said. These are some of the stories that bring the nightmarish reality to light.

◆ ◆ ◆

Unchecked anti-gay harassment was the most pernicious and precarious aspect of "Don't ask, don't tell." There was reason to take these threats seriously. In 1992—the year before the initial debate on gays in the military, and the year before Michelle and I launched SLDN—sailors murdered Petty Officer Allen Schindler while he was on shore leave in Sasebo, Japan.

Schindler had just come out to his commander and reported the harassment he was facing on the ship. Two shipmates followed him one evening and beat him so badly that every organ in his body was destroyed. His face was beaten to a pulp.

"The whole time I waited for his body to return, I had dreams of holding my son and kissing him goodbye," said his mother, Dorothy Hajdys. "But I couldn't do that because he had no face."[225]

Schindler's case underscored not just the dire consequences of unchecked harassment, but the Navy's attempts to cover up wrongdoing. Hajdys pressed the Navy for information about her son's murder but was stonewalled repeatedly.[226] Without her knowledge, the Navy convened a court-martial and convicted Airman Charles Vins, who was sentenced to only 78 days in prison in return for his cooperation. Later, Airman Apprentice Terry Helvey, who stomped Schindler to death, pleaded guilty to murder and received a life sentence.

Every year, sailors who have been convicted to serve more than 30 years can get a clemency hearing to consider a reduction in their sentence. Sailors are eligible for parole after serving only 10 years. Helvey never demonstrated remorse.

Hajdys launched a campaign to obtain a million letters urging the Navy to not grant clemency. SLDN partnered with her, launching a GoCard postcard campaign (a popular advertising gimmick that placed racks with postcards in restaurants and bars that patrons could grab). We placed tens of thousands of post-cards featuring her son's story in restaurants across the United States. The interest was overwhelming.

We quickly helped Hajdys collect more than 25,000 signatures of people who opposed clemency for Helvey.[227] The names and email addresses we gathered helped to build our grassroots data-base. We carried crates of signatures to the clemency board.

SLDN's Kirk Childress, a man with the energy and light of a hummingbird, said of the clemency board members: "They know the murder was brutal; they know it was even worse because it was one shipmate against another. What they don't understand is why they get nine crates of mail about it. It touches a nerve because any gay person knows what it's like to be afraid of anti-gay violence."[228]

Helvey has not received clemency. He is currently serving his life sentence at a federal prison in Greenville, Illinois.

◆ ◆ ◆

One client told us soon after President Clinton announced "Don't ask, don't tell" that gay service members all felt as if they had a bullseye painted on their backs. Another said that a fellow sailor declared war on "Clinton's Navy," signaling that it was now okay to target gay service members. It is difficult to imagine how horrifying it is to be under constant threat for being who you are.

"Don't ask, don't tell" required gay service members to remain in a dark closet of absolute silence, impervious to taunts, insinu-ations, attacks, threats, and assaults. This is just a sampling of the taunts that they heard or saw, as published in our annual reports:

"Die Fag." "Kill all fags." "You're going to die." "You can't hide, fag." "You will be killed." "We're going to kill you." "We're going to get you." "You sick fucking dyke!" "That dyke is going to fry." "That fag [Matthew Shepard] deserved to die." "We don't need queers around here." "What are you going to do about it, fag?" "You're dead, you dick-sucking faggot." **"There's nothing wrong with beating up gays."** "If I find a gay guy on this ship, I would throw him overboard." "There's nothing to do in Sasebo unless you are a homo killer." "You'd better not be queer because in the Navy we kill our fags." "If I ever saw two guys kissing, I'd beat them with a baseball bat." "We can't wait to get out to sea so that we can throw you overboard." **"I hate homosexuals."** "If you find one ... beat the shit out of him." "If I ever find out for sure you're a fag, I'll kick your ass." "There are three things I hate: liars, thieves and faggots." "If I catch you around town, I'm going to kill you." "There are accidents in divisions. Sometimes people die. When word gets out, you may be one of those." **"You're a dead faggot."** "Whip his faggot ass." "Rump ranger." "Pussy sucker." "You're a man in women's fatigues." "Let's go to a gay bar and fuck some queers up." "Stupid dykes." "You twisted freaks." "We should kill them all." "I wish San Francisco would burn to the ground." "I will send you home in a box." "Cocksuckers." "Fudge-packers." "Watch your back, faggot." "Pole smoker." "Faggots die out in the field." "Flaming faggot." "Fruity." "I'm going to stomp your brains out." "Rainbow warrior." "Fruit loops." "You're being watched." "Watch your ass." "Your time will come." "Lock your door at night." "Visualize blowing up a gay bar." **"Put all fags on an island and nuke it."** "I'm going to snap your fucking neck." "You'll go home in a body bag." "Sissy." "Fucking freak." "There's no way to hide." "You know there's nowhere to run."

◆ ◆ ◆

What do you do when you find a note in your barracks that says "DIE FAG" on Christmas Eve? That was the predicament faced by Sean Fucci, a pensive, taciturn, detail-oriented airman who would later work for SLDN. He had shrugged off a prior doodle with the words "Smiley Fag." Now, though, he thought his life might be in danger.[229]

Fucci—scared, not knowing what to do—called Michelle at her home on December 24, 1995. He had permission to leave, but had nowhere to go and no funds to get a hotel room. She scrambled and found him off-base housing. She then doggedly tracked down the commander during the holidays to take action.

The commander referred the matter to the Air Force's Office of Special Investigations, which declined to investigate the threats without more substantial evidence. In a memorandum for record, the commander wrote, "I contacted OSI and learned that they had no interest in investigating the incidents.... It is an issue of anonymous intimidation for which there is not much that can be done...."[230]

Investigating anonymous threats is challenging and may have led nowhere, but it was clear to us that the OSI didn't even try. Fucci's case highlighted how fearful service members are when threatened and how vulnerable they feel when their case is not resolved. He was discharged for being gay because he came out to save himself.

◆ ◆ ◆

Former Marine Lance Corporal Kevin Smith can also testify to the double-edged sword of anti-gay harassment when commands do not know the rules or do not take appropriate steps to ensure the safety of their troops. On September 26, 1997, he was assaulted by two men outside a gay bar in San Angelo, Texas.

He decided not to press charges. "I did not want the military to learn about the attack. I feared that the circumstances surrounding the attack would be used as an excuse to initiate an investigation into my sexual orientation," he said.[231] And he was right, because when the platoon sergeant found out about the incident through other means, he warned Smith, in a way that Smith found less than reassuring, that an NCIS investigation into the assault would be "very thorough." Smith was discharged.

◆ ◆ ◆

In August 2000, soldiers at Fort Jackson, South Carolina, assaulted Private First Class Ronald Chapman, a 19-year-old from Massachusetts, after a drill sergeant called Chapman a "faggot." What a leader says matters.

"Taking their lead from a scene from the 1987 film *Full Metal Jacket*, the attackers snuck-up on Chapman during the middle of the night as he slept," E.A. Barrera wrote in *East County Magazine*. "Known as a 'blanket party,' the other soldiers repeatedly hit him with blankets stuffed with economy sized soap bars."[232]

Chapman described the attack in a letter to his parents: "I have some bad news for you. I got beat up last night. Someone came to my bed—a group of someones—and they were hitting me with blankets and soap. I am aching all over my body. My whole body hurts. I can't tell anyone because they left no marks. Who'll believe me? I can't believe this all has happened. Who did I hurt?"[233]

◆ ◆ ◆

An Army private burned down the house of Lieutenant Colonel Steve Loomis in 1996. The Army discharged the arsonist, as would be expected—but it also discharged Loomis. The reason? A civilian fire marshal found a homemade sex tape in the ashes and turned it over to Loomis's commander.[234]

The Army didn't stand by Loomis, or help him rebuild his house. Instead, he was discharged for conduct unbecoming an officer. His "other than honorable" discharge prevented him from securing his pension and accessing veterans benefits. It also damaged his civilian job prospects, as employers are loath to hire a veteran whose discharge carries that characterization.

Loomis had not come out to his command for 20 years. He strictly compartmentalized his life. That was the thing under "Don't ask, don't tell"—any evidence that you were gay, even off duty and off base, was fair game. SLDN tried to persuade the Army to allow Loomis to retire early and preserve his pension, but—unlike our successes with Lieutenant Steve May and Master Chief Petty Officer Timothy McVeigh—the secretary of the Army did not show mercy.

As SLDN's Kirk Childress explained, "He's a victim of a felony—an arsonist torches his house—but instead of reacting by saying 'What can we do to help,' the Army says, 'We're going to have to discharge you.'"[235]

Loomis's discharge, in July 1995, "looks particularly vindictive," said Representative Barney Frank, who the month before had introduced legislation to decriminalize certain consensual adult sexual activities. "A guy with a grudge did something to him, which led someone else to make a report to the Army. Loomis didn't tell, and he wasn't bothering anyone."[236]

◆ ◆ ◆

Senior Airman Lauren Hough had her car torched and faced unrelenting harassment and death threats. Her command turned a blind eye.

In 1999, during Exercise Bright Star in Egypt, she found the words "die you fucking dyke" written on the window of her government vehicle. After returning from Egypt to Shaw Air Force Base in South Carolina, she found a note on her car: "God hates queers and so do we, die you fucking dyke." She reluctantly decided not to report the newest threat, fearing that doing so would lead to an investigation against her.

The threats continued. A few weeks later, two of the tires on her car were slashed. Then her car was torched, destroying it. She reported the death threats and the arson.

After she bought a new car, another threat appeared: "gun, knife, bat. I just can't decide which one. It's not over dyke." One of her supervisors called her a "fucking rug muncher."[237]

The Air Force Office of Special Investigations never investigated the incidents against her—but her commander pursued criminal charges, alleging that she had set the fire to her own car in order to defraud her insurance company.[238] Neither the Sumter County, South Carolina, sheriff's department nor the insurance company found any evidence of wrongdoing on her part.

Nevertheless, the Air Force prosecuted her for fraud, rather than investigate the multiple threats on her life because others perceived her as a lesbian. A court-martial found her not guilty.[239] The judge reportedly told her to come to him directly if she faced further retaliation by the command. Instead, fearing for her safety, she left the Air Force and a career she loved.

◆ ◆ ◆

Specialist Brad Powell, a member of the North Carolina Army National Guard, reported in 2002 that a noncommissioned officer had instructed his unit on how to throw a hand grenade by visualizing "blowing up a gay bar."[240] Powell overheard another NCO tell soldiers that "the only way to decrease our nuclear arsenal is to put all fags on an island and nuke it."[241] Yet another said, "The only thing a good fag needs is a good fag bashing."[242]

Powell came out to escape the harassment and was discharged. No one was disciplined for the misconduct.

◆ ◆ ◆

Navy Airman Paul Peverelle served as an openly gay man, but not by choice. He came out to his command on the USS *Enterprise*, where he was part of an F-14 squadron, in April 2001 because of the pervasive anti-gay harassment aboard the ship and because he wanted his superiors to "know that this great work—and effort—is coming from a gay man."[243]

His commander refused to discharge him, believing, without evidence, that Peverelle was simply trying to avoid service. Once again, a commander was blaming the gay sailor rather than addressing the harassment.

Four weeks later, Peverelle, along with the rest of the crew, deployed for a six-month tour of duty. Then came 9/11, and the *Enterprise* was ordered to join the forces fighting the war against terrorism.

While at sea, Peverelle told some friends that he was gay—but he was careful not to broadcast it too widely, given the atmosphere on the ship. His commander outed him, though, and his sexual orientation became common knowledge.

Again, what a leader does matters. Harassment followed. "I actually had two guys in my berthing area call me 'faggot,' 'gay bitch,' and 'ass licker,' threatening to 'beat my ass the next chance they get,'" he told us.[244] His commanding officer did nothing to stop the reported harassment.

Shortly thereafter, an Associated Press photographer snapped a photo of a missile inscribed with the words "High Jack This Fags [sic]." It is not uncommon for service members to write messages on bombs, but the anti-gay message reflected the ship's culture.

Rear Admiral Stephen R. Pietropaoli, the head of the Navy's public affairs office, dismissed the epithet as "an isolated incident" and a "spontaneous act of penmanship." But he also condemned the graffiti and said, "The Navy does not tolerate discrimination of any kind."[245]

When the *Enterprise* returned to Norfolk to a hero's welcome, the Navy discharged Peverelle.

◆ ◆ ◆

"Don't ask, don't tell" produced a lot of stupid. In 2005 it was reported that a decade before, the Air Force had commissioned research on aphrodisiacs that could be used in bombs that would turn the enemy gay.[246] The theory was that the presence of openly gay troops would undermine the enemy's morale and cohesion and make them easier to defeat.

The researchers apparently had never heard of Sparta, Lesbos, or the Band of Thebes, let alone the gay Americans serving in our armed forces.

That same year, SLDN also uncovered a secret Pentagon operation that was spying on civilian LGBT organizations. A subsequent Freedom of Information Act request by SLDN uncovered the extent of the surveillance.

A gay "kiss-in" on the campus of the University of California, Santa Cruz, was described by the Department of Defense as a "credible threat" of terrorism.[247] OUTLaw, a gay advocacy group at New York University's law school, was classified by the Pentagon as "possibly violent." NBC News reported that Pentagon investigators had spied on groups at William Paterson University of New Jersey and the State University of New York at Albany. Their primary concern was the students' opposition to the "Don't ask, don't tell" policy. We were the queer and present danger.

In a statement released by SLDN, I said, "The Pentagon seems to constantly find new and more offensive ways to demean lesbian, gay, bisexual, and transgender people. ... First, we were deemed unfit to serve our country, despite winning wars, medals, and the praise of fellow service members. Then, our sexual orientation was suggested as a means to destabilize the enemy. Now, our public displays of affection are equated with al-Qaeda terrorist activity. It is time for a new Pentagon policy consistent with the views of 21st-century America."[248]

◆ ◆ ◆

Petty Officer First Class Larry Glover's attempts to protect younger sailors from anti-gay harassment led to threats of negative performance evaluations.[249] Glover had served for 15 years. He had earned 10 medals, including a Navy and Marine Corps Achievement Medal for having risked his life to save a $77 million plane from going over the side of an aircraft carrier in high seas.[250]

"I went from two commands that were not too bad to one that was pure hell," he told *The Nation*.[251] That was the Russian-roulette nature of "Don't ask, don't tell" leadership: You could serve well, even openly, in some commands without concern; in other commands, life was miserable.

"I witnessed chief petty officers using terms like 'the little fag,' 'the little butt-bandit,' 'ball breath,'" he said. "One kid had a complete nervous breakdown—I took him off the ship crying."

Glover contacted SLDN to assess his options. Despite his 15 years of service, he decided that he had no choice but to leave. He came out to his commander and was discharged, giving up $850,000 in pay and retirement benefits he would have been due if he had served for 20 years.

Looking back on his experience, Glover had one thought: "We've got to fix this policy—we just *have* to."[252]

CHAPTER 21

LESBIAN-BAITING

A particularly pernicious result of harassment, both before "Don't ask, don't tell" and under it, was its disproportionate impact on women, resulting from a convergence of gender discrimination, sexual harassment, and homophobia. The pre-"Don't ask, don't tell" witch hunts at Parris Island and aboard the USS *Norton Sound*, USS *Dixon*, USS *Yellowstone*, and USS *Grapple* all targeted women.

In 1990, Michelle was the co-author of a groundbreaking article in the *Harvard Women's Law Journal*[53] that described "lesbian-baiting," where women were accused of being lesbian in retaliation for reporting sexual harassment, or simply for being a woman in a non-traditional career field. Men stereotyped women in the armed forces as either "dykes" or "whores," and women were caught in the vise of proving their heterosexuality—what poet Adrienne Rich called the culture of "compulsory heterosexuality."[254]

The Pentagon's data is clear: In the 10 years after the announcement of "Don't ask, don't tell," women comprised, on average, 14 percent of the armed forces—and 30 percent of the gay discharges.[255] One of our first cases provided a stark example of what our clients had to endure.

In 1994, while serving in South Korea, Private First Class Shannon Emery was threatened with criminal charges for sodomy and sexual misconduct after filing a complaint against male soldiers who had attempted to sexually assault and rape her.[256] In one incident, a male soldier threw Emery up against a wall, pinned her hands above her head, and said, "Let's fuck." She and other women were forced to run a gauntlet of catcalls, lewd comments, and other forms of harassment when they attempted to go from their rooms to the women's latrines. In retaliation for her reporting them, the accused men spread rumors that Emery was a lesbian, and the commander backed his men.

As we noted in our second annual report: "The command tried to force her to confess to being gay. She refused. The command threatened her with prison if she did not identify suspected lesbians in her unit. She refused. The command started discharge proceedings against her based on the same trumped-up allegations. She still refused to buckle."[257]

Emery spent $4,000 on telephone bills and Federal Express charges. Her mother, Debbie, worked for at least 15 hours a week on behalf of her daughter, spending almost $6,000 on long-distance bills and faxes. Michelle worked on the case every day for six months.

"If we hadn't gotten involved, she would have been rail-roaded out of Korea and out of the Army," Michelle said. "That's crystal-clear."[258]

Through the assistance of Senator Patty Murray, who represented Emery's home state. we were able to extract her from South Korea. The charges were dropped, and Emery flourished in her Army career. I told Murray that the commander had even accused her of being a lesbian for supporting Emery. Her eyes popped with incredulity.

The Army eventually held the commander accountable, but not for what he did to our client. Instead, he was disciplined after driving a forklift, while intoxicated, into stacks of cargo on the base and destroying them.

"What I don't like," Emery told her hometown newspaper, "is they could kick out anyone in the military by saying she was gay. All you have to do is start enough rumors."[259]

◆ ◆ ◆

The Air Force discharged Senior Airman Sonya Harden, who was serving at Eglin Air Force Base in Florida, based solely on an allegation that was later recanted. The accuser admitted that the two had been in a dispute over money when she claimed that Harden was in a lesbian relationship. Though Harden should not have had to do so, she presented former boyfriends to testify on her behalf at the discharge board, but to no avail.[260] She was discharged—yet another example of how "Don't ask, don't tell" was a weapon that could all too easily be used against others.

At an event with SLDN supporters, Harden described her ordeal. "The first thing SLDN did was save my life," she said. [261] She then broke into tears.

◆◆◆

Petty Officer Second Class Nicole Barbe called SLDN because she could not trust her command with her life. She joined the Navy in 1995 and was assigned to the weather-forecasting service. At her assignments in Biloxi, Mississippi, and Kingsville, Texas, she encountered a barrage of anti-gay harassment, directed at her and others. She told *The Nation* that an instructor would make jokes about "dikes in the water," then turn to her and say, "Don't get too excited about that word." After that, she said, someone "wrote a message on my car that said, 'You suck dick and eat pussy'"[262]—the classic paradox of "whores" and "dykes." She tried to report the hostile climate and the harassment, but after three superior officers had harassed her, she "didn't feel there was anybody among my chiefs who'd back me up if I was assaulted."[263]

Her concerns were well-founded. Having come out to her commander, which necessitated discharge under "Don't ask, don't tell," the inquiry officer assigned to her case launched a wide-ranging investigation. He outed Barbe to dozens of service members at two bases, soliciting information about her sexual identity and sexual conduct[264]— a classic "homosexual question-naire" intrusion.

Surprisingly, he recommended retention, concluding that "[h]er continued presence in the Navy is consistent with the Navy's interest in good order and discipline and morale."[265] Even though she had been outed to her unit because of his inquiry, he admonished her to keep her sexual orientation a secret.

During a work-related dinner, Barbe's supervisor, Master Chief Petty Officer Robert Tyo, asked her in front of her peers and their spouses why she had not brought a date, clearly goading her.[266] He had previously threatened to punish her if she made "any missteps."[267]

Barbe was facing sexual harassment, anti-gay harassment, and being forced into the box of compulsory heterosexuality on pain of penalty. After SLDN intervened, the Navy discharged her.

Like several other clients, Barbe worked for us for a brief period after her discharge. She then moved to New Orleans and became a police officer.

SLDN came to her rescue one more time in a funny, sad, and horrifying moment. While on patrol in New Orleans after Hurricane Katrina, she and her fellow officers came under fire and were trapped on the rooftop of a building. She called our communications director, Steve Ralls, and asked if we could alert CNN, figuring that the presence of news media might provide the distraction needed to resolve the situation. Within five minutes, Anderson Cooper arrived on a fan boat, reporting live.

◆ ◆ ◆

There were other incidents in which SLDN was not involved, but they were classic lesbian-baiting cases reported in the news. In 1996, retired Army Sergeant Major Brenda Hoster accused the Army's top enlisted man, Sergeant Major of the Army Gene McKinney, of sexual misconduct. Anonymous allegations that

Hoster was a lesbian surfaced almost immediately in the *Los Angeles Times*. Shortly thereafter, McKinney's attorney accused Hoster of being a lesbian and questioned her friendships with female Army colleagues.[268]

Also in 1996, Air Force Lieutenant Kelly Flinn, the first female B-52 pilot, was questioned out of the blue by investigators about whether she was in a lesbian relationship at the same time that she was under investigation for adultery with a man. In response to a reporter's question about the interrogation, Flinn remarked on the lesbian-baiting dynamic at work: "The fact that I wasn't dating openly sparked rumors that I was homosexual. ... You can't win."[269]

The bottom line: If you were a woman, straight or gay, there was nowhere to hide under "Don't ask, don't tell."

CHAPTER 22

LOUISVILLE SLUGGER

Nothing in my law school training prepared me for the day that Michelle and I called Pat Kutteles to tell her that her beloved son had been murdered because he was believed to be gay. But we did it because we had to, and the course of events that ensued produced the first seismic shift in the battle to repeal "Don't ask, don't tell."

Barry Winchell was 21 years old and stood 6-foot-2—a strapping young man with a swallowed-the-canary grin. As a teenager, he was an Eagle Scout and a member of the Rocket Club. He played the piano and bass guitar, and was in a heavy metal band. Academically, he struggled, having been diagnosed with attention deficit disorder and dyslexia.[270]

The Army offered discipline and opportunity, and for Winchell, life was finally on track: He was a member of Delta Company,

Second Battalion, 502nd Infantry—part of the prestigious 101st Airborne Division at Fort Campbell, Kentucky. He was uncannily adept at mechanics. He told a superior one day that a manual incorrectly described how to build an engine, and he was right.

He was the top marksman in his unit, and his fellow soldiers started calling him "Top Gun."[271] He wanted to fly Black Hawk helicopters. He was preparing to apply to warrant officer school.[272] In the weeks before his murder, he was nominated for Soldier of the Month.[273]

Two soldiers crushed Barry Winchell's dreams. One, Private Calvin Glover, attacked him with a Louisville Slugger because he thought Winchell was gay. The other, Specialist Brian Fisher, goaded Glover into the attack on his sleeping roommate. It was around 2 a.m. on July 5, 1999.

Rhonda White, co-director of the Coalition for Justice in Nashville, Tennessee, contacted SLDN four days later. Soldiers at Fort Campbell had called her, telling her that a soldier on the base may have been killed for being gay. She needed help verifying the facts and navigating the military.

That afternoon I was driving in my 1983 red Datsun 280ZX past verdant cornfields to the Delaware shore for some weekend sun. Michelle called me around 3 p.m.

"Dixon, we may have another Allen Schindler on our hands."

Michelle was shaken, but calm, focused, determined. She felt personally responsible for every client we had—not literally, but emotionally. These were her people. She was their commander. The report of a soldier being killed by another soldier was among the worst news any commander could receive.

"What happened?"

"We got a call from activists in Nashville. They say that a soldier, Private First Class Barry Winchell, was killed this past weekend. He was stationed at Fort Campbell. They have reason to believe he was gay, and fear that the Army is trying to cover it up."

"Shall I turn around?"

"No. We need to get the facts first—check it out."

"What do we know?"

"Not much yet. Winchell's death is being reported on the news as the result of a physical altercation on the Fourth of July. Maybe that's the end of the story. But a Nashville activist told us that Barry was dating a performer at The Connection, the local gay dance club in Nashville, and they are concerned that Barry was targeted for being gay."

"We need to be careful here. We can't call it a hate crime if it wasn't."

"Exactly. I have asked Kathi and Gary to fly out to Nashville tonight to see what they can find out. I wanted to clear the expenses with you."

"Absolutely. Keep me posted. This is important."

Kathi Westcott was a fierce, compassionate, meticulous staff attorney at SLDN. She headed our investigative team. She and Gary Norcross, an SLDN volunteer and a former Air Force assistant chaplain, flew to Nashville and drove almost two hours to Fort Campbell, a sprawling 100,000-acre base straddling the Tennessee/Kentucky border.

On Saturday, July 10, they pulled up to the guard station at the base entrance. Gary rolled down his window. He was a southerner, from Waynesboro, Virginia, and could charm the dew off a honeysuckle, as Blanche DuBois on *The Golden Girls* might say. With a smile creasing his face, and a wink in his eye, he flashed his military ID, showing that he had served in the Air Force, and told the guard, "Me and my fiancée are thinking about getting married on the base and wondered if we could visit the base chapel." The guard waved them through.

(There was a wonderful irony that a lesbian and a gay man were waved through the gates because they pretended to be a heterosexual couple running to the altar. The guard probably should have questioned why an airman wanted to be married on an Army base.)

Gary and Kathi asked soldiers on the base if they had heard about the murder. Some had; most had not. Most did not know the details. They had more luck at a gay bar near the base. (Yes, there are gay bars on the Tennessee/Kentucky border.) Some of the patrons had heard about the murder and the rumors that it was gay-bashing. They expressed concerns about the level of anti-gay harassment that they had witnessed on the base. But no one had details.

Gary and Kathi asked that anyone with information call them. They distributed our business-card-size legal rights cards, which gave our phone number and advised service members targeted under "Don't ask, don't tell" to "Say Nothing. Sign Nothing. Get Legal Help." We had distributed tens of thousands of those cards at Pride days throughout the country and had placed the same language as advertisements in the *Army Times*, the *Air Force Times*, and the *Navy Times*.

Gary and Kathi returned to Nashville, where they met with Rhonda White and other local activists. They also talked with Calpernia Addams, a pre-operative transgender performer at The Connection, whom Winchell had been dating. On stage, Addams was a rabble-rousing crowd pleaser. Off stage, she had a tremulous elegance and poise.

A Navy veteran, Addams had served as a combat medic in Saudi Arabia during the Gulf War. Upon leaving the Navy, she began her transition from male to female.

The two had been dating for three months. They held hands, went to the movies, sat at coffee shops, and were intimate.[274] "We found something in each other that made us happy and kept the dark side of existence a little farther away from our demanding, difficult lives," Addams wrote on her website.[275]

On the evening of July 4, Addams was competing in the Tennessee Entertainer of the Year contest. She wore a beaded black pantsuit and lip-synched to Sinead O'Connor's haunting rendition of "Don't Cry for Me, Argentina" while playing the violin riffs herself.[276] At 2:30 a.m. on July 5—as her boyfriend lay bleeding to death on a cot in the hallway outside his room—she was crowned the winner. She wouldn't learn of Winchell's murder until later that day, when she turned on the television and heard the catastrophic news.

When Addams spoke with Kathi, she was composed, stoic, and determined. But she was also grief-stricken, having lost—in a brutal, savage fashion—the first romantic relationship of her life as a woman.

"I met Barry three months ago. He and some other soldiers had come to see the show."

She paused and reflected. "Barry was real quiet. Shy. Handsome. Strong."

She described the beginnings of the relationship: "We started to see each other. He would come to the shows on weekends and usually stay in my dressing room, reading manuals on helicopters and such. We'd go to the movies. Have coffee. It was really nice."

"Did Barry talk about being harassed?" Kathi asked.

"Barry told me that his roommate was teasing him about being gay. Fisher. Specialist Fisher. Fisher came with Barry to the bar sometimes.

"Barry would just tell him to cut it out," Addams added. "He didn't want to make a big deal about it. I knew it was getting to him. But Barry's motto was just to 'suck it up.'"

Kathi: "Did other people on the base know?"

"Yes. Brian Fisher, obviously. Other soldiers came to the bar with him, too—we had the best music in town! But it made the rumors spread."

After several days at Fort Campbell and in Nashville, Kathi returned to Washington. We didn't know whether Winchell had identified as gay. We didn't know the full details of the murder. What actually had transpired on the evening of July 4 and the early hours of July 5? What was the motivation?

What we did know was that Winchell was perceived as gay at Fort Campbell by a not insignificant number of soldiers; that soldiers had concerns about anti-gay harassment on the base; and that Winchell had expressed concerns to Addams and others about the increasing harassment he was experiencing. If he had been murdered because others thought he was gay, then it was a hate crime. A hate crime is based on the intent of the perpetrator—not the sexual orientation of the victim, and not the gender of his lover.

We knew from news reports that Glover had been arrested in connection with the murder. Soon afterward, we learned that Fisher was arrested as well.

We needed more information. I recalled the advice of Marylouise Oates, one of our early mentors. She was a former reporter for the *Los Angeles Times* and the wife of Bob Shrum, one of Washington's most powerful Democratic operatives. As we sat in her Georgetown townhouse one afternoon in 1993, she said, "Make one mistake with the press, and you're through."

Kathi stopped by my office. Leaning on the door frame, she said, "I hate to ask this. But can we afford to do this?"

"Yes," I replied firmly.

"I ask because this is one case." Kathi was always persistent. Yes/no answers never sufficed; even detailed explanations didn't always satisfy her. But her questions were also good ones and on point.

"We don't know where it will lead," she continued. "We are stretched beyond our capacity responding to calls from help from so many others. How can we do this?"

At the time, we had three staff attorneys, each handling hundreds of client intakes each year, with at least 50 open matters at any time.

"We cannot afford not to," I said. "There are times when an important event occurs, and we have to respond. We have to step up. This is one of those moments."

"But what if it isn't one of those moments?" Kathi asked.

"We won't know that unless we delve into this. Who else will do it? Who else knows the military justice system, 'Don't ask, don't tell,' Pentagon officials, the history of Allen Schindler's murder, but us?"

"No one."

"So we have to do this. If we discover that the murder was only a drunken brawl, as the Army claims, we will pull back, but your preliminary report back from Nashville suggests that there is more. We have to find out."

Recognizing an opportunity can be a defining moment for an organization or an issue. Opportunities like this one are big and symbolic. They force you to reallocate your resources. They may make the public reassess its own views. Winchell's murder was a moment that could possibly shake the foundations of "Don't ask, don't tell."

◆◆◆

The next day, Kathi told Michelle and me, "The press knows. A local television station plans to run a story at the end of the week that Barry's murder may have been a hate crime. Barry's parents don't know. What should we do?"

"We have to call them," Michelle responded. "Do we know how to reach them?"

"I'll try to find out," Kathi said.

Within hours, she reported that she had the phone numbers for Winchell's brother, Ian, and his parents in Kansas City, Missouri.

"Let's call Ian first and get his advice," said Michelle, who had good instincts. "He may know how best to proceed with his parents."

I sat in front of Michelle's desk, and dialed the phone number, 8-1-6.... We were on speakerphone.

"Hi, Ian. This is Michelle Benecke and my colleague, Dixon Osburn. We are from a group called Servicemembers Legal Defense Network in Washington, D.C. We have heard about your brother's death, and we want to tell you first of all how very sorry we are for your and your family's loss."

"Thank you."

Michelle continued: "We have some news about your brother's death that we wanted to share with you and get your guidance on whether and how to tell your parents.

"We learned that a local TV station in Nashville plans to do a story about the death later this week. The reporters have information that this may have been an anti-gay hate crime. We haven't talked to the reporters; we don't know what information they have. But we thought you and your parents would rather hear from a friendly voice about the news rather than hearing it first in the press."

Ian remained quiet.

Michelle took a deep breath and went on: "Here is what we can do to help you and your family if you are interested. It is completely up to you. Our group, Servicemembers Legal Defense Network, provides free legal services to those hurt by 'Don't ask, don't tell.' We know the military's legal system very well. We know how the investigation into your brother's death is likely to unfold, and what the legal options are for the command, depending on what the investigation finds."

"Are you saying that Barry was gay?" Ian asked in a way that was neither surprised nor accusatory—a reaction that was very helpful.

"We don't know," I said. "What we know at this point is that there were rumors that he was, that he had frequented a local gay club on some occasions, and that he had been dating a performer at the club. The local news station is likely going to report those facts.

"We don't know whether this is a hate crime or not. We have been asked by members of the local community to see if we can find out the facts. We tend to be very cautious in assessing the facts because we do not want to make any false suppositions."

"Okay," Ian said. "So what do you want me to do?"

I was relieved that he was willing to engage.

"You tell us," I replied. "Would you like us to talk to your parents? Would you like to tell them? We at least thought you should know."

"Let me think about it," he said. "Thanks."

He hung up the phone. Michelle and I sat across the desk from each other, arms folded, staring, grim-faced.

"I hate this," I said.

"Yeah," Michelle said. "I think we did the right thing."

Within 10 minutes, the phone rang. I was still in Michelle's office. It was Pat Kutteles, Winchell's mother.

How do you tell parents that their dead son might have been gay? And that his death may become front-page news as a result of his being gay, or at least being perceived as gay? They have already had their hearts ripped out of their chests; now they were having the rug pulled out from under them as well. Who was their son? If he was facing harassment, why had he not told them? If he was gay, why didn't he tell them?

Pat was a psychiatric nurse. She was a salt-of-the-earth woman with deep compassion. Her husband, Wally, was a Korean War veteran.

I remember how faint Pat's voice was on the other end of the line. It took every ounce of energy just for her to speak, but she was the strong one. Wally was mostly quiet.

Pat's voice reminded me of my mom's voice in 1972 when she told me at 6 a.m. that my brother had been killed in a car accident seven hours before. He was 18; I was 7. I asked in a sweet innocence that comprehended the meaning of death even at that tender age, "But who will teach me how to ride my bike now?" I knew what death was and how it completely devastates families.

Michelle reiterated how sorry we were for their loss. We told them what we knew so far, and what the press was likely to report. We offered to fly to Kansas City to speak with them in person. "Okay," Pat said, quietly but with conviction.

Two days later we arrived in Kansas City. We met Pat and Wally, Ian, and an uncle at the uncle's law office—a small, unassuming one-man shop. There wasn't much air in the room, or maybe it just felt that way.

Pat and Wally chain-smoked their way through the conversation. Pat slumped in her chair, drained by sleepless nights and grief. Wally was agitated, more upright, his face tense, but the same tears stained the edges of his bloodshot eyes.

Michelle and I again went over the facts that we knew. We told them that we wanted to be respectful and helpful to the extent that they wanted our help. It was clear that Pat wanted to size us up. Why were activists trying to get involved in this case? What was our motive?

Michelle explained the process of the murder investigation.

"The Army has said that Barry's death was the result of a physical altercation, a drunken brawl. They have arrested two of the soldiers in Delta Company in connection with the murder. The first step is that CID [the Army criminal investigative command[277]] will conduct an investigation to determine the facts and evidence. That report will inform whether any criminal charges are preferred against Calvin Glover, Justin Fisher, or anyone else.

"The commander at Fort Campbell, Major General Clark, will make the decision about what charges to prefer and against whom. If there are criminal charges, there will be an Article 32 hearing, which is the equivalent of an arraignment, followed by a court-martial. The commander will appoint members of what is the equivalent of the jury. The commander also has the authority to enter into plea bargains."

"That's good to know," Pat said.

"You should also know that you have rights as the family," Michelle continued. "You can ask to see a copy of the CID report. You can express opinions about the sufficiency of criminal investigation. You can ask questions about any stage of the process. You can attend the hearings. The decisions are left to the commander, but you can be engaged."

"Okay," Pat said.

Michelle went on, steady and measured. "We know of one other case possibly like this one. It was the case of Seaman Allen Schindler. In 1992, he was brutally murdered for being gay in Sasebo, Japan. The Navy tried to cover it up as a random attack in a public park. A civilian investigator dug up the truth. Two sailors from Allen's ship had stalked him and killed him. He was beaten so severely that his mom could only recognize him from a tattoo on his arm."[278]

"We are not presupposing any of the facts in your son's case," I added. "The Army has been firm that this was a tragic result of an altercation. The Army has been adamant that there was no anti-gay animus involved. We don't know. But we do know that Barry had expressed concern about increasing harassment, and that others thought he might be gay because he was dating Calpernia. Understanding the motive behind the attack will be essential in proving guilt if this goes to a court-martial."

"Calpernia has sent us some of Barry's things," Pat said—a revelation that she was aware of a connection between her son and Addams.

Wally tapped into his own pride as a veteran: "The Army has been up-front with us. I don't have any reason to second-guess the Army."

"I'm not saying that you do," I replied. "We are just letting you know about the criminal investigative process, your rights, and the prior precedent that should at least make us vigilant."

Pat said, "Well, I appreciate that."

"We know Allen's mom," Michelle said. "If you would like to speak to her at some point, I am sure she would be willing."

"Okay. Let me think about that," Pat said.

The meeting ended. Michelle and I gave them room to grieve—and to consider what we had told them. We just wanted to demonstrate that we were honest brokers and would help as much, or as little, as they allowed. They would set the terms. Advocates and politicians sometimes rush to judgment to support a belief or cause. Expediency must give way to due diligence.

◆◆◆

Over the next few months, everything Michelle and I said about Winchell's death at the outset proved true. The Army had to backtrack from its explanation to Pat and Wally that the death was the result of a brawl. It was premeditated murder. Evidence emerged that he was indeed being harassed because he was perceived as gay, and that it was much more extensive than previously known. The Army repeatedly bungled the investigation and prosecution; but for SLDN's persistence, justice may not have been served.

The preliminary report of the Army's criminal investigation was notable for its incompetence. The Army simply confirmed that there had been a barbecue on July 4, that everyone had been drinking, and that Glover had picked a fight with Winchell and later killed him. Case closed. We already knew that there was more to the story. After our visits to Nashville and to Fort Campbell, some of the soldiers who knew Winchell called us and told us more of what had happened. We tried to help steer the Army in the right direction.

Michelle and I drove to Quantico, Virginia, to meet with the head of the CID to discuss the preliminary report. We always sought to address our concerns with the highest authority. We knew that if we were to convince the local criminal investigators to redo the report, we would first have to convince the commander at headquarters. We also knew that we needed a more probing investigation if the cause of Winchell's death was not to be whitewashed.

I have always appreciated how open true leaders are to different points of view, even if it was clear that the CID commander was not happy to see us question the probity of his investigators' report. I tackled the heart of the matter.

"Did your investigators ask anyone whether Private First Class Winchell was taunted for being gay?" I asked him. "Who did the taunting? What was said to Winchell? What did others do to Winchell? Do we know from witnesses how Winchell responded? Did Winchell report the harassment to anyone, including the chain of command? Did Glover say anything about Winchell being gay? Did Fisher?"

"Look, we investigated this as a possible murder," the CID commander responded. "We are not investigating all these other claims."

"I appreciate that, sir," I said. "But what I am suggesting is a line of questions that goes to the heart of motive for murder. Motive. That will be crucial for the convening authority, the prosecutors, the military judge, the jury.

"It will also help with public perception, sir," I added. "The press has already reported that Private First Class Winchell's murder may have been a hate crime, and any investigative report that fails to examine that as a possible motive will be seen as omitting a key factor.

"So," I continued, "without prejudging what your investigators may find, is it possible to requestion some of the witnesses to lock down the motive behind the attack?"

He did not agree to our request. Officials rarely commit to do what you ask. They have to consult with others, weigh the risks and benefits. When they are sworn in, CID agents pledge that, at all times, they will "seek diligently to discover the truth, deterred neither by fear nor prejudice." In this case, Michelle and I had to remind them how to discover the truth.

Ultimately, the Army asked many of the questions we proposed, as it reinterviewed witnesses two and three times, according to further transcripts of the record of investigation. Despite emerging evidence of persistent anti-gay harassment against him, a Fort Campbell spokeswoman, Major Pamela Hart, told reporters that if Winchell had felt threatened, he could have talked to his superiors or to the post's Equal Opportunity Office.[279] It was, again, always the fault of the gay person for failing to do something.

In a call the day before the Article 32 hearing where Glover would be arraigned, the head of the CID insisted to me that there was no evidence that Winchell's murder was a hate crime. He and the Fort Campbell spokeswoman should have spoken with the witnesses.

◆ ◆ ◆

On December 12, 1999, Kathi Westcott and I arrived at the small courthouse at Fort Campbell for Glover's court-martial. It was a trailer with low ceilings, fluorescent lights, and fake wood paneling. It was not the sort of marbled hall of justice that spoke gravity and reverence. This felt more like an inconvenience.

I had alerted Major Hart, apparently to her surprise, that there would likely be significant media interest. The base arranged for a second trailer for the media. Addams arrived in her red pickup truck. Pat and Wally arrived and hovered by the back entrance, where they chain-smoked through their grief and anxiety. CNN and NBC had set up satellite feeds. Reporters from *The New York Times* and other news outlets were ready.

The pivotal testimony came from Sergeant Michael Kleifgen, Winchell's section leader. He confirmed what we had been documenting through our own interviews and warning CID about.

"Pretty much everybody in the company called him derogatory names,"[280] Kleifgen said of Winchell. "Basically, they called him a 'faggot' and stuff like that, I would say, on a daily basis. A lot of times, he was walking around down in the dumps."[281]

Kleifgen generally considered the taunts typical Army hazing. But he testified that he thought that his immediate superior, First Sergeant Roger Seacrest, went too far when he said was going to "get that faggot." [282] It was one thing to haze; it was another to turn against a good soldier and cause him professional harm. Kleifgen reported Seacrest to the company commander, Captain Daniel Rouse, and to the base's inspector general.

"I filed a formal complaint," Kleifgen said. "Nothing was done about it. It was basically blown off."[283]

From the back of the room, a public relations officer said, "Oh, shit!" and scampered out of the trailer to do damage control.

The details emerged about the days leading up to the murder, and what had happened on the night in question. The story had broken. Winchell's murder was a hate crime. Here is what happened.

◆◆◆

On July 3, a hot Saturday afternoon, the guys from Delta Company gathered around a keg in front of the barracks to kick back a few brews and shoot the shit. Glover was trying to hold court and prove himself a badass.

He was an 18-year-old kid with a troubled past. He had dropped out of high school and was placed in a youth facility— twice. After getting his GED, he enlisted, receiving an age exception because he was only 17.[284]

That day, he was drunk, boasting about taking meth, using cocaine, and robbing banks.

Glover was "trying to impress us to show us how tough he was," recalled Private First Class Arthur Hoffman. "He was loud in a bragging type of way. Really pushing it."[285]

Having heard enough, Winchell said what everyone was thinking: "Glover, take your drunk cherry-ass to bed."

"Do you want to fight, faggot?" Glover swatted at Winchell, trying to knock the beer bottle out of Winchell's hands.

"I don't want to fight you, Glover," Winchell said.

"Faggot!" Glover was having difficulty standing. He tried punching Winchell, but his arms flailed in the air. "Faggot! Come on, faggot!" Swing and a miss. "Show us how tough you are! Faggot."

Finally, Winchell dropped his beer bottle, hit Glover in the face with his palm three or four times, and pinned him to the ground. Glover was squirming and cussing. Two soldiers separated them.

Winchell tried to make amends. "It's cool, right?"

"It's not cool," Glover said. "I could fucking kill you."[286]

Winchell was shaken—not because of the fight, but because of the taunts. He had been enduring daily epithets. His Army brothers called him "rope smoker," "butt pirate," "faggot." He had confided to a friend, Specialist Lewis Ruiz, that he thought the harassment was coming to a boiling point, but he didn't know how to contain it.

Winchell started crying while walking back to his barracks room. "Why do people have to push me to that point?" he asked aloud.[287]

Glover followed him part of the way. "It ain't over! I won't let a faggot kick my ass!"

Fisher, Winchell's roommate, liked to get under people's skin. He seized the moment to goad Glover. "How does it feel to have your ass kicked by a faggot?"[288]

"Fuck you," Glover shot back.

Fisher had apparently started the rumors about Barry Winchell.[289] He had told Kleifgen that he saw Winchell making out with a guy at The Connection. What he didn't tell Kleifgen is that he was the one who had encouraged Winchell to go to the

194

bar and even accompanied him there on several occasions. He acknowledged that he had made out with one of the performers. It would subsequently come to light that one night, Winchell awoke to find Fisher caressing his feet.[290] It is possible that Fisher was dealing with his own sexuality at the time and perhaps was trying to deflect suspicions from himself to Winchell.

On July 4, Fisher picked up where he had left off the night before. Leaning out his barracks-room window, he yelled down to Glover, "I'm gonna tell everyone at work next week that you got your ass kicked by a faggot."[291]

"Fuck you!"

That night the Delta Company gang gathered again around the concrete picnic table, drinking beers from a keg. Soldiers report that Glover and Winchell were surprisingly amicable. They played wiffle ball. Winchell showed Glover how to juggle. It appeared that all was forgiven. But as the evening wore on and the alcohol took hold, Glover's mood started to shift. The beer keg was a powder keg.

Though underage, Glover had been drinking heavily—17 beers, by one account.[292] Fisher kept trying to dig under Glover's skin, bit by bit.

"I can't believe you got your ass kicked by a faggot,"[293] Fisher said, laughing. "How does that make you feel? What are you going to do about it?"

Glover took the wiffle ball bat and smashed it against the keg several times, venting anger and frustration.

At around 11:30 p.m., with the keg drained, Fisher took Glover to an on-base store and bought two 40-ounce bottles of malt liquor.[294]

Meanwhile, Winchell went to bed, as had most of Delta Company. It was his night to take care of the company's mascot, Nasty, an Australian cattle dog. He set up a cot in the hallway outside the room he shared with Fisher because he knew how Fisher would react if the dog made any mess in the room; once, when Winchell was smoking in the room, Fisher smashed his face with a dustpan, splattering blood on the wall.

Winchell needed stitches,[295] but he refused to press charges, trying to just get along. "Suck it up," he would say. Fisher refused to let Winchell wash the bloodstain from the wall—a reminder of what could happen to him if he crossed Fisher again.

Fisher joined Glover in Glover's room. Fisher started in again.

"Everyone is going to think you're a pussy. Winchell is talking shit about you behind your back. What are you going to do about it?"[296]

Fisher and Glover walked back to the room that Winchell and Fisher shared. It was spartan but sufficient. The space included two bedrooms and a common bathroom and sink. As they walked by Winchell, who was asleep on the cot in the hallway, Glover growled, "What is that faggot doing sleeping out here?"[297]

Inside the room, Fisher turned on the soundtrack to Gus Van Sant's 1998 remake of the film *Psycho*.[298] The hard metal beats pounded. They drank the malt liquor. Fisher picked up a baseball bat he owned and stroked it. He swung it in short chopping motions, as if he was preparing to step up to the plate.

"He thought he was his own personal crime boss," Private First Class Nikita Sanarov would later testify at Glover's trial. "He was always plotting his own crimes. He liked to plot revenge on someone who had stolen something of his—handcuffing the guy, plunging his head in a tub, and burning a cigarette into his flesh.

He liked the idea of interrogating someone like that. He wanted to be the Man."[299]

Fisher was a fan of gangster flicks, like *Scarface* and *Reservoir Dogs*. He could have included in that list Robert DeNiro's portrayal of Al Capone in *The Untouchables*; in the film, Capone crushes the skull of a rival with a baseball bat.

The *Psycho* beats kept pounding. Fisher handed the bat to Glover, who started swinging it like Fisher had—in short chopping motions.[300]

"How does your face feel?" Fisher asked. "How did it feel to have your ass kicked by a faggot?"

"Fuck you!" Glover responded, growing angrier. "I ought to go outside and fuck him up."[301]

Fisher replied calmly, "Go outside and kill that motherfucker."[302]

It was about 1:30 a.m. Everyone else on the floor was in their room, asleep. Winchell was on the cot outside, his head facing the wall.

Glover approached Winchell without hesitation. He raised the Louisville Slugger and brought it crashing down on Winchell's head. He did it again, and again, and again, three to five times. Blood sprayed all the way up the wall to the ceiling. It gushed from Winchell's ears, mouth, and nose. Forensics experts testified later that his skull was crushed like an eggshell.

Glover returned to the room. "I did it," he boasted.

"This just stays in the family," Fisher said. "You and me are in the family."[303]

Both were calm. Fisher used the sink to meticulously clean the blood off the bat.

"Let's go outside and have a cigarette," Glover suggested.[304]

As they left, Glover turned to Winchell and said, "Look who got their ass kicked now, faggot. You won't be kicking anybody's ass now, faggot."[305]

He hit Winchell in the face.

Fisher heard gurgling sounds, which spooked him. Winchell was alive, but just barely. The cot was soaked in his blood.

"Is he dead?" Fisher asked.[306]

Glover lifted Winchell's head and dropped it.

"He's dead."[307]

At that moment, it dawned on Fisher that they had committed murder and could go to jail. He needed to save his skin. They had to cover their tracks.

"What are we gonna do now?" Fisher asked urgently. They thought about dumping the body in the river, but couldn't find Winchell's car keys.[308]

"You better get the fuck out of here," Fisher said,[309] adding that Glover should dispose of the evidence and say nothing.

Glover ran out of the building. He threw his blood-soaked clothes and a pair of gloves in a dumpster. He ran back to his room, in another building, to wash the blood off his body.

Fisher came up with an alibi—that he had discovered Winchell and was the one who was calling for help to save him. He started yelling: "Winchell, Winchell, come on, get up!"[310]

His shouts woke up Private First Class Jonathan Joyce,[311] who lived on the floor below. Joyce ran upstairs, saw Winchell, then ran back downstairs and called 911. He called 911 five times[312] but couldn't get through because, unbeknownst to him, calls to 911 could not be made from inside the barracks. He finally found a payphone to call 911. Emergency personnel arrived forty-five minutes later.

Fisher was back on the third floor, screaming, "Help! Help! Help!" He set off the fire alarm, alerting everyone to the emergency. "Help!"

Soldiers asked him what had happened. He said he didn't know; he had just found Winchell there.

When the ambulance arrived, Winchell had "raccoon eyes"— extensive bruising and discoloration that indicated a basal skull fracture and massive hemorrhaging.[313] He had suffered irreversible brain damage. Fifteen to 20 soldiers watched as paramedics loaded Winchell into the ambulance and took him to the hospital at Fort Campbell; from there he was transported to Vanderbilt Medical Center in Nashville. Fisher yelled as the ambulance pulled away, his mood shifting darker, "No balls! No balls!"[314]

Glover returned to the scene. He was wearing a pair of black shorts; a white T-shirt was draped over one of his shoulders. "How did it happen?" he asked.[315] No one knew.

The Army called the murder a result of a "physical altercation."

On December 9, 1999, the Army convicted Glover of premeditated murder and sentenced him to life in prison.

On January 9, 2000, Fisher pled guilty to lesser offenses— obstruction of justice, lying to investigators, and serving alcohol to a minor—and was sentenced to 12½ years in prison, of which he served only seven.

◆ ◆ ◆

Over the objections of both Winchell's family and SLDN, Major General Robert T. Clark, the commanding general at Fort Campbell, signed off on a lenient plea bargain with Fisher. It dropped the original charges in exchange for his cooperation in the trial against Glover. If he had been found guilty of the original charges, which included participating as a principal to premeditated murder and acting as an accessory after the fact, he could have received the maximum sentence: life in prison.[316]

One troubling fact of military justice is that the commanding general of a base gets to decide what charges are preferred against a service member accused of a crime, determines whether to accept a plea bargain, and picks the members of the jury. The situation is rife with conflict of interest.

We are seeing the same concerns about conflict of interest raised in the context of sexual assault in the armed forces. Traditionalists have argued that sexual harassment and sexual assault charges should be left to the chain of command to resolve—not only because commanders are in the best position to assess the credibility of the initial allegations, but also because respect for the chain of command is essential to good order, discipline, and morale. Others argue that the armed forces have repeatedly failed to adequately address claims of sexual assault and harassment. The bigger story, which has yet to be addressed, is whether the base commander should be the decision-maker in legal matters or whether, for all criminal charges, there should be an independent process.

A charitable reading of Clark's decision to enter into a plea bargain with Fisher is the adage "A bird in the hand is worth two in the bush." Obtaining Fisher's testimony against Glover assured that Glover would be severely punished. Without it, the prosecution may have been concerned that its case was not solid.

A less charitable reading is that Clark didn't want two extended trials, one for Glover and one for Fisher, which would have prolonged the negative publicity and might have also highlighted other command failures.

Under Clark's leadership, the base had not installed a functional 911 system; that delayed medical help reaching Winchell by 45 minutes.[317] The hospital at Fort Campbell was rated one of the worst in the Army.[318] Underage drinking was rampant.[319] A *60 Minutes* segment broadcast on January 17, 1999, more than five months before Winchell's murder, revealed that domestic violence at the base was significant.[320]

A prolonged trial may have shown that discharges of gay soldiers at Fort Campbell alone skyrocketed from 17 in 1999 to 160 in 2000[321] as a direct result of Clark's orders.[322] Without basis, Clark blamed the increase on gays "seeking an easy way out of the Army."[323] Once again, it was the fault of gay service members for what happened to them.

Major Paul Gott, the doctor who treated Winchell at the base hospital, came out to his commander because he could not reconcile the animosity under Clark's leadership with his good conscience. His heart-wrenching letter read:

> "I am writing to inform you that I am gay.... I had the misfortune to be the surgeon on call the night Private First Class Winchell was brought to the emergency room at Fort Campbell. The obvious brutality and hatred that must have motivated his attacker struck me deeply. In the days that followed, the knowledge that the attack was an anti-gay hate crime filled me with outrage and disgust. Yet I remained silent. Imagine the stress and anxiety of working in an environment where the brutal murder of a person simply for being gay was the topic of casual conversation.... [T]he response I

perceived was that it was a ... not unexpected consequence of gays serving in the military. I am sure I am
not alone among gay servicemembers who sat silently
through these conversations with a sense of nausea and
fear.... I can no longer, in clear conscience, be silent and
bear witness to the ongoing harassment and violence
faced by gay service members."[324]

Clark never told his soldiers after the murder that "anti-
gay harassment" was wrong. He did not order the flag at Fort
Campbell to be flown at half-mast, as is customary when a
soldier dies on the base. In a memorandum issued months after
Winchell's murder, Clark wrote: "Respect for others is an Army
Value and a cornerstone of discipline and esprit de corps. All soldiers will be treated with dignity and respect."[325] Clark's failure
to address anti-gay harassment specifically, given the magnitude
of information about anti-gay harassment that was then on the
record, was inexplicable.

SLDN documented every misstep. Clark refused to let gay
soldiers at the base report harassment anonymously by hotline
to an inspector general coming to the base to inspect the situation, saying that it was not in the "best interest" of the command.
He issued a direct order placing The Connection, the gay bar in
Nashville that Winchell had frequented to see Calpernia Addams,
off limits, making it a criminal offense to go there.[326] "Don't ask,
don't tell" specifically allowed military personnel to go to gay
bars, but violating Clark's direct order made doing so punishable
by jail.

Clark refused a request by SLDN to place an ad in the base
newspaper, *The Fort Campbell Courier*, to advise service members

how to report harassment safely.[327] "We do not believe running this advertisement is in the best interest of the command and its soldiers," the base's public affairs office told us.[328]

He also temporarily suspended access from base computers to SLDN's website, where soldiers could have obtained information and legal resources concerning "Don't ask, don't tell."

It's no surprise that anti-gay harassment continued unabated in the aftermath of the murder. Specialist Michael McCoy, one of Winchell's good friends, observed increased anti-gay epithets, comments, and graffiti at Fort Campbell, including soldiers who mocked the murder. During a training exercise, he heard an infantry soldier call other soldiers "faggot" if they gave incorrect answers. Another soldier added, "That's right, and I will beat you with a baseball bat."[329] These statements were made in the presence of noncommissioned officers, none of whom spoke up or intervened.

On other occasions, McCoy observed anti-gay graffiti in public areas on the base.[330] One drawing, on the wall of a Family Support Center restroom, was of a large baseball bat with the words "FAG WHACKER" prominently inscribed in the middle of the bat—a purposeful drawing mocking Winchell's murder and indicating the degree of anti-gay sentiment allowed to flourish at the base. Graffiti at a post recreation center read "All Fagets [sic] in the Army will be killed." Both the Family Support Center and the recreation center are heavily used common areas at Fort Campbell; officers and enlisted leaders could not have missed seeing the anti-gay sentiment.

Another soldier, Private Javier "Cortland" Torres, told us that his sergeant briefed his unit on "Don't ask, don't tell" a month after

Winchell's murder. The sergeant called the class a "fag briefing" and referred to gay soldiers as "fags."[331] When Torres expressed concern about how one soldier could turn on another, a soldier said, "So what if [Winchell] was killed. He was gay." And "Who cares? He was just a fag." The soldiers then turned on Torres and asked him if he was gay, too.[332]

Torres also reported that a staff sergeant had led his unit on a run, singing a chilling cadence: "Faggot, faggot, down the street. Shoot him, shoot him 'til he retreats."[333]

◆◆◆

Lieutenant General Jack Keane, the commanding general at Fort Bragg, North Carolina, faced a comparable situation, but he handled the matter very differently. After skinhead soldiers murdered two Black civilians, he immediately made a public statement that he deplored racial violence to assure the entire community that such behavior was unacceptable. He then invited community leaders to meet with him, asking for their help in determining what else he could do to minimize the possibility of another such crime.

At Fort Campbell, Clark blamed the victim, and took steps to ensure that lesbian, gay, and bisexual service members were made even less welcome under his command—reinforcing the climate that led to Winchell's murder in the first place.

Clark denied any failure of leadership. He retired in December 2006; a month later, he told the *San Antonio Express News*: "I'll just say there's a lot of character assassination that went on with that that was disconcerting to say the least."[334] He told Pat and

Wally Kutteles to their face that he blamed them for putting him and his family through a difficult time.

Clark's next two successors took a significantly different approach. Major General Richard A. Cody assumed command at Fort Campbell on June 10, 2000, "in ceremonies marked by the military pageantry of music, cannons firing, helicopter flyovers and 16,000 troops of the division and support units passing in review."[335] Two months later, we had a situation. We asked Cody to intervene to protect the safety and careers of two soldiers.

Sergeant Matthew Laxton, a 21-year-old infantryman, had recently arrived from his last duty assignment in South Korea and was stunned by the intensity of anti-gay fervor within his unit, including dismissive comments about Winchell's murder.[336] He confided in his platoon sergeant that he was gay and sought advice on what he could do to ensure his safety. With his platoon sergeant's support, Laxton disclosed his sexual orientation to his company commander, Captain Edward Brady, who demanded that Laxton "prove" he was gay and did nothing to investigate anti-gay harassment. When the platoon sergeant overheard Brady call Laxton a "pole-smoker," he reported Brady's misconduct up the chain of command. In response, Brady threatened to lower the platoon sergeant's official performance evaluation.

SLDN assisted Laxton in filing a complaint with the base's inspector general; we also asked Cody to intervene. He acted swiftly, issuing a personal reprimand to Brady and protecting the platoon sergeant from retaliation—sending a clear signal to the soldiers that such behavior would not be tolerated. Laxton was discharged.

In late 2000, Cody invited SLDN to brief one hundred officers. He required every battalion-level commander and command sergeant major to attend a mandatory meeting to discuss Barry Winchell's case and to make recommendations to prevent such a tragedy from occurring again.

"We share a common goal of ensuring that all Fort Campbell soldiers—straight, gay, lesbian, and those perceived be gay or lesbian—are treated with dignity and respect,"[337] he wrote in a memorandum to SLDN. (It's notable that he used "gay" and "lesbian" rather than "homosexual"—simultaneously a small detail and a huge cultural shift.) Finally, Fort Campbell had a leader who weighed in against violence and harassment against suspected lesbian, gay, and bisexual soldiers. That didn't mean that the command climate changed overnight. Gay discharges continued to surge, but we had an ally with whom we could work to try to turn things around.

Cody invited SLDN to the base twice in 2001. Kathi Westcott and another SLDN staff attorney, Jeff Cleghorn, a former Army major who had served in military intelligence, briefed him on the findings in SLDN's annual report, especially as they pertained to Fort Campbell, soon after it was published in March. Jeff went back in August, this time escorting Pat and Wally Kutteles. It was the first time they had returned to the base since the trials. The parents visited the barracks where their son had lived—a moment that brought pain, sorrow, and connection. They were encouraged by the steps Cody had taken to address the base's anti-gay culture.

Cody's successor, Major General David Petraeus, also invited SLDN to meet with him. While gay discharges at the base had dropped from a high of 222 in 2001 to 92 in 2002, the number remained unacceptably high.[338] Jeff returned to Fort Campbell and explained our concerns about the harassment at the base, the climate of fear that had ensued, and the alarming discharge rate.

"I am committed to doing all I can to ensure that all my troopers are treated with dignity and respect and are able to serve their nation in an environment that is safe—free from harassment of any form," Petraeus assured him.[339]

It didn't surprise me that a decade later, Petraeus—now a four-star general—supported the repeal of "Don't ask, don't tell." You never know when the relationship you build one day becomes key years later.

◆ ◆ ◆

The Army inspector general was ordered to investigate the situation at Fort Campbell. We provided as much detail as we could about ongoing harassment, given that soldiers were terrified to say anything. The officer in charge of the review team confirmed that he would report any service members found to be gay during the course of investigating anti-gay harassment, further alienating the Army from the truth.

Lieutenant General John M. LeMoyne, the Army's deputy chief of staff for personnel, briefed me on the findings when the report was done. He came to SLDN's office, which had moved to 16th and K Streets Northwest, just north of the White House. LeMoyne said the report had concluded that there was no systemic and pervasive anti-gay climate at the base, only isolated incidents.

Clark felt vindicated. He shouldn't have. Despite its conclusion, the report verified the anti-gay harassment that Winchell had faced, the anti-gay cadences during physical training runs, and the anti-gay graffiti in public spaces.[340] It also found that anti-gay "joking and bantering" occurred among soldiers "on a regular basis," LeMoyne told me.

He then looked at me, and the light bulb turned on. "Huh," he said. "I guess we are going to have to treat those comments as harassment now?"

"Yes, sir," I replied. "That is the point."

LeMoyne later told Aaron Belkin, founding director of the Palm Center, that he had changed his mind about "Don't ask, don't tell" and supported repeal.[341] (The Palm Center, founded at the University of California, Santa Barbara, in 1999 as the Center for the Study of Sexual Minorities in the Military, is an academic center dedicated to scholarly research on LGBT military service.)

◆ ◆ ◆

Tragedy can be an opportunity, but one must tread those grounds lightly and respectfully. There is a difference between seizing an opportunity and being opportunistic.

We did not immediately proclaim that Winchell's murder was a hate crime. At the outset, we said that there was evidence indicating that it *could* be a hate crime, but that the facts had to be developed. We gave the Army room to do its own investigation. We gave ourselves time to piece together the facts. Had we declared that Winchell was gay and that this was a hate crime, and it proved to be untrue, we would have lost all credibility.

To this day, I do not know for sure whether Barry Winchell was gay. According to trial transcripts, his friend, Lewis Ruiz, testified that Winchell had come out to him and his wife, but he was not out to his parents or closest friends, so it isn't clear just what he had communicated to others. Pat asked me once why her son would not have come out to her if he was gay, knowing that she would have been supportive. "He may not have known himself yet if he was," I replied. "It was too early."

What is clear is that he was a young man who was probably exploring his sexuality with a beautiful transgender woman. What the facts bore out, though, is that his fellow soldiers perceived him as gay—and that is, in part, what motivated Glover's attack and why it was a hate crime.

As Fisher's trial concluded, Michelle and I asked Pat whether she would be willing to read a statement to the press. We helped her draft it but told her that she had complete authority over the text to ensure that it reflected her sentiments. We had not asked Pat and Wally to do anything up to that point; we knew that they needed to grieve and to let the legal process work. We were prepared for them to walk away, and no one would have blamed them if they had. Michelle and I had done our best to be honest brokers, and we were proven right at each turn.

"I'm ready," she said with conviction, sitting behind a small conference table. "I will do whatever you want me to do. It's what Barry would want."

And she did. "The SLDN helped immensely in finding out what really went on," she told *The New York Times*.[342]

From that moment, Pat and Wally were on the front lines, pushing for repeal of "Don't ask, don't tell." They walked the halls of Congress. They spoke at events around the country. They sat for interviews with *The New York Times*, *The Washington Post*, and *NBC Nightly News*. Their activism with SLDN paved the way for major policy changes. The Anti-Defamation League honored them at its annual Concert Against Hate at the Kennedy Center in Washington on November 15, 2011, and I was there cheering them on.

We assisted Pat and Wally in filing a Military Claims Act against the Army for the wrongful death of their son. The Army denied the claim.[343] In a terse one-page letter, it said that Winchell's murder was "incident to military service." I don't know many soldiers who would enlist if being killed by another soldier in your unit is part of your service commitment.

◆◆◆

Barry Winchell's murder was one of the first turning points in the battle to repeal "Don't ask, don't tell," as it underscored the tragic consequences of a law that forced service members into silence and gave cover to those who would harass, intimidate, and kill. Vice President Al Gore, who was running for the Democratic presidential nomination to succeed Clinton, announced that "Don't ask, don't tell" should be repealed,[344] as did Senator Bill Bradley, who was also running for the nomination.[345]

Clinton, for the first time, started to backtrack on his commitment to his "honorable compromise," calling the law "out of whack."[346] Four years later, in a letter to SLDN written at my behest for our annual gala, he would conclude, "Simply put, there is no evidence to support the gay ban."

Before denouncing "Don't ask, don't tell" in December 1999, Gore called Pat and Wally to express his sincerest condolences. It is something I had asked his campaign to do. Before he did so, I got a call from Gore's campaign manager, Donna Brazile, as I was riding on a bus back to Georgetown. She spoke a mile a minute.

"Dixon, I'm calling to say that Vice President Gore is going to call the Kutteleses. This is important. I know there are rumors about me. I'm not ready for that. But this is important."

All I had time to say was "thank you" before she hung up. I thought to myself, "Huh. She just came out to me." She had recently told *The Washington Post*, "If I had a personal life, I'd have a sexual orientation."[347] She would later come out.[348]

Months later, the Army sent Pat a package with her son's personal belongings, which had been held as part of the investigation. She was upset that the box was in disarray. It appeared that his things had been haphazardly thrown into the box—not carefully and meticulously arranged, as one would expect per military protocol. It showed disrespect. But one item caught her attention, and she called to tell me about it.

She had opened her son's wallet to find an SLDN legal rights card. He had our legal rights card. Winchell had known about SLDN before his murder. If he had called us, would we have been able to prevent the horrific tragedy?

Pat could not see me on the other end of the phone line, tears streaming down my face.

"I knew there was a reason Barry brought you to me," she said.

CHAPTER 23

SHIN-KICKER

From the outset, the strategy to repeal "Don't ask, don't tell" was to dismantle the statute brick by brick, and let the pillars crumble. We demonstrated how the policy was eroding unit cohesion through divisive witch hunts, intrusive investigations, and unchecked harassment—all of which resulted in the loss of patriotic Americans serving their country.

At the same time, we were building, block by block, a new foundation that would support service members after "Don't ask, don't tell" repeal. We had secured President Clinton's executive order to end sexual orientation discrimination in security clearances and the Deutch memo setting terms for recoupment against gay ROTC members; reversed the ban on HIV+ service members; and gotten another executive order, this one providing for a limited psychotherapist privilege. We ended the practice of witch hunts and criminal prosecutions.

No set of policy achievements prior to repeal, however, was more important than those designed to curb harassment. We knew that we would have to fundamentally shift the military's culture if "Don't ask, don't tell" was to be successfully repealed.

In our first annual report, published in 1995, we predicted that if the Pentagon took no steps to combat harassment, another service member would be murdered, just as Allen Schindler had been. I wish we had not been correct. The harassment our clients endured was brutal enough.

The regulations implementing "Don't ask, don't tell" stated that "the armed forces do not tolerate harassment of any kind against any service member." But that wasn't enough, because it didn't specify what kinds of harassment were wrong. As in Barry Winchell's case, many of his fellow soldiers took anti-gay hazing as the norm. No big deal.

Our strategy was to document case after case of anti-gay harassment, collect the data, tell the stories, and use those as levers to pursue policy change. Even people who didn't like gays and lesbians agreed that physical and verbal harassment were wrong.

Michelle and I took as our solemn responsibility to do everything we could to protect all service members, straight and gay, from anti-gay harassment. After four years of making our case to Pentagon officials, we had our first breakthrough.

We met with the Defense Department's under secretary for personnel and readiness, Edwin Dorn, in 1995, 1996, and 1997 to report the findings from our annual reports. We laid out the grim statistics of anti-gay harassment we had recorded. The incidents escalated year over year.

At our meeting in 1997, Michelle said, "I remember in my command, sir, when our base commander called us in and immediately chewed us out. 'I watched as you filed into this room,' he said. 'I had placed a Coke can and litter outside the door, and not one of you stopped to pick it up. We are all responsible for the order and discipline at this base, and each and every one of you failed.'

"That lesson has always stuck with me, sir. Ending harassment is everyone's responsibility, but leadership from the top is essential."

"The armed forces strive to uphold the dignity and respect of every service member," Dorn replied. "We do not tolerate harassment of any kind. Why do we need more guidance?"

"Sir, because no one knows that the ban on harassment includes anti-gay harassment," I said.

"But the 'Don't ask, don't tell' regulations specifically state that harassment will not be tolerated."

"The caveat is in a footnote, sir, that no one has read," I responded. "And even if they have read it. sir, no one gets that using words like 'faggot,' 'dyke,' 'die fag'—words our clients hear every day—equals harassment."

In late March I received a letter from the Pentagon. I opened the envelope and discovered a one-page policy memorandum, dated March 24, 1997.[349] There was no accompanying note or letter.

I wondered why the memo had been sent to me. It was addressed to the highest levels of command and intended for distribution. I read it several times and understood that Dorn had done what we had asked him to do: He had published new policy guidance to try to limit anti-gay harassment.

Dorn hadn't told us that his office had prepared the memo, or even contemplated publication of such guidance, despite our many requests and proposals of language. As with the head of the CID in the Winchell case, officials rarely agree to do what you ask because they might not be able to deliver. Sometimes you have to let the process work—and it's very uncomfortable, because you're not in control. The process isn't linear. It isn't transparent. Leaders send conflicting messages. Sometimes they don't follow through.

Here, the new policy memorandum simply arrived in the mail. It was one of Dorn's last acts before accepting a position as dean of the Lyndon Baines Johnson School of Public Affairs at the University of Texas at Austin.

The memo instructed commanders to investigate anti-gay threats and lesbian-baiting, not the service members who report it. It was the first to identify anti-gay threats as a potential problem, though we thought that the use of the word "threats" to describe harassment set the bar too high for the varied types of harassment that service members experienced.

It also alerted commanders to the phenomenon of lesbian-baiting—where women, regardless of their sexual orientation, were accused of being lesbian in retaliation for reporting sexual harassment or rebuffing sexual advances, as had occurred with Army Private First Class Shannon Emery, our client in South Korea. It was the first time that any public official, let alone a government document, had acknowledged lesbian-baiting.

I walked down the corridor, handed the memo to Michelle, and waited to see her reaction.

"What is this?" she asked

"We got it!" I smiled broadly.

She read it again. "Holy crap!" We high-fived.

◆◆◆

Though we received the memo, no one else in the military did.[350] The Pentagon did not distribute it.

More persistence was needed. Through conversations with military defense attorneys, commanders, and clients in the field, we documented the abject failure to distribute the guidance and train service members in what it meant. We pushed again.

We made some progress in getting increasing recognition from policy leaders that lesbian-baiting was sexual harassment. In May 1997, the Senate Armed Services Committee addressed this form of harassment for the first time:

> "The committee is concerned by an increasing number of reports that service members who refuse to participate in improper sexual activities or who report improper sexual activities by others are being labeled as being homosexual as a form of retaliation. Such labeling is especially insidious in its secondary effects which frequently include additional harassment, humiliation, ostracism, and, in extreme cases, improper investigation for homosexuality."[351]

The committee report "urges the Department of Defense and leaders at all levels" to "ensure that no individual experience [sic] the need to submit to unwanted sexual advances or harassment for any reason" and to permit individuals to report inappropriate activities without fear of retaliation.[352] The report further expressed the committee's concern that "the right to investigate individual conduct is not used as a threat or abused in any manner."[353]

Four months later, the Army's Senior Review Panel Report on Sexual Harassment noted that "[f]emale soldiers who refuse the sexual advances of male soldiers may be accused of being lesbians and subjected to investigation for homosexual conduct."[354] Further, the report continued, "Women accused of lesbianism believe that the mere allegation harms their careers and reputations irreparably."[355]

Given the serious risks involved in reporting lesbian-baiting, it is significant that the panel itself did not specifically survey or question soldiers about it. Soldiers raised this issue on their own initiative in focus groups, as well as in other venues, during panel members' visits to Army bases.[356]

The Dorn memo lay dormant. We asked the Pentagon to review "Don't ask, don't tell" implementation, challenging both civilian and military officials to make their own assessment of whether commanders were asking, harassing, and pursuing service members in violation of the law. Having already documented widespread asking, harassing, and pursuing, we were turning the argument into one about leadership—or the lack thereof.

In April 1998, we got our wish. A report instigated by the Hickam Air Force Base witch hunt was used by the Pentagon as a departure point for a broader review of the policy's implementation and our reports of anti-gay harassment.

The report conceded that the services had not distributed Dorn's memo. Once again, though, the Pentagon downplayed the extent of anti-gay harassment, asserting that commanders in the field had simply not indicated to higher-ups that it was a problem.

Nevertheless, the Pentagon did not simply order that the Dorn memo be reissued; it also clarified that the ban on harassment included not just "threats," but forms of anti-gay harassment that were lesser than threats.

Significantly, the report called for harassers to be called out: "[I]n reissuing the memorandum providing guidelines for investigating threats against service members based on homosexuality, the Department should include language to make clear that harassment of service members based on their alleged or presumed sexual orientation is unacceptable and that service members who engage in such harassment will be held accountable."[357]

It wasn't clear how far the Pentagon would go, or if it even understood the issue at hand; after all, you can't state that harassment is not a problem and, at the same time, issue guidance governing it. That sends mixed signals to the field. The memo called on each service to develop and incorporate anti-gay harassment provisions in its regulations.

The call to action went unheeded once again. The Pentagon did not distribute the memo on anti-gay harassment. In 1999 we spoke with Rudy deLeon, Dorn's successor as under secretary for personnel and readiness. He agreed to meet with us and update us on progress being made in implementing anti-harassment provisions. Michelle and I were told that the meeting would be with just us, deLeon, and one or two of his assistants.

We arrived at the Pentagon Metro entrance and were escorted not to deLeon's office, but to a large conference room. Waiting for us were officials from the Pentagon general counsel's office, the Army and the

Air Force; staff members for Vice President Al Gore and Representative Barney Frank; and Andy Tobias, the treasurer of the Democratic National Committee, who had written two popular memoirs about growing up gay. DeLeon and a coterie of advisors arrived as we sat down.

Michelle and I looked at each other. This was not the meeting we had planned. As deLeon arrived, Michelle whispered to me, "Any change of plan?"

"No," I said. But this was different because it was more formal.

In meetings like this, sometimes Michelle took the lead, and sometimes I did. This time it was my turn. I took a deep breath and commenced.

"Under Secretary deLeon, thank you for agreeing to the meeting. We appreciate the efforts the Pentagon and services have been taking to try to calibrate implementation of 'Don't ask, don't tell,' and specifically efforts to try to address anti-gay harassment. When we last spoke, we made a series of specific requests, and we wanted to take this opportunity to check in with you about those efforts.

"Have you had a chance to follow up with the Army in its promulgation of regulations pursuant to the Dorn memo?"

"No. I do not have anything to report back on that."

"Have you followed up with the Navy on its anti-gay harassment policies?"

"No."

"How about the Air Force?"

"No."

"Sir, I am a little concerned because the purpose of this meeting was to assess the status of implementing the anti-gay harassment policies. Could you give us a timeline when you expect the services to implement the guidance?"

DeLeon's face was turning as red as his hair. He was clearly upset. That was too bad. I was not intentionally embarrassing him. He didn't do what he said he would. I was trying to get information and agreement on next steps.

What made my task more difficult was that underneath the table, Michelle was kicking my shin with the heel of her shoe. I caught my breath once. I glanced at her, but she didn't look at me. Her gaze was fixed on deLeon, and she was calm and smiling.

Opportunities to engage with top-level officials are rare. It is important not to squander them, hold back, or mince words. It is equally important to be professional, fact-driven, and persuasive.

DeLeon promised that he would have answers at our next meeting and glared at one of his aides. He had not been properly prepped, and I am sure that he had a word with his aides afterward.

He then began a lofty speech to the dozen or so assembled. "I am pleased that today gays can serve without discrimination, and that we are continuing to make further progress ..."

I interrupted. "Mr. Under Secretary, with all due respect ..."

Michelle kicked me again. I winced.

"If I have not been clear up to now, let me be clear now," I said. "There is one thing that you must take away from this meeting. 'Don't ask, don't tell' is a law of discrimination, pure and simple. You cannot say that gays are serving without discrimination, nor that we are making progress.

"Gay Americans who come out or are discovered through interrogations or forced out of hiding by harassment are banned from our armed forces by law. Now we are not here today to discuss the wisdom of the law or to ask you to change the law. We know you can't. That is up to Congress.

"We are simply here to ask you to live up to the few promises made in the law that, if enforced, would make the lives of gay Americans slightly less intolerable while serving our nation. That is it. But please, do not tell us that 'Don't ask, don't tell' is some civil rights breakthrough. It is far from that."

Shaken, deLeon finished his remarks as quickly as he could, thanked everyone for attending, and stood up. We all stood up, shook hands, and left.

Andy Tobias approached me. "Great job! He needed to hear that!"

"You don't think it was too strong?" I asked.

"No. He needed that. Excellent."

From Michelle came a sigh of relief. I rubbed my shin.

◆◆◆

Barry Winchell's murder in July spurred further action. Policymakers often act only in crisis. But in the five years leading to this moment, Michelle and I had laid the groundwork, documenting the increasing harassment, the Pentagon's failure to act, and the steps necessary to correct the course.

The first step: Defense Secretary William Cohen finally succeeded in distributing the Dorn memo on August 13, 1999,[358] a month after Winchell's murder and only days after highly charged testimony in the Article 32 hearing of the accused murderer, Calvin Glover. Cohen also ordered each of the services to conduct training to prevent anti-gay harassment.

"I think they realize at the Pentagon that this just can't be swept under the rug," a senior Clinton administration official, speaking on condition of anonymity, told *The New York Times*.[359] "There's a recognition there that this problem of gay harassment is worse than they thought."

The guidance was issued only because of the murder and the uproar it caused. Notably, the new iteration of the Dorn guidelines required prompt investigations into allegations of anti-gay harassment and stated that those reporting the harassment should not be investigated for doing so.[360]

While the new guidelines were welcome, they continued to fall short in important respects—for example, they dropped the language about lesbian-baiting that was in Dorn's original memo.[361]

They also didn't specify where to report harassment. We immediately wrote to Cohen, urging the Pentagon to permit gay service members to report harassment through the same channels as service members who weren't gay—to their commanders, mental health counselors, inspectors general, chaplains, and equal opportunity advisors, among others.[362]

A senior Army officer who helped to develop the training program on harassment issues told *The Washington Post* that the equal opportunity advisors—assigned to every command team to advise on race relations—had been specifically instructed *not* to address issues of anti-gay harassment.[363] (In late 2000, the Pentagon reversed course and ordered the Defense Equal Opportunity Management Institute to train all equal opportunity advisors on how to respond to reports of anti-gay harassment.[364])

Lastly, despite the promise against retaliation, the guidelines did not make clear that the military should not discharge service members who, while reporting harassment, revealed that they were gay or who were found out to be gay.[365]

In addition to the gaping holes in the new policy, each of the services approached training differently—and inadequately.[366] Neither the Pentagon nor the services made their training protocols available to us, but we obtained copies from service members and military lawyers. The fact that SLDN had infiltrated the ranks in less than seven years, and had built such trust and credibility, was remarkable.

The Air Force produced a two-hour lesson on military law, covering prohibitions on desertion, dereliction of duty, and other military crimes, along with its policy on gays.[367] That did not send a supportive message.

The Navy developed a slide show on building trust in which only two of the 25 slides addressed how anti-gay harassment undermined trust.[368] Strike two.

Unlike the other services, the Army designed a briefing specifically on "Don't ask, don't tell," but just one of the 15 slides addressed specific types of anti-gay harassment, such as anonymous threats, name-calling, and anti-gay graffiti.[369] Multiple officers tasked with giving the briefing told us that the slides were confusing.[370] At one briefing, a superior officer asked the instructor, First Lieutenant Paul Sprague, whether he was gay.[371] At the end of that briefing, a senior enlisted soldier stood up and told an anti-gay joke.[372] Afterward, a soldier approached Sprague and said he used to "seek out homosexuals" in New York City's Greenwich Village neighborhood and beat them up.[373] Ironically, Sprague was gay; as he was awarded his third Army Achievement Medal, he came out and was discharged.[374] Strike three, though the Army's briefing had the most potential.

None of the trainings mentioned Barry Winchell.

As one high-ranking Army officer said, "This is not sensitivity training for homosexuality."[375] While acknowledging some problems with implementation, the chairman of the Joint Chiefs of Staff, General Hugh Shelton, defended "Don't ask, don't tell": "It is a law that, I think, strikes the proper balance between the requirement for good order and discipline in the military and individual rights."[376] Shelton would weigh in again in the final moments of the 2010 debate on "Don't ask, don't tell," but not helpfully.

SLDN had repeatedly urged leadership and accountability. In the aftermath of Winchell's murder, despite the missteps, those ideals started to take hold. Honoring a long-standing SLDN request, each service secretary and chief issued a statement that preceded or accompanied the new guidelines.

The Navy said: "Respect for the individual is paramount. Commanding officers must not condone homosexual jokes, epithets, or derogatory comments, and must ensure a command climate that fosters respect for all individuals."[377]

The Marine Corps said: "As all Marines learn in their earliest basic training, mistreatment of any Marine is incompatible with our core values and is unacceptable conduct that must be dealt with quickly and appropriately by commanders."[378]

The Air Force said: "Harassment, threats, or ridicule of individuals or groups based on real or perceived differences, including sexual orientation, have no place and will not be tolerated."[379]

The Army said: "Harassment of soldiers for any reason, to include perceived sexual orientation, will not be tolerated. Commanders at every level will take appropriate action to prevent harassment of or threats against any member of the Army."[380]

SLDN applauded these statements, calling them "an important development that will, finally, signal to commanders in the field that they have the support of their top leaders to prevent anti-gay harassment."[381]

CHAPTER 24

HATE CRIMES

The second achievement in the aftermath of Barry Winchell's murder was President Clinton's executive order updating the military's *Manual for Courts-Martial* by providing for sentence enhancement in violent crimes motivated by hatred and bias, including anti-gay, racial, or gender bias.[382] We secured this hate-crimes provision in the military a decade before Congress passed, and President Barack Obama signed, the national Hate Crimes Prevention Act in 2009.

Clinton wanted to do something to underscore his opposition to hate crimes and harassment of Americans. Winchell's murder provided that moment—and, as I did with the rule on psycho-therapist privilege (also part of this executive order), I helped the hate crimes sentence enhancement rule come to life.

The vehicle to obtain the executive order had been set into motion two years earlier. On May 6, 1997, the Joint Service Committee on Military Justice, an inter-agency body responsible for updating military law and legal procedures, issued a recommendation to amend the *Manual for Courts-Martial* to provide for sentence enhancement in cases of hate crimes involving sexual orientation, among other factors.

I read the proposed rule in the *Federal Register*. We had not been alerted that such a proposal was even being considered; it came fully from within the Pentagon. I submitted comments supporting it and provided statistics and narratives about harassment and hate crimes based on sexual orientation in the armed forces, all documented in our cases.

In November 1997 I attended the White House Conference on Hate Crimes. It didn't address hate crimes in the military, so I raised the issue directly with Attorney General Janet Reno. I hoped that she would persuade Clinton to issue an executive order on hate crimes, because that was within his power to do. I do not know if she ever spoke to him about it.

In July 1999, three weeks to the day after Winchell was murdered, Michelle and I wrote to the president, demanding that he "immediately sign an executive order amending the *Manual for Courts-Martial* to provide sentence enhancement in anti-gay hate crimes." I followed up by calling Richard Socarides, the White House liaison on gay and lesbian issues, asking him to make the executive order "pop." He was unaware of the proposed hate crimes rule.

He called me the day before he submitted the executive order to the president for his approval. He asked me if I was sure that I wanted Clinton to sign it. "Absolutely," I said. And it was done. It was that simple.

The fact that Secretary of Defense William Cohen had accepted the Joint Service Committee recommendation concerning sentence enhancement in hate crimes gave the matter the greatest legitimacy. Not one member of Congress objected when Clinton signed the executive order. In early 2001, as the George W. Bush administration was reviewing Clinton's executive orders with an eye toward preserving them or rescinding them, Bush kept the order governing hate crimes. This was another big policy win for the new kid on the block, now almost six years old.

CHAPTER 25

LITTLE EARS

On December 13, 1999—five days after Calvin Glover was convicted of the premeditated murder of Barry Winchell at Fort Campbell, Kentucky—Secretary of Defense William Cohen ordered the Office of Inspector General to conduct a survey of service members to determine whether anti-gay harassment was indeed a problem.[383]

We initially criticized his order, concerned that any report by the OIG would severely undercount the actual harassment in the services and dismiss what our clients experienced daily. How could anyone who witnessed or experienced anti-gay harassment feel comfortable reporting it in a climate that supported the harassment and discharged those discovered to be gay?

Our concerns were well-founded.

We documented that an administrator at one base where the survey was distributed specifically prevented a gay service member who was being discharged from filling it out. At another base, the administrator reviewed the responses as they came in, subverting any effort at confidentiality.

Even without that scrutiny, the survey allowed service members who had nothing to report to skip to the end within five minutes and leave the room—meaning that those who had something to report remained in the room, under the scrutiny of other service members and monitors.

Perhaps most significantly, the survey also had no mechanism by which it could measure the anti-gay harassment experienced by lesbian, gay, and bisexual service members as compared to straight service members. "Don't ask, don't tell" prevented asking service members if they were gay and would not let gay service members identify themselves.

Our confidence flagged as the Pentagon signaled, yet again, that anti-gay harassment just wasn't a big issue.

"What has been alleged is that there is a lot of harassment of homosexual service members within the military,"[384] Pentagon spokesman Kenneth Bacon said on December 9, 1999, the day Glover was sentenced to life in prison. "We have always said that every time we have clear evidence of harassment, we will investigate that. ...

"We don't believe that there has been escalating harassment of gays in the military, and I don't believe that the evidence shows that. ... [I]t's not an issue that generally comes up, that this is a problem for commanders."

He would be proven wrong, and he would later admit it.

Despite its limitations, the harassment survey—conducted at

38 installations and on 11 ships and submarines—documented widespread anti-gay harassment in the services.[385]

"We need to do more work on this policy," Bacon said during a March 24, 2000, briefing about the survey results. "In short, offensive comments about homosexuals were commonplace, and the majority believed that these offensive comments were tolerated to some extent within the military."[386]

The specifics were actually even more startling. Among them: 80 percent of service members had heard derogatory anti-gay remarks during the past year; 37 percent had witnessed or experienced targeted incidents of anti-gay harassment; 9 percent reported witnessing or experiencing anti-gay physical assaults. [387]

That last statistic was particularly surprising. If 9 percent of our 1.5 million active-duty service members had witnessed or experienced anti-gay physical assaults, that meant that 135,000 service members had witnessed or experienced the worst of anti-gay harassment. The Department of Defense said that the survey of more than 71,000 service members was not statistically significant and could not be generalized to the full force. Who were they kidding?

The OIG report confirmed SLDN's own findings over the previous six years: Anti-gay harassment was a problem. Still, it did not result in any immediate policy changes. We pushed again. We enlisted support from Congress.

In May 2000, Representative Barney Frank and Senator Max Cleland, who had lost both legs and one arm during Army service in Vietnam, sent "a tart letter to Defense Secretary Cohen pointing up the failure to implement antiharassment training in the armed forces in a meaningful way."[388] Cohen would act, but there was another battle brewing at the same time.

◆◆◆

Major General Robert Clark, the commanding general at Fort Campbell at the time of Winchell's murder, was appointed to become the vice director of operations for the Joint Chiefs of Staff at the Pentagon once his command ended on June 10, 2000.[389] The transfer, which did not include a promotion in rank, was still a position of prominence, and it met with swift rebuke.

Frank penned an even stronger letter on June 7, 2000, signed by 28 Democrats, including House Minority Leader Richard Gephardt, and two Republicans, Connie Morella and Mark Foley. The letter called "the Pentagon's failure to curb harassment 'disgraceful' [and] denounc[ed] the promotion of Clark, the Fort Campbell commander."[390]

The Pentagon responded by naming Clark as the deputy commanding general, Fifth U.S. Army, in San Antonio, Texas. He was not nominated for promotion to lieutenant general—a small victory for accountability, though a short-lived one.

◆◆◆

With the controversy surrounding Clark's next posting mitigated, but the issue of how to curb harassment unresolved, Cohen announced the formation of an intra-service working group to study the issue further and recommend whether policy changes were needed. We were concerned that the committee was a delay tactic or that it would simply whitewash the inspector general's findings.

The committee refused to meet with Michelle or me or any of our clients. Its members had no mechanism to identify or interview lesbian, gay, or bisexual service members who would be discharged if they came out. Instead, they invited us and other interested parties to submit written recommendations for consideration.

Michelle and I drafted our response. We provided specific recommendations and reinforced them by having members of Congress weigh in with the same or similar language. Specifically, we recommended that the Pentagon: (1) allow service members to report anti-gay harassment without fear that those reports would lead to an investigation into their sexual orientation or be used as a basis for discharge; (2) identify personnel to whom service members could report and discuss harassment in confidence, without fear of repercussions; (3) define anti-gay harassment clearly, so that service members know that harassment includes not only physical assault, but also anti-gay epithets, anti-gay march cadences, graffiti, and the like; and (4) hold accountable those who engage in anti-gay harassment.

We enlisted the support of former Assistant Secretary of Defense Lawrence Korb, who had served in the Reagan administration, and Edwin Dorn, the former under secretary for personnel and readiness in the Clinton administration, to try to create the space for service members to report harassment without fear of discharge.

"My primary concerns," Korb wrote to the committee, "are the ongoing harassment of service members by their supervisors and peers and the lack of safe places for service members to turn within the military if they are facing harassment, medical or mental health problems or seeking spiritual guidance."[391]

Dorn wrote this:

"Recent reports have indicated that physicians, EEO personnel, inspectors general and law enforcement personnel believe that they are obliged to turn in service members who reveal their sexual orientation when they report anti-gay harassment, or who are discovered to be gay during an investigation into the reported harassment. If these practices occur, then they have the effect of punishing the victim. This is not what I anticipated or intended when I was involved in the development of DoD's 1997 anti-harassment guidance."[392]

We got a bootleg copy of the committee's draft report from a member of Congress—and were pleasantly surprised. The Anti-Harassment Action Plan contained 13 points, including seven of the recommendations we had made. Notably, its first mandate was for the Department of Defense to "adopt an overarching principle regarding harassment including based in *perceived sexual orientation*"[393] (emphasis added). It further defined harassment to include "mistreatment, harassment, and inappropriate comments or gestures." It ordered that the new directive make clear that commanders and leaders would be held accountable for failure to enforce the directive. It required commanders to inform personnel of other "confidential and non-confidential avenues to report mistreatment." The draft plan was nearly a home run.

There was one part of the near-final plan that stuck in our craw. It would reiterate that gay service members would be discharged if they disclosed their sexual orientation.

To us, this remained the heart of the problem in violence prevention. How could service members report that they were being harassed for being gay without saying "I am gay"? The pin-headed lawyers, of course, argued that gays should simply say, "I am being harassed because I am *perceived* as gay." Corporal Kevin Blaesing had figured that out, but other gay service members would not.

The evening before the Pentagon published the plan, I got a call from Carol DiBattiste, under secretary of the Air Force and the chair of the intra-service committee. I was standing on the corner of Massachusetts Avenue and 22nd Street, Northwest, as buses whizzed by.

"We are planning to release our report on harassment tomorrow morning, and I wanted to give you a heads-up," she said.

"Yes, ma'am," I said. "Thank you. I have seen a copy of the report."

"You have?" she asked, surprised. It's always good to have multiple sources when the primary source, the Pentagon, is being less than transparent.

"Yes, ma'am, and I would appreciate it if you could delete one item," I replied, going straight to the heart of our concerns. I didn't want the opportunity to slip away.

"Could you please delete the section telling gay service members that they will be discharged if they say they are gay? They already know that. What they don't know is whether they can report harassment without fear of being discharged if they are not careful in what they say and how they say it."

"P.T. Henry says I shouldn't trust you," she said. Henry was the assistant secretary for manpower and Reserve affairs. I didn't know if what she said was true. Perhaps DiBattiste was worried that no good deed goes unpunished.

"If I delete that line," she continued, "will you promise me you will support the report when it is issued tomorrow morning?"

I paused for a moment, a knot in my throat.

The report didn't go as far as we would have liked. I was concerned that I was making a commitment without sign-off from Michelle. But this was the moment. On a street corner in Dupont Circle. With buses and car horns. Where I had to say "yes" or "no." The report adopted seven of our long-standing recommendations.

"Yes, ma'am, we will."

Too often, activists complain when they don't get all that they want, rather than celebrate significant achievements. It is important to thank leaders when they move in the right direction.

I called Michelle to let her know. This was another major policy victory in less than seven years. We were putting teeth into the meager regulatory promises Bill Clinton had made.

We got a bonus when the Anti-Harassment Action Plan was announced the following day. In announcing the new regulations, Cohen stated that anti-gay harassment harmed "unit cohesion."[394]

This was a breakthrough. If anti-gay *harassment* hurt unit cohesion, it was not a big step to argue that anti-gay *discrimination* did as well. Therefore, "Don't ask, don't tell," which codified discrimination against gays, actually undermined military readiness, turning on its head the central argument for the gay ban.

After the plan was announced, the services began educating their personnel about anti-gay harassment. General Eric Shinseki, the Army chief of staff, trained the members of the Joint Chiefs of Staff. Each service secretary and chief issued statements calling for efforts to end anti-gay harassment.

The Navy said: "Respect for the individual is paramount. Commanding officers must not condone homosexual jokes, epithets, or derogatory comments, and must ensure a command climate that fosters respect for all individuals."

The Marine Corps said: "As all Marines learn in their earliest basic training, mistreatment of any Marine is incompatible with our core values and is unacceptable conduct that must be dealt with quickly and appropriately by commanders."

The Air Force said: "Harassment, threats or ridicule of individuals or groups based upon real or perceived differences, including sexual orientation, have no place in the United States Air Force and will not be tolerated. ... Each of us has an individual responsibility and professional obligation to do his or her best to prevent harassment of any nature and to immediately correct it if it occurs."

The Army said: "Harassment of soldiers for any reason, to include perceived sexual orientation, will not be tolerated. ... Commanders at every level will take appropriate action to prevent harassment of or threats against any member of the Army."

On May 1, 2001, the Army published *Dignity & Respect: A Training Guide on Homosexual Conduct Policy*.[395] Several months before, P.T. Henry had invited Michelle and me to his office at the Pentagon to preview the book and provide comments.

The information in the book, presented in cartoon-style images, was notable for two things. It was the first and only guidance to troops about "Don't ask, don't tell" that tried to explain the schizophrenic law in simple terms. It also stands out as a frozen-in-time graphic symbol of blatant discrimination[396] as it describes how gay service members must be discharged from the Army when discovered.

Still, the statements from the service chiefs, which SLDN had called for since 1993, signaled to commanders in the field, in very specific terms, that they had the support of their top leaders in taking steps to prevent anti-gay harassment.[397] The Anti-Harassment Action Plan marked the most significant regulatory advance in the area of military anti-gay harassment. By fundamentally starting to shift the culture inside the armed forces, it was also one of the most important preconditions to repeal of "Don't ask, don't tell."

The plan didn't halt all harassment, though it started to mitigate it as some commanders were held to account—an insight that started even before final guidance was issued.

In October 1999, three months after Winchell's murder, Lieutenant Colonel Edward Melton sent an email to his subordinates and his superior at the Marine Corps Air Ground Combat Center in California, informing them of his opinion of gay people.[398] The e-mail concerned how to apply the "Homosexual Conduct Policy" and stop anti-gay harassment. Melton wrote:

> "Due to the 'hate crime' death of a homo in the Army, we now have to take extra steps to ensure the safety of the queer who has 'told' (not kept his part of the DOD 'Don't ask, don't tell' policy). Commanders now bear the responsibility if someone decides to assault the young backside ranger. Be discreet and careful in your dealings with these characters. And remember, little ears are everywhere."

One of those "little ears" on his distribution list immediately forwarded that email to us. CNN was airing it within the hour. Melton was disciplined and transferred.[399]

As Assistant Secretary of the Navy Carolyn Becraft explained in a letter to Barney Frank, "After reviewing the investigation, Major General [Clifford L.] Stanley ordered Melton relieved of his duties as executive director of the Marine Corps Communications Electronics School, and he was reassigned as a special projects officer without supervisory duties. He subsequently retired on July 1, 2000."[400] (Like so many other leaders mentioned in this book, Clifford Stanley will return for an important role in implementing the "Don't ask, don't tell" repeal.)

♦♦♦

We didn't always achieve accountability—most notably with Major General Clark. In the fall of 2002, President Bush nominated him for promotion to lieutenant general. SLDN organized a coalition to oppose his promotion, including the National Organization for Women, People For the American Way, and the Democratic National Committee.[401]

P.T. Henry tried to pressure me to drop SLDN's opposition to Clark's promotion. He argued that it would cause us to lose credibility and access.

"I can't do that, sir," I replied. "Look, it's not up to SLDN to determine whether Major General Clark gets his third star or not. The Senate has every right to review his record, and they should look at his total record. SLDN is highlighting deficiencies in his record that they should take into account."

Henry understood that we had come to a principled position.

Clark's promotion didn't make it to the Senate floor before the end of the 107th Congress. Having successfully lobbied against it, we hoped that Bush would not renominate Clark in the next Congress, but he did, in March 2003.

The Senate had never denied promotion to a general, let alone questioned his fitness to lead based on his handling of anti-gay harassment. For 14 months—the time frame covering his first and second nominations for promotion—senators debated his leadership and the rampant anti-gay environment under his watch.[402]

As Clark was being grilled before the Senate Armed Services Committee, one colleague said that you could hear the voice of Edward Kennedy booming down the halls of the Russell Senate Office Building. Susan Collins told *NBC Nightly News* that "[t]here is compelling evidence that there were problems at this base."[403]

On the Senate floor, Kennedy said that after Winchell's murder, "from all the evidence we have seen, he did not even once speak out against the specific problems of anti-gay harassment and anti-gay violence, or implement any training for the soldiers against it." Indeed, he said, Clark "chose to deny that any problem existed."[404]

"What is going to happen to all the other gay and lesbian soldiers out there?" asked Mark Dayton, a Democrat on the Armed Services Committee. "What kind of message are we sending to them?"[405]

While the Senate eventually approved Clark's promotion in November 2003, the debate brought the issue of anti-gay harassment in the military to the Senate floor for the first time in history. Military leaders were put on notice that congressional leaders would no longer turn a blind eye to the military's anti-gay harassment and intransigence in enforcing the law more fairly.[406] As Tom Oliphant of *The Boston Globe* observed, "At the top of [the] chain of command at Fort Campbell sat General Clark. Instead of being held responsible for what happened to a soldier in good standing under his command, he is being promoted."[407]

Barry Winchell's murder opened the public's eyes to the reality of federally imposed discrimination and paved the way for new rules governing anti-gay harassment and hate crimes. We would have never succeeded in repealing "Don't ask, don't tell" if the Pentagon had not started to address anti-gay harassment beforehand. We were responsible for identifying the problems and the solutions.

While Winchell's murder was the first significant event changing the political debate, it wasn't the last. There was still work to be done. Yet, as *The Nation* very kindly observed as SLDN marked its seventh anniversary, "It's amazing how much this small legal-aid group has accomplished already."[408]

That view was shared by Deb Price of *The Detroit News*: "SLDN has repeatedly forced the Pentagon not just to take notice, but to change."[409] We were making progress.

GAME CHANGERS

CHAPTER 26

REFRAMING THE DEBATE

One of the game-changers in the effort to repeal "Don't ask, don't tell" was the about-face in the public narrative about military service by openly lesbian, gay, and bisexual people.

In 1993, respected generals like Colin Powell and Norman Schwarzkopf warned that the presence of openly gay service members would undermine unit cohesion and military readiness. The courts accepted that proposition in challenges to the law's constitutionality. No one ever offered evidence to support that assertion—an indication of the deeply ingrained prejudices toward gay Americans at the time.

One of the mistakes made by the Campaign for Military Service in 1993 was to argue that ending the gay ban was mainly a matter of civil rights. It was, of course, about equality, but that wasn't a sufficient argument. Americans are willing to sacrifice civil liberties for our national security—but when our top generals warned that openly gay service members would degrade our security, the costs of lifting the ban outweighed the benefits.

Michelle and I knew when we started SLDN that we had to turn that narrative on its head; what hurt unit cohesion and military readiness was the ban, not the presence of openly lesbian, gay, and bisexual service members. Our argument benefited from being true, but we knew that we had to offer the evidence to prove it.

In our first annual report, published in 1994, we wrote: "In cases where courts have allowed lesbian, gay, and bisexual service members to serve openly, there have been no problems. In fact, the opposite has proven to be true." That same year, syndicated columnist Anna Quindlen noted: "It's the legal challenges to the policy that have exploded the underlying rationale, that unit cohesion would crumble if gay men and lesbians openly served. ... Predictions that unit cohesion could not survive honesty about sexual orientation were simply wrong."[410]

Colonel Margarethe Cammermeyer, Commander Zoe Dunning, Lieutenant Paul Thomasson, Captain Rich Richenberg, Petty Officer Keith Meinhold, and Sergeant Justin Elzie had all demonstrated that openly lesbian, gay, and bisexual service members enhanced their units' effectiveness.

At the same time that we were contending that the presence of openly gay service members contributed to unit cohesion, we argued that commanders who flouted the regulations undermined readiness. Our annual reports, our clients, and the military's own documents provided the evidence.

Our arguments took hold. *The Boston Globe* editorialized in 1997, only four years into the new law, "The worst 'Don't ask, don't tell, don't pursue' violations merit an executive office bellow of 'Cut it out!'"[411]

Andrew Sullivan wrote in *The New York Times*: "Is it too much to ask that this President finally live up to his own words?"[412]

One of Barry Winchell's fellow soldiers said it well—that murder destroyed any illusion that Winchell was part of a "band of brothers."[413] Even Secretary of Defense William Cohen conceded that anti-gay harassment undermined unit cohesion.

Concurrently with the arguments that gay service members contributed to readiness and that the failure to stop asking, pursuing, and harassing undermined it, we could then pivot and argue that the law itself was to blame. "Don't ask, don't tell" in any incarnation eroded good order, discipline, and morale, the essence of unit cohesion and military readiness.

In our third annual report we argued, "Spending time and resources to ferret out hardworking men and women who might be gay takes away from mission readiness and reveals a misguided set of priorities."[414] Two years later, we said, "The report concludes that, as military leaders struggle with critical retention and recruiting shortfalls, they can ill-afford to violate the letter and intent of the policy, or to continue to let the valuable contributions of lesbian, gay, and bisexual service members be frittered away by indifference or outright hostility."[415] In our next annual report, published the year after Barry Winchell was murdered, we asserted: "Congress should repeal the ban on openly gay service members because the policy hurts military readiness, and it kills."[416]

As I told CBS News when the Pentagon announced additional training after Winchell's murder, "It's hard to implement a policy fairly that at its root is base discrimination."[417]

In response to our eighth annual report, published in February 2002, editorial boards around the country weighed in. The *Chicago Tribune* said, "The 1993 'Don't ask, don't tell' policy to prevent discrimination against gays in the military has been a failure from the start. [T]he Bush Administration ... ought to lift the ban on gays in the military."[418] *The San Diego Union-Tribune* said, "'Don't ask, don't tell' is clearly an unworkable policy. It would appear that [it] is based on no more than 'mere prejudice.'"[419] *The Tennessean* said, "This policy must end."[420] *The Washington Post* wrote, "This policy is an enormous waste of human resources."[421]

The Washington Post returned to this topic in another editorial the next year: "'Don't ask, don't tell' works against our military preparedness, is unfair to patriotic Americans and, as a policy, has failed miserably. It must be repealed."[422]

Also in 2003, Tom Oliphant wrote in *The Boston Globe*, "The rationale for the [gay ban] had always been that the presence of homosexuals in the military somehow undermined 'unit cohesion' and morale. ... The reality, increasingly, is that in practice this rationale is undermined by experience."[423]

We used our annual reports to deliver a dose of reality. Michelle described our strategy this way: "Over time, our aggressive presence would start to change the climate. Our goal was to ward off investigations and create some safe space for military members to live their lives. ... Over time, the rationale for DADT—that known gay people harmed unit morale and cohesion—would be proven to be the lie that it was."[424]

Elizabeth Kier, an assistant professor of political science at the University of California at Berkeley, offered an analytical basis undercutting the unit cohesion rationale. The evidence, she wrote in the highly respected journal *International Security*, suggested that unit cohesion was based on units working together on common tasks, not on the social backgrounds of their constituent members.[425]

The military readiness rationale was only one argument we had to shift to build support and win repeal. Michelle and I were also fighting a social context that was fraught in 1993 from a society that looked upon gay Americans with approbation and an LGBT community that distrusted the military.

♦ ♦ ♦

In 1993, the public still viewed lesbian, gay, and bisexual Americans as criminals, mentally ill, and sinners. We were viewed as criminals because the laws of many states and the military's Uniform Code of Military Justice punished consensual sex between members of the same gender. It would not be until 2003, in *Lawrence v. Texas*, that the U.S. Supreme Court reversed its 1986 decision (*Bowers v. Hardwick*) that upheld state sodomy laws.

We knew that we had to get the military to either remove Article 125, which criminalized "unnatural carnal copulation with another person of the same or opposite sex," from the UCMJ, or at least determine that it was irrelevant. A driving theory of "Don't ask, don't tell" was that coming out was tantamount to announcing criminal intent.

Some critics, then and now, view lesbian, gay, and bisexual people as sinners. Appearing before the House Armed Services

Committee in May 1993, Brigadier General James Hutchens, an Army chaplain who was active in the National Association of Evangelicals, called homosexuality "a moral virus" that could diminish unit cohesion.[426] After "Don't ask, don't tell" became law later that year, the anti-gay evangelical movement gained strength—first seeking to overturn or prevent nondiscrimination ordinances and then promoting state constitutional amendments to prevent marriage equality. Consistent with Hutchens's views, the military chaplaincy played a significant, though underreported, behind-the-scenes role in advocating for "Don't ask, don't tell" in 1993.[427]

Michelle and I minimized religious opposition with three strategies. First, we did not cede the moral argument. Frank Kameny had coined the phrase "gay is good" in the 1960s. We highlighted the moral goodness of lesbian, gay, and bisexual patriots who were willing to shed blood to defend our freedoms.

Second, in our original language to repeal "Don't ask, don't tell," we crafted a religious exemption that permitted clergy to act according to their faith, but also allowed civil military policy to dictate personnel choices.

Third, we built support among religious communities. As we pushed for legislation to move forward, we created a military chaplains council, headed by an Army chaplain, Colonel Paul Dodd, to conduct outreach among religious groups in the military.

Michelle and I also leaned on the Metropolitan Community Church, a Protestant denomination founded by Vietnam veteran Troy Perry to minister to the LGBT community and its allies. He invited us to address MCC's biennial convention in Atlanta in 1994. He told us that there were many LGBT veterans among his church's members, and he knew we would be well received. Michelle and I agreed that she would deliver the speech in Atlanta, as she was a devout member of MCC.

There were two thousand people in the audience when we took the stage. It was beautiful and welcoming. Michelle spoke.

"As a soldier stationed at Fort Bliss, in El Paso, Texas, I would get off duty some Fridays and immediately head to the airport. I would take the first Southwest Airlines flight to wherever it was going to get out of El Paso. I would go to Phoenix, Dallas, San Antonio, or Austin. The one thing I could count on was attending church on Sundays at a local MCC, where I could let down my guard and be myself. And you have no idea how important that was to me."

At this point, she choked back tears. "Hallelujah!" rang up from the crowd. Perry raised his hands and shouted, "Feel the pain!" I stood there next to Michelle wondering, "What the hell am I going to do now?" I hugged her and asked if she would like me to continue. She sobbed and nodded.

I was not a regular churchgoer. I had no prepared speech.

"What Michelle is telling us today is the story of family," I riffed.

"Amen!" one person shouted. That gave me some courage.

"We know all too well the pain of being disowned by our families when we come out as lesbian, gay, bisexual, or transgender. What not all of us know is that the pain is doubled when you are kicked out of the military. You see, the military teaches troops that it will take care of its own. The military is your family. And when you get kicked out for being gay, it's like having your own family throw you out of the house."

My voice started to rise and tremble. "That is why we turn to MCC!"

"Hallelujah!"

"Because MCC is our *chosen* family!"

"Amen!"

"You will not kick us out!"

"Amen!"

"You will not turn your backs on us!"

"Amen!"

"You will love us!"

"Hallelujah!"

"You will love us in Phoenix! You will love us in Austin! You will love us in Dallas!"

"Praise the Lord!"

The spirit had seized me. Michelle stood, eyes wide in amazement. I took her hand and raised it into the air to the chorus of hallelujahs.

Praise goes to Troy Perry, who founded a spiritual outlet for tens of thousands around the world when few congregations and communities were accepting, creating a safe space for our soldiers, sailors, airmen, marines, and coastguardsmen.

◆◆◆

In addition to viewing us as sinners and criminals, some critics viewed us as sick, diseased, or disordered. The American Psychiatric Association listed homosexuality as a mental disorder in its diagnostic manual until 1973,[428] when it removed "homosexuality" and added "sexual orientation disturbance" to describe people "in conflict with" their sexual orientation. That term remained until 1987,[429] only six years before the enactment of "Don't ask, don't tell."

Robert Maginnis, a national security analyst with the Family Research Council and a retired Army lieutenant colonel, typified that view. "The reason why homosexuality has raised a red flag ... is because in all healthy societies, homosexuality is recognized as a pathology with very serious implications for a person's behavior," he told the *Los Angeles Times*. "And even more importantly for security concerns, this is a behavior that is associated with a lot of anti-security markers, such as drug/alcohol abuse, promiscuity and violence."[430]

During a Commander's Call on the Homosexual Conduct Policy in November 2001, an Air Force colonel conducting the briefing told his subordinates, "Homosexuality is like alcoholism, thievery, lying, and is not tolerated in the military."[431]

In 2010, as the Senate Armed Services Committee debated repeal, Republican Saxby Chambliss warned that allowing gays to serve openly would create a military susceptible to "alcohol use, adultery ... and body art."[432] The conflation of being gay and tattoos was a new and unexplored line of pathology.

There was no evidence supporting the view that gay Americans were biologically deficient, but that didn't prevent such claims from being made. The view that "gayness" was an illness dissipated in the currents of discourse as more people came out at home, at work, and in popular culture. Those cultural shifts were another game-changer.

◆ ◆ ◆

Michelle and I also had to fight anti-militarism and elitism in the LGBT community. "Much of the community leadership," I once said, "had come from the white middle or upper class and had been part of or strongly influenced by the antiwar and feminist movements. Marriage was seen as patriarchy to be torn down, and there was general antipathy to the military."[433]

The Nation observed, "Many left-wing gays were uncomfortable at seeing precious energies squandered in combat for the right to serve in a military they disdained and distrusted."[434]

Soon after the enactment of "Don't ask, don't tell," a leader of one gay rights organization said at a fundraiser for her organization, "I never understood why gays and lesbians would want to serve anyway." I made a beeline to Margarethe Cammermeyer, the highest-ranking lesbian to challenge the military's ban, who stood there with a fixed smile, and said, "We will make this right."

The internal resistance persisted, even as Michelle and I made progress. At the Millennium March on Washington for Equality in 2000, we had to literally barge through the organizers to get on to the stage at the very end of the day, hours after we had been scheduled to appear and despite promises for a more prominent role. We had with us retired Army Major General Vance Coleman, the first general to address a gay rights rally, and Pat Kutteles, whose son, Barry Winchell, had been killed the previous year. The organizers had polled the LGBT community, and gays in the military remained one of the highest concerns of the community, but LGBT leaders sidelined the issue, as they often did.

We were told that they allowed Ellen DeGeneres to speak well beyond her time allotment. She has been an inspiring leader since coming out in 1997. But on that day, I was devastated as our two speakers (Michelle and I severely cut our own remarks) poured their hearts out to the remaining 50 or so attendees, instead of the hundreds of thousands who had marched and would have been inspired by their message.

It was the first time Pat had spoken at a public event about her son. "Barry never told me about the harassment he was facing," she said. "When things got tough, Barry would always say to me, 'Suck it up and drive on, Mom.'

"Barry knew that I loved him. If he was gay and finding this part of himself, I know that he would have told me when the time was right for him. As a psychiatric nurse, my life's work has focused on kids, including gay kids who have been rejected by their parents. This rejection is heartbreaking, and I shared this with all three of my sons as they were growing up. I wanted my sons to know that our love for them is unconditional. If you love your child, whether gay or not, you're going to fight for him. I loved my son very, very much."

Big donors also not infrequently asked why our clients didn't choose another career. Why would anyone willingly choose to serve in an organization that did not want them? Few understood that for many Americans who have not had the same financial and educational opportunities that they had, the military is the way up and out.[435] Few understood that ending the ban was also a matter of racial justice, as African Americans found opportunity in the military when it was denied elsewhere. The armed forces were also an incredible proving ground for youth who, if successful, were given tremendous leadership responsibilities at a young age.

As one client described it, joining one of the uniformed branches was an escape route from both a stunted economic situation and from "a small town in East Tennessee in the middle of the Bible Belt—for me, it was a way of getting out to see the world."[436]

Petty Officer Keith Meinhold, one of the heroes of repeal, told *The Miami Herald* why he chose the military: "I joined the Navy before graduation. I wasn't doing well; I hated high school. I knew college wasn't an option. The Navy was available to me. It was either that or continue working in a furniture warehouse in Stuart."[437]

In her *New York Times* bestseller, *Leaving Isn't the Hardest Thing*, SLDN client Lauren Hough wrote: "For people like ... me, the military's the only chance we have of getting out of our shithole towns and our miserable destiny of maybe making middle management at the meatpacking plant or the Piggly Wiggly."[438]

National gay rights leaders also marginalized the work Michelle and I did by failing to see the broader implications of what we were getting done. Their groups held annual retreats in Laguna Beach, California, to discuss movement strategy; despite our entreaties, Michelle and I were never invited.

Yet we didn't let the internal movement obstacles get us down. It just made us dig in harder for our men and women in uniform to ensure that they had the strongest advocate possible.

Thus, in addition to making our case against "Don't ask, don't tell," Michelle and I had to dismantle the social constructs that demonized the existence of people like us. We had to demonstrate to the public at large that gay Americans are moral and good. We had to convince the LGBT community that equality demanded our support for those seeking to marry or to serve in the military, even if we would not make that choice ourselves. We had to break the classism of elite leaders who deprioritized what mattered to many in LGBT communities of color and those who grew up in rural America. We had to convince the public, Congress, and military leaders that it was "Don't ask, don't tell" that undermined unit cohesion, not gays serving openly. Those strategies were rooted in telling the stories of the brave men and women we served.

◆◆◆

Our success in building support was reflected in the polls. We had a monumental task in front of us.

An Annenberg poll in 1992 found that only 16 percent of male service members supported gays in the military.[439] In 1993, according to an unscientific poll of 478 soldiers conducted by military sociologists Charles Moskos and Laura Miller at two bases in Texas, Fort Bliss and Fort Hood, 90 percent of respondents said they would be "uncomfortable" serving with a gay soldier.[440] A poll Miller conducted the next year found that 75 percent of male respondents and more than 40 percent of female respondents opposed gays serving openly.[441] In 1999, 76 percent of senior officers opposed gays serving openly, according to the Triangle Institute for Security Studies.[442] In 2000, another Annenberg poll found that support for and opposition to gays in the military among junior enlisted personnel was split at 50 percent for each view.[443]

When the Pentagon released its report on "Don't ask, don't tell" in 2010, one of the most striking findings was that 70 percent of service members said that the impact of allowing gays to serve openly would be positive, mixed, or of no consequence.[444] We saw the shift in attitudes up close.

In 2001 I was invited to speak to 550 Naval Academy senior midshipmen in the Leadership, Ethics and Law section. I asked SLDN staff attorney Paula Neira to speak in my stead because she was a fellow ring-knocker, an affectionate term for Naval Academy graduates. I sat in the front row as she "challenged the midshipmen to consider a future where, during their service to the Navy, the ban on openly gay personnel was dismantled and their leadership would be integral to the successful integration of lesbian, gay, and bisexual personnel into the ranks."

Paula was a hit, and the midshipmen swarmed around her after her remarks, indicating an increasing comfort with lesbian and transgender Americans. Paula had herself transitioned from male to female after leaving the Navy.

Ken Lynch, a self-identified heterosexual aviation operations officer, typified the changing attitudes. In 2003, he wrote to *Navy Times*, "I couldn't care less whether the guy who pulls me out of a burning airplane is straight, gay, or into Velveeta."[445] The dramatic shift in support inside the military was necessary for repeal to take hold.

The positive shift in public opinion outside of the military was equally impressive. FiveThirtyEight analyzed public opinion between 1993 and 2010 based on ABC News/*Washington Post* polls, which asked the same two questions every year.

The first question, which FiveThirtyEight called "restrictive," asked: "Do you think homosexuals who do NOT disclose their sexual orientation should be allowed to serve in the military?"[446] This question reflected "Don't ask, don't tell."

The second, which FiveThirtyEight called "permissive," asked: "Do you think homosexuals who DO publicly disclose their sexual orientation should be allowed to serve in the military?"[447] (An aside: I don't like the wording of the questions because using the clinical term "homosexual"—instead of "lesbian, gay, or bisexual"—tends to suppress positive responses.)

Despite my concerns, the 17-year timeline of responses is instructive. According to FiveThirtyEight, "In 1993, 44 percent of Americans approved of service by gays and lesbians who publicly disclosed their sexual orientation; by 2008"—the year after I left SLDN—"the percentage had risen to 75 percent. This rise by more than 30 percentage points is remarkable, especially compared with trends on other civil rights issues for gay Americans."[448] That figure held through 2010.

Support for gays serving who did not come out of the closet "rose by 15 percentage points in the same period, to 78 percent, from 63 percent."[449]

When "Don't ask, don't tell" was implemented, nearly 40 percent of Americans supported a complete ban on gays serving, open or closeted. By 2008, opposition had shrunk to 22 percent. By 2010, it was 18 percent.

There were two reasons for the seismic shift in opinion. First was the drip-drip-drip of stories, data, and analysis produced by SLDN that repeatedly highlighted the contributions of lesbian, gay, and bisexual service members to our nation's security. In addition, events like the murder of Barry Winchell shocked the nation.

Then there were the larger cultural shifts in support of gay Americans. Michelle and I knew that our strategy to repeal "Don't ask, don't tell" rested inside a greater context of social change. Social change and political strategy benefit from biofeedback, and in the 17 years leading to the repeal of "Don't ask, don't tell," our persistent public campaign helped transform society, just as the changes in the public's opinion about gay Americans transformed politics.

The positive shift in public opinion was another game-changer, but politicians are remarkably impervious to polls when they want to be. The overwhelming bipartisan public support for policies to address gun violence, police reform, election reform, and climate change are frequently obstructed in Congress, mostly by

Republicans. Hence, the shift in narrative and opinion on gays in the military was necessary—but it wasn't sufficient.

◆ ◆ ◆

Also important in changing hearts and minds was popular culture. It produced the currents on which public and military opinion in support of gays serving openly in the armed forces shifted dramatically over 17 years. While smart litigation and political advocacy was essential in securing the repeal of "Don't ask, don't tell," the cultural revolution helped normalize gay Americans and contributed to greater acceptance.

In 1994, one year after "Don't ask, don't tell" was enacted, Arthur Dong produced *Coming Out Under Fire*, a documentary based on the 1990 book of the same name by Allan Bérubé. Through interviews, the film brought to life the stories of lesbian, gay, and bisexual World War II veterans. It showed the joy men and women from across the United States discovered in finding others like themselves, and the pain of being sent home in shame (or so it was seen at the time) if unmasked. The film added to the growing recognition of gay Americans, including those from the Greatest Generation, who had served our nation honorably.

In 1995, NBC aired *Serving in Silence*, which told the story of our Military Advisory Council member, Margarethe Cammermeyer, and her partner, Diane Divelbess, and depicted how the gay ban threated to derail Cammermeyer's career. Starring Glenn Close and Judy Davis and produced by Barbra Streisand, it received three Emmy Awards and was one of the biggest breakthroughs in LGBT film.

One of SLDN's more ambitious events was to host the premiere of *Serving in Silence* at San Francisco's Palace of Fine Arts in February 1995. Having started operations barely two years before, what were we thinking? We didn't have enough donors nationally to fill the thousand seats in the theater. We were blessed by the talents of Alix Sabin and others as event producers *extraordinaire*, with deep contacts in the Bay Area. The event sold out. I had just one production note: As the credits rolled, I wanted Cammermeyer to be standing on the stage, a spotlight illuminating her. The crowd went wild.

I had the privilege of also attending the New York premiere. It benefited the Lambda Legal Defense and Education Fund, which had represented Cammermeyer in her successful court fight. I sat down in the theater and quickly felt two eyes boring into me. I turned around.

"Hi! I'm Rosie!" she said.

"Yes, Ms. O'Donnell," I replied. "I know who you are, and it's great to meet you." Elevator speech ready, I told her about SLDN and Cammermeyer's role on our Military Advisory Council, just as the lights dimmed.

At the post-film reception, I had the chance to briefly meet Glenn Close. She was much more interested in my lavish praise of her performance than she was to hear about SLDN—but you never know who may become an ally.

In 2008, Peter Singer, a senior fellow at the staid Brookings Institution, published a monograph cheekily titled "How *The Real World* Ended 'Don't Ask, Don't Tell.'"[450] He began by noting that in 1992, the same year that presidential candidate Bill Clinton proposed the idea of gay, lesbian, and bisexual Americans serving openly in the military, "MTV famously launched the story of 'seven strangers, picked to live in a loft, and have their lives taped, to find out what happens when people stop being polite ... and start getting real.'" A year later, Clinton's idea "had mutated into the policy known as 'Don't Ask, Don't Tell.' ... In contrast to Clinton's policy, MTV's new show thrived."

The Real World: New Orleans, which aired in 2000, featured a "Don't ask, don't tell" storyline: The charismatic and handsome Danny Roberts was dating an Army Ranger. MTV obscured the officer's face so the Pentagon could not track him down and discharge him. In 2003, after he left the military, Paul Dill revealed his identity on an MTV special.[451]

In 2001, Marc Wolf brought his one-man show *Another American: Asking & Telling* to Washington. He developed the play after driving cross-country, interviewing dozens of veterans who were both for and against "Don't ask, don't tell." He interviewed me and Michelle as part of his research, identifying stories he could tell and ensuring that he understood the law.

He retold the stories in a series of vignettes that gave the audience a deep appreciation for the horrors that lesbian, gay, and bisexual service members faced and the opinions of those who believed in the ban. Marc won an Obie Award for his off-Broadway show. He also won the Helen Hayes Award, the equivalent prize for theater in the nation's capital.

I was his date for the Helen Hayes Awards and enjoyed the ceremony held at the Kennedy Center. When the presenter announced Marc's name, he sat stunned in his seat.

I leaned over. "You won. Get up." He sat there.

I punched him in the arm and exclaimed, "You won! Get up!"

He sprung up and walked on to the stage.

What struck me, though, was not that he had won. After all, his play is amazing, and is included in an anthology titled *Plays That Shaped a Century*. What struck me was that when he acknowledged SLDN in his remarks, there was sustained applause and cheers.

I looked around the large theater and asked myself, "Who are these people? How do they know about SLDN?" I realized that our work was seeping into the political consciousness of the public well beyond those who came to SLDN fundraisers.

In 2003, SLDN client Reichen Lehmkuhl (who now goes by the last name Kuhl) and his then-partner Chip Arndt won season four of *The Amazing Race*[452]—a show that has garnered 15 Emmy Awards[453] and millions of viewers.

In interviews and in a 2006 autobiography, *Here's What We'll Say: Growing Up, Coming Out, and the U.S. Air Force Academy*, the former Air Force captain captured the double life gays had to live while serving our nation.

"I was living my own doppelganger every single day," he wrote. "I had my secret gay life and I had my open 'normal' life, with a beautiful girlfriend and a pressed uniform. Everyone believed that avoiding the punishment for being caught in a gay bar was worth the lies we would have to tell."[454]

In a 2003 interview with *Metro Weekly*, he described the threats he faced while serving and what SLDN meant to him:

> "I called on SLDN when I was a lieutenant at a Los Angeles Air Force Base. Some female enlisted person decided that I was gay because of something that I had said. I happen to think that she was monitoring my emails, actually—emails that were going

back and forth from me and Chip.... [Fortunately] nothing did come of it. But I still called SLDN because it was a potentially hazardous situation and I got scared. And I'll tell you, I felt so comfortable under their wing, knowing that someone was looking out for me. They said, 'It's okay.' They had a book—a survival guide—FedExed to me. It explained what all my rights were, what I should do, how I could get in trouble, how I couldn't. It just made me feel so good, I'll never forget it. It felt like falling off a building and someone catching you on this very, very soft pillow."[455]

That same year he also told *The Boston Globe*: "I think SLDN will be responsible—mark my words—for lifting the ban on gays in the military. And it's going to have a huge social impact, not just on the military, but everywhere." [456]

What he did not share until later was that he was sexually assaulted while at the Air Force Academy by several guys who put a hood over his head. Because of "Don't ask, don't tell," he felt that he could not report the crime.[457]

He spoke at SLDN's national gala, the annual Hollywood Hills pool party, and a cocktail party in Palm Springs. I recall one story he shared about his grandmother, who he says was one of the first female pilots in World War II. He said he was afraid of coming out to her because of their shared military service.

"Are you sure?" she asked him.

"Yes, I am," he said.

"Then be the best gay you can be," she replied.

Also in 2003, the premium cable network Showtime aired *Soldier's Girl*—the love story of Barry Winchell and Calpernia

Addams.[458] Their relationship was a stark contrast to the vitriol Winchell experienced from the two soldiers at Fort Campbell who killed him because they thought he was gay. The American Film Institute named *Soldier's Girl* as one of the 10 best television programs of the year.[459] It also won a Peabody Award, given for presentations of "stories that defend the public interest, encourage empathy with others, and teach us to expand our understanding of the world around us."[460]

On her website, Addams describes what the film captured: "I was a showgirl, he was in the Army, both of us at defining moments in our lives, and we fell into an intense, private relationship almost immediately. ... We only had a short time together, enough time to begin to hope that things could progress and life could change from loneliness to love, and then he was murdered by two fellow soldiers."[461]

Four years later, *Lifetime* aired *Any Mother's Son*, about the brutal murder in 1992 of Petty Officer Allen Schindler, starring Bonnie Bedelia as Allen's mother, Dorothy Hajdys.[462] SLDN premiered the film in Chicago.

"The biggest reason I wanted the movie made was because I wanted people to understand how hard it was for me to come to grips that Allen really was gay, and to realize that gays aren't these weirdos that you see," Hajdys told television critics during a press conference about the film. "They are very loving and caring people. And for people to realize that Allen could have been any mother's son."[463]

In 2007, Showtime's drama *The L Word*, about the intertwined lives of a group of lesbians and bisexuals living in Los Angeles, introduced a "Don't ask, don't tell" storyline. Rose Rollins portrayed Tasha Williams, a soldier in the National Guard who had served in Iraq and was simultaneously dealing with post-traumatic stress disorder and being threatened with discharge after a fellow soldier accuses her of being a lesbian. We honored the show at our 2007 gala with the Randy Shilts Visibility Award,[464] named for the author of *Conduct Unbecoming*.

We proposed honoring Rollins and the show's producer, Ilene Chaiken. The entire cast wanted to come, but we couldn't afford to cover those costs. They came anyway because they wanted to be part of the growing movement. Joining our honorees that night were Cybill Shepherd, Marlee Matlin, and Pam Grier.

Matlin, who is deaf, said (and signed), "It is absolutely f–ing wrong to deny any citizen the right. ... Marriage equality and overturning 'Don't ask, don't tell' go hand in hand."[465] She echoed what Michelle and I had first postulated in 1993—that the military and marriage were the linchpins for equality.

In an interview before coming to Washington for the award presentation, Shepherd said, "I have this enormous respect for people with the courage to go where other people haven't gone and set the example of defying 'Don't ask, don't tell' and other types of discrimination. ... It's hard to believe that in this day and age we still have this kind of discrimination and we're depriving ourselves at a time when we desperately need these great, good people who have the expertise and are willing to serve their country. ... Let's shoot ourselves in the foot a few more times."[466]

While these productions brought to life the experience of lesbian, gay, and bisexual service members, other shows truly permeated the culture. In 1997, Ellen DeGeneres came out on her eponymous ABC comedy—a move that, according to Peter

Singer, may have "short-circuited her popular sitcom and movie career at the time."[467] Six years later, though, she launched *The Ellen DeGeneres Show*, which has won 64 Emmys[468] and for years was one of the most popular shows on daytime television.

President Obama presented DeGeneres with the Presidential Medal of Freedom in 2016, saying, "It's easy to forget now—when we've come so far, where now marriage is equal under the law—just how much courage was required for Ellen to come out on the most public of stages almost 20 years ago.... Just how important it was, not just for the LGBT community, but for all of us to see somebody so full of kindness and light, to see somebody we liked so much ... challenge our own assumptions."[469]

Will & Grace aired from 1998 to 2006. It was a top 20 show for half of its run and won 18 Emmy Awards. In 2012, in an appearance on NBC's *Meet the Press*, Vice President Joe Biden said that he credited *Will & Grace* with changing Americans' "evolving" attitudes toward gays, adding that the show "probably did more to educate the American public than almost anything anybody has ever done so far."[470]

Not everyone saw the evolution of these attitudes, thanks to popular culture, as something positive. In 1996, Justice Antonin Scalia decried the culture wars in a scathing dissent in *Romer v. Evans*, the 6-3 Supreme Court decision striking down as unconstitutional an amendment to Colorado's constitution that prohibited local governments from making efforts to protect gays, lesbians, and bisexuals against discrimination.

"The Court has mistaken a Kulturkampf for a fit of spite," Scalia wrote, arguing that the growing acceptance of lesbian, gay, and bisexual Americans would override the religious beliefs of others.[471]

Scalia was wrong to assert that religious beliefs trump civil rights, though it remains to be seen where the Supreme Court will ultimately land on that proposition. He was correct, however, that America was battling for its better angels, and the cultural revolution that depicted gay Americans as part of the fabric of the nation played a crucial role in the fight.

CHAPTER 27

HOW MANY AND HOW MUCH

One of the most important game-changers in the debate on "Don't ask, don't tell" was data. The biggest data set that was missing in 1993 was an accounting of how many gays, lesbians, and bisexuals were serving in the military. It was easy, though disingenuous, for supporters of the ban to argue that the gay population was insignificant and that the military effectively rooted out almost all gays.

Because service members risked discharge if they came out, few were able to participate in the congressional hearings or public debate in 1993, and few would be able to when the policy was debated anew. While SLDN's storytelling provided a powerful personal account of the damage done by "Don't ask, don't tell," we needed hard data.

Gary Gates, a social scientist at the nonpartisan Urban Institute in Washington, helped crack the nut. He analyzed the 2000 census—the first one that allowed respondents to indicate if they were living in a spousal relationship with someone of the same gender—and cross-tabulated that data with veteran status. From that, he determined that there were approximately one million gay veterans in America, including those who had served in significant numbers in World War II, the Korean War, the Vietnam War, and the Persian Gulf War.[472]

One of my favorite moments at the SLDN gala on October 23, 2002, was honoring five gay World War II veterans who were met with a long, well-deserved standing ovation. One was Frank Kameny, the father of the modern gay rights movement.[473] More than a quarter-century before Michelle and I founded SLDN, he and Barbara Gittings, an early activist for lesbian rights, had organized marches at the Pentagon for the right of gays to serve openly.

Frank was lovingly ornery and bellicose, dressed in a well-worn sports coat. He was a staunch friend of SLDN, arguing from the podium at one of our fundraisers that denying gays the right to serve openly was "tantamount to aiding and abetting the enemy, which is treason, for which I will gladly provide the rope!"

In World War II, Frank was in England, Germany, France, and Holland, where he served in front-line combat. He was in Czechoslovakia during its liberation. "During World War II," he said, "I knew for what I was fighting. Over the years since, I have come to know even better for what I fought."[474]

Another World War II honoree that night was Dr. John Cook from Richmond, Virginia. John took part in the Normandy invasion, landing on Omaha Beach, and was awarded the Croix de Guerre by the French government.[475] He served in the Army Medical Corps, staffing a hospital unit that followed General Dwight D. Eisenhower's headquarters. John was later transferred to England, where he set up a 3,000-bed hospital to treat injured troops. John's partner of 50 years, Dr. Waverly Cole, served as an army physician in Heidelberg, Germany, after the war.[476]

In his southern drawl, John told the story of when he and Waverly met: "It was shortly after the waaah, and I heard there was a dahctah that was going to be at the paaahty, and I said, 'I'm going to meet this dahctah.' And we've been together evah since." Waverly nodded in agreement.

John was nervous about doing an interview before the gala, where he would be honored as a gay World War II veteran.

"Dixon, I don't know if I should do this interview," he told me. "You know that Waverly's mom, who is 93 years old, lives with us, and we are not out to her."

"John," I said, "you have been together for 50 years, living in the same house. I bet she knows."

"You are probably right!" His eyes popped open, delighted at the insight. He laughed, and he did the interview. His partner's mother was none the wiser, though likely wise enough.

◆ ◆ ◆

Since Gary Gates had cracked the code of how many gay veterans there were, I asked if he could determine the current number of gays and lesbians serving. SLDN provided a grant to support his research. In a report published in 2004, he concluded that there were approximately 65,000 gay Americans serving our country.

Lesbian, gay, and bisexual service members were no longer invisible. They were a number. They equaled 13 Army brigades,[477] or enough sailors to staff all our aircraft carriers,[478] or two-thirds of the military force in Afghanistan at its peak.[479]

Now that SLDN had hard data in hand, the question was no longer whether gays should serve in our armed forces, but how commanders should treat the ones who were already serving. Do you treat patriotic Americans with dignity and respect, or do you force them behind a wall of secrecy and threaten them with punitive action for being honest about themselves?

It doesn't take a skilled human resources officer to know that mistreating a significant percentage of your workforce dampens productivity. Many members of Congress would acknowledge this reality in the 2010 debate on gays in the military by describing the question as whether gays should "serve openly," not whether they should serve at all.

Gary went on to become the research director at UCLA Law School's Williams Institute, a public policy center examining issues of sexual orientation and gender identity. Two years later, I asked him whether we could extrapolate the number of gay service members who might have joined the armed forces if "Don't ask, don't tell" didn't exist. He concluded that forty thousand gay Americans might have joined our armed forces, all things being equal, bringing the lesbian, gay, and bisexual force to 100,000 strong.

Gary found that during the years that the military draft was in place, the percentage of gay men serving our country roughly equaled their percentage of the overall population. Once the draft ended in 1973, however, the percentage of gay men joining the all-volunteer forces dropped significantly. One could hypothesize that the drop resulted in part from the government discrimination. The military could amplify its forces by 40,000 troops if it stopped discriminating.

He then took the analysis one step further to determine how many lesbian and gay service members left the armed forces annually either by not reenlisting or by resigning their commissions, rather than being discharged under "Don't ask, don't tell." He determined that between three thousand and four thousand lesbian and gay service members left every year under the radar, silent casualties of "Don't ask, don't tell."

In 2007, military leaders urged Congress to provide for an increase in force strength of up to 80,000 service members because of the stresses placed on the armed forces by the wars in Iraq and Afghanistan. To meet its recruiting needs, the Army had already raised the maximum age for enlistment to 42, lowered the educational requirements, and increased the number of moral waivers granted, allowing criminals, gang members and skinheads, like Calvin Glover, to join. The Army also offered bonuses of $40,000 or more for enlistment and reenlistment. Other services also offered bonuses and decreased eligibility criteria to boost recruitment.

Governors were concerned that the overseas deployments of their states' National Guard units were threatening their ability to respond to needs at home, such as fighting forest fires and responding to natural disasters, like Hurricane Katrina. Reservists were legitimately complaining that their civilian jobs were threatened because they had been deployed multiple times, contrary to the expectation that their longest deployment would be one year. Families expressed concerns about the impacts of multiple deployments. One military spouse said of the extended deployments for her husband versus the continued discharge of gay service members, "I don't think it's fair ... when there are people wanting to go over there."[480]

Yet despite the personnel shortfall and the impact of the increased operational tempo on military readiness, the Pentagon and Congress said "no thanks" to qualified, mission-critical lesbian, gay, and bisexual service members. The point was driven home by a clever campaign organized by Jacob Reitan and Haven Herrin under the auspices of Soulforce and Right To Serve.[481] With their assistance, openly gay young adults who were willing to join the military went to dozens of recruiting stations around the country in 2006 asking to enlist, only to be turned away at the door.

In March 2007, former New York City Mayor Rudolph Giuliani, who had announced his candidacy for the Republican presidential nomination the month before, stated that the policy on gays in the military should not be changed during wartime.[482] Senator John McCain made the same argument in 2010. I believe that you should always urge change when the need is greatest. The demands placed by the wars in Afghanistan and Iraq meant that our nation needed all qualified volunteers to serve, including lesbian, gay and bisexual patriots. These conflicts made Americans keenly aware of our national security, the sacrifices required by our men and women in uniform, the drain that multiple deployments were placing on families, and the important contributions of all our troops—including those who were gay.

Statistics are powerful. Data removes the emotion from argument. Commanders no longer had to say whether they liked or disliked gay troops. They had to confront the reality that they were in command of a significant population. If they wanted to recruit and retain talent, the military had to create a work environment that was conducive to their success. Otherwise, the services would lose the people they needed the most—Arabic linguists, sharpshooters, and intelligence officers.

♦♦♦

The second data point that had some persuasive power was the cost tag of "Don't ask, don't tell." Every year, starting with our first annual report,[483] SLDN estimated the cost of gay discharges, using 1992 General Accounting Office data.[484] We published the cost data in our annual reports, and the media picked up on it.

In our 10th and final annual report, SLDN cited a *Government Executive* story that placed the cost of adding 10,000 soldiers (9,682 service members had been kicked out for being gay in the first 10 years[485]) at $1.2 billion.[486] These cost figures allowed us to argue in meetings on the Hill that for the same amount of money lost through these discharges, the Army could buy interceptor body armor vests to outfit all its troops.[487]

The GAO (which changed its name in 2004 to the Government Accountability Office) updated its cost estimates in 2005, days before the Military Readiness Enhancement Act—the initial effort at repeal—was introduced in Congress.[488] It reported that in the decade from fiscal year 1994 (when "Don't ask, don't tell" was implemented) through fiscal year 2003, the costs of recruiting and training service members to replace those kicked out for being gay amounted to more than $190.5 million—and that figure did not include the costs of investigations, pastoral care, separation functions, and discharge reviews.[489]

A year later, a University of California blue-ribbon commission, chaired by former Secretary of Defense William Perry and organized by the Palm Center at the University of California, Santa Barbara, also produced a cost analysis. Its report, which covered the same decade as the 2005 GAO report and corrected some "oversights in GAO's methodology," found that the cost of discharging gay service members under "Don't ask, don't tell" and retraining their replacements was at least $319.6 million— 68 percent higher than GAO's estimate.[490] In August 2010, the Palm Center updated that blue-ribbon commission report, noting that UCLA's Williams Institute had recalculated the numbers to include the four years since the commission's report was released. The total: more than $555 million.[491] All of these estimates we believed were low, based on our analysis as well as the report in *Government Executive*—but however the numbers were calculated, the final bill was eye-poppingly large.

CHAPTER 28

ARABIC LINGUISTS

On September 11, 2001, I arrived at work around 8:45 a.m. Minutes later, American Airlines Flight 11 crashed into the north face of the World Trade Center's North Tower. Our communications director, Steve Ralls, herded us quickly into the conference room to watch the breaking news.

The *Today* show's Katie Couric was reporting that something had flown into the building—perhaps a sightseeing plane. At 9:02, United Airlines Flight 175 crashed into the south face of the South Tower. "This is a coordinated terrorist attack," I shouted.

Around 9:35, one of our attorneys, Kathi Westcott, called from her apartment along Interstate 395 and said that she had just seen an American Airlines plane fly unnervingly close to her building. Within seconds, NBC's Pentagon correspondent, Jim

Miklaszewski, was telling viewers that the building was shaking, but he didn't know specifically what had happened.

I turned to my staff. "They are attacking Washington. We have to leave now. Gather what you need and go home immediately. I'll be in touch on when we can reassemble."

I made sure everyone had left and the doors were locked. As Vice President Dick Cheney was being escorted by the Secret Service to an underground bunker (President Bush was in Florida), I walked out of our office on K Street, a few blocks north of the White House, into the bright crisp light of a gorgeous autumn day. Lobbyists, lawyers, White House staff, nonprofit trailblazers—they were all still walking to work, smiling, laughing, humming, oblivious for the moment to how the world had changed.

I walked 45 minutes to my rowhouse in Georgetown and turned on the television. In the late afternoon, I attempted a run along the C&O canal, and stopped midway, dry-heaving. We knew, some quite well, several people who were in the Pentagon. Most survived; one did not. Lieutenant General Timothy Maude, the highest-ranking military officer killed in the attack, was the Army deputy chief of staff for personnel and its point person on "Don't ask, don't tell." He helped develop and implement the services' most comprehensive anti-harassment training program and was one of the first Army leaders to meet with the parents of Barry Winchell after he was murdered.[492]

Eighteen months later, President Bush launched the war in Iraq, and it occurred to me that now was the time to repeal "Don't ask, don't tell." While Bush had said that he was a "'Don't ask, don't tell' man,"[493] Vice President Dick Cheney, while serving as secretary of defense in 1991, had called the rationale for the prior gay ban a "bit of an old chestnut."[494]

I called Barney Frank, one of our staunchest supporters in Congress, and asked, "Should we push for repeal of 'Don't ask, don't tell' now? It seems to me we can demonstrate the strongest need for all hands on deck, and we now have overwhelming popular support." In one decade, the opinion polls had shifted dramatically in our favor.

Frank responded brusquely, "Where are the votes?" The call ended.

He was correct. We didn't have the votes.

Republicans controlled both the White House and the House of Representatives, and were trying to prohibit same-sex marriage through a constitutional amendment. Frank underscored a lesson I already knew: You need to count the votes in the House and the Senate to see if you can win. If you don't have the votes, keep your powder dry.

The war in Iraq, however, focused national attention on our armed forces and on the ability of the United States to meet its national security interests. It and the ongoing war in Afghanistan would provide plenty of opportunities to educate the public—and their representatives in Congress—how "Don't ask, don't tell" hurt military readiness.

It was a case of simple arithmetic, as well as needed skills. As I wrote in SLDN's eighth annual report, "It has never been more obvious than in the weeks and months following September 11th that this policy weakens our military, deteriorates our readiness and undermines the morale and cohesion of our troops."[495]

◆ ◆ ◆

As I was ushering staff out of our offices, Army Specialist Cathleen Glover was on lockdown at the Defense Language Institute in

Monterey, California.[496] Only halfway through her studies, she and her classmates were watching Al Jazeera, the Arabic-language news network based in Qatar, and furiously translating what was being said.[497] Her study of Arabic had just become much more valuable. Her sexual orientation made her expendable.

Like many lesbian, gay, and bisexual service members who joined the armed forces, she thought she could compartmentalize her life. Her partner moved to Monterey to be with her, but the stress of hiding strained the relationship beyond the breaking point. In a poignant column for *The Monterey Herald*, she wrote: "The truth is, none of us realizes how difficult it is to lead a double life in which a relationship must be conducted behind closed doors and ... lies."[498] Her closest friend at DLI, a fellow linguist, received orders for Fort Campbell, Kentucky. He decided to come out and be discharged rather than join the installation where Barry Winchell had been murdered.[499] Glover, an SLDN client, ultimately decided she could not hide who she was, and the Army discharged her for it.

Attending DLI at the same time was another Arabic linguist, Private First Class Alistair Gamble. He and his boyfriend, who also was a linguist, were caught in the same room during a surprise inspection at 3:30 a.m. The Army found a Valentine's Day card[500] and photographs of them showing affectionate, but not sexual, contact[501] that became the basis for discharging them both. Two months later, without consulting us, Nathaniel Frank of the Palm Center broke the story about our client in *The New Republic*.[502]

We were concerned about how sex in the barracks (or the inference of it) would play in the media. Though the Army had also caught men and women in the same room during that 3:30 a.m.

barracks sweep, evenhanded administration of the rules did not apply to gay soldiers. At SLDN, we were developing a broader story about the linguist discharges—one that might not place Gamble in the predicament of explaining why he had his boyfriend in his room. Fortunately, the potential salaciousness of the story was a non-issue, and that in itself was a little noticed breakthrough.

SLDN was assisting seven Arabic linguists in 2002, and we hoped we had achieved an important change in practice. The Army told two of our clients, Private First Class Julie Evans and Private First Class Patricia Ramirez, that they would be retained despite being out lesbians.[503]

The victory was short-lived. Several weeks later, DLI officials reopened their cases, digging for additional evidence against them, contravening the investigative limits. Investigators allegedly threatened other service members with disciplinary action if they didn't cooperate. Evans and Ramirez, like the others, were ultimately discharged.

Army Sergeant Bleu Copas, an Arabic linguist at Fort Bragg, North Carolina, was discharged in 2006 as a result of an anonymous tip that he was gay. He had signed up to serve our nation, he said, "out of a post-9/11 sense of duty."[504] Investigators never identified his accuser.[505]

In a segment on Copas's story, *The Daily Show* noted that the military had raised the recruiting age, accepted people with criminal records, and accepted high school dropouts and people with low IQs to fulfill recruiting requirements, but "had to draw the line somewhere"—and that line kept gay crypto-linguists on the other side.[506] Copas addressed an SLDN gala in Arabic, driving home the point of what had been lost to our nation.

The discharge of linguists from DLI was not a new phenomenon. As Randy Shilts described in *Conduct Unbecoming*, there had been routine purges of gay Americans in the foreign language fields, including Arabic linguists.[507] In 1991, during the Gulf War, the National Security Agency called "people up who had been kicked out for being gay ... begging them to come back to work" because there was a shortage of qualified Arabic linguists.[508]

SLDN had warned of problems at DLI for years. As we noted in our sixth annual report, the institute had engaged in a witch hunt in 1999 that resulted in the discharge of 14 service members. The institute was discharging not just Arabic linguists, but those who spoke Farsi and Korean—the languages in the countries (Iraq, Iran, and North Korea) that only three years later would come to comprise President Bush's "axis of evil." (I cheekily noted in SLDN's ninth annual report that the "loss of essential personnel is disturbing news in any language."[509])

In 2002 and 2003, the Department of Defense discharged 32 Arabic linguists for being gay.[510] Those discharges, in our time of greatest need for their skills, symbolized the utter failure of "Don't ask, don't tell." According to a 2002 GAO study, the critical shortfalls in linguists, both in the Army and in other government agencies, have "compromised U.S. military, law enforcement, intelligence, counterterrorism and diplomatic efforts."[511]

In November 2002, Barney Frank called DLI's discharge of nine gay linguists "the new height of stupidity."[512] That same month, *The Washington Post* wrote in an editorial: "The desire to defeat al-Qaeda has been preempted by an apparently more important priority: continuing the irrational discrimination against gay men and lesbians who would serve this country."[513]

In February 2007, Representative Gary Ackerman, a member of the House International Relations Committee, asked Secretary of State Condoleezza Rice why her department had not hired the Arabic linguists fired by the Pentagon to fill its need for trained linguists. During a June 3, 2007, debate for the Democratic candidates seeking their party's 2008 presidential nomination, Senator Hillary Clinton cited the discharge of Arabic linguists as a reason she supported the repeal of "Don't ask, don't tell."[514]

The Tipping Point, by Malcolm Gladwell, uses the word "stickiness" to describe when a moment takes hold because of some event or message. Arabic linguists became shorthand for the idiocy of "Don't ask, don't tell." In 2010, the story of Dan Choi, a West Point graduate who spoke Arabic, featured prominently in the final push to repeal "Don't ask, don't tell."

◆◆◆

While the symbolism of discharging Arabic linguists was indelible, SLDN's analysis of gay discharges found that linguists were not the only mission-critical personnel being discharged during the Afghanistan and Iraq wars. For example, the Pentagon's 2004 discharges included at least 41 health care professionals, 30 sonar and radar specialists, 20 combat engineers, 17 law enforcement agents, 12 security guards, and seven biological and chemical warfare specialists.[515]

The data helped Congress and the public to grasp how our national security was being harmed by "Don't ask, don't tell." As one observer noted, "Armed with the energy of public opinion ... and now a legislative strategy that focuses more on national security than on social philosophy, the movement to overthrow the military's 'Don't ask, don't tell' law keeps gathering momentum."[516]

CHAPTER 29

POPPYCOCK

The public announcement by Brigadier General Keith Kerr, Brigadier General Virgil Richard, and Rear Admiral Alan Steinman that they were gay—in *The New York Times*, no less[517]—coincided with the 10th anniversary of "Don't ask, don't tell" and marked another turning point in the debate. At the time, they were the highest-ranking officers to acknowledge their sexual orientation.

The Pentagon could no longer argue that gays had not served at the highest ranks of the military. The Pentagon could not deny their stellar contributions to our armed forces. The Pentagon was put on the defensive as to why any officers should be forced to hide the truth about themselves as a condition of military service.

I first met Keith Kerr at a cocktail party in 1995, the year he retired from the California State Military Reserve after having previously spent 31 years in the Army and the Reserves. I asked to meet with him later, and he graciously invited me and SLDN board member Zoe Dunning, the Navy officer who had prevailed at her discharge hearing, to his house in San Francisco where he lived with Alvin, his partner of more than 20 years.

Keith was a handsome, gravel-voiced man in his 70s. He wore his heart on his sleeve, though his words were deliberate and considered. He always had a cultural or literary reference that drove his point home. He had a penchant for golden retrievers and bonsai.

"Sir, I am going to lay all of my cards on the table," I told him. "I want you to join our Military Advisory Council. And I want you to come out."

He looked at me as if I was from Mars.

Keith is of an older generation where you just didn't come out. He was not out to his family or to any of his military buddies, at least officially.

"I will not force you to do anything," I said. "You will do it on your own timeline. Your confidence remains with me. But I want you to know my game plan so you don't think I have a hidden agenda."

Two weeks later, Keith joined our Military Advisory Council, but he didn't come out publicly. Many members of the council were not gay, so there was no legitimate inference to be made.

Several years later, Keith's partner, Alvin, died of liver failure. He was a priest in the Episcopal Church, another institution that for years had forced men into the closet as a condition of service. Keith was bereft. He told me that he was deeply moved that several retired generals had attended the funeral. He told me that they had come to his home and had known Alvin.

He told me that he was not out to them. I told him that he *was* out to them, and that their presence was a sign of love and acceptance far beyond what he had realized.

After a few days, Keith called me. He wanted to come out and tell his and Alvin's story. "No," I replied. "You are in too much pain. You are grieving. You will not be able to handle the calls and questions that may result from coming out right now. Wait. Grieve. Take time."

I met Virgil Richard in 2000 at his small ranch-style two-bedroom home in Austin, Texas, where he lived with his partner, David. Virgil was a retired Army general straight out of Central Casting: receding hairline, barrel-chested, with a ruddy face from harvesting wheat in Oklahoma at his family's farm and spending days in the Texas sun. He was married to a woman throughout his 32-year military career and had three sons, but realized late in life that he was attracted to men. After he retired in 1991, he filed for divorce and fell in love with a man.

Virgil was very comfortable in his own skin. He had taken to the gay community in Austin like a duck to water, and immediately became involved in activities. I didn't ask him to do anything when we first met, but he was the first general officer I approached when I wanted all three to come out together.

Alan Steinman came out of the blue—well, out of the fax machine. I was working late one evening when a fax emerged from the paper feed. It read: "I am a gay admiral. Call me if I can be of assistance." That was the best fax I ever received.

I called him immediately. He said that he had recently retired and that he wanted to come out and make a difference, but he had a few questions first. Those questions stretched over two years.

Alan was tall and lean, an emergency-medicine specialist and an expert on sea survival and hypothermia. He lived in Dupont, Washington, near the Army base at Fort Lewis, and had taken a slightly different path from his colleagues. He started out as a physician in the Public Health Service, which comes under military personnel policies only during time of war. Yet because of that remote possibility, many gays in the PHS remain closeted. Some are selected to join the Coast Guard; Alan was one, and he served for 25 years, retiring as its director of health and safety.

He had two critically important questions for anyone considering coming out in the armed forces under "Don't ask, don't tell" after retirement. First, he wanted to know if the military could take away his pension.

Theoretically, that was a possibility. Practically, it was not. To cut his pension, the Defense Department would have to recall him to active duty (perhaps even bring the PHS under Pentagon authority), convict him of a crime, and include in the penalty a reduction in pension.

The Pentagon had never taken such a drastic measure against any of the tens of thousands of gay service members who had come out after military service, including some, like Colonel Margarethe Cammermeyer, who had been quite visible in the public eye. We could not guarantee zero risk, but the risk was minimal.

The second question was how he should answer questions about his personal life. Had he ever engaged in sex with a man while on active duty, in violation of the Uniform Code of Military Justice? Could he get into trouble for those answers? Would it be sufficient for him to decline to answer personal questions as a matter of privacy?

There were two approaches, we told him. The first was to be fully forthcoming about his relationships. We are all human. We date; we break up. We have families, and we share joys and sorrows. The full story is a human story.

There is also the story of the pain endured because of "Don't ask, don't tell." Alan talked about parking his car in Virginia and taking the Metro to go to gay bars in the District of Columbia, ensuring that military police would not find his car and its military sticker near a gay establishment. Almost every gay, lesbian, and bisexual person who served during the ban will tell you that he or she changed the pronouns of his or her boyfriend or girlfriend or spouse when talking with their buddies to hide the fact that they were in a same-sex relationship. For example, I once met Chris, the partner of a closeted gay soldier. When the partner was deployed to Iraq, he referred to Chris in conversation with his friends as "Christina."

The second approach was to not discuss any relationships at all. By de-sexing any conversation, you run less risk of raising the question of whether you engaged in sex in violation of the Uniform Code of Military Justice, and you present no reason for the Pentagon to recall you to active duty to charge you with violating Article 125 or other provisions of the UCMJ.

Yes, you could lie about any sexual relations you had while serving. But lying is included in the catch-all "conduct unbecoming," a criminal offense in the military. It's ironic that the military did not at that time see "Don't ask, don't tell" as anathema to the services' honor codes, which called on all personnel to adhere to the core values of honesty, integrity, and candor.

My staff and I spoke with Alan many times over the next two years. We reviewed the legalities. We conducted media training. We helped him get used to the types of questions he would face and the sort of answers that might be most appropriate and comfortable for him. We provided the same training for the two retired generals.

I decided that the 10th anniversary of "Don't ask, don't tell"—December 2003—was the right hook for these extraordinary individuals to come forward and tell a story that had not been told before. *The New York Times* agreed to interview them.

I first approached Virgil Richard and told him I wanted all three men to do it together. He said "yes," without hesitation, saying he had been thinking about it for some time.

Four years later, in praising the work I had done at SLDN, he choked up, saying, "He *made* me come out." I realized that his decision to participate in the *Times* interview was not as easy as his command decision on the phone with me had seemed to indicate.

Next, I called Alan, who also agreed quickly.

The last person I asked was Keith. There was a long pause on the phone, and he finally said in his gravelly voice, "Well, if you think it will help the cause ..." His voice tapered off.

The story appeared in *The New York Times* on December 10, 2003.

A network morning show asked to interview Virgil the next day. We prepared him with talking points. When asked what he thought of "Don't ask, don't tell," he said, "I think it's poppycock."

I laughed out loud. It was not one of our talking points. "Poppycock" is not part of the command lexicon. I asked Virgil why he had used that word.

"I was trying to think of a word that people did not hear all of the time, something that would make them stop and listen," he said. It's akin to using the word "gobbledygook" or "cattywampus." The general knew what he was doing. He made his message stick.

The next month, *People* honored Keith, Virgil, and Alan by naming them, as a group, among the magazine's 100 Most Influential People of 2003.[518] When introducing any one of them at later events, I joked that I was happy to present one-third of one of the most influential Americans in 2003.

At a cocktail party in San Francisco in 2004, Keith explained why he had finally decided to publicly acknowledge that he was gay. "When Dixon first asked me to come out seven years ago, I thought he was crazy," he said. "I would never do it. But he asked me to join the Military Advisory Council. I looked in the mirror, and asked, 'What have you done for the gay community?' And the mirror responded, 'Nothing.' So I agreed.

"Then Dixon asked me to come out in *The New York Times*. When he asks you to do something, it isn't small." He chuckled and winked to the crowd. "So I looked in the mirror again and asked, 'What have you done for the gay community?' The mirror replied, 'Not much.' So I agreed."

The sky did not fall. The military did not crumble. The press was overwhelmingly positive. Keith, Virgil, and Alan all had some long-standing associates who bristled, but each reported that most of the reaction was supportive.[519]

The fact that two brigadier generals and a rear admiral came out in 2003 paved the way for others to do the same.

CHAPTER 30

THE MAGNIFICENT SEVEN

Most notably, seven retired O-6s came out on March 16, 2007. O-6s include colonels in the Army, the Air Force, and the Marine Corps and captains in the Navy and the Coast Guard. Never before had so many high-ranking retired officers come out all at once. When I met them, I asked each of them to join SLDN's Military Advisory Council, joining the initial cohort that Michelle and I had recruited in 1993.

One of the most remarkable things about these seven officers coming out at the same time was how unremarkable it was. No major media outlet wanted to report on it. Not *The New York Times*, not *The Washington Post*, not *USA Today*. Not The Associated Press. No major television network. They all were of the view that of course there are gay colonels and captains.

Their attitude showed that we had been enormously successful in turning the tide of the debate, but we also ran the risk of not being able to demonstrate how "Don't ask, don't tell" continued to ruin careers and undermine national security.

The LGBT media understood the significance of what these men and women had done. *The Advocate*, the leading LGBT news magazine, called them "the magnificent seven."[520] Communities without power are always looking for heroes—a well that must be constantly replenished.

We also had a hook: Four days before, in an interview with the *Chicago Tribune* editorial board, Marine General Peter Pace, the chairman of the Joint Chiefs of Staff, said he believed that "homosexual acts between two individuals are immoral and that we should not condone immoral acts" by allowing gays to serve openly.[521] The stories of the "magnificent seven" stood as a sharp rebuke to Pace's comments.

◆◆◆

Captain Joan Darrah joined the Navy in 1973. She was in the Pentagon on 9/11—in fact, the hijacked American Airlines jet crashed into the room where she had led an intelligence briefing only minutes before,[522] and seven of her colleagues were killed. The event shook her to her core. She wrote this about her experience:

> "In the days and weeks that followed, I went to several funerals and memorial services for shipmates who had been killed. Most of my co-workers attended these services with their spouses whose support was critical at this difficult time, yet I was forced to go alone.

"As the numbness began to wear off, it hit me how incredibly alone Lynne would have been had I been killed. The military is known for how it pulls together and helps people; we talk of the 'military family' which is a way of saying we always look after each other, especially in times of need. But none of that support would have been available for my partner, because under 'don't ask, don't tell,' she couldn't exist.

"In fact, Lynne would have been one of the last people to know had I been killed, because nowhere in my paperwork or emergency contact information had I dared to list her name.

"This realization caused us to stop and reassess exactly what was most important in our lives. During that process, we realized that 'don't ask, don't tell' was causing us to make a much bigger sacrifice than either of us had ever admitted. Eight months later, in June 2002, I retired after more than 29 years in the U.S. Navy, an organization I will always love and respect."[523]

Colonel Andy Leonard served in the Army for 30 years in a variety of active and Reserve roles. Primarily an intelligence officer, he also had infantry, special forces, military and sports parachute, and foreign language training, and was a scuba diving instructor. As a military diplomat during the Vietnam War, he advised against an invasion of Laos, perhaps preventing what could have been another disastrous war. As an intelligence analyst, he briefed the chairman of the Joint Chiefs of Staff and executive branch leaders in the White House Situation Room.

I met Andy at one of SLDN's fundraisers. He was nervous. I welcomed him warmly and thanked him for joining us. I then asked him if he knew of any other openly gay colonels.

He shook his head vigorously, as if that were an impossibility.

"Come this way," I said. SLDN served as a connector for officers who thought that they were the only one.

I had known Mike Rankin since 1993, when I was at the Campaign for Military Service. He had spent 24 years as a medical officer in the Navy and Navy Reserve, retiring as a captain. He was an FOB, a Friend of Bill (Clinton), and had served as Arkansas' commissioner of mental health during Clinton's first term as governor.

Now that Clinton was president, Mike was one of the quiet leaders urging his old friend to live up to his pledge to lift the ban on gays serving our country. He told Clinton that he should speak up as John F. Kennedy had after the racial bombing in Birmingham, Alabama, when he said, "If an American, because his skin is dark, cannot ... enjoy the free and full life which all of us want, then who among us would be content to have the color of his skin changed and stand in his place?"[524] Mike told me that his request to Clinton was a plea for empathy. Clinton told Mike that he would reread Kennedy's speech—and never invoked Kennedy's civil rights legacy for gays in the military.

Mike frequently held barbecues at his home in Arlington, Virginia, and invited me and Jeremy to join him and his military buddies. He asked me to speak to a Northern Virginia gay democratic alliance and gave me the most humbling introduction I've ever received. He described his military career and contrasted it with my civilian background. He then compared me to King Christian X of Denmark, who, so the story goes, wore a yellow Star of David during the Holocaust in solidarity with his country's Jews. While that story isn't true, the United States Holocaust Memorial Museum notes that it "conveys an important historical truth ... [that] both the King and the majority of the Danish people stood by their Jewish citizens and were instrumental in saving almost all of them from Nazi persecution and death."[525]

Rightly or wrongly, Mike told the audience that it took special courage for a civilian to defend his military brothers and sisters. That was an introduction I strived to live up to every day.

Sadly, he succumbed to Alzheimer's disease in September 2017. I was honored to speak at his memorial service in San Francisco a month later. He was a past president of Congregation Sha'ar Zahav, and the synagogue was filled with people who knew and loved him. I was grateful to hear about a part of his life that I knew nothing about, and it reminded me how we all know only pieces of each other. In turn, I was the only one there who knew anything about his heroic efforts to repeal "Don't ask, don't tell," and the congregants were glad to stitch another piece of his life story into the quilt of that day.

I also had known another San Francisco resident, Navy Captain Robert Dockendorff, since 1993. He was an active supporter of the Campaign for Military Service and was well known among the San Francisco LGBT community.

He had served as a supply corps officer in Vietnam. He survived an attempt to court-martial him after an anonymous activist in San Francisco "scattered newsletters bearing his picture from a gay function in front of the officer barracks on Treasure Island," but retired soon thereafter.[526]

I got to know Colonel Stewart Bornhoft in San Diego, and there was no doubt when I met him that he was ready to join the cause. A West Point graduate, class of 1969, he volunteered for Vietnam. In April 1995, after the bombing of the Alfred P. Murrah Federal Building, he was sent to Oklahoma City, where he served as defense coordinating officer—the secretary of the Army's representative and the on-site decision-maker for Department of Defense support during the rescue and recovery effort.

In March 2007, addressing a crowd in front of the Capitol in Washington, he reflected on his years of service. He specifically cited the West Point Cadet Prayer:

> "Strengthen and increase our admiration for honest dealing and clean thinking, and suffer not our hatred of hypocrisy and pretense ever to diminish. Encourage us in our endeavor to live above the common level of life. Make us to choose the harder right instead of the easier wrong, and never to be content with a half-truth when the whole can be won.

> "Endow us with courage that is born of loyalty to all that is noble and worthy, that scorns to compromise with vice and injustice and knows no fear when truth and right are in jeopardy."

Then he asked the hundreds assembled, "How do you reconcile that prayer with a policy which demands that you equivocate when asked the simple question: 'Hey, how's it going? What'd you do this weekend?'"

Navy Captain Sandy Geiselman was the only female battalion commander in the first coed class at Officer Candidate School.

Being the first, or only, woman to serve in a particular assignment became a pattern in her naval career, which culminated in her being the first woman to serve as director of the White House liaison office for the secretary of the Navy. She was also selected to command three different Reserve units, one of which was called up for the Gulf War.

Colonel Paul Dodd retired from the Army in June 1998. He was a chaplain, serving 20 years on active duty and 10 years in the Army Reserve and National Guard. At one point he was senior pastor of Memorial Chapel at Fort Myer, Virginia, where he preached to the military leadership, including many general officers. He subsequently became command chaplain for the United States Army Medical Command.

I am forever grateful that Paul presided over the funeral of Chief Master Sergeant David Guy-Gainer, another member of SLDN's Military Advisory Council, who had tragically taken his own life. The Master Chief, as he liked to be called, was always rallying the spirits of others, and he loved nicknames. When he learned that my favorite cookie at age eight was a snickerdoodle, made by a colleague of my dad's in Cleburne, Texas, my name forever changed. "Hey, Snickerdoodle! How're you doing?" he would ask when he checked in with me. I was also immensely grateful for Dodd's counsel when my mother passed away in 2005 and I had to gather my thoughts for her eulogy.

In the last years of "Don't ask, don't tell," Paul led an effort to reach out to military chaplains, who had adamantly opposed gay service in 1993, to encourage them to rethink the issue.

◆◆◆

The Advocate said the timing of seven senior officers coming out as gay just after the chairman of the Joint Chiefs spoke out against gays serving openly "reflected well on the savvy of Servicemembers Legal Defense Network."[527] We would win another ally in response to Pace's prejudice, as momentum to repeal "Don't ask, don't tell" gathered strength.

CHAPTER 31

GENERAL POWELL CALLED

Michelle and I knew when we founded SLDN that for "Don't ask, don't tell" to be repealed, we would have to either win the support or neutralize the opposition of Colin Powell—the chairman of the Joint Chiefs of Staff in the early 1990s, when the policy was making its way into law.

Powell was one of the more vocal critics of President Clinton's pledge to end the ban on gays in the military. During the 1993 debate over "Don't ask, don't tell," he stood on the steps of the Pentagon to report how many phone calls he had received in opposition to allowing gays to serve openly. He told the Senate Armed Services Committee that the service of openly gay troops would harm unit cohesion. He argued that race was a "benign characteristic"[528] and being gay was not. Congress agreed.

Michelle and I met Powell at the Arlington, Virginia, head-quarters of America's Promise, a nonprofit dedicated to the well-being and empowerment of youth that Powell founded after retiring from the Army in 1993. He was being asked about the efficacy of "Don't ask, don't tell" when he appeared on the Sunday talk shows, so I contacted him in 1997 with an offer to brief him on its current implementation. He agreed to see us.

I wanted to tell him that his stance in 1993 was fundamentally wrong, but I also knew a simple truth: You cannot change some-one's mind by telling them that they are wrong. You have to let them reach that conclusion on their own, over time, based on evidence. We were still in our earliest days of building our case against the law and amassing our data. The question was whether we could find common ground on which to build a new consensus.

My theory was that Powell, as well as Clinton, genuinely believed that "Don't ask, don't tell" was a better policy than the one before it, and that it allowed gay Americans to serve with greater freedom and latitude than the rules had previously allowed. After all, a Defense Department directive on standards for enlistment, released after the policy became law, stated that sexual orientation was no longer a bar to service and that a person's sexual orienta-tion was a "personal and private matter."[529]

"General Powell," I said, "we have received nearly a thousand calls from service members who have been impacted by 'Don't ask, don't tell.' The service members we assist come from every branch of the armed forces; they are stationed worldwide; they range from junior to senior enlisted and junior to senior officers. Men and women. We have documented that most are being asked point-blank about their sexual orientation in contravention of 'Don't ask.'"

"That's not supposed to happen," he said.

"Marine Lance Corporal Kevin Blaesing was turned in by his psychiatrist for asking questions about his sexuality in his attempt to figure out his sexual identity. He was discharged as a result."

"That shouldn't be happening," he confirmed.

"I gather that you agree that the new rules under 'Don't ask, don't tell' were designed to provide a zone of privacy for gay service members where they could be out to friends, family, and doctors, but not to commanders or in a visible and public way." (In 1993, Powell had testified before Congress: "We will not ask, we will not witch-hunt, we will not seek to learn orientation."[530])

"Yes," he concurred.

"Well, that is not happening, sir. We could use your help to adjust the course."

That was our first conversation.

We might have been able to better enforce some of the meager gains under "Don't ask, don't tell" if we had been able to prevail upon Powell to help us, but he wasn't ready.

In 2003, he told *Teen Ink* magazine that while discrimination is wrong, "I think it's a different matter with respect to the military, because you're essentially told who you're going to live with, who you're going to sleep next to."[531]

Four years later, he called me, prompted by an opinion essay in *The New York Times* that I had sent him. "Second Thoughts on Gays in the Military"—written by retired Army General John Shalikashvili, Powell's successor as chairman of the Joint Chiefs—called for repeal of "Don't ask, don't tell."[532] Like Powell, Shalikashvili had supported "Don't ask, don't tell," but he had changed his mind.

The column had not popped up out of the blue; Aaron Belkin of the Palm Center had asked Shalikashvili to write it.[533] The request came after multiple meetings and conversations coordinated by Alan Steinman, who lived near Shalikashvili.

The retired general met first with Steinman alone, then on separate occasions with Steinman and me, Steinman and Belkin, and Steinman and several openly gay service members who risked their careers to meet with him.

Pondering the life stories and experiences of the openly gay service members, Shalikashvili turned to me and asked, "I understand why lifting the ban is good for the gays. But why is it good for the Army?"

This is where data came in handy.

"Sir, according to the United States census, there are 65,000 gay troops serving our country, and there are more than a million gay veterans," I said. "The question for you as a commander is this: How do you want to lead your soldiers? Do you want them to live honestly, or do you want them to lie? What is best for unit cohesion—truth or dissembling? Holding on to the best, or discharging them just because they happen to be gay?"

The integrity argument, both for the individual and for the institution, is what would ultimately persuade Admiral Mike Mullen, the chairman of the Joint Chiefs from 2007 to 2011, that it was time to repeal "Don't ask, don't tell."[534] For now, though, Shalikashvili nodded, but he didn't commit.

In December 2006, the Palm Center published the results of a Zogby poll showing that 73 percent of returning Iraq and Afghanistan military personnel were comfortable with gay Americans and that 23 percent of them also reported knowing a service member in their unit who was openly gay. The poll was risky because we didn't know what the findings would be, but Belkin and I both agreed it was better to know the results than not. The Zogby poll finally clinched it for Shalikashvili. Neither Belkin nor Steinman had told me about his column, but I credit them for making it happen.

Powell and I spoke for 45 minutes. "I agree with General Shalikashvili that America has changed and is ready for gays to serve openly," he said.

I almost fell out of my seat. Here was the moment I had been waiting for. My heart was pounding. I wanted to yell down the hall to tell my staff to come into my office to hear the historic pronouncement. Powell was going to stand with Shalikashvili and call for repeal of "Don't ask, don't tell." We could get another opinion column, or he could simply affirm his support on a morning show. This could be the tipping point.

Then came the "but."

"I am not convinced, however, that military commanders are ready for that change."

That was, in part, his argument in 1993 when he forcefully argued against President Clinton's proposal to let lesbians and gays simply serve openly.

My head hit the desk. I took a deep breath.

I asked him if he was aware that military opinion, not just public opinion, had changed significantly since 1993. (He should have been; I had sent him the data.)

He had but remained steadfast that he didn't think that military *leaders* were there yet. He believed that while the views of younger generations had shifted, those of the senior leaders who had risen through the ranks had not—and their leadership would be essential if and when the ban was lifted. As Eric Schmitt reported in *The New York Times* in January 1993, during the heated debate on gays in the military, "In the military chain of command, officers and enlisted personnel take their cues on social issues like sexual harassment and racial discrimination from their superiors."[535]

Powell urged caution: "I agree with General Shalikashvili that Congress should not push for repeal now."

He was referring to this sentence in Shalikshvili's essay: "By taking a measured, prudent approach to change, political and military leaders can focus on solving the nation's most pressing problems while remaining genuinely open to the eventual and inevitable lifting of the ban." Powell read the line to mean that Congress should be open to eventual repeal but should remain focused now on more "pressing problems."

"I read that line differently, sir," I responded. "I believe that what he is saying is that Congress should not push for repeal until the votes are there. Believe me, as someone who wants to see 'Don't ask, don't tell' repealed, I don't want us to be premature in our efforts. We do not want a repeat of 1993. We want to win.

"I wouldn't advocate for a vote today, but I think it is fair for Congress to hold hearings and start the dialogue again. That's why Representative Meehan has introduced a bill that would repeal 'Don't ask, don't tell'—to get the ball rolling."

Powell paused. He agreed.

I then put it on the line—one decade after I had started my conversation with him. I asked Powell for his support. "Sir, you will be a critical voice on 'Don't ask, don't tell' when it comes up for debate again. I need you to support repeal if we are going to win. Do you know that?"

"Yes," he said.

On August 8, 2007, he wrote to me, saying that one of his greatest regrets regarding "Don't ask, don't tell" was that the rules had become statutory, constraining the defense secretary and the commander in chief from changing them. As I read his words, I thought, "Then why didn't you fight for that in 1993, rather than let Sam Nunn codify the ban?" I recognized, though, that he was expressing regret and was open to the way forward.

Finally, on February 5, 2010, 10 months before final repeal of "Don't ask, don't tell," Powell released a statement: "If the chiefs and commanders are comfortable with moving to change the policy, then I support it. Attitudes and circumstances have changed. Society is reflected in the military. It's where we get our soldiers from."[536]

His words reflected exactly what he had told me three years prior—that repeal could succeed because society had changed, but only if the chiefs and commanders would also support the change. The stage was set.

CHAPTER 32

REINFORCEMENTS

LGBT veterans' decisions to come out strengthened the resolve of our straight allies to speak up on our behalf as well. In addition to Shalikashvili, two retired Army leaders—General Wesley Clark and Lieutenant General Claudia Kennedy—spoke out for repeal, as did two former Republican lawmakers: Alan Simpson, who had retired from the Senate in 1997, and Bob Barr, who lost reelection to the House of Representatives in 2002. Some of these relationships took time to build; others spontaneously materialized. Some started in the strangest of places.

With Claudia Kennedy, it was at a hair and nail salon. I had called her out of the blue to introduce myself and our work, and she graciously agreed to meet. I first saw her at First Star, a nonprofit organization dedicated to helping abused and neglected children, where she served on the board of directors. Our second meeting was at a salon where her husband was having a pedicure while they were in town.

Kennedy was the first woman in the Army to reach three-star rank. As deputy chief of staff for intelligence, she oversaw policies and operations affecting 45,000 people stationed worldwide and a budget of nearly $1 billion. A true beacon of hope for all our women in uniform, she proved that the barriers to women in the military were falling. After she retired in 2000, she became an analyst for MSNBC and CNN and wrote *Generally Speaking*, a best-selling memoir of her Army career.

One would have hoped that she would have immediately joined the bandwagon supporting repeal of "Don't ask, don't tell." She had faced discrimination and harassment throughout her career; as she was leaving the Army, she filed a sexual harassment complaint against a fellow general, showing that sexism was prevalent even at the highest echelons of the service.

But she wasn't an immediate supporter of repeal. Like Powell and Shalikashvili, she wasn't sure if gays should be allowed to serve—and even if they were, she didn't know under what conditions. She told me, somewhat pained, one day, "Dixon, I know I should support you. And I don't know why I can't. I should stand up for what is right. You just need to give me more time."

I gave her more time. I would touch base every three months or so with new information about "Don't ask, don't tell." One day, after a story broke about the discharge of a gay Arabic linguist, she emailed: "Did you see the story about the Arabic linguist being kicked out for being gay? That is outrageous!" I knew we were making progress.

In 2004 I was in Boston at the Democratic National Convention, volunteering with the LGBT caucus, some of whose members had given or raised substantial sums of money. A number of prominent Democrats were scheduled to drop by to thank the group for their support, but they weren't showing up. There was a growing chorus of dissatisfaction at being taken for granted.

Chris Neff, an SLDN staff member who was also at the convention, told me that Kennedy was speaking across the hall to the Veterans Caucus. I told him to see if she would be willing to speak to us, as a favor to me. Never faint of heart, Chris walked boldly into the Veterans Caucus room and asked her. She said yes, perhaps without really understanding what she had agreed to do.

I met her as she crossed the hallway from the Veterans Caucus to the LGBT Caucus. "I don't know that I can do this," she said. "What should I say?" I gave her the taking points: (1) the Pentagon is kicking out two to four service members every day for being gay; (2) John Kerry, who was being nominated at the convention as the party's presidential candidate, has pledged to repeal "Don't ask, don't tell"; (3) thank you for your support. I gave her options that allowed her to be technical—and to declare John Kerry's support, not hers.

I introduced her so the civilians would know that she was a superstar and that their support for the party commanded the highest respect. Kennedy took the microphone.

"Thank you for letting me come and speak to you," she said. "I know what it is like to be discriminated against. I know you know what it is like to be discriminated against. And it is wrong. Everybody knows that gays are serving our country. We should be treating gays equally like everyone else. That is what the military does. And that is what John Kerry has said he will do."

Kennedy received thunderous applause. As we walked out of the room, she said, "Dixon, I said a lot more than I thought I would. Thank you."

Two years later, I asked her to keynote our 2006 national gala.[537] She agreed. Then she waffled. She called me three weeks before the dinner and said, "Dixon, I just can't do it. I've been working nonstop. I'm tired. I need to pull back. I am canceling all my commitments. I'm sorry." I didn't doubt that she felt like she was running on empty.

I took a deep breath. "I understand how tired you must be. You are just amazing. Of course, this will put us in a bind. The invitations have already gone out with your name and photo on it. You are on our website. You know, I have a letter on my desk that I just got in the mail yesterday. (I did. Scout's honor.)

"It's from a woman who is coming to the dinner. She is currently serving in the Army. Let me read it to you. She says, 'I have never come to one of your dinners because I am in the Army. But if Lieutenant General Kennedy has the courage to speak up on our behalf, I will have the courage to come to the dinner. Thank you for all you are doing.'" I stopped.

There was a very long pause. "Okay," she said. "I'll do it. I have to."

I thanked her profusely, hung up the phone, and bought her a spa package to help her rejuvenate.

At our national dinner, she exuded Army green. She was smart, a bit wonky, but she walked the Army walk and talked the Army talk. She said:

> "Army values are taught to soldiers from their earliest days in the Army. Those values are loyalty, duty, mutual respect, selfless service, honor, integrity, and personal courage. We teach our soldiers that these are

the values we expect them to live up to. I believe that as an institution, our military needs to live up to the values we demand of the service members. Military leaders need to respect all service members. We need to recognize that loyalty and selfless service are exhibited equally by service members of every color, gender, and sexual orientation.

"When we ask people to hide something important about their identity, it is a challenge to their integrity and to the integrity of the institution.

"It is also disrespectful to them and to those with whom they serve. When we say, 'You are good enough to serve in Iraq, but you may not be openly gay,' we break trust with all of our service members. The Army has a credo that we will leave no soldier behind. It is found in the Soldier's Creed, and we believe it. On the battlefield, we act on this—we leave no soldier behind. How is the situation of the gay soldier any different?"[538]

I think Kennedy got as much out of our national dinner as we did. While she had come to the intellectual conclusion that "Don't ask, don't tell" should be eliminated, I don't think she had felt it in her bones. At the dinner, she found 700 lesbian, gay, and bisexual service members, spouses, and allies, cheering her on. She found young enlisted men who were out to their units and happy. She found women whom she had commanded but hadn't known that they were lesbian. She found service members who had been kicked out and lost everything.

The dinner helped her reaffirm that she had made the right decision. She told me, "Dixon, I know so many people here tonight." I replied, "Now you really do."

◆◆◆

Wesley Clark came out in support of gays in the military prior to his announcement that he was running for the Democratic presidential nomination in 2003. He had served as Supreme Allied Commander of NATO and the head of U.S. European Command from 1997 until 2000 and had also headed U.S. Southern Command.

Appearing on *Meet the Press* on June 15, 2003, he said this about "Don't ask, don't tell": "I don't think it works. Essentially, we've got a lot of gay people in the armed forces, we always have had, always will. And I think that ... we should welcome people that want to serve."[539]

Clark's comments, like Kennedy's, did not materialize spontaneously. They happened because we had pushed the right levers and laid the right groundwork.

I had met with Clark only once, at a fundraiser for his presidential exploratory committee, before he made those comments. Political fundraisers are terrible venues to discuss policy because you get only seconds to engage with the candidate, but he asked me to step out of the receiving line and wait so we could speak. When we did, he focused on me like a laser for several minutes as I explained the reasons the armed forces were now ready for change. He then thanked me and promised to continue the dialogue, but made no commitments.

I approached allies at the Democratic National Committee, telling one of them, "General Clark is about to declare his candidacy for president. There needs to be frank talk about his position on gays in the military. Al Gore supported repeal in 2000.

Every leading candidate today, from John Kerry to Howard Dean to Richard Gephardt, supports repeal. We cannot have a leading candidate in the Democratic Party backpedal on this, especially a retired general."

Clark subsequently announced his support for gays serving openly in the armed forces.

◆ ◆ ◆

Good leaders are always willing to listen.

The road to getting Alan Simpson's support was a short one. Before I contacted him, he had come out in favor of gay equality in a number of contexts other than the military. It wasn't clear, though, where he would stand on "Don't ask, don't tell." He was a veteran, had voted for "Don't ask, don't tell" in 1993, had chaired the Veterans Affairs Committee, and had served on the Iraq Study Group.

I wrote him a letter—several letters, actually, spanning six months. He finally wrote back: "I like your letters. Give me a call."

We spoke. He asked, "Did you ever hear about the letter I sent to Fred Phelps?" Phelps was a disbarred lawyer and Baptist minister whose life mission was to protest funerals of people who had died of AIDS; or had been victims of hate crimes, like Matthew Shepard; or had died in in Iraq and Afghanistan (because they died serving on behalf of a nation that has not condemned homosexuality).[540] He proselytized that "God hates fags" and "homosexuals are going to hell."

I told Simpson that I hadn't heard about his letter to Phelps. He said, "Well, I wrote him and said, 'Reverend Phelps, as a man of God, I wanted to let you know that some asshole out there is using your good name to say terrible things.'"

Simpson agreed to write an opinion essay in support of repeal and asked that I coordinate with Charles Francis on drafting language for him to consider. Francis was the founder of the Republican Unity Coalition—a group that that brought together leading conservatives, straight and gay, in support of gay equality. Simpson served on his board.

But to the media, the growing chorus in support of repeal was, by now, nothing new. Alan Simpson was a retired senator whose views on gay issues were well known to have evolved. Paper after paper declined to publish his column. We remained hopeful that its moment would come.

Marine General Peter Pace's statement that the Pentagon should not condone "immoral acts" by allowing gays to serve openly not only allowed us to publicize the story of the "magnificent seven," it created the opportunity to publish Simpson's essay in *The Washington Post*. He wrote:

> "Is there a 'straight' way to translate Arabic? Is there a 'gay' Farsi? My God, we'd better start talking sense before it is too late. We need every able-bodied, smart patriot to help us win this war. ... This policy has become a serious detriment to the readiness of America's forces as they attempt to accomplish what is arguably the most challenging mission in our long and cherished history."[541]

The New York Times reported three months later that Pace's comments may have contributed to President Bush's decision not to renominate him for a second term as chairman of the Joint Chiefs.[542] His successor would be none other than Admiral Mike Mullen, who as chairman ushered in repeal of "Don't ask, don't tell."

◆ ◆ ◆

Bob Barr—a rabid foe of gays when he served in Congress—also changed his views on gays in the military.[543]

In 1996, he was the author and primary sponsor of the Defense of Marriage Act. It barred federal recognition of marriages (which included, among other things, military benefits for spouses) except those between a man and a woman. The American Civil Liberties Union made headlines by retaining Barr as a consultant[544] after he left Congress. On March 30, 2004, he testified before the House Judiciary Committee—a panel on which he had served—against amending the Constitution to ban marriage equality for gay Americans.[545] While he still supported DOMA, his position was rooted in a federalist view that marriage laws should be left to the states. (He ultimately embraced marriage equality and apologized in 2008 for his role in the Defense of Marriage Act.[546])

I called Anthony Romero, the head of the ACLU, shortly before the November 2006 elections to explore whether Barr might reverse his opposition to "Don't ask, don't tell."

He did. In a column for *The Wall Street Journal,* published three months after Simpson's essay, he wrote:

"The bottom line here is that, with nearly a decade and a half of the hybrid 'Don't ask, don't tell' policy to guide us, I have become deeply impressed with the growing weight of *credible military opinion* [emphasis added] which concludes that allowing gays to serve openly in the military does not pose insurmountable problems for the good order and discipline of the services. ...

"Why? First, true *conservative political philosophy* [emphasis added] respects the principles of individual freedom and personal privacy, particularly when it comes to what people do in private. The invasive investigations required to discharge a service member are an unconscionable intrusion into the private lives of American citizens. Worse, while supporters of 'Don't ask, don't tell' claim the policy only regulates behavior and not identity, the distinction is disingenuous. A service member could be discharged for being overheard remarking that 'I can stay later today since my partner will be taking the dog for a walk.'"[547]

What one can glean is that Barr had reconsidered his opinion because other opinion leaders had done the same. Shalikashvili, Simpson, and others had created the room for someone with staunch conservative credentials, like Barr, to take a stand. It is also clear that SLDN's annual reports on "Don't ask, don't tell," which had seeped into the public consciousness, had an impact. The gay ban was not a policy of discretion, but an "unconscionable intrusion" into privacy. Barr ultimately concluded that a law that said one could be gay, yet prohibited anyone from talking about it or acting upon it, was disingenuous.

◆ ◆ ◆

One of my final actions before I left SLDN was to secure a statement from former President Jimmy Carter calling for repeal of "Don't ask, don't tell." Having succeeded in securing pledges for repeal from every Democratic presidential candidate since Bill Clinton, and having gotten Clinton to walk back his support for "Don't ask, don't tell," I wanted to close the loop and ensure that Carter stood for repeal as well. His administration had drafted the gay ban that existed before "Don't ask, don't tell," and it was time for both to be rebuked.

I asked Andy Tobias, the Democratic National Committee treasurer (and the guy who praised my performance before Rudy deLeon while Michelle kicked my shin), if he could make the request. He did. In a letter to SLDN in May 2007, Carter wrote, "'Don't ask, don't tell' is the only law in America today that regulates a group of citizens, then prohibits them from identifying themselves and speaking up on their own behalf. Gay soldiers, sailors, airmen, and marines are unable to tell their Member of Congress or their commander that the policy is an abject failure and they are living proof because they will face discharge. Those who defend our liberties and freedoms deserve better."[548] Given Carter's human rights record, which had only grown since he left office, no one was surprised by his statement. It didn't generate a lot of attention, but the historical import was significant.

◆ ◆ ◆

The Palm Center, in a powerful and complementary move, exponentially grew support from retired generals and admirals by carefully and methodically reaching out, asking them to sign a letter supporting "Don't ask, don't tell" repeal. In November 2007, 28 retired generals and admirals called on Congress to repeal the policy, citing evidence that 65,000 gay men and women were serving in the armed forces and that there were over a million gay veterans.[549] By July 8, 2008, 52 retired generals and admirals signed the letter calling for repeal of "Don't ask, don't tell."[550] By November 17, 2008, about two weeks after Barack Obama was elected president, 104 retired generals and admirals signed a similar statement.[551] The goal was to break any idea that general officers and flag officers were a monolithic block opposing equality.

The endgame for repealing "Don't ask, don't tell" was drawing nearer.

CHAPTER 33

LAWRENCE

The courts were indifferent, at best, and hostile, at worst, to lesbian, gay, and bisexual service members in denying initial challenges to "Don't ask, don't tell." We needed a precedent that would shake them out of their tunnel-vision deference to the military.

The turning point was *Lawrence v. Texas*,[552] a 2003 Supreme Court decision that struck down state sodomy statutes. *Lawrence* provided an opportunity to relitigate the constitutionality of the military's sodomy statute, as well as the constitutionality of "Don't ask, don't tell."

Prior to *Lawrence*, the armed forces had repeatedly upheld the constitutionality of Article 125 of the Uniform Code of Military Justice, which made "unnatural carnal copulation ... with another person of the same or opposite sex" a crime. Under Article 125, oral sex even between married heterosexual adults was a criminal offense, punishable by up to five years in prison for each offense. The lead case upholding that statute was *United States v. Fagg*, decided in 1991 by Chief Judge Walter T. Cox III.[553]

The military's jurisprudence was based on *Bowers v. Hardwick*, a 1986 Supreme Court case that upheld the constitutionality of a Georgia law criminalizing oral and anal sex between consenting adults. In *Lawrence,* the justices, by a 6-3 vote, overturned *Bowers,* holding that it was wrongly decided then and bad law now.

In sweeping language, Justice Anthony Kennedy wrote for the majority: "Liberty presumes an autonomy of self that includes freedom of thought, belief, expression, and certain intimate conduct. The instant case involves liberty of the person both in its spatial and more transcendent dimensions. ...

"The petitioners are entitled to respect for their private lives," he continued. "The State cannot demean their existence or control their destiny by making their private sexual conduct a crime. Their right to liberty under the Due Process Clause gives the full right to engage in private conduct without intervention of the government."[554]

The continued validity of the military's sodomy law was now in doubt. The constitutional validity of "Don't ask, don't tell" was also in doubt.

There were eight challenges to "Don't ask, don't tell" after it became law in 1993. The cases eventually reached the U.S. Courts of Appeal for the Second,[555] Fourth,[556] Eighth,[557] and Ninth[558] Circuits. All the courts ruled that the gay ban was not unconstitutional, resting their decisions explicitly or implicitly on *Bowers.* They reasoned that if it was constitutional to prohibit consensual oral and anal sex, it was also constitutional to prohibit someone from saying "I am gay," since that was credible evidence that the person had a propensity to engage in conduct that could be constitutionally proscribed.

While "Don't ask, don't tell" said gays could rebut the presumption that they would engage in sex with a person of the same gender, that was always a farce, as the Dunning memo and the *Richenberg* decision[559] made clear early on—and as the courts clearly discerned.

The courts never addressed the fact that saying "I am straight" could also provide credible evidence that the person would violate Article 125. Nor did they address why it would be appropriate to ban one class of persons but not others for expressing their sexual identity. The courts never addressed why a statement of sexual orientation for gays, but not straights, resulted in harm to unit cohesion, holding time and again that civilian judges had to defer to the judgment of the military, even when the military judgment was backed by no evidence. Since *Lawrence* made it no longer constitutionally permissible to discriminate against a class of persons for their intimate sexual conduct, it stood to reason that it would no longer be permissible to discriminate based on statements of sexual orientation. The Supreme Court's decision opened a door that had been closed.

The battle against the military's sodomy statute was immediately joined. There were two dozen cases in the military system where service members had been convicted of consensual sodomy. One, *Marcum v. United States*, was already before the Court of Appeals for the Armed Forces, the highest appellate court in the military legal system and one rung below the Supreme Court.

Air Force Technical Sergeant Eric Marcum had been convicted in May 2000 of several offenses, including forcible sodomy and nonforcible sodomy. His appeal was based, in part, on the Supreme Court's ruling in *Lawrence*, and SLDN filed an amicus brief urging the court to overturn the sodomy statute and declare Article 125 unconstitutional. In an unusual move, and with the permission of Marcum's lawyer, the court asked us to argue the portion of the case addressing the sodomy statute's constitutionality. Typically, those who file amicus briefs are not asked to speak.

This wasn't our first effort to repeal Article 125. On March 13, 2001, SLDN's legal director, Sharra Greer, testified before a blue-ribbon commission that was making recommendations on modernizing the 50-year old Uniform Code of Military Justice. The commission was headed by none other than Walter Cox, who had written the majority opinion in *U.S. v. Fagg*.

Sharra urged the Cox Commission to repeal Article 125. She provided evidence that the sodomy statute was selectively enforced and unfairly targeted lesbian, gay, and bisexual service members. "It is too easy for a jilted lover or angry roommate to bring allegations of sodomy and end the career of a service member for engaging in consensual sexual activity," she told the panel.

In May 2001—the 50th anniversary of the UCMJ, and two years before *Lawrence*—the Cox Commission recommended repeal of Article 125, calling sodomy prosecutions "arbitrary and even vindictive."[560] (The commission convened again eight years later and made the same recommendation, since the military court decisions post-*Lawrence* had not yet unequivocally declared Article 125 dead.)

In our argument to the Court of Appeals for the Armed Forces, we presented the conclusions of the first Cox Commission. We detailed the history of the sodomy prohibition, showing that the military had, in 1947, simply adopted the sodomy ban then existing in Maryland law—the model for the UCMJ. Most states had sodomy provisions in force in 1947, and Congress sought to make the military's laws comparable to state laws. That was no longer the case.

The court's decision in *Marcum* wasn't a home run, but it was a ground rule double. The judges upheld Marcum's conviction and didn't overturn Article 125, but their ruling held that *Lawrence* applied to the military and that courts reviewing sodomy convictions had to conduct a "searching constitutional" inquiry to determine whether the convictions should be upheld. Complicating matters, though, was the fact that Marcum had also committed fraternization by having sex with a subordinate. The court inferred a lack of consent; as a result, the judges ruled, *Lawrence* was not relevant to this case since it applied only to consensual sex.

Still, using the *Marcum* precedent, the Army quickly overturned at least three sodomy convictions. The Navy overturned at least one.

The court's decision was really a dodge; it could have explicitly struck down Article 125 as it applied to consensual sexual acts. There are other provisions of the UCMJ that punish fraternization. Leaving Article 125 intact only created delay or confusion. But the decision did establish a strong presumption that Article 125, as it applies to consensual activities, was invalid.

The partial success in *Marcum* was crucial as we moved forward to relitigate the constitutionality of "Don't ask, don't tell." The crux of the government's argument in support of banning openly gay Americans from military service is that the United States has the right to criminally punish gay sex, and it therefore has the right to administratively discharge all openly gay Americans from the armed forces as a prescriptive measure. We could now argue that, under *Lawrence* and *Marcum*, the military doesn't have the right to criminally punish gay sex—and therefore the government also couldn't discriminate against gay Americans for saying who they are.

◆◆◆

In 2006, one year after we had launched our legislative strategy to repeal "Don't ask, don't tell," SLDN filed *Cook v. Rumsfeld* (later known as *Cook v. Gates*) before the U.S. District Court for the District of Massachusetts, as its appellate court—the U.S. Court of Appeals for the First Circuit—had never considered the constitutionality of the gay ban.

We brought a case that represented multiple branches of service and a full range of the horrors experienced under "Don't ask, don't tell." We interviewed 200 clients to assess who should be part of the lawsuit. Our 12 plaintiffs had more than 65 years of service and six dozen medals of commendation and other honors. All had served during the war on terrorism. Three had served in direct support of operations in the Middle East. Among our plaintiffs were men and women, officers and enlisted. They were all exceptional veterans who served our nation with distinction.

The named plaintiff was Army Specialist Tommy Cook, an expert in ground surveillance intelligence. He had deployed to Kuwait and was ready to deploy to Iraq. When he heard his sergeant say, "If I ever found out someone in my crew was gay, I would kill him," he decided to report the threat. In doing so, he outed himself—and a month later, he was discharged.[561]

Military tradition ran strong in Cook's family: His great-great-grandfather served in the Civil War, his great-grandfather in World War I. His grandfather was also in ground-surveillance intelligence but hadn't seen combat.

After leaving the military, Cook became a nurse and moved to New York during the COVID-19 pandemic to serve our nation once again.

Sergeant First Class Stacy Vasquez was one of the Army's top recruiters, kicked out at a time when the service was struggling to meet its recruiting goals. Her case demonstrated how the Army was shooting itself in the foot because of "Don't ask, don't tell." She served for a brief period as SLDN's paralegal[562] and stood alongside Speaker of the House Nancy Pelosi on December 21, 2010, as Pelosi signed the bill repealing "Don't ask, don't tell" that would be sent to the White House for President Obama's signature.

Navy Lieutenant (junior grade) Jen Kopfstein was a surface warfare officer and served openly for two years on the USS *Shiloh*, patrolling the Pacific coast with her crew after the 9/11 attacks. Two captains under which she served testified at her discharge board that she was an exemplary junior officer and that "Don't ask, don't tell" was a bad policy. In her last fitness report, Captain W.E. Dewes lauded her as a "trusted Officer of the Deck and the best ship handler among her peers." Her "sexual orientation has not disrupted good order and discipline onboard USS *Shiloh*," he wrote.[563]

Air Force Captain Monica Hill, whose partner died of brain cancer on 9/11, joined the case. She had dreamed of becoming the surgeon general of the Air Force when life, death, and the ban intervened.

David Hall and Jack Glover were among the top students in their ROTC unit at the University of Alaska in Anchorage when they were discharged for being gay after a student in whom Hall had confided reported their relationship to superiors.[564] Jeremy and I visited them in Anchorage the summer before the case was filed and hiked with Hall in the hills near the Matanuska River. Hall would later join SLDN's staff. In 2013, he was asked to be a citizen co-chair of the Presidential Inaugural Committee.[565]

While serving aboard the USS *Bridge* in Southwest Asia, Navy Petty Officer First Class Derek Sparks was falsely accused of engaging in sex with two other men.[566] It didn't happen, and witnesses could vouch for Sparks's whereabouts.[567] Despite the lack of evidence, the investigation convinced Sparks to leave the Navy. He told a local paper, "The Navy's core values—honor, courage and commitment—don't go along with hiding who you are."[568]

Joining these plaintiffs were equally stellar individuals who had been discharged under "Don't ask, don't tell": Army Private Megan Dresch, who served in the military police; Air Force Second Lieutenant Laura Galaburda, a physician specializing in family medicine; Private Jennifer McGinn, who joined the Army two months after 9/11; Coast Guard Seaman Justin Peacock; and Army Captain James Pietrangelo, an infantryman who served in the Gulf War and rejoined the armed forces after graduating from law school.

In addition to the star plaintiffs, we had lined up star litigators from Wilmer Cutler Pickering Hale and Dorr, including Stuart Delery, who would later serve as assistant attorney general for the Civil Division and then acting associate attorney general, the third-highest position in the Justice Department.[569] He was also the highest ranking openly gay person in the department's history. Other future stars on our litigation team were Maura Healey, who would later be elected attorney general of Massachusetts, and Ali Nathan, who would become a District Court judge in the Southern District of New York. I was a bit gobsmacked and humbled at a litigation meeting when former Solicitor General Seth Waxman walked into the room and praised my work. How did he know of my work?

Any one of our clients' stories should have convinced a reasonable person that the law hurt military readiness and deprived our armed forces of talented, patriotic Americans. We thought we had a slam-dunk case. As legal analyst Dan Abrams observed, "I think it may be time to say goodbye" to the ban on gays in the military: "[A]s a constitutional matter, I think it's tough to reconcile *Lawrence v. Texas*, that decision, with the military's policy."[570]

We had asked Judge George A. O'Toole Jr. for a trial so we could lay out in methodical detail the evidence against "Don't ask, don't tell." He declined our motion. He then ruled against us, once again deferring to the military's assertions, without evidence, that the presence of openly gay service members undermined unit cohesion.[571] The U.S. Court of Appeals for the First Circuit affirmed O'Toole's decision in June 2008.[572]

The courts circumvented *Lawrence* by concluding that while Texas did not have a rationale to punish sex between consulting adults, the military did—despite *Marcum*. Those rulings reinforced my belief that Congress was our only avenue.

◆◆◆

While SLDN's case failed, other challenges gained traction. The first was *Witt v. Department of the Air Force*.[573] Major Margaret Witt was a Reservist flight nurse who had served 18 years in the armed forces. From 1997 to 2003, she was in a committed relationship with a civilian, and maintained a home with the woman about 250 miles from the base where she was assigned. In July 2004, she was told she was under investigation for being gay; four months later, her superiors told her that they were beginning separation proceedings.

In March 2006, she was advised that a discharge action was being initiated and that she had the right to an administrative hearing. The next month, she filed suit in U.S. District Court for the Western District of Washington, contending that "Don't ask, don't tell" violated the equal protection clause of the Constitution, substantive due process, and procedural due process.

The court dismissed her suit, saying that it failed to state a claim, and she appealed to the U.S. Court of Appeals for the Ninth Circuit.[574] In July 2007, amid these legal proceedings, she was given an honorable discharge.

On May 21, 2008, 18 days before the *Cook* decision, the Ninth Circuit ruled against Witt's challenge, under *Lawrence*, to the overall constitutionality of "Don't ask, don't tell." But unlike the First Circuit's ruling in *Cook*, the Ninth Circuit returned the case to the district court, asking it to determine whether "Don't ask, don't tell," as applied to her individually, was unconstitutional, given that the Supreme Court had "struck down the statute as applied to anyone engaging in homosexual conduct."[575]

The Ninth Circuit held that, at the very least, *Lawrence* required the government to demonstrate on the record that any person it sought to discharge for being gay had disrupted unit cohesion. In *Cook*, the First Circuit dismissed our "as applied" challenge, holding that challenging the application of the law in individual cases was tantamount to challenging the underlying constitutionality of the law.

Under the First Circuit analysis of the "as applied" challenge, which was not an unreasonable analysis, it was difficult to see how Witt's case would survive on remand to a district court that had already ruled against her once. Yet the Ninth Circuit poked an important hole into the original premise of "Don't ask, don't tell": Where was the evidence that it undermined unit cohesion? It should not be conjecture or opinion, even of well-respected leaders, but actual evidence of disruption caused by the presence of someone who is honest about their sexual orientation.

In early 2009, as the Obama administration was settling in, I wrote a letter about Witt's case to White House Counsel Greg Craig (one of SLDN's original honorary board members) and Defense Secretary Gates. I argued that the government should not seek Supreme Court review, since the Ninth Circuit had not ruled against the constitutionality of the law. The administration followed this advice, though it's not clear that my letter had any impact.

I also argued that the government should not litigate the case further at the district court. The Ninth Circuit had handed it a victory of sorts. If the military had to conduct individual fact-specific determinations of whether a gay service member undermined military readiness, it would spend inordinate resources on those cases—and would likely lose almost all of them. As a matter of policy, the standard was unworkable.

The government didn't accept that advice, and the remanded case went to trial in September 13, 2010, three months before Congress voted to repeal "Don't ask, don't tell."

On September 24, Judge Ronald Leighton ruled in Witt's favor and ordered the Pentagon to reinstate her.[576] On November 23, one week before the Pentagon published a study concluding that lifting the gay ban was doable, the government appealed Leighton's decision to the Ninth Circuit Court of Appeals. Once "Don't ask, don't tell" was repealed, the case was rendered moot.

◆◆◆

A second case, *Log Cabin Republicans v. United States*,[577] also found success where SLDN's case had not. Heard before Judge Virginia Phillips of the U.S. District Court of the Central District of California, the suit contended that the "Don't ask, don't tell" statute was, in all applications, unconstitutional.

Phillips agreed, ruling on Sept. 9, 2010, that the statute violated the First and Fifth Amendments to the Constitution and proposing a permanent injunction on its enforcement. A month later, after hearing from both sides, she issued that injunction, effective worldwide, banning the discharge of gays from the military.

Rejecting significant testimony from the defendants about how "Don't ask, don't tell" harmed military readiness, she wrote: "[T]he Act's restrictions on speech not only are broader than reasonably necessary to protect the Government's substantial interests, but also actually serve to impede military readiness and unit cohesion rather than further these goals"—the very argument SLDN had been advancing for 17 years.

One of the odd quirks of that case is that it almost didn't happen.[578] When it was filed in 2004, the original judge on the case, Judge George Schiavelli, dismissed it without prejudice because the Log Cabin Republicans—an organization of LGBT conservatives—had not identified any member who had suffered an injury under "Don't ask, don't tell." I had urged the group's executive director not to file the case for that reason, as well as the fact that the Ninth Circuit had issued a series of decisions upholding "Don't ask, don't tell," making its argument harder to prevail.

Log Cabin refiled the case, identifying two members of the organization harmed by "Don't ask, don't tell"—an "honorary member," Alex Nicholson, who was being trained in counterintelligence when he sought the assistance of his superiors to stop rumors that he was gay and was discharged from the Army in March 2002, and "John Doe," a lieutenant colonel on active duty. The optics of filing as "Log Cabin Republicans" (and not the names of the two individuals) weren't ideal, but the court granted standing.

Schiavelli was seriously injured in an escalator accident in 2005,[579] and the case went into a black hole. In 2008, he stayed the lawsuit, pending final disposition of the *Witt* case. While the stay was in effect, he resigned from the bench, and the case was reassigned to Phillips.[580] A nonjury trial was held over two weeks in July 2010.[581]

"We have been surprised at every stage of this," Nicholson said after Phillips issued the injunction. "We thought the judge would follow every other pattern the other judges have followed: deference to the military."[582]

The *Log Cabin* and *Witt* cases applied pressure to the political process at a critical juncture: If Congress wasn't going to repeal "Don't ask, don't tell," the courts just might take action, through an injunction, that would have the same effect. Gates repeatedly pleaded with Congress to repeal "Don't ask, don't tell" to give the Pentagon the time to roll out revised regulations in an orderly fashion, rather than in a court-directed fashion.

It's not clear that either case would have ultimately prevailed on appeal, given previous court decisions, but the timing of these two cases and their favorable opinions added to the growing chorus for repeal.

◆◆◆

SLDN had one other case in the wings. On August 11, 2010, *Fehrenbach v. United States* was filed by SLDN and counsel from Morrison & Foerster before the U.S. District Court for the District of Idaho,[583] along with a motion for an expedited hearing.

According to the complaint, Air Force Lieutenant Colonel Victor Fehrenbach faced imminent discharge after more than 19 years of service, threatening the pension that retiring service members receive after 20 years. He was trained as a fighter weapons systems officer, flying the F-15E Strike Eagle, and served in Kuwait and Qatar following the Gulf War. In 2008, eight days before he was to deploy to Afghanistan,[584] he was falsely accused of sexual assault by a civilian who had made similar claims against other service members.[585] While those allegations were dismissed within three weeks, the Air Force continued its investigation into his sexual orientation.[586]

The case had not gone to trial when "Don't ask, don't tell" was repealed at the end of the year. Fehrenbach also was standing with Speaker Pelosi when she signed the "Don't ask, don't tell" repeal legislation; he retired from the Air Force the following year.

ENDING DON'T ASK, DON'T TELL

C. DIXON OSBURN

CHAPTER 34

STORMING THE HILL

The endgame started in 2001 and culminated in 2010. From 1993 to 2000, SLDN focused on providing direct legal aid to service members who were hurt by "Don't ask, don't tell." We documented their stories. We effectively ended the practice of witch hunts and substantially reduced the harassment our clients were facing. We educated the public and started seeing dramatic shifts in public opinion in favor of gays serving openly in the military. Where we could secure them, we pushed for policy victories. We called out the Pentagon for its failed leadership in failing to stop the witch hunts and harassment. Increasingly, pundits and decision-makers were adopting our framing of the issue: "Don't ask, don't tell" hurts military readiness.

Michelle left SLDN at the end of 2000, having put her heart and soul into our work, 24/7, for seven years. In that year's presidential election, Texas Governor George W. Bush defeated Vice President Al Gore, fulfilling my premonition when we launched SLDN that an anti-gay Republican would succeed Clinton and make a third presidency the earliest when we could realize repeal. I considered whether I should join Michelle in pursuit of new challenges so that SLDN could have fresh leadership, but I also thought that the organization needed continuity—so I redoubled my commitment, literally, for another seven years. Those who pursue social justice must invest for the long term, because civil and human rights don't come about overnight. Social justice requires long-term strategy and relationships so that when the moment presents itself, you can seize the opportunity.

In 2001, SLDN started to shift its game plan and resources, because I could foresee a time when Congress could repeal "Don't ask, don't tell" despite the Bush presidency. The board and staff agreed. Over the next four years, we consciously reduced the legal staff from four attorneys to two, plus a paralegal. We added a legal database to better track our cases, making intakes and data collection more efficient. We added a junior lobbyist, and then a senior lobbyist. At each step I checked in with Sharra Greer, our implacable legal and policy director. I could never read her poker face, so I always asked what she was thinking. I needed to know if we were staying true to our clients. She knew that we were pushing the edge of what we were capable of doing but agreed with our strategy.

The year 2003 was the 10th anniversary of the enactment of "Don't ask, don't tell." It also was proving to be an opportune time to kick off our legislative strategy. A Gallup poll conducted that year found that 79 percent of Americans supported gays serving openly in the armed forces,[587] up from 43 percent in 1993.[588] SLDN estimated that the Pentagon had deployed as many as 10,000 lesbian, gay, and bisexual service members to Afghanistan, Iraq, and other locations in the Middle East.[589] All of our major military allies, including the United Kingdom and Israel, had lifted their bans. U.S. troops were serving alongside openly gay troops of our allies in Afghanistan and Iraq, and in joint operations with United Nations and NATO forces.[590] Our troops were serving alongside openly gay civilian operatives from the Department of Defense, the Central Intelligence Agency, the National Security Agency, and others. The Palm Center produced peer-reviewed reports concluding that the presence of openly gay troops from Canada,[591] Australia,[592] and Britain[593] was a nonissue in our allied forces and in joint operations.

The war in Iraq was straining the capacity of the Army, the Marine Corps, the National Guard and the Reserves. The Pentagon was still discharging up to two service members every day for being gay, which, predictably, was 40 percent fewer than before the war. Among those being discharged were gay service members in specialties the Pentagon deemed critical, including Arabic linguists. Two retired brigadier generals and one retired rear admiral—Keith Kerr, Virgil Richard, and Alan Steinman—had all come out as gay. The cost of the ban was staggering, as shown in our annual reports and in other reports produced by the Palm Center and the GAO. Evidence showed that "Don't ask, don't tell" was a failed policy. Popular support for nondiscrimination was mounting.

We officially launched our Freedom to Serve campaign in 2003.[594] It included a bill to repeal "Don't ask, don't tell" and a coordinated lobbying campaign. We branded our local fundraisers "Freedom to Serve" to match our vision that lesbian, gay, and bisexual Americans should be able to serve freely, defending the freedoms that they swore to protect. We produced ads and placards with bold images of our clients, draped in the American flag or holding pins and medals, with the taglines "Let Him Serve," "Let Her Serve," "Let Them Serve," and "Here to Serve."

We drafted legislation, coordinating our efforts with Marty Meehan, a Democrat on the House Armed Services Committee. We called it the Military Readiness Enhancement Act—MREA, pronounced "Maria." (At one of our gala dinners, channeling my best Mother Abbess in *The Sound of Music*, I sang, "What do you do with a solution like Maria?" A pundit covering an SLDN event once wrote that my "dorkism ... only further endeared him to the crowd," which made me smile.[595])

MREA would repeal "Don't ask, don't tell," and replace it with a law of nondiscrimination. It specifically made benefits concessions to comply with the Defense of Marriage Act (marriage equality was banned at the time) and ensured that chaplains would not face persecution for their individual religious beliefs regarding sexual orientation.

It did not overturn transgender discrimination because "Don't ask, don't tell" was a law that specifically referenced sexual orientation. We were concerned that we would make the situation worse for transgender service members should members of Congress use our bill as a vehicle to convert the regulations governing transgender service into statute. (That's what happened when President Clinton tried to lift the ban in 1993: Lawmakers intervened to make it a statute that only Congress or the courts could overturn.)

The secretary of defense retained the authority to change the regulations governing transgender service; it was even possible, we thought, that ending transgender discrimination could precede repeal of "Don't ask, don't tell," depending on whether a future administration would be more favorable than Congress. We consulted extensively with leaders of the transgender community, who agreed with our strategy—but since they had excoriated the Human Rights Campaign for not including transgender Americans in the Employment Nondiscrimination Act, they preferred to provide quiet support. The strategy to end transgender discrimination ultimately worked as planned, though there were obstacles along the way.

We knew that we would have to build support for repeal of "Don't ask, don't tell" over several years in Congress, perhaps much longer, and that an actual bill was the best vehicle to do so. Members of Congress do not commit to hypothetical legislation but will sign up as co-sponsors to something on paper.

With our support (and thanks to our behind-the-scenes efforts), the Military Readiness Enhancement Act was introduced in the House of Representatives in 2005, 2007, and 2009, and in the Senate in 2010. We always knew that its original language and intent might not survive, and we were prepared with backup plans, including language that repealed "Don't ask, don't tell" and returned regulatory authority to the Department of Defense—General Powell's preferred outcome in 1993. In each session of Congress, more members signed on. We secured 122 House sponsors in 2005, 149 in 2007, and 192 in 2009. In 2010, for the first time, a companion bill with 33 co-sponsors was introduced in the Senate.[596] Momentum was building.

Meehan was our champion in 2005 and 2007. He agreed that the issue had to be positioned first as one of national security, and then as one of civil rights. He embraced our introduction strategy—a press conference where he would be surrounded by three generals and an admiral. He agreed with our title for the bill: the Military Readiness Enhancement Act, signifying that this was legislation to support national security. He invested the time required as the bill's lead sponsor, calling his colleagues and building support.

Meehan had long demonstrated passion for this issue. In 1993, as a freshman congressman, he introduced an amendment that would have killed enactment of "Don't ask, don't tell" as a law and left it to the secretary of defense to adjust the regulations on gays in the military. The amendment failed, and Congress removed the secretary of defense's discretion to regulate this personnel matter.

Some who thought "Don't ask, don't tell" was a step forward failed to recognize that Congress made it much harder to change the policy because it was a law, not a regulation. Future presidents could not, as Clinton had sought to do, issue an executive order to end the discrimination without igniting a constitutional showdown over whether the executive or legislative branch had plenary authority to regulate military personnel matters. Future secretaries of defense could not suspend military regulations on gays to end discrimination or boost retention, even given the strain of military capacity caused by the Afghanistan and Iraq wars.

In the mid-1990s, I asked Meehan to speak to a small group of SLDN's major donors. It was a hot July day, and just before the event started, the air conditioning conked out. As sweat streamed down his face and mine, Meehan told the group that repeal of "Don't ask, don't tell" was one of his top three issues. "I want to be able to look my grandchild in the eye one day and tell her we made the world a better place," he said.

Pennsylvania Democrat Patrick Murphy, who in 2010 would lead the final push in the House for repeal, said much the same thing when asked why he cared so deeply.

"It's pretty simple," he said. "I have two little kids who are five and two, and I want them to be proud of what their daddy fought for when he had the chance to serve his country."[597] Having fought enemy fire in Iraq, he would face death threats at home for leading the repeal effort.[598]

◆◆◆

The hardest days are those where your personal and professional worlds collide. One of those days for me was March 1, 2005.

We were making plans to announce the repeal bill the next day. We had arranged for three generals and an admiral to come into town for the press conference. We had lined up an exclusive with *The New York Times*, to be followed by an Associated Press story. Everything was clicking.

But Meehan's press secretary broke our press embargo and leaked the story to *The Boston Globe*, the congressman's hometown paper. That ended the arrangements we had made with *The Times* and the AP. It also threatened to undermine the press conference and massive outreach effort that had been planned for months. Allies do not always do what is smart.

Word then came that Meehan was having second thoughts about going forward with the introduction. He wasn't abandoning the idea; he just had other things he wanted to do—or so his staff said. I immediately placed a call to his office and asked him to get back to me promptly.

As I tried to reach Meehan, my stepmother called. My 74-year-old father, who lived near Houston, had significant blockages in the arteries of his brain and complete occlusion in several coronary arteries. The doctors were recommending immediate open-heart surgery the next day and were advising that the surgery carried a serious risk of stroke or death.

My chest tightened. That was just a little too much to bear. So, as I called Meehan's office once again, I went online to determine how early and how quickly I could get to Houston for the surgery if that moved forward. I called my sister to see if she could come from her home in Laguna Beach, California, for the surgery. She couldn't. I spoke with my mother, who had been divorced from my father for 20 years and was living with my sister, to let her know what was happening. She was battling stage 4 lung cancer, and it felt as if Mom and Dad were now in a macabre competition.

I tried to calm Steve Ralls, our director of communications. He was thin as a wisp, a bundle of energy with bottle-blond hair and a Madonna fetish. He was one of the best communications professionals in the business. Sharp, quick, funny, responsive, he was the Radar O'Reilly in SLDN's MASH unit. He was now apoplectic as months of media strategy and preparation were coming unraveled.

Steve was being pummeled by reporters who were angry at him for the leak. He said it was not his doing and tried to assuage them. The reporters, however, rightfully expected full coordination among legislative partners. Many papers decided not to run a story. Where the story ran, it was relegated to the back pages.

I scrambled to fully delegate the next day to Sharra. Like Steve, Sharra is one of the best leaders I know. She is a Zen master of lists and strategy—always organized, always prepared, ensuring that the trains are moving on time despite endless interruptions.

I didn't want to miss the bill's introduction. The initial co-sponsor list included 52 names, significantly more than we had anticipated. It was going to be one of SLDN's biggest days. But I had a firm rule for myself and my staff: family and health come first. The work will always be here. You are surrounded by wonderful colleagues who will drop what they are doing to help in time of need.

Meehan called me back.

"Congressman," I said, "we have three generals and an admiral coming into town tomorrow, and we have a big press conference lined up. These VIPs do not have any flexibility. I want to make sure that we are moving forward as scheduled with the introduction tomorrow."

"Yes, we are. I'm looking forward to it." Meehan's staff had gotten it wrong, or perhaps he had caught wind of our concern. (As it turned out, my father's surgery was postponed, and I was able to be present for his two successful operations later that summer. My mother passed away on Veterans Day.)

The next day, as scheduled, Meehan announced that he was introducing the Military Readiness Enhancement Act—the legislation that would repeal "Don't ask, don't tell." He was flanked by Alan Steinman, Keith Kerr, and Virgil Richard—and another retired brigadier general, Evelyn Foote, who served as the first female commander of Fort Belvoir, Virginia, in 1988 and 1989. Repealing "Don't ask, don't tell," she said, was "a critical way to begin bringing the military into the 21st century."[599]

Our strategy was noticed. "Smart," wrote political blogger Steve Benen, who would later become a contributor to *Washington*

Monthly and a producer for *The Rachel Maddow Show*. "It's not about civil rights; it's about a stronger military. It has nothing to do with discrimination, and everything to do with military readiness. We're not concerned about homophobia; we're concerned about keeping highly trained translators on [the] job, screening intercepts that may include terrorist plots that could kill Americans."

Meehan, he added, deserves "a lot of credit—he's not only pushing the right bill at the right time, he's playing the politics perfectly."[600] Behind every smart politician is a smart NGO.

Deb Price, a columnist who wrote about gay issues for *The Detroit News*, noted in 2006 that SLDN's "modest, pragmatic approach toward getting rid of 'Don't ask, don't tell' is the most likely way the ban will be lifted and a repeat of the painful crisis of 1993 avoided."[601]

We were deliberately bipartisan from the outset. Ileana Ros-Lehtinen, a Florida Republican, said this of the gay ban: "I don't think it works. And we've spent a lot of money enforcing it. ... We investigate people. Bring them up on charges. Basically wreck their lives. People who've signed up to serve our country. We should be thanking them."[602]

We grew the co-sponsors list from 52 to 122 through the dedicated advocacy of our policy director, Sharon Alexander, and our annual "lobby day," an event we launched in 2003. We asked our supporters who had the time and inclination to join us in Washington to educate their senators and representatives about the imperative of "Don't ask, don't tell" repeal. The call to duty was met.

We were rigorous in our approach. We trained our supporters for a full day on the in and outs of Congress. We wanted them to know what to expect going into the meetings; we helped them craft the best talking points tailored to their experience and their member of Congress. SLDN met with more than 100 offices in 2003,[603] including 18 of the 25 members of the Senate Armed Services Committee.

One of my favorite moments in 2005 came as I was escorting Keith Kerr and Virgil Richard in the Senate office buildings. We happened to run into Senator Hillary Clinton, who was surrounded by another group. I asked the generals if they would like to speak with her, and they eagerly nodded. To them, she was a rock star.

"Sirs," I said, "I don't know if we can do it, but hold on." I waited for the second that Clinton started to pivot away from the group, then asked in a stentorian voice, "Senator Clinton, do you have time to speak with two generals today?"

She came right over with her trademark warm smile. The best members of Congress understood the importance and stature of generals. To her, *they* were the rock stars.

I turned to the generals and said, "Sirs, tell Senator Clinton why you are here today." They immediately launched into crisp talking points about the failure of "Don't ask, don't tell."

Without missing a beat, she replied, "Bill was so stupid to go with 'Don't ask, don't tell.' It is a terrible policy. Let me know what I can do to help."

The office of Senator Kay Bailey Hutchison, a Republican from Texas, did the opposite. Instead of talking with her, Virgil and I—her fellow Texans—stood in the hallway and spoke with a low-level staffer. She received a tart letter from me after the incident. It is possible to disagree without being disagreeable.

◆◆◆

In 2007, we geared up for the second introduction of the Military Readiness Enhancement Act, again with Meehan at the helm, accompanied by our coterie of generals and admirals. It too almost got derailed—not by an errant press secretary, but by the intervention of the Human Rights Campaign, which asked the congressman to not go forward.

Meehan called me. "Human Rights Campaign says the bill should not go forward. You've got to work it out and let me know."

"Yes, sir. There must be some confusion. I'll get back to you shortly."

I was stunned. David Smith, a top official at the Human Rights Campaign, had told Meehan that our bill would upstage their efforts to secure an overall nondiscrimination bill and a hate crimes bill. Meehan, appropriately, did not want to mediate internecine wars.

Smith's message was more strident than what his boss, Joe Solmonese, had said when LGBT leaders met in 2006 to discuss the prospects of LGBT equality legislation. Solmonese said that the priorities for the Human Rights Campaign were—and for the LGBT community should be—passage of the Hate Crimes Act and the Employment Nondiscrimination Act. ENDA would provide civilian job protection against anti-gay discrimination.

"Joe," I said, "I would like to offer a friendly amendment. I think you are exactly right that ENDA and the hate crimes bill will likely get to a vote first, and SLDN stands full-square behind you on that, but we would be wise to keep in mind that you never know what external event or spark of energy might ignite support for a different bill, and we should make sure we are able to align around that moment.

"For example, what if a gay Special Operations officer finds bin Laden and is then discharged? That could ignite such outrage that the public demands repeal of 'Don't ask, don't tell.' Let's just be ready."

(As it happened, the hate crimes bill became law first, in October 2009,[604] 14 months before "Don't ask, don't tell" repeal. ENDA, later called the Equality Act, never passed. In 2020, the Supreme Court ruled in *Bostock v. Clayton County* that LGBT discrimination in the workplace was unconstitutional sex discrimination under Title VII of the Civil Rights Act of 1964.[605])

I was appalled by Human Rights Campaign's subterfuge. We had been coordinating the reintroduction strategy with our allies for months, through our Freedom to Serve roundtable. I convinced Solmonese that the reintroduction of the Military Readiness Enhancement Act would in no way impair their legislative strategies, which we supported, but David Smith wanted something. He demanded that a representative of the Human Rights Campaign participate in the events accompanying the reintroduction of the legislation.

The speaker they proposed was Staff Sergeant Eric Alva, the first marine injured in the war in Iraq and a gay man. Alva is a dynamic guy, with energy exuding from every pore. He had served in the Marine Corps for 13 years. On March 21, 2003—the first day of Operation Iraqi Freedom—he was in a convoy to Basra with his battalion, in charge of 11 marines, when he stepped on an improvised explosive device and lost his right leg. His closest friend ran to help him, and another IED detonated and severely injured him. That is unit cohesion. That is one buddy looking after the other. Some knew he was gay. Sexual orientation didn't matter. The military awarded Alva a Purple Heart. President Bush and Secretary of Defense Donald Rumsfeld visited him in the hospital.

I agreed without hesitation. Though the Human Rights Campaign's underhandedness was wrong, Alva was a star, and his story was important. We had to check our egos and outrage at the door for the greater good. I also knew that we would need the help of the Human Rights Campaign as we neared the finish line.

Along with the reintroduction of the bill, we sponsored a rally in front of the Capitol. Joining me on stage were Representatives Tammy Baldwin and Barney Frank, Keith Kerr, Virgil Richard, Joan Darrah, Frank Kameny, and many more. Supporters hoisted signs urging that the ban be lifted. I gave a call to action, fist in the air, with the white Capitol dome and crisp blue skies behind me.

Again, our strategy was getting noticed.

"There has been an agenda in the sense of a long-term strategy, not unlike the carefully plotted strategy of Thurgood Marshall and others in the civil rights movement that ended formal racial segregation," Michael Kinsley wrote in *Time*. "It was a brilliant decision to start with the military rather than attempt to outlaw discrimination generally or push right away for gay marriage. Twenty years from now, maybe sooner, gays will have it all."[606] While it was not our view that the movement was leading with the military strategy, I was humbled by the comparison to a civil rights icon.

The Human Rights Campaign wasn't the only challenge from our allies. After reintroduction of the Military Readiness Enhancement Act, the Palm Center's Aaron Belkin decided to float a different bill—one that would exempt only Arabic linguists who were gay from discharge under "Don't ask, don't tell."

Without telling us, he started lobbying Meehan and two more Democratic congressmen, Gary Ackerman and Steve Israel, to introduce a linguist waiver bill. Meehan again called me to find out what was going on.

Belkin's view was that an Arabic linguist waiver bill had a high chance of success. Kicking out Arabic linguists during wartime had received tremendous publicity, and it symbolized the failure of "Don't ask, don't tell." He argued that getting the bill passed would put the proverbial camel's nose under the tent and lead to full repeal.

His argument had a certain appeal. Compromise is one of the hallmarks of legislative strategy. But you have to be careful not to suck the oxygen out of the room, or you'll choke off the bigger goal. The question is: How do you distinguish between the two scenarios?

A compromise bill is good if it's all you can get and it doesn't harm the longer-term goal. The linguist waiver bill would have been seen as a proxy for "Don't ask, don't tell," and it potentially would have killed momentum for the larger repeal effort. Some members of Congress might have taken the position that a vote for the waiver bill would fix the only problem in the current law. Others might have seen their vote on the waiver as all that can, or should, be done for the next five or 10 years. And in 2007, it was doubtful that we could muster enough votes even for a linguist bill.

From an operational standpoint in the armed forces, the linguist waiver also would have been unworkable. "What do you do with Arabic linguists who get promoted to other duty assignments that do not include linguistics?" I asked Belkin. "Do the gays get fired then? What does the commander tell the Soldier of the Quarter who comes out as gay but is not a linguist? Will the commander say, 'I'm sorry, but the law requires me to discharge you, but I must keep the mediocre linguist?'" Disparate treatment undermines unit cohesion.

Belkin made his proposal while the Military Readiness Enhancement Act was before the House for only the second time. If the 2008 elections produced results favoring our position, all signs pointed to gathering momentum in the House and the Senate for full repeal. Those predictions came true. If we had pushed for a vote on a compromise—the linguist waiver—in 2007, it could have been disastrous for repeal efforts.

To our great surprise, Meehan decided to leave Congress several months after introducing the Military Readiness Enhancement Act to accept a job as chancellor of his alma mater, the University of Massachusetts at Lowell. We needed to find a lawmaker to act as a point of contact for other members of Congress to add their names to the bill as co-sponsors. Ellen Tauscher, a Democrat who sat on the House Armed Services Committee, stepped up to lead the effort.[607]

In July 2008, that panel's military personnel subcommittee, chaired by Susan Davis, held the first hearings on "Don't ask, don't tell" since the policy's inception in 1993. Witnesses in favor of repeal included Joan Darrah of the "magnificent seven," Eric Alva, and retired Major General Vance Coleman. Coleman is the heroic figure whom organizers of the Millennium March on Washington for Equality in 2000 tried to erase from the program, the first general ever to address a gay rights rally. He, like Joan Darrah, served on SLDN's Military Advisory Council.

The unifier for the hearing was SLDN's arch-enemy, Elaine Donnelly, president of the Center for Military Readiness (to my colleagues, I called it the Center for Military Disarray). An acolyte of Phyllis Schlafly, her mission in life was to oppose gays and women in the military. She warned the subcommittee that if the gay ban was lifted, the military would be rife with "inappropriate passive/aggressive actions common in the homosexual community," "exotic forms of sexual expression," and "HIV positivity," among other dire prospects. She warned of the "San Francisco left, who want to impose their agenda on the military."

One committee member, Democrat Vic Snyder, called Donnelly's statement "just bonkers" and "dumb," Bringing up HIV, he added, was "inappropriate."

"By this analysis," he said, "you know what we ought to do. We ought to recruit only lesbians for the military, because they have the lowest incidence of HIV in the country."

Chris Shays, a Republican who was one of our earliest champions, also laid bare her false claims. When Donnelly told the lawmakers that she "respects the service of Captain Darrah, General Coleman, Sergeant Alva, everybody who serves in the military," he responded: "How do you respect their service? You want them out."[608]

As Dana Milbank wrote in *The Washington Post*, "Donnelly achieved the opposite of her intended effect."[609]

I was there for that hearing and saw we were getting closer to the day that repeal could happen. Julie Kruse, who was one of SLDN's fearless lobbyists and helped put the hearing together, was smiling from ear to ear. All the years of education and hard work were paying off. The 2008 elections would prove to be a final pivot to victory, though not without twists and turns.

CHAPTER 35

STOP LOST

The momentum for repeal continued to build. Gay discharges were dropping as the United States fought two wars in Iraq and Afghanistan. The number of cases where commanders retained openly gay personnel continued to grow. *The Boston Globe* reported that the military retained 12 openly lesbian, gay, and bisexual service members in 2003, 22 in 2004, 36 in 2005.[610] SLDN sent letters to commanders who retained openly gay service members, congratulating them for being civil rights heroes.

Army Sergeant Darren Manzella was the epitome of the competent, well-regarded openly gay soldier who put a lie to the belief that his mere presence would weaken military readiness. He was out to his Army buddies and had even introduced them to his boyfriend.

In 2006, while serving at Fort Hood, Texas, he started getting anonymous emails and calls warning him that he was being watched and to "turn the flame down." Seeking advice, he went to his lieutenant and "told"—and the lieutenant reported the conversation up the chain of command.[611] That triggered an investigation, during which Manzella held nothing back, even submitting photos of him and his boyfriend. His unit knew that he was gay and rallied around him.

The Army's conclusion: He wasn't gay. He was told to get back to work. "I thought it was a big step when they told me that they were going to retain me," he told CNN.[612]

Manzella's unit was sent back to Iraq later that year. The Damocles sword of "Don't ask, don't tell" still hung over him, though, and he didn't know if his current commander—or a new one—would try to discharge him.

SLDN contacted Manzella while he was deployed to see if he would be willing to tell his story to *60 Minutes*.[613] SLDN counseled him on the pros and cons of doing the interview, notably that coming out in such a public fashion would likely trigger discharge, despite his prior retention. He decided that it was worth the risk.

But how could he be interviewed while he was serving in Kuwait? The Army would never grant permission, nor would it allow *60 Minutes* to show up on the base uninvited. Steve Ralls, SLDN's communications director, came up with a plan.[614]

Manzella signed up to run in the Army marathon in Kuwait. At a predetermined point, he veered off-course to a waiting car that whisked him to a hotel, where he changed into civilian clothes and met with correspondent Lesley Stahl. After the interview, he changed back into his running clothes, the crew doused him with sweaty water, and the car whisked him back so he could cross the finish line.

Once the segment was broadcast, the Army could no longer pretend that Manzella wasn't gay, or that "Don't ask, don't tell" was a law with an on-off switch. He was discharged six months later and became one of the many vocal advocates for repeal.

In August 2013, as he was pushing a stranded vehicle from the road, Manzella was struck by a car and killed. I attended his service at St. John's Episcopal Church on Lafayette Square across from the White House. Brigadier General Tammy Smith, the first open lesbian to attain the rank of general after the ban was lifted, gave the eulogy, saying that she "carried a piece of his courage in her heart every day."

◆◆◆

Barack Obama's election in November 2008 presented a new opportunity to press for the repeal of "Don't ask, don't tell." During the campaign, he had mentioned repeal more often than any other LGBT issue. Aware of Obama's interest, Mike Mullen, the chairman of the Joint Chiefs of Staff, formed a five-person working group so that he could better understand "Don't ask, don't tell" and how it had evolved since 1993.[615] His preparation would pay dividends when he was asked to testify before the Senate Armed Services Committee in 2010.

Obama was joined in office by a strong Democratic majority in the House and the Senate, ushered in by an economy teetering on the brink of depression and anger over the Bush administration's lies about the reasons for the Iraq War.

Speaker of the House Nancy Pelosi met with LGBT leaders prior to the inauguration. The consensus among their groups, with the Human Rights Campaign in the lead, was to prioritize hate crimes and employment non-discrimination legislation over "Don't ask, don't tell."[616] In June, *Stars and Stripes* reported that "an official with the House Democratic leadership said the House is committed to repealing 'don't ask' but has agreed with civil rights groups to put new hate crime legislation and a workplace non-discrimination bill on the legislative calendar before taking up the military issue."[617] In August, seven months into the new administration, the Human Rights Campaign's Joe Solmonese said that he saw "a road map of six-month windows: the hate crimes bill, then the Employment Non-Discrimination Act, then 'Don't ask, don't tell.'"[618] The failure to prioritize "Don't ask, don't tell" in 2009 could have derailed repeal.

The White House also didn't prioritize "Don't ask, don't tell," though it signaled repeatedly that it remained committed to repeal. Obama entered office with an economy in free fall and plans for significant overhaul of the health care system. As for "Don't ask, don't tell," wrote Bryan Bender of *The Boston Globe*, the White House "does not want to ask lawmakers to do it until the military has completed a comprehensive assessment of the impact that such a move would have on military discipline. Then, the president hopes to be able to make a case to members of both parties that overturning the 1993 law would be in the best interest of national security."[619] By doing so, Obama hoped to avoid the "fierce resistance from lawmakers and commanders" that Clinton had encountered when he proposed lifting the gay ban in 1993. And while there was, as Bender noted, good reason for the

Obama administration to move cautiously on the issue, there was a critical caveat to that strategy: "A delay," said Nathaniel Frank of the Palm Center, "could let opposition fester and build."[620]

On March 2, Ellen Tauscher reintroduced the Military Readiness Enhancement Act in the House of Representatives. It was the third time that the House would consider the bill, but the first since the chamber was put in Democratic hands.

I was concerned about the launch. Unlike in 2005 and 2007, it didn't feature a press conference with the lead sponsor surrounded by retired generals and admirals. Instead, it was held at a progressive think tank, the Center for American Progress.

The optics weren't ideal, but they weren't bad. Speakers included Lawrence Korb, a CAP senior fellow, an assistant secretary of defense in the Reagan administration, and an SLDN ally; Nathaniel Frank, whose compelling book *Unfriendly Fire* (which documented the failure of "Don't ask, don't tell," drawing heavily on SLDN's work) was published that same day;[621] and the Human Rights Campaign's spokesman, Eric Alva. I was glad to see the increased commitment from the Human Rights Campaign and the Center for American Progress, two heavyweights in the political fight ahead, but concerned that while SLDN's historic fingerprints were everywhere, its visibility was not. The Military Readiness Enhancement Act, after all, was the bill drafted by SLDN.

News of Obama's intent to study "Don't ask, don't tell" and then push for its repeal was made clear in early interviews. On the same day that Tauscher reintroduced MREA, a White House spokesman, Tommy Vietor, said, "The president supports changing 'Don't ask, don't tell.' As part of a longstanding pledge, he has also begun consulting closely with Secretary Gates and Chairman

Mullen so that this change is done in a sensible way that strengthens our armed forces and our national security."[622]

That same month, though, Gates offered a cautionary note about timing of any substantive conversation about repeal, saying he preferred to "push that one down the road a little bit" and raising concerns in the LGBT community about the sincerity of the efforts underway.[623]

In April, Obama, Gates, Pentagon general counsel Jeh Johnson, Attorney General Eric Holder, Solicitor General Elena Kagan, White House senior advisor Valerie Jarrett, and Marine General James Cartwright, vice chairman of the Joint Chiefs of Staff, met in the Roosevelt Room at the White House to discuss how to respond to the Ninth Circuit's decision in *Witt*.[624] The court had ruled that the military must provide fact-specific evidence as to how a lesbian service member undermined unit cohesion and had remanded the case to the lower court for further review.

The White House wanted Pentagon collaboration on its plans for repeal, but there was significant resistance among senior uniformed leaders. Johnson recalled that in the first 30 days of the Obama administration, the judge advocate general of the Air Force, Lieutenant General Jack Rives, had told him that the Pentagon had to immediately petition the *Witt* decision to the Supreme Court. "There's a storm a-coming here," Johnson thought.[625]

Kagan, whose office argues the government's position in cases before the Supreme Court, asked for the Pentagon's views on whether to ask the justices to review *Witt*. It was Johnson's task to articulate the Pentagon's position. Obama left it to the Pentagon to decide, but the position was carefully negotiated with Holder. The decision, expressed in an April 20 letter, was to let the district court and the Ninth Circuit hear the case again before determining whether a petition to the Supreme Court was necessary.[626]

On April 2, a Pentagon spokeswoman, Cynthia Smith, confirmed that Gates and Mullen "are discussing how to move forward on this issue and discussions are still ongoing."[627] An April 16 article in *The New York Times* confirmed that Gates had begun discussions with the president and Mullen.[628]

On May 21, the Pentagon's chief spokesman, Geoff Morrell, said that Gates and Mullen were "working to address the challenges associated with implementation of the president's commitment," which would be done in "a way that is least disruptive to our troops."[629] Three days later, Mullen told *This Week with George Stephanopoulos*:

> "The president has made his strategic intent very clear. That it's his intent at some point in time to ask Congress to change this law. ... And so I've had discussions with the Joint Chiefs about this. I've done certainly a lot of internal, immediate staff discussions about what the issues would be. ... And what I also owe the president, and I owe the men and women in uniform, is an implementation plan to achieve this based on a timeline that would be set, obviously, after the law is changed."[630]

What is critical to note was that Obama had asked his top defense officials not to debate *whether* lesbian, gay, and bisexual service members should serve, but to study *how* to implement repeal once Congress had voted to do so. This was a monumental sea change, made possible by the years of groundwork laid before.

Around that same time, I met with Brian Bond, the deputy director for White House public engagement and the former executive director of the Gay & Lesbian Victory Fund. We sat on a park bench in Lafayette Park across from the White House, near the statue of Friedrich Wilhelm von Steuben, a Prussian general recruited by George Washington to serve in the Continental Army. Von Steuben was the author of *Regulations for the Order and Discipline of the Troops of the United States*, which remains the core doctrine for military good order and discipline today.[631] It is also widely believed that he was gay.[632]

"How do we get this done?" Bond asked me, referring to repeal.

"You have to have Pentagon buy-in before moving forward," I said. "You must get Gates and Mullen to support and lead the repeal effort in Congress. Then Congress will follow, and so will the chain of command. This is critical. Convince the military leadership and move when they can lead the fight."

◆◆◆

On May 2, *The Washington Post* published a column by Richard Socarides, President Clinton's LGBT liaison, challenging Obama to be the fierce advocate he had pledged to be during the campaign.[633] On May 4, Obama's national security advisor, retired Marine General Jim Jones, told the *Post* that he had advised the president not to add "Don't ask, don't tell" repeal to his "already full plate," and the president had taken his advice.[634] On May 7, *The New York Times* reported growing frustration among the LGBT community regarding Obama's inaction on gay rights.[635]

That same day, the White House invited members of some prominent LGBT organizations to meet with Deputy Chief of

Staff Jim Messina to discuss legislative strategy on hate crimes as well as "Don't ask, don't tell."[636] Coming out of the meeting, the Human Rights Campaign's Joe Solmonese said, "They have a strategy. They have a plan"[637]—but never said exactly what that plan was.

Tobias Wolff, the top LGBT advisor to the Obama campaign, offered insight on the president's cautious approach: "I think he has a genuine sense that in order to move these issues forward, you need broader buy-in than you are going to get if you poke a stick in too many people's eyes." [638] In other words, he wanted to get Pentagon buy-in and then move.

On May 11—two months after MREA was reintroduced, but before it could gain any legislative traction—the Palm Center released a report calling on Obama to issue an executive order invoking stop-loss authority to immediately suspend all gay discharges pending repeal.[639] A stop-loss order is the involuntary extension of service beyond the term of enlistment during a national emergency. The strategy was based on a legal memo, commissioned by the Palm Center, concluding that the president had the authority under stop-loss to immediately suspend discharges under "Don't ask, don't tell."

Aaron Belkin explained that his strategy was to "bash" Obama into action.[640] The month before, *Newsweek* columnist Anna Quindlen had called on the president to issue an executive order.[641] The Center for American Progress echoed the recommendation in a report published on June 17.[642] Five days later, Democrat Alcee Hastings and 76 other House members sent a letter to Obama, urging him "to exercise the maximum discretion legally possible ... until Congress repeals the law ... [and] that you direct the Armed Services not to initiate any investigation of service personnel to determine their sexual orientation."[643]

The president, as commander in chief, could have issued an executive order suspending "Don't ask, don't tell" discharges until Congress acted. Any stop-loss order, though, would have been viewed as an attempt to repeal "Don't ask, don't tell" by executive fiat.

If Obama had invoked the stop-loss authority to halt discharges of gay service members, it is likely that Gates and Mullen would have opposed it, given their desire to conduct an orderly review and acclimate the armed services to the change. Gates was highly concerned about the courts overturning the ban by judicial fiat, so executive fiat would have fared no better in his estimation. Not having top military buy-in would have been fatal.

John McCain, the top Republican on the Senate Armed Services Committee, was adamantly opposed to repeal. I was concerned that he, or another member of Congress, would file a lawsuit to stop the executive order from being implemented, and would ask for, and likely obtain, an immediate injunction so that the court could adjudicate the merits of the dispute between Congress and the executive branch. Courts are loath to disrupt the status quo— in this case, the gay ban—unless there is an exigent circumstance.

Those calling for the executive order would argue that America was fighting two wars, presenting a national security emergency that ending the ban could alleviate. Nothing had changed from 2008 to 2009, however, except a pledge by the president to end the wars. President Bush had issued a stop-loss order after 9/11, at the height of a national security emergency, but it didn't include gay service members. The Army order, for example, specifically stated that "soldiers in violation of the Army's homosexual conduct policy are exempt from the stop-loss."[644] In "Think Before You Tell," a story in *The Advocate*, SLDN had even warned service members not to come out.[645]

Critics of the executive order would argue that "Don't ask, don't tell" was informed by the Pentagon, duly passed by Congress after much deliberation, and signed into law by the president, and that an executive order could not undo the will of Congress. They would further argue that the Constitution grants Congress the exclusive authority to raise and fund the Army and the Navy, and that courts have repeatedly held that such authority extends to establishing personnel policies, including "Don't ask, don't tell." In more than a dozen cases specifically litigating "Don't ask, don't tell," the courts reasoned that their powers were limited when reviewing laws, passed by Congress, that regulated military personnel matters.

The Obama administration could counter that the president also has constitutionally granted authorities to promote officers and to lead as commander in chief, that those authorities are heightened when the United States is at war, and that the statutory authority to issue a stop-loss order should override congressional authority in regulating personnel policy during time of war. As a candidate, Obama had specifically run against the concept of a unitary executive—the basis for many of the Bush administration's most egregious policies, including torture, rendition, and secret prisons.

The Palm Center's Nathaniel Frank dismissed the White House's view that "a legislative solution was more 'durable,'" calling it "unconvincing."[646]

"Some think Clinton's mistake that year [1993] was to move too quickly on this issue, without consulting the military," Frank wrote in *The New Republic*. "Indeed, it seems this has become the current White House's rationale for delay. But this is the wrong lesson. ... Clinton's error was not moving too quickly—it was moving too slowly. Indeed, it was during his proposed six-month 'time-out' that religious conservatives hijacked the debate, eroded public support for change, and defeated the president." [647]

In my view, Frank misunderstood the lesson from 1993, as well as Obama's conviction. Back in 1993, I would have agreed with Frank. I thought that Clinton had blundered by not immediately issuing an executive order ending the gay ban and ordering his top commanders to fall in line. But it is clear that Sam Nunn, then the chairman of the Senate Armed Services Committee, and others would have marched forward with a legislative ban, overturning any short-lived executive order.[648] Indeed, Senate Minority Leader Bob Dole, with the support of the Joint Chiefs of Staff, was threatening to ensure that the ban became law by placing it as a rider on the Family and Medical Leave Act legislation.[649]

The issue in 1993 and 2009 was not about timing, but about overcoming political objections. A *Washington Post* editorial noted that "the political heat Mr. Obama would face for doing so without first getting the military and key congressional constituencies on board would be intense."[650]

Yet the notion that Obama could and should issue an executive order gained traction and fueled frustration in the LGBT community, derailing energy needed to build support for repeal in Congress. At a conference in Dallas in May, an activist who had never worked on the gay ban issue told me, "You don't know what you're talking about" regarding stop-loss. The Palm Center called my opinion "uninformed."[651]

The media piled on, too. Rachel Maddow, the openly lesbian MSNBC host and the daughter of a retired Air Force captain, repeatedly chastised Obama for not issuing an executive order, accusing him of not being the "fierce advocate" he claimed he would be.[652]

"Gay leaders have been in a slow burn through much of the spring, distressed about the Obama administration's failure to press for immediate repeal of the military's 'Don't ask, don't tell' policy prohibiting openly gay men and women from serving," Ben Smith and Josh Gerstein wrote in *Politico*. "Some also chafed at the White House's refusal to suspend forced discharges of gay military personnel."[653] The newly formed California-based online petition group Courage Campaign generated over 100,000 signatures calling for a moratorium on firings.[654]

In an interview with NPR in 2011, Belkin ultimately reflected on his tactic: "I criticized the president early in his administration for moving slowly on DADT. But with three and a half years of hindsight, I give him credit. He was right to get the military's buy-in, and to move to repeal in a deliberate way."[655]

But in the heat of the moment in 2009, Obama stood in the crosshairs of the LGBT movement, and he didn't do himself many favors to quell the revolt.

When he didn't recommend including "Don't ask, don't tell" repeal (not an executive order) in the annual National Defense Authorization Act, SLDN led a march on the White House on June 23, then organized a protest two days later at a hotel where the Democratic National Committee was holding a major LGBT fundraiser.

This was a shift in tactics. SLDN had held rallies in front of the Capitol but, until now, had not conducted a direct-action protest against the president in front of the White House. I had left SLDN two years before, passing the baton to Aubrey Sarvis, an Army veteran who had previously been staff director and chief counsel of the Senate Commerce Committee and a high-powered lobbyist for Verizon.[656] I continued to play a behind-the-scenes role when useful, but Aubrey led the charge for repealing "Don't ask, don't tell" in the final three years.

An Associated Press report on the protest outside the fundraiser noted that "[s]ome gay donors had called for a boycott [of the fundraiser] after Obama's Justice Department, in a court filing, compared gay marriages to incest."[657] Others threatened to cut off the "gay ATM"[658] until the administration made real progress on equality issues. Demonstrators outside the hotel carried signs calling attendees "Gay Uncle Toms."[659] Vice President Joe Biden, the event's keynote speaker, acknowledged the controversy and promised the guests that he and Obama had every intention of supporting LGBT equality.

Michelangelo Signorile, a reporter who followed the LGBT movement closely, ripped into me on air for accepting the invitation to the DNC fundraiser. He tapped into the emerging *zeitgeist* that gays should stop supporting the DNC and the president until there were affirmative laws and policies that ended the discrimination we faced. I told him that I supported both the protesters, who should continue to apply pressure on the administration and Congress to act, and our friends inside the administration who were trying to move the ball forward. He told me on the air I could not do both. I said we would have to agree to disagree. That evening, I stood in solidarity with SLDN outside the hotel and thanked the veterans in attendance who were pushing for repeal. Then I headed inside, where I lobbied the insiders.

Four days later, the White House commemorated the 40th anniversary of the Stonewall riots with an East Room reception attended by gay and lesbian advocates.[660] In a nod to the protesters, Obama encouraged them to keep the pressure up: "Don't judge me by my words, but by the promises I keep." I told Obama that he should move more quickly and put Gates and Mullen in the lead before Congress. It would take another six months.

◆◆◆

Meanwhile, concerns arose on Capitol Hill when Obama nominated the repeal bill's primary sponsor, Ellen Tauscher, as under secretary of state for arms control and international security. Supporters were left scrambling to find new congressional leadership at the very time when most advocates thought we had the best chance to push for repeal.

On July 8, Patrick Murphy stepped up to lead the repeal efforts in the House. His leadership did not come about by accident. Two months after he was elected to the House in 2006, I met with him at the Renaissance Weekend in Charleston, South Carolina, a big confabulation for progressive thinkers. Over lunch, I talked to him about "Don't ask, don't tell" and told him that we needed his leadership.

Murphy represented the new generation of young Iraq War veterans—an Army paratrooper who had served in combat, had served with gay Americans, and thought the policy made no sense. The seed was planted. It bore fruit in 2009 as he approached Tauscher and Pelosi about assuming leadership on the bill, even though no one in the LGBT community (other than me, two years earlier) had approached him.[661]

Murphy meticulously garnered support and co-sponsors, but the legislation was stuck. Ike Skelton, chairman of the House Armed Services Committee and a long-standing foe of gays in the military, opposed considering the bill in committee.

There was no sister bill in the Senate. There also had been no Senate companion bill in 2007 or 2008, and precious time to build support had been lost. Before I left SLDN, I had lined up several possible Senate sponsors, including Chuck Schumer, Ron Wyden, and Russ Feingold. My ideal lead was Joe Lieberman, who had been Al Gore's running mate in 2000 and was now an independent who caucused with the Democrats. He was a military hawk with a strong record of working across the aisle and a champion of civil rights, but he wasn't ready in 2007 to take the lead.

Hillary Clinton offered to be a lead sponsor in 2008 but was rebuffed by SLDN after I had departed. I thought that there would be great irony in having her undo what her husband had wrought, even knowing that her sponsorship would be short-lived as she pivoted toward a presidential run. In February 2009, Ted Kennedy said that he planned to introduce a bill in the Senate but was looking for a Republican co-sponsor before doing so.[662] (He had said the same thing to us in 2005.) Sharra Greer, SLDN's law and policy director, made the pitch to him as he played fetch with his dog, Splash, in his office. SLDN announced that Kennedy would be the lead, but by then, the public knew that he had brain cancer and that, sadly, he would not be leading the charge.

Kirsten Gillibrand, who was appointed to Hillary Clinton's Senate seat after Clinton resigned to serve as Obama's secretary of state, announced in July that she was planning to offer an amendment to the National Defense Authorization Act that would block funding of "Don't ask, don't tell" investigations, effectively ending the law, but never introduced it due to a lack of support.[663] Aubrey Sarvis, who had been advocating to use that legislation as a means of repealing "Don't ask, don't tell," said, "I thought it was a long shot from the very beginning."[664]

Gillibrand then announced she was working with Murphy and Kennedy to develop support for repeal legislation and would be among the original co-sponsors of the bill when it was introduced.[665] Kennedy died on August 25, and no bill was introduced in the Senate in 2009.

Gillibrand said she did not want to introduce legislation until she had secured 60 votes to overcome a filibuster.[666]

I thought a bill should have been introduced in the Senate in 2007; if it had been, the groundwork would have been laid by 2009. Instead, activists were still floundering when Obama took office, and they continued to misdirect energy against the president, rather than toward the Senate. Barney Frank told *Roll Call* on April 27 that Congress should wait until the next year— 2010—to vote on repeal. "We haven't done the preliminary work, the preparatory work," he said. "It would be a mistake to bring it up without a lot of lobbying and a lot of conversation."[667]

Aaron Belkin published a blistering polemic on July 27 criticizing the LGBT movement for failing to pressure Obama to issue a stop-loss order.[668] He accused "gay and gay-friendly activists" of derailing his proposal and "taking the foot off the gas pedal."[669] He argued that suspending gay discharges and allowing gays to serve openly would force ultimate repeal because it would be impossible for the Pentagon "to put the toothpaste back in the tube."[670] Of course, both Presidents George H.W. Bush and Bill

Clinton had done just that—suspended gay discharges and then reinstated them. SLDN appropriately responded that the president's main role "should be to lean on Congress."[671]

Belkin was right that time was slipping away, but wrong, I would submit, in his political strategy. *Politico* covered Belkin's criticism under the headline "Friendly fire," indicating how he was shooting his allies.[672]

Despite the lack of a Senate bill in 2009, Majority Leader Harry Reid breathed some life into repeal. On September 24, he sent letters to Gates and Obama, urging them to "bring to Congress your recommendations on DADT."[673]

He wrote that he had been inspired by Lieutenant Daniel Choi, whom he had met at a Human Rights Campaign dinner in Las Vegas. Choi was a West Point graduate, had served in Iraq, and was an Arabic linguist. The Army was seeking his discharge after he came out. Reid said he had also met Lieutenant Colonel Victor Fehrenbach, an 19-year Air Force officer who had flown missions against the Taliban and al-Qaeda. The Air Force was discharging him after he was outed by a third party.

But hanging over these efforts was a sense of inertia on the part of the White House. That began with a pre-inaugural statement by Obama spokesman Robert Gibbs that "there are many challenges now ... so not everything will get done in the beginning" and specifically mentioning "Don't ask, Don't tell."[674] During a June 17 press briefing, Gibbs said that the president remained committed to repeal but added, "We are working on a large amount of things"[675]—yet another in a series of administration comments that did not create the fullest confidence in Obama's actual commitment.

I believed strongly that for "Don't ask, don't tell" to be repealed, the stage in Congress had to be set in 2009 for action in early 2010, before the lawmakers got caught up in the midterm elections. The focus and pressure on the president to issue an executive order and the failure to lobby Congress frittered away precious time.

◆◆◆

On October 1, *Joint Force Quarterly*, a prestigious security journal, published "The Efficacy of 'Don't Ask, Don't Tell'" by Air Force Colonel Om Prakash.[676]

It was not the first time that someone in the military had gained notice for an article criticizing "Don't ask, don't tell." In 2007 a West Point cadet won "best thesis" award for arguing that the policy should be scrapped.[677] Prakash's essay, which would have been reviewed by the Office of the Joint Chiefs of Staff before publication, raised the critical profile significantly.

In his essay, which won the 2009 Secretary of Defense National Security Essay Competition,[678] Prakash concluded that "after a careful examination, there is no scientific evidence to support the claim that unit cohesion will be negatively affected if homosexuals serve openly." [679] He based his assessment on an analysis of several factors echoing the messages that SLDN had deployed since 1993—unit cohesion and personal integrity.

Prakash noted that "Don't ask, don't tell" requires service members to keep their sexual orientation a secret, which "has led to an uncomfortable value disconnect as homosexuals serving, estimated to be over 65,000, must compromise personal integrity ... [and] has placed commanders in a position where they are expected to know everything about their troops except this one aspect."[680] The question on everyone's mind was whether this signaled how 2010 would unfold or was just another thoughtful analysis that would be quickly forgotten.

On October 28, Obama signed into law the Matthew Shepard and James Byrd Jr. Hate Crimes Prevention Act, which had been attached as a rider to the National Defense Authorization Act. Shepard was a gay student who was tortured and murdered near Laramie, Wyoming, in 1998, the same year that Byrd, a Black man, was tied to a truck and dragged to death by white supremacists in Jasper, Texas. The Human Rights Campaign's first legislative priority had been achieved.

In December, Joe Solmonese discussed repeal strategy with Lieberman.[681] On December 24, at a birthday party for White House Communications Director Dan Pfeiffer, Obama approached Brian Bond, placed his hand on his shoulder, and said, "We are going to end 'Don't ask, don't tell.' We have a little bit of work to do still, but we are going to get it done."[682]

CHAPTER 36

MURPHY AMENDMENT

On January 27, 2010, in his State of the Union address, President Obama made this pledge: "This year, I will work with Congress and our military to finally repeal the law that denies gay Americans the right to serve the country they love because of who they are. It's the right thing to do."[683]

White House Chief of Staff Rahm Emmanuel had notified Gates about that pledge in advance, but the announcement caught Mullen by surprise.[684] Fortunately, he had been preparing for this moment for 18 months, having formed a working group to study the issue soon after Obama, as a candidate, pledged that if elected, he would repeal "Don't ask, don't tell."[685] The president then called Mullen and Gates to the White House and told them that "this would be a priority. He got no objections."[686]

The pledge had a serious defect, though: timing. Two weeks earlier, the Human Rights Campaign had held a tense meeting at its headquarters regarding an upcoming White House meeting. The timeline for repeal, the group told advocates, would not be up for discussion.[687]

The Human Rights Campaign had seized the leadership reins, and LGBT leaders met with Obama shortly thereafter. Why the Human Rights Campaign had not insisted on a timeline that would actually achieve repeal is perplexing. SLDN tried to figure out how to get the community out from being backed into a corner.

SLDN's Aubrey Sarvis praised Obama's State of the Union pledge and called on him to include repeal in the National Defense Authorization Act for fiscal year 2011, as "that is probably the only and best bill where DADT can't be killed this year."[688] A few days later, Jim Messina, deputy White House chief of staff, met with LGBT groups to discuss strategy. He didn't invite SLDN, apparently angered that Sarvis had called on the administration to include repeal in the defense authorization bill. He told the advocates that repeal would not be included in that legislation and that no action would be taken until the Pentagon had completed a study. According to *The Nation*, "Messina spoke of the difficulty of ending DADT in the midst of two wars, a remark many of the activists in the room found offensive. The Pentagon needed time to survey the troops on the impact of repeal, Messina said, which wouldn't be done until December"[689]—meaning that the White House wasn't considering repeal until 2011.

The *Washington Blade* placed blame squarely on the Human Rights Campaign: "You can't fault HRC for having White House access, but excluding experts from key meetings smacks of either petty turf wars or appeasement and pandering to an administration looking to retaliate against its critics. HRC shouldn't have played along and instead insisted on bringing Sarvis."[690]

LGBT bloggers responded by leading a "blog swarm" targeting the Human Rights Campaign, demanding that Obama commit to repeal in 2010 and taking the lead in working with Congress to make that happen.[691] Unlike the previous emphasis on issuance of an executive order to effectively repeal the law, this made great sense, because it focused on how to achieve the legislative goal within the critical window of opportunity. Either the White House hadn't forecast the possibility that Democrats could lose control of Congress in 2011, or it didn't care if "Don't ask, don't tell" became a casualty of the midterm elections.

Six days after the State of the Union address, Mullen and Gates supported Obama's call for repealing "Don't ask, don't tell" in testimony to the Senate Armed Services Committee. It was the first time that a sitting chairman of the Joint Chiefs of Staff had called for an end to the discrimination facing lesbian, gay, and bisexual service members in the armed forces.

"I have served with homosexuals since 1968," Mullen told the committee. "Everybody in the military has, and we understand that. ... No matter how I look at the issue, I cannot escape being troubled by the fact that we have in place a policy which forces young men and women to lie about who they are in order to defend their fellow citizens. For me, it comes down to integrity—theirs as individuals and ours as an institution."[692]

John Ullyot, a former spokesperson for the committee's Republicans, told *Politico* what I knew—that Mullen's support would make congressional opposition more difficult. "Republicans are in many ways better off not going to the mat over something that is supported by Secretary Gates, Admiral Mullen, and many in uniform and is rapidly becoming a non-issue for younger generations of voters," he said.[693]

As columnist Deb Price wrote, "The absolute worst nightmare of diehard defenders of Don't Ask, Don't Tell has become reality: They're now fighting the Pentagon, including the chairman of the Joint Chiefs of Staff."[694]

(In an interview 10 years later, Mullen said that what he had heard in two small focus groups helped to solidify his views.[695] In one, a marine sergeant told him that his "best battle buddy" from two tours in Iraq had come out after he had left service. "I don't care about his being gay," the sergeant told Mullen. "He was a great marine." In the other, an O-6 described how "Don't ask, don't tell" forced service members to come to work every day and lie.)

In his opening statement to the committee, Gates put the issue this way: "The question before us is not whether the military prepares to make this change, but how we must—how we best prepare for it. We've received our orders from the commander in chief and are moving out accordingly."[696]

He told lawmakers that he would ask the RAND Corporation to update a 1993 study on gays in the military and would conduct a separate review of the issues involved in implementing repeal, due "by the end of the calendar year." That review, he said would be conducted by a working group headed by the Pentagon's general counsel, Jeh Johnson, and General Carter Ham, commanding general of U.S. Army Europe. He also said he would explore how to enforce current policy in a "fairer" manner.[697] (In fact, he had already asked Johnson to examine how to make the "Don't ask, don't tell" regulations more consistent with the original intent to not ask, pursue, or harass service members.[698])

There were two ways to read Gates's testimony. One was that he and Mullen needed time to acclimate the services to the change, ensure that they could head off any rebellion, and truly understand all of the issues that a change in the law would affect, including housing, benefits, and other equal opportunity matters. The other was that he was trying to kill repeal. As *HuffPost's* Ryan Grim and Kerry Eleveld have noted, "'Study' meant one thing in Washington: delay."[699]

I worried about delay. I dashed off a note to Brian Bond at the White House reminding him that the issue had been studied to death for five decades. The Pentagon had published the Crittenden report in 1957, reports by the Defense Personnel and Security Research Center in the 1980s, and the RAND report in 1993. The GAO had produced several reports, the Palm Center dozens. All concluded, one way or another, that the Pentagon could, and should, welcome the service of openly lesbian, gay, and bisexual service members. Further study was unnecessary.

More to the point, I told Bond that the timing of the study—which now had a due date of December 1[700]—would put publication after the elections at the earliest or into the next Congress, which would all but kill repeal. To me, it looked like the Pentagon was trying to appear supportive of repeal while clearly undercutting the president's ability to accomplish it. That is how it appeared to many in the LGBT community as well. Anger continued to grow.

So did support for repeal. The day after Mullen and Gates appeared before the Senate Armed Services Committee, an old antagonist of ours, Colin Powell, issued this statement: "I fully support the new approach presented to the Senate Armed Services Committee this week by Secretary of Defense Gates and Admiral Mullen, Chairman of the Joint Chiefs of Staff. I will be closely following future hearings, the views of the Service Chiefs, and the implementation work being done by the Department of Defense."[701] He acknowledged that times and attitudes had changed, a testament to the years of communications he and I had had.

That night, Patrick Murphy, who had introduced the repeal bill in the House the previous year, was a guest on *The Rachel Maddow Show*. "How important is General Powell's change of heart on this subject?" Maddow asked.

"Absolutely huge," he replied.[702]

That's why I had built that relationship with Powell over all those years.

Powell's support opened more four-star doors. Asked on *Meet the Press* on February 21 whether soldiers in the field cared whether their comrades were gay, General David Petraeus, the head of Central Command and perhaps the most dynamic general since Powell, drew on personal experience. "I served in fact in combat with individuals who were gay and who were lesbian in combat situations and, frankly, you know, over time you said, 'Hey, how's, how's this guy's shooting?' Or 'How is her analysis,' or what have you," he said. In other words, sexual orientation was irrelevant.[703]

The next day, at a Pentagon briefing, Army General Raymond Odierno, who led the surge in Iraq, said in response to a question about "Don't ask, don't tell" repeal, "My opinion is everyone should be able to serve."

The chairman of NATO's Military Committee, Italian Admiral Giampaolo Di Paolo, told CNN's Wolf Blitzer that NATO welcomed openly gay service members, and that there was no issue with respect to military readiness or unit cohesion.[704]

The support from these military leaders gave permission to others on active duty and those in Congress to support repeal. Even Dick Cheney, who was President George H.W. Bush's defense secretary and George W. Bush's vice president, weighed in, telling *This Week* on February 14: "I see that ... Mike Mullen, the chairman of the Joint of Chiefs of Staff, has indicated his belief that we ought to support a change in the policy, so I think—my guess is the policy will be changed."[705] That was a nice Valentine's Day gift. I had reached out to Cheney in the mid-1990s, when he was CEO of Halliburton, but he never agreed to meet.

Finally, on March 3, Joe Lieberman and Carl Levin, the chairman of the Senate Armed Services Committee, introduced the Military Readiness Enhancement Act—the first time the Senate would consider the legislation.[706] Aaron Belkin had criticized Levin's lack of leadership on "Don't ask, don't tell." What he didn't understand is that Levin rarely sponsored legislation that would be considered by the committee he led. As I had explained to the *Washington Blade* two months before, Levin was "somebody who's very much a consensus-builder within the Senate Armed Services Committee. ... So if it's not percolating up in the Senate Armed Services Committee, he's going to be more reluctant, even as he believes that the law should repealed, and right now you don't have the bubbling-up within the Senate Armed Services Committee."[707] Now, Levin was on board as repeal gained traction.

I had long thought that Lieberman would be the perfect person to sponsor the repeal of our bill, and he had finally agreed to do so. "I've been asked by both the White House and the advocacy groups within the gay-rights community to be the lead sponsor, and I'm glad to do it," he said.[708]

The White House had been recruiting Lieberman for this role since at least the previous October.[709] SLDN had been speaking with him since 2000, when he was the Democrats' vice presidential candidate. He clearly supported "Don't ask, don't tell" repeal even then. SLDN's staff had met with his staff many times, trying to secure his support to lead repeal efforts in the Senate. He was willing, but he was waiting for the right time.

Mike Bauer helped to cement his participation. A quintessential connector, Mike was an indefatigable fundraiser and the go-to guy in Chicago for any Democrat. As a result, he earned some deep appreciation and opened some doors.

He also helped us with an important Chicagoan—Barack Obama. Mike was one of the first to join Obama's campaign committee when the likelihood of the first-term senator's winning the Democratic presidential nomination was seen as a long, long shot. He made sure that candidate Obama's positions on "Don't ask, don't tell" were crisp, clear, and thoughtful. In February 2008, Obama issued an open letter in which he called for "Don't ask, don't tell" repeal. The 2008 Democratic Party platform called for repeal as well, reflecting many of SLDN's long-standing talking points.[710] When Obama became president, Mike's work made all the difference, laying the groundwork to ensure that "Don't ask, don't tell" would be a priority.

Mike had also raised a lot of money for Lieberman, with whom he also shared a passion for Jewish causes. Lieberman knew him well enough that one time, when he saw Mike at a function, he made a beeline to congratulate him and his husband on their recent wedding in Canada. Mike saw Lieberman at an event at the end of 2006 and said he wanted to see him in person one of the next times he was in Washington. Lieberman agreed without reservation.

When they met, Mike asked Lieberman to consider stepping up as the lead Senate sponsor of the Military Readiness Enhancement Act. He had his pitch, partially from repeated conversations with me and partially through his own synthesis of what he thought the senator would respond to. He debriefed me over oysters at Hank's Oyster Bar on Capitol Hill.

He asked Lieberman to be the lead because there was simply no other senator who had the moral authority on matters of both national security and civil rights. Lieberman also was one of those senators who could bring Democrats and Republicans together on this issue.

Lieberman agreed to be at least a co-sponsor at the bill's introduction and said he would consider being the lead sponsor, but he didn't make a final commitment until early 2010, thanks to ongoing conversations with SLDN and the Human Rights Campaign. I am so grateful for Mike's leadership.

◆◆◆

Levin wasted no time. He scheduled a committee hearing for March 18, just two weeks after introducing the repeal bill. Star witnesses included two SLDN clients—former Navy Lieutenant (junior grade) Jen Kopfstein, who had served openly for two years before being discharged over the objections of her commanders, and a new and emerging voice, former Air Force Major Mike Almy, who had been in charge of large swaths of Iraqi air space during the Iraq War and was discharged after someone illegally searched his personal email account and found evidence that he was gay.

I was surprised that the witness list didn't also include brass who would testify about the need to repeal "Don't ask, don't tell," or other experts. The opposition witness, after all, was retired Marine General John "Jack" Sheehan, a former commander of U.S. Atlantic Command. He told the committee that the Netherlands' policy allowing gays to serve openly contributed to the inability of Dutch troops serving as a United Nations protection force to prevent the horrific Srebrenica massacre, in which the Serbian military killed more than 8,000 Bosniak men and boys in 1995.[711] His outrageous comment drew a deserved rebuke from the Netherlands.

Soon after the hearing, another top marine expressed his bias. In an interview with the website Military.com posted on March 26, the Marine Corps' commandant, General James Conway, said he "wouldn't ask our marines to live with someone that's homosexual if we can possibly avoid it. And to me that means we've got to build [barracks] that have single rooms."[712]

Two major veterans organizations also opposed repeal. In February, echoing its position from 1993, the American Legion said, "Now is not the time to engage in a social experiment that can disrupt and potentially have serious impact on the conduct of forces engaged in combat."

The Veterans of Foreign Wars also was critical: "The VFW is fully aware that societal norms regarding homosexuality have changed since the 1993 passage of [the ban], but what is considered acceptable by civilians must not be blindly imposed on a military institution that the great majority of society chooses not to join."[713]

Despite the groundbreaking testimony by Mullen and Gates in February, and by gay service members in March, many senators were hedging their bets—something that might have been averted if a bill had been introduced sooner and activists had focused their attention on Congress. Now, the activists had their work cut out for them.

Virginia Democrat Jim Webb was a swing vote, and an important one: He was a former Navy secretary, a decorated Marine Corps officer, and a senator from a state with a significant number of military bases. "I don't want to predict at all where this is going to go," he said.[714] Alaska Democrat Mark Begich said he would wait for the Pentagon to complete its investigation: "I'm leaving it to the military to help us guide us through."[715] The Human Rights Campaign and SLDN were also concerned about the votes of lawmakers from Arkansas, Indiana, Montana, Nebraska, Nevada, New Hampshire, North Dakota, Ohio, and South Dakota.[716]

Maine Republican Susan Collins swung both ways, saying that while she supported the notion that "Don't ask, don't tell" should be reviewed in light of changed circumstances since 1993, she also wanted to see the Pentagon's study.[717] No other Republican at this point was ready to commit to repeal.

The hearing also exposed a possible rift in strategy among the groups lobbying for repeal. The Human Rights Campaign favored a stand-alone bill, as did I.[718] SLDN favored attaching the bill to the National Defense Authorization Act.[719] The problem with the

NDAA strategy was that differences in the House and Senate versions of the bill would get reconciled at a conference involving the chairmen and the ranking members of the Armed Services Committees. Only Levin supported repeal. John McCain, the top Republican on the Senate panel, and the House committee's chairman and ranking member, Ike Skelton and Howard "Buck" McKeon, opposed it, so there was legitimate concern that repeal could be dropped from the final version of the legislation.

There was also a difference in how best to make the case. As the *Washington Blade* reported, "Last week's Senate Armed Services Committee hearing occurred alongside other events that brought attention to 'Don't ask, don't tell,' including Servicemembers Legal Defense Network's lobby day on Capitol Hill; the Human Rights Campaign's rally on Freedom Plaza with comedian Kathy Griffin;[720] and an act of civil disobedience by gay U.S. Army Lt. Dan Choi, who handcuffed himself to the White House gates in protest of the law."[721] SLDN went for substance; the Human Rights Campaign went for celebrity; and Get Equal, which had launched only weeks before, went ACT UP—adopting the tactics of the legendary direct action organization working to end the AIDS pandemic.

◆ ◆ ◆

The anger at Obama for his failure to be more visible, vocal, and active in pursuit of repeal continued to grow. While he and his administration had been working diligently behind the scenes to enlist the support of Mullen, Gates, and Lieberman, and consistently expressed support for repeal, it wasn't enough for a community that had been sidelined and disappointed too often.

Robin McGehee launched Get Equal to try to hold the president's feet to the fire.[722] As she explained, she wanted to take the lessons from the civil rights movement in the 1960s and create iconic moments, like Rosa Parks on the bus or the march across the Edmund Pettus Bridge. Her icon was Dan Choi, a West Point graduate who had served in Iraq and spoke Arabic.[723] He had come out to Rachel Maddow on March 19 and March 20, 2009 (two nights because the audio cut out in the middle of the first show),[724] and had just co-founded Knights Out, a gay alumni network of West Point graduates, with Sue Fulton, an inspiring officer whom I had known at the 1993 Campaign for Military Service.[725] The Palm Center had paired its stop-loss demand with Choi's imminent discharge.[726]

Choi was fresh, eloquent, and uncompromising. The image of him in uniform handcuffing himself to the White House fence made great copy every time he did it—in March,[727] April,[728] and November 2010.[729] In May 2010, he also launched a seven-day hunger strike to protest "Don't, ask, don't tell."[730]

There were those who worried about the imagery. Some were concerned about having a relatively young officer as the front man. Others feared that Choi had flouted military regulations by wearing his uniform, and that his disregard for military protocol undermined his narrative. It wasn't clear if his supporters knew how to advise him properly, and it was likely that even if "Don't ask, don't tell" was repealed, Choi had torpedoed his chances to return to service.

The choice and the risk were his. He was willing to take the risk because he believed deeply in the cause. I salute him for that commitment. I was worried that with the White House protests, too much attention was once again being diverted away from Capitol Hill, but I was grateful that Choi spoke out all around the country, galvanizing supporters.

The anger continued as the White House refused to explicitly call for "Don't ask, don't tell" repeal. *Politico* reported in April that the White House was quietly urging members not to vote on repeal that year, intensifying frustrations.[731]

Brian Bond was on the hot seat during a May 1 panel at the Equality Forum in Philadelphia. When pressed on repeal, he read a prepared statement reiterating Obama's "unequivocal" support but noting that the president wanted to wait until the Pentagon completed its study of the law.[732]

Prepared statements don't inspire much confidence. *Washington Blade* editor Kevin Naff responded, "I find it deeply troubling that the administration will not say that it supports Congress taking a vote this year on 'Don't ask, don't tell.' ... That is deeply disappointing."

Panel moderator Jarrett Barrios, president of the Gay & Lesbian Alliance Against Defamation and a former SLDN board member, said, "We are impatient and, I think, a lot of the folks out there are impatient. ... Whether it was the 'fierce advocate' speech, or whether it was the campaign, we heard a little bit more zeal than we feel right now."[733] The impression left was that the community was being managed, even if that wasn't the intent.

The Equality Forum contretemps was followed by another White House protest the next day. Organized by Get Equal and led by Dan Choi, the crowd of 300 protesters "shouted out the Pledge of Allegiance to the six people handcuffed to the fence. After reciting the last line of 'with liberty and justice for all,' attendees repeated the refrain, 'For all! For all!'"[734] People at the rally carried signs reading "Mr. Obama, what's the holdup?" Howard Dean, who had run for the Democratic presidential nomination in 2004 and then served as chairman of the Democratic National Committee, joined the protest. "We can't afford to lose any talented people," he said, "and to kick talented people out of the military because they happen to be gay or lesbian makes no sense at all."[735] More protests would follow.

Some worried that direct confrontation would backfire. As one commentator, Eric Etheridge, lamented, "I wish that Obama's progressive critics would learn to distinguish between pressing hard for the issues they care about and attacking the character of the president when he doesn't seem to be sufficiently supportive of those positions. This is not just a matter of accuracy and good manners, but also one of strategic calculation."[736]

◆◆◆

Defense Secretary Robert Gates perplexed activists because he proved both champion and obstacle during the push for repeal. David A. Graham, writing in *The Atlantic*, perhaps put his finger on why when he reported that Gates "never relied on the soaring rhetoric of rights and justice that people like Obama used. Gates spoke with the dry, careful language of a bureaucrat."[737]

On March 25, Gates delivered what he had promised in his previous Senate testimony: revised "Don't ask, don't tell" regulations intended to be "fairer and more appropriate." The Pentagon's general counsel, Jeh Johnson, had been crafting them for months. The new rules included: (1) raising the rank of an officer who is authorized to initiate a fact-finding inquiry or separation proceeding regarding homosexual conduct to a general or flag officer in the service member's chain of command; (2) raising the rank of an officer who is authorized to conduct a fact-finding inquiry to the level of lieutenant colonel, Navy commander, or above; and (3) excluding the use of confidential information in discharges, including statements made to lawyers, clergy members, mental health professionals, and others.[738]

The last bullet point was something for which SLDN had long advocated. If Clinton, Powell, Nunn, and others truly believed that "Don't ask, don't tell" carved out a zone of privacy that allowed some wiggle room for gay Americans to live and breathe, certainly it meant that they could be honest about who they are to some folks. The first two points simply moved authorization for investigations from service secretaries to officers in the chain of command, which was a difference without meaning. Most activists didn't realize that extensive inquiries already required sign-off by the service secretary, a rule that SLDN had obtained a decade before.

On April 30, it appeared that Gates was backtracking, though he was in fact consistent with his original testimony. "I strongly oppose any legislative action" before completion of the Pentagon review on December 1, he wrote in a pointed letter to Skelton. Members of the armed forces "must be afforded" the chance to share their "concerns, insights and suggestions."[739]

There was immediate blowback from the LGBT community. Brian Bond felt the heat in Philadelphia. Aubrey Sarvis issued a scathing statement, saying that SLDN "strongly repudiates any delay game." *The Washington Post's* Jonathan Capehart wrote that the Gates letter "is a stark reminder for me that pressure on the president is paramount if the repeal is to get done."[740] On May 21, *The Hill* reported that the White House continued to back Gates's plan for legislation only after the Pentagon study had been completed.[741]

◆◆◆

Gates's letter concerned not only the LGBT community, but members of Congress intent on repeal. It was clear that Skelton wouldn't move forward on including language repealing "Don't ask, don't tell" in the House version of the National Defense Authorization Act. Gates had drawn a line: He would not support repeal until the Defense Department study was completed.

Something new was needed. "The White House is facing a budding revolt over its carefully crafted strategy for repeal ... that would have pushed the decision past the November election," Michael Riley of *The Denver Post* wrote on April 20, adding that the 2010 elections would be the toughest election cycle in years for the Democrats.[742]

SLDN proposed a "60-60-60" plan. "We delay repeal for 180 days after the president signs the defense bill to ensure a timely transition to open service and an orderly implementation," Sarvis said.[743]

Chris Johnson of the *Washington Blade* explained how the plan would work: "Gates would retain authority for discharges immediately upon the legislation's passage. An estimated 60 days later, the Pentagon working group would make its recommendations on December 1. After an additional 60 days passes, the Defense Department could issue guidelines on implementing open service, and 60 days later, the services can issue their own regulations."[744] The Human Rights Campaign's David Smith called delayed implementation "essential" to achieve legislative success this year.[745]

The Center for American Progress thought that delayed repeal wasn't enough; repeal had to be contingent on certification by the Pentagon that it could work. CAP's Winnie Stachelberg floated the contingency idea to Lieberman, who thought that it could help secure the votes from the Senate Armed Services Committee that were needed to add repeal to the defense authorization bill.[746] Contingency was also crucial to securing support from the White House and the Pentagon, even though both had rhetorically said that the question was not about whether to repeal "Don't ask, don't tell," but how.

The Palm Center's Aaron Belkin was on board with delayed implementation, but he argued that the gay and lesbian communities should make even more substantive concessions. He cited a 2008 report prepared by a commission of retired generals and admirals that, among other things, recommended returning "authority for personnel policy under this law to the Department of Defense," arguing that "optimal policy sometimes collides with political reality."[747]

I had denounced the report's recommendations when it was issued in 2008, noting that the Military Readiness Enhancement Act "would not only not only repeal Don't Ask, Don't Tell, but codify a law of non-discrimination to protect lesbian, gay and bisexual service members."[748] The Palm Center proposal was premature in 2008. It remained unclear why Belkin would take non-discrimination off the table now.

While he claimed that groups backing repeal were on board with his proposal, most were not. Only Winnie Stachelberg was also of the view that Congress might not support the non-discrimination language.[749]

On May 24, the White House brought together leading congressional Democrats and LGBT leaders to hammer out a compromise. The result was the Murphy amendment, named after Patrick Murphy, the lead sponsor of "Don't ask, don't tell" repeal in the House.

The Center for American Progress produced draft language with the assistance of Wilmer Hale partner Jamie Gorelick, the former Pentagon general counsel who had helped to implement "Don't ask, don't tell" under President Clinton.[750] House Majority Leader Steny Hoyer's office won approval on the new language from Gates, Pelosi, Levin, Lieberman, and the White House.[751]

The strategy was to attach an amendment to the NDAA that would repeal "Don't ask, don't tell" legislatively, but the repeal would take effect only after the Pentagon working group completed its report and the secretary of defense, the chairman of the Joint Chiefs, and the president certified to the Senate and House Armed Services and Appropriations Committees that ending "Don't ask, don't tell" could be done without any deleterious effect on military readiness. That was CAP's strategy. Notably, though, it stripped out the non-discrimination language from the Military Readiness Enhancement Act. That was Belkin's strategy.

Belkin claimed that he "did not know why the non-discrimination language was removed."[752] But two days before the Murphy amendment compromise, *The Washington Post* published another op-ed by General Shalikashvili in which he urged Congress to support repeal "while avoiding action on a non-discrimination statute."[753]

Some repeal advocates were livid; some hedged their bets; others celebrated. "It's not anything that SLDN volunteered to give up," said Sarvis, who at the same time called the compromise a "dramatic breakthrough." "I want to get what's realistic and I want to get something that will ensure that service members can serve openly as soon as possible," he said.[754]

Joe Solmonese of the Human Rights Campaign was more optimistic: "Today's announcement paves the path to fulfill the president's call to end 'Don't ask, don't tell' this year and puts us one step closer to removing this stain from the laws of our nation."[755]

A *Los Angeles Times* editorial warned that this was less than the full rejection of "Don't ask, don't tell" that was warranted. Alex Nicholson, one of the plaintiffs in *Log Cabin Republicans v. United States* and a leader of the LGBT advocacy organization Servicemembers United, said that removing the non-discrimination language was "unnecessary" to secure support for repeal.[756] The Palm Center's Nathaniel Frank would concede in 2013 that removing the non-discrimination provision had not been necessary to win repeal.[757]

On May 24—the day of the White House meeting—Levin, Lieberman, and Murphy exchanged letters with Peter Orszag, the director of the Office of Management and Budget.[758] The lawmakers' letter announced the compromise and asked for the administration's support. Orszag, in return, said that while "ideally" the Pentagon review would be completed before Congress voted on repeal, "the Administration is of the view that the proposed amendment meets the concerns raised by the Secretary of Defense and the Chairman of the Joint Chiefs of Staff."[759]

In a somewhat petulant concession, the Pentagon's chief spokesman, Geoff Morrell, said that Gates "continues to believe that ideally the DOD review should be completed before there is any legislation to repeal the 'Don't ask, don't tell' law. With

Congress having indicated that is not possible, the secretary can accept the language in the proposed amendment."[760]

On May 27, the House of Representatives voted 234-194 to adopt repeal language as an amendment to the National Defense Authorization Act. Murphy had bypassed Skelton and the Armed Services Committee and secured permission from the Rules Committee for a vote on "Don't ask, don't tell" repeal as an amendment to the NDAA. The vote demonstrated strong support for repeal.

Murphy said that leading up to the vote he was in weekly, sometimes daily, contact with SLDN and the Human Rights Campaign to count votes and plot next steps.[761] He was armed with stories and data from SLDN and district-by-district poll numbers from the Human Rights Campaign.

On October 3, 2018, at an event celebrating SLDN's 25th anniversary, Pelosi recalled that on the day of the House vote, she turned to three liberal Democrats—Barney Frank, Maxine Waters, and Jerry Nadler—and said, "This is an historic moment."

Waters, she said, responded, "We will finally repeal 'Don't ask, don't tell.'"

"No," Pelosi replied. "You three are voting for the defense bill for the very first time."

On the Senate side of the Capitol, the Armed Services Committee voted 16-12 to attach the repeal amendment to that chamber's version of the NDAA. Vice President Biden spent the week leading up to the vote calling his former Senate colleagues, urging them to support repeal.[762] All that was needed was for the full Senate to pass the legislation and lobby to ensure that the language wouldn't be removed during conference.

Then, crickets. The Senate didn't vote on the National Defense Authorization Act in May or June or July or August. That wasn't unusual; the vote on the annual must-pass legislation not infrequently occurs later in the year. But the midterm election season was heating up, and it was becoming clear that the Republicans would regain control of the House of Representatives—and possibly the Senate—in 2011. If Congress didn't repeal "Don't ask, don't tell" now, the window could close for years to come. The anger and frustration were palpable.

The news grew seemingly worse in early July, as the Pentagon announced that as part of its study it would now survey 400,000 troops and their families about what they thought of gay people. The survey used the clinical term "homosexual" in some of the questions, which some said would result in negative responses. The questions asked straight troops what they would do if a gay person was in the shower, and whether they would bring their spouse to a social function if openly gay service members were present.

Was this Gates throwing another wrench into the works? The behind-the-scenes compromise in drafting the survey, according to one official, was to use the word "homosexual" when the question asked for factual response and "gay" when trying to elicit a more emotional response.[763]

SLDN warned that LGBT service members could not answer the questionnaire without risk of being identified and discharged. This was the same warning I had issued when Defense Secretary William Cohen ordered a survey about anti-gay harassment in 1999, following the murder of Barry Winchell.

My concern remained valid and was ignored. Pentagon spokeswoman Cynthia Smith confirmed that the law "is still in effect, and if someone were to out themselves, we would have to begin the discharge process."[764] Not only did the questionnaire increase risk for LGBT service members, but the Pentagon potentially suppressed their participation by announcing that careless responses would be punished.

The survey was also unprecedented. The Pentagon didn't survey white troops about racial integration, or men about opening the service academies or ships to women. The Pentagon didn't survey opinions during World War II on whether German Americans or Japanese Americans should serve, or whether American Muslims should serve following 9/11. The survey, which cost the Pentagon more than $4 million (greater than SLDN's annual budget), was, to quote retired Brigadier General Virgil Richard, "poppycock."

Or was it? On an issue as combustible as "Don't ask, don't tell," there is some logic to asking troops the shower question in order to address, head-on, concerns raised by critics. But would any result satisfy critics? As much as I thought the survey was a bad idea, I also knew what had happened the last time the Pentagon administered a survey—one assessing the level of anti-gay harassment. Those results were breathtaking in demonstrating how much harassment service members were experiencing, and they spurred the Pentagon to take action. I hoped for another breathtakingly good response here.

◆ ◆ ◆

SLDN launched Stories from the Frontlines to galvanize support for repeal. The campaign built on Voices of Veterans, a campaign I had conducted several years before. Each testimonial captured a distinct perspective on why Congress should repeal "Don't ask, don't tell."

The central animating message was that "Don't ask, don't tell" hurts military readiness. But the reasons why the law undermined unit cohesion varied, and what resonated with decision-makers varied. The winning message could be the loss of mission-critical skills, the staggering costs of the policy, the support of straight allies, inequality, opportunity, shared responsibility, or something else. It was important to hit them all.

Major Mike Almy, one of the great voices to emerge at the end of the repeal fight, wrote:

> "Stationed in Oklahoma, I was named officer of the year for my unit of nearly 1,000 people. ... During my career, I deployed to the Middle East four times. In my last deployment, I led a team of nearly 200 men and women to operate and maintain the systems used to control the air space over Iraq.... Shortly after I left Iraq—during a routine search of my computer files—someone found that my [service] was supported by the person I loved—a man. The email—our modern-day letter home—was forwarded to my commander. I was relieved of my duties. ... I was given a police escort off the base as if I were a common criminal. ... Despite this treatment, my greatest desire is still to return to active duty as an officer and leader in the United States Air Force, protecting the freedoms of a nation that I love; freedoms that I myself was not allowed to enjoy while serving in the military."[765]

Major General Vance Coleman, a straight ally who had served when troops were segregated, bore witness once again:

> "Mr. President, I know what it is like to be thought of as second-class, and I know what it is like to have your hard work dismissed because of who you are or what you look like. I also know what a difference it made to me and others when President Truman eliminated segregation in the armed forces and placed qualification ahead of discrimination.
>
> "As a retired Army commander, I also know how disruptive it is to remove a trained skilled member from a unit. In Korea, I had a sergeant first class in my unit who was gay. It was no secret. He was in charge of the unit's communication. He was essential to our performance and our survival, and he was damn good at his job. If I had to remove him, our unit's effectiveness as well as morale most certainly would have been harmed."[766]

An active-duty military chaplain said, "We went to foreign lands to wage war to liberate people so they would not have to live in the fear of waiting. But citizens of our own land who served nobly, who died to secure freedoms which they would never profit from, must live in fear, waiting for justice."[767]

In July, the Human Rights Campaign announced a grass-roots campaign to increase support for both "Don't ask, don't tell" repeal and the Employment Non-Discrimination Act.[768] The efforts focused on 10 states with key lawmakers whose votes on repeal were critical.[769] The 19 million emails sent to members and supporters nationwide, calling on them to take action on "Don't ask, don't tell," generated over 625,000 emails to members of Congress urging repeal. The campaign also collected almost 50,000 pro-repeal handwritten communications to Congress and conducted more than 1,000 grassroots lobby visits, both in Washington and in lawmakers' district offices.[770]

HRC also funded the Voices of Honor tour[771] in partnership with Servicemembers United. Co-founder Alex Nicholson had approached SLDN in 2006 to help finance the organization's Call to Duty Tour,[772] but we didn't have the discretionary funds. In addition to making a small donation, I told him that SLDN could be a fiscal sponsor and provide administrative, finance, and media support. He called me a Nazi. I admired his initiative.

The Voices of Honor tour had officially launched one year before[773] with Patrick Murphy as chairman and Eric Alva as one of the principal spokespersons. The Human Rights Campaign had placed Eric on an exclusive retainer starting in 2007, meaning that his talents and message could not be shared without its approval. Now the Voices of Honor tour had the deeper pockets of the Human Rights Campaign behind it, and there was an agreement on which cities to hit to maximize impact. It made stops in more than 50 locations across the country, concluding with a Veterans Lobby Day co-sponsored by more than 70 other organizations, with hundreds of lesbian, gay, and straight veterans lobbying members of Congress.[774]

In 2010, I was working for Human Rights First at its headquarters directly across from the Capitol, and I was on the Hill frequently, lobbying against torture and the U.S. military prison at Guantánamo Bay, Cuba. I smiled as I saw young vets arrive with SLDN materials and copies of Nathaniel Frank's book *Unfriendly Fire*. "Go get 'em," I thought.

◆◆◆

One of the surprising grassroots scores was Lady Gaga. When her Monster Ball tour brought her to Washington on September 7, she told her team that she wanted to meet with gay veterans. She had read about the *Log Cabin* case and asked what she could do.

David Hall, one of SLDN's plaintiffs in *Cook v. Gates* and an SLDN staff member since 2006, was a huge Gaga fan and leaped at the opportunity.

Lady Gaga asked David if he and other LGBT veterans could join her in Los Angeles at the MTV Video Music Awards. Former SLDN staff member (and another *Cook* plaintiff) Stacy Vasquez and two former clients, Mike Almy and Katie Miller, walked Lady Gaga down the white carpet, were interviewed on MTV, and sat behind her at the ceremony, where she won eight awards (out of 13 nominations) and wore the infamous "meat" dress. Lady Gaga subsequently recorded multiple videos[775] for SLDN and encouraged her "little monsters" to speak up.[776]

She traveled to Maine to rally voters in support of "Don't ask, don't tell" repeal, calling homophobia "the real threat to unit cohesion."[777] Susan Collins was still not fully committed to repeal, and she didn't like the shove. She said she would vote based on what her constituents thought, not on a rock star's opinion.

I had been critical of celebrity endorsements. I thought Magic Johnson was not as persuasive as the chairman of the Joint Chiefs in advocating for repeal of the ban on service members who were HIV+. I didn't think that deploying comedian Kathy Griffin at a rally on the same day as the Senate hearing on "Don't ask, don't tell" was as effective as SLDN's lobby days with veterans who could tell their personal stories to their representatives and senators.

But Lady Gaga was different. This was targeted, it raised SLDN's profile at a critical time, and it mobilized 314,446 "monsters" to click on SLDN's "Take action" page.[778] It had impact.

♦♦♦

On September 21, Senate Majority Leader Harry Reid scheduled a vote on the National Defense Authorization Act. Inexplicably, he framed the bill authorizing $726 billion in military spending not as a vote for our troops, or as a vote for our defense against terrorism, or as a vote for weapons and personnel needed to secure our freedom, but as a vote on whether gays should serve openly in the military. The LGBT advocates did the same. So did the press. This bill was about our security. Was it really in our nation's best interest that some senators would jeopardize our national security solely because of their unsubstantiated fear of gays?

John McCain announced that he would filibuster the legislation. Rather than force him to do exactly that for hours and hours and hours, painting him as out of touch, willing to sacrifice a must-pass bill because of his views toward gay Americans serving our nation, Reid meekly filed for a motion to invoke cloture—a procedure to end debate and move to a vote.

At the start of the new session of Congress in 2009, Reid had announced that legislation would require 60 votes because

Minority Leader Mitch McConnell had said he would obstruct all Democratic bills. McConnell proudly proclaimed that his only legislative goal was to make Barack Obama a one-term president,[779] and it is stunning that the Democrats just went along.

McConnell's tactics broke with years of Senate comity, and rather than force Republicans to do their job, Reid simply acceded. As a result, according to an analysis by Swarthmore College professor Richard Valelly, "majority rule in the Senate ... seemed to metamorphose into supermajority rule by the 111th Congress. This change—the advent of a 60-vote requirement for legislation—turned the Senate into a major battleground for DADT repeal."[780]

Reid would ultimately prove to have a stronger backbone than I thought.

The cloture vote failed. While the motion to break the filibuster received 57 votes in favor, it fell three short of the 60 required. The filibuster prevailed. Susan Collins voted with McCain,[781] as did two Democrats, Blanche Lincoln and Mark Pryor. Republican Lisa Murkowski did not vote. As these senators prevented a vote on the defense authorization bill, Bill Clinton told CBS's Katie Couric that he regretted enacting "Don't ask, don't tell."[782]

Some activists held out hope that McCain would end his filibuster if the Pentagon study concluded that repealing "Don't ask, don't tell" was appropriate. Four years earlier, appearing on MSNBC's *Hardball*, he had told host Chris Matthews: "The day that the leadership of the military comes to me and says, 'Senator, we ought to change the policy,' then I think we ought to consider seriously changing it."[783] He had reiterated that position as a presidential candidate in 2008.[784]

A ban on gays in the military, though, was part of the Republican Party platform.[785] I also knew that McCain was dug in, something the new crop of activists had forgotten. I had tried to engage him, as I had engaged General Powell, and he sent me a letter in May 2007. In it, he asserted:

> "I believe polarization of personnel and break-down of unit effectiveness is too high a price to pay for well-intentioned but misguided efforts to elevate the interests of a minority of homosexual servicemembers above those of their units. Most importantly, the national security of the United States, not to mention the lives of our men and women in uniform, are put at grave risk by policies detrimental to the good order and discipline which so distinguish America's Armed Services. For these reasons, which have nothing to do with my personal judgments about homosexual behavior, I remain opposed to the open expression of homosexuality in the United States military."[786]

McCain cultivated a reputation as a maverick. I know because I worked with him on other issues. At Human Rights First, one of my tasks was to close the military prison at Guantánamo Bay. McCain said at a Senate hearing I attended, "Wouldn't it be an act of courage if we were to close Guantánamo?"

I made a beeline to his staffer and asked if his boss had flip-flopped again. I promised to deliver the needed votes if he stood by that statement. I did. And he did. We didn't close Guantánamo, but Congress included language in that year's defense authorization bill that permitted the transfer of prisoners who had been vetted by the intelligence agencies. The prison population dropped from 179 prisoners to 40. On "Don't ask, don't tell," would McCain stand by the sentiments expressed to me or to Chris Matthews?

Activists were scrambling to figure out why the cloture vote had failed. Why didn't they have the 60 votes? Had Harry Reid miscalculated? The GLBTQ Archives project reported:

> "When it was revealed that President Obama had lobbied not a single senator to vote in favor of breaking the filibuster and that the day after the vote Vice President Biden flew to Arkansas to attend a fundraiser for blue dog Democrat Blanche Lincoln, who had joined the filibuster, many gay activists came to the conclusion that the entire vote was a charade so that Democrats could pretend they were trying to repeal DADT even as they were not."[787]

Reid said that he might attempt to bring up "Don't ask, don't tell" repeal after the midterm elections in November, during the lame-duck session. McCain promised to filibuster any such effort.[788] The failed attempt to repeal "Don't ask, don't tell" left the LGBT community feeling that the promises made by the administration had fallen short, as they had feared for months.

At the same time, brave service members continued to share their stories in the hope that they would make a difference. In 2013, during a Pentagon LGBT Pride Month event, Valerie Jarrett recalled that in the midst of the Senate debate over "Don't ask, don't tell," she met at the White House with several active-duty gay and lesbian service members and veterans who had been discharged. "I'll never forget the young woman who said she and her girlfriend lived in a perpetual state of fear of accidentally saying the wrong thing or doing something that might give away their secret," Jarrett said. "I'll never forget the veteran who said he couldn't even be honest about who he was with his own family, because he didn't want to ask them to lie for him."[789]

◆ ◆ ◆

Precious minutes ticked by. Congress went on a pre-election recess. The nation went to the polls in November, electing all 435 members of the House of Representatives and one-third of the Senate. The Democrats held on to the Senate by a slim majority but lost the House. As a result, the House would not repeal "Don't ask, don't tell" in the next Congress, and there would not be enough votes in the Senate to overcome a filibuster. By any measure, the Democrats suffered what President Obama called a "shellacking." One of the casualties was Patrick Murphy. "The drive in Congress to repeal the military's 'Don't ask, don't tell' policy appears all but lost for the foreseeable future," Laura Meckler wrote in *The Wall Street Journal.*[790]

Congress returned to Washington in November for the lame-duck session, which usually lives up to its name. Not this time: The Democrats decided to pursue one of the most consequential agendas of any lame-duck session in history. Priorities included the National Defense Authorization Act, a nuclear weapons treaty with Russia known as New START, a spending bill, tax breaks for the middle class, and the DREAM Act, which would give legal status to undocumented immigrants who were brought to the United States as children.[791] "Don't ask, don't tell" repeal was also in the mix.

Some Senate Democrats were cautious. "I think we're going to have to kind of come to grip with the realities of how much time is left and what's real and what can really pass," John Kerry told *Roll Call*.[792] Mark Udall warned, "If we don't get this job done this year, I think it could be years before we have another opportunity."[793]

Joe Lieberman and Susan Collins called on the Pentagon to immediately release its study on repeal. Lieberman announced that he had secured 60 votes to overcome a filibuster: "Based on the statements by Senators Collins and [Richard] Lugar and others privately, I am confident we have more than 60 votes prepared to take up the defense authorization bill with the repeal of 'Don't ask, don't tell.'"[794]

On November 15, three groups threw a wrench into the plans. OutServe, a newly formed Facebook group for gay service members; Knights Out, the West Point gay alumni group co-founded by Dan Choi; and the Palm Center argued that Congress should pass the defense authorization bill "whether or not the repeal of 'Don't ask, don't tell' is included."

"There is nothing more important than loyalty to those with whom we serve," they said in a joint statement. "This means ensuring that no one issue interferes with funding the courageous and selfless work our fellow service members are doing around the world."[795]

Levin conceded that the NDAA would be easier to pass without "Don't ask, don't tell" in it, and he wanted the defense bill passed.[796]

SLDN, the Human Rights Campaign, the Center for American Progress, and Servicemembers United issued a joint statement rebuking the three organizations: "Under no circumstances should DADT repeal be stripped from the underlying defense authorization bill."[797] One LGBT commentator said what many were thinking: "This is just becoming insane, and more proof that we are our own worst enemies."[798] Fred Sainz, a spokesman for the Human Rights Campaign, said the three groups were "good people who are extremely naive legislatively."[799]

I often wondered why those in the LGBT community turned against one another, even though they shared a common purpose. Stories are complicated. You look for heroes and villains. It's not that easy to demarcate. I have always preferred to assume the best of intentions all around.

Yet movements too often find themselves in circular firing squads. SLDN board member Paul Smith, an Army officer who became a social worker, offered this theory. "It's internalized fear," he said. "We don't want to trust anyone but ourselves with our lives on the line. We think we can do it better, and we will fight hard to do it."

In a boost for repeal efforts, *The Washington Post* secured the results of the Pentagon survey of 400,000 active-duty and Reserve troops about gays serving openly in the armed forces, reporting on November 11 that more than 70 percent of the respondents said that the effect of ending "Don't ask, don't tell" would be positive, mixed, or nonexistent.[800] The leak to the *Post* prompted an inspector general's investigation.

The Center for American Progress said that there were 10 senators who had said that they would await the Pentagon study prior to making a decision on repeal, including Republicans Lindsey Graham, Judd Gregg, and John McCain. Aubrey Sarvis was more sober in his assessment, noting that there have been "no concrete changes yet on the positions of the senators and senators-elect."[801]

White House officials and senior aides to Harry Reid met with gay-rights activists on the evening of November 17, reiterating the president's and the Senate majority leader's commitment to repeal "Don't ask, don't tell." Neither Obama nor Reid attended.[802]

CHAPTER 37

THE PENTAGON STUDY

Gates released the Pentagon study on "Don't ask, don't tell"[803] one day early, on November 30—exactly 17 years after President Clinton had signed "Don't ask, don't tell" into law. The symbolism cut both ways. Was this date to mark a continuation of the gay ban or a break from it? Was there even time left on the calendar to get the job done?

Two and a half months before, I had met with Jeh Johnson, the Pentagon's general counsel and co-chair of the review group, and a group of retired generals to discuss Guantánamo. After the main agenda, Johnson asked the generals what the Pentagon should do when two service members—one gay, one straight—refused to work with the other. Major General Paul Eaton, who had led the effort to train Iraqi troops in 2003 and 2004, responded succinctly, "I think that question was asked and answered in 1948," referring to President Harry S. Truman's decision to integrate the troops. It was perhaps the most succinct nod to equality I'd heard.

Johnson, who is Black, chuckled, and said, "I asked the same question of a drill sergeant at Camp Lejeune. He said, 'Sir, you see that pile of dirt over there? I would give them a shovel and order them to dig. They can stop when they agree to work together or they drop.'" I knew then that the report would turn out well, but would it come in time?

Doug Wilson, the Pentagon's assistant secretary for public affairs and a member of the team that implemented repeal, recalled a similar story. At Fort Hood, he asked members of a tank crew what they would do if "Don't ask, don't tell" was repealed and one of the crew said he was gay.

"The first person said, 'Well, my brother's gay, so it doesn't matter.' The second person said, 'Well, you know, I have so many friends who are gay from high school. It doesn't matter.' The final person said, 'What matters to me is if this thing is burning, I want someone to be able to pull me out, and I don't care what their orientation is.'"[804]

Overall, the study cost about $9 million,[805] more than three times SLDN's annual budget. The 256-page report concluded that while there may be some "limited and isolated disruptions" in the short term, over the longer term, "with a continued and sustained commitment to core values of leadership, professionalism, and respect for all, we are convinced that the U.S. military can adjust and accommodate this change, just as it has others in history."[806]

It noted that any concerns raised about gays serving openly were "exaggerated and not consistent with the reported experiences of many service members." It found that 69 percent of the respondents said they had already worked with someone they believed to be gay or lesbian. Of those, "92 percent stated that the unit's 'ability to work together' was 'very good,' 'good,' or 'neither good nor poor.'"[807]

Repeal, Gates said at a December 1 press conference, "would not be the wrenching, traumatic change that many have feared and predicted."[808]

The next day, Mullen told the Senate Armed Services Committee, "Back in February ... I said that I believed the men and women of the armed forces could accommodate such a change, but I did not know it for a fact. Now I do. And so, what was my personal opinion is now my professional opinion."[809] Mullen, like Shalikashvili before him, could now make an even more persuasive argument for repeal—one backed by data.

The study was based on exhaustive consultation by the Comprehensive Review Working Group, led by Johnson and General Carter Ham and comprising 68 staff from across the Department of Defense and each of the military services. Forty-nine were in uniform (officer and enlisted); 19 were civilians. In addition to the nearly 400,000 questionnaires that solicited information, views, and data on "Don't ask, don't tell" (and resulted in 115,052 responses—"one of the largest surveys in the history of the U.S. military"), the working group "conducted 95 face-to-face 'information exchange forums' at 51 military bases and installations around the world, where we interacted with over 24,000 service members." More than 150,000 questionnaires were sent to military spouses; 44,266 responded. In addition, an anonymous online "inbox" collected 72,384 comments from service members and their families.[810]

In an interview, Johnson noted that initially there was significant resistance to repeal—critics believed that it was an act of political correctness to fulfill a campaign promise. What was clear, he said, "was that the views on 'Don't ask, don't tell' had been frozen in time since 1993."[811]

He said he hadn't known what the outcome of the survey would be. "I was driving in Martha's Vineyard when I got the call about the survey results," he told me. "I pulled off to the side of the road because I didn't want to drive off the bluffs."[812] When the results showed that repeal would be a non-issue, "I was pleasantly surprised."

The comprehensive review enabled both Mullen and Gates to unequivocally support repeal. It was now the eleventh hour. Gates declared it a "matter of urgency" that the Senate, in the last weeks of its lame-duck session, vote to repeal the law.[813]

"As we have seen this past year, the judicial branch is becoming involved in this issue, and it is only a matter of time before the federal courts are drawn once more into the fray," he told the Senate Armed Services Committee on December 2. "Should this happen, there is the real possibility that this change would be imposed immediately by judicial fiat—by far the most disruptive and damaging scenario I can imagine, and the one most hazardous to military morale, readiness and battlefield performance."[814]

Mullen agreed. "I worry that unpredictable actions in the court could strike down the law at any time, precluding the orderly implementation plan we believe is necessary to mitigate risk," he said.[815]

The *Witt* decision had made "Don't ask, don't tell" implementation already impractical. It required the services to make individual evidence-based determinations that a service member was causing disruption to unit cohesion, rather than a blanket statutory proscription against gay service. Judge Virginia Phillips's short-lived worldwide injunction on discharges of gay service members in the *Log Cabin Republicans* case had highlighted the shifting legal sands. Lieutenant Colonel Victor Fehrenbach had filed another challenge to "Don't ask, don't tell" in August and was awaiting trial.

Invoking judicial intervention as a reason to act was a thin reed on which to hang an argument. No appellate court had ever ruled "Don't ask, don't tell" unconstitutional. The Pentagon now had a road map on how to implement repeal. If the military could move 150,000 troops halfway around the world to fight an enemy, certainly it could administer a new personnel policy if ordered by a court. The call to arms against judicial intervention made a convenient excuse for why action had to be undertaken immediately. Congress is adept at escaping inconvenient truths or relying on convenient excuses.

Simultaneously with the Pentagon study, the RAND Corporation published an update of its 1993 study on gays in the military. Bernard Rostker, whom I had met when he served as assistant secretary of the Navy for manpower and Reserve affairs under President Clinton, was the lead consultant on the review, and I was among the experts interviewed. RAND had reviewed the studies published by SLDN and the Palm Center in the 17 years since its earlier report. The second report agreed with the first: "The research concludes that there would be little impact on recruiting and retention of military personnel and on unit cohesion and performance."[816]

Levin swiftly scheduled hearings. Gates, Mullen, Johnson, and Ham appeared on December 2. The next day, the committee heard from Marine General James Cartwright, the vice chairman of the Joint Chiefs of Staff, and the five service chiefs—Army, Navy, Air Force, Marine Corps, and Coast Guard.

David Gardner of *The Daily Mail* reported on their testimony.[817] Cartwright testified that the "warrior ethos" in service outweighed personal differences, like sexual orientation. Admiral Gary Roughead, the chief of naval operations, said 76 percent of sailors were either neutral or positive about having openly gay colleagues, making it feasible to repeal "Don't ask, don't tell." The Coast Guard commandant, Admiral Robert Papp, also said repeal wouldn't be a problem.

The Army's chief of staff, General George Casey, was more cautious, saying, "I believe that the law should be repealed eventually" but the question "is one of timing." He predicted that repeal would create "a moderate risk to our military effectiveness." General Norton Schwartz, the Air Force chief of staff, concurred, saying it wouldn't be "prudent" to implement repeal "in the near term" and suggested waiting until at least 2012. The Marine Corps' commandant, General James Amos, remained adamantly opposed: "Repeal has strong potential for disruption at the small unit level, as it will no doubt divert leadership attention away from an almost singular focus of preparing units for combat."

All testified, however, that they would implement the new policy if Congress voted to repeal "Don't ask, don't tell."[818] That was the victory. The officers would salute their commander in chief.

John McCain's intransigence on principle stood in sharp contrast to General Ham, the working group's co-lead. "When asked Tuesday by lawmakers in a closed briefing, Ham reportedly said he is personally opposed to homosexuality," *The Washington*

Post reported.[819] Professionally, however, he understood that the majority of service members looked at the issue differently. "If this changes, I've got to do this," he told the *Post*, noting that he was the commander of U.S. Army Europe as well as the working group's co-chair. "I can't put my signature on something that's contrary to what I think. If I didn't believe what's in that report, I wouldn't have signed it."[820]

When I spoke with him several years later, he said, "I had to go where the evidence led, and not let my religious views get in the way." I was told that Ham was particularly moved by the anonymous emails from lesbian, gay, and bisexual service members collected as part of the Pentagon review. I find it extraordinary, and a mark of leadership, when someone can acknowledge bias, be open to the possibility that the rest of the troops do not share that bias, and understand that bias does not serve the military well. The best leaders are those who are open to challenging their own views—the path followed during this process by General Shalikashvili, Lieutenant General Kennedy, and so many others.

The political sands started shifting favorably. Republicans Olympia Snowe, Lisa Murkowski, and Scott Brown all signaled that they would now join Susan Collins in breaking the filibuster and voting for repeal. John Ensign's staff also indicated that he would support repeal.[821]

Brown had been more opposed to repeal than many had thought. I had organized a meeting with him and four generals to discuss Guantánamo on September 14. He came in late, leaned back in his chair, and put his boots on the table, which did not impress the generals. He derided the "social agenda" of those trying to add "Don't ask, don't tell" to the defense bill. I quickly advised Colonel Andy Leonard and Brigadier General Keith Kerr at SLDN to mobilize Massachusetts voters and not take his vote for granted. They mobilized, and Brown's opinion evolved.

"Having reviewed the Pentagon report, having spoken to active and retired military service members, and having discussed the matter privately with Defense Secretary Gates and others, I accept the findings of the report and support repeal based on the secretary's recommendations," he said on December 3.[822]

The support of Lisa Murkowski was based on timing. SLDN clients David Hall and Jack Glover had been her constituents in Alaska when they were discharged, and they met with her. She had promised in 2005 that she would back repeal if it had a real chance of success. In 2010, it did. "America is the loser when it denies those who are willing to make great sacrifices demanded of our men and women in uniform the opportunity to do so on grounds of sexual orientation," she said on December 8.[823]

◆◆◆

McCain's filibuster of the National Defense Authorization Act—with repeal attached to it—was still in effect. Senate Majority Leader Harry Reid set another cloture vote for December 9. Because this legislation authorizes funding for military spending in the next fiscal year, it is one of the few bills to pass Congress in bipartisan fashion. It is also typical that the majority and minority agree on a certain number of amendments to be considered before a final vote.

Reid had been negotiating with Collins over the number of amendments that could be added to the bill and the hours of debate that would be allotted. In return, he hoped that she could deliver enough Republican votes to invoke cloture.[824] She had previously voted to support the filibuster not because she opposed repeal, but because she wanted to ensure that Republicans had due opportunity to offer amendments.

Reid scheduled the vote without finalizing any deal with Collins, reasoning that Republicans didn't have enough support to strip the repeal language. He thought they "surely wouldn't be craven enough to block an entire annual defense bill" over "Don't ask, don't tell."[825] He was wrong.

Collins was surprised by Reid's maneuver and rushed to the floor. She still wanted the opportunity to add amendments, but Reid told her that given the full legislative agenda for the rest of the lame-duck session, the time to act was now.[826] This time she sided with Reid on the cloture vote; Murkowski and Brown didn't, despite their support for repeal. With 60 votes needed to invoke cloture, the effort to end McCain's filibuster fell short by three votes.

The death knell was sounding. Richard Socarides, President Clinton's advisor for gay rights, called the failed cloture vote "a political train wreck."[827] *Stars and Stripes* reported that "gay rights advocates ... may have to wait years for another chance."[828] NPR's Ari Shapiro said, "Everybody I talked to, from activists to Capitol Hill staffers, can describe the moment they knew 'Don't ask, don't tell' would never be repealed." The director of Servicemembers United, Alex Nicholson, wrote in his memoir, "We were finally at the end of our rope."[829] The Human Rights Campaign issued a press release saying that "Don't ask, don't tell" was dead: "It appears Congress won't repeal 'Don't ask, don't tell' this year."

Even Collins was downbeat, telling *The New York Times*, "I'm sad to say I think the chances are very slim for getting it through."[830]

Gates, traveling in the Middle East, told reporters on his plane that he was "disappointed" in the vote and warned that if Congress did not succeed with repeal, "my greatest worry will be that then we're at the mercy of the courts and all of the lack of predictability that that entails."[831]

The next week, Dan Choi, the gay West Point graduate who had handcuffed himself to the White House fence multiple times to protest "Don't ask, don't tell," was admitted to the psychiatric ward at a Veterans Administration hospital. In an email, he told supporters that he had experienced a "breakdown and anxiety attack."[832]

"My breakdown was a result of a cumulative array of stressors," he wrote, "but there is no doubt that the composite betrayals felt on Thursday, by elected leaders and gay organizations as well as many who have exploited my name for their marketing purposes, have added to the result."[833]

CHAPTER 38

HAIL MARY

House Majority Leader Steny Hoyer started to develop a Plan B in the days before "Don't ask, don't tell" repeal failed for a second time in the Senate.[834] He was reading the tea leaves. He believed that there were now sufficient votes in both chambers to pass a stand-alone repeal bill—my original plan.

The idea was planted by the Human Rights Campaign's legislative director in mid-November.[835] Hoyer sensed that removing the repeal language from the National Defense Authorization Act would overcome the concerns of Republicans who simply wanted an opportunity to amend that legislation with provisions unrelated to "Don't ask, don't tell."

Hoyer spoke with five Republican senators to see if his assessment was correct. Susan Collins, Lisa Murkowski, Olympia Snowe, and George Voinovich all said they would support repeal. Only Richard Lugar said no.[836]

He then called Harry Reid, his counterpart in the Senate, to inform him of his plan. "Commitment would overstate what he gave me," Hoyer said of Reid in an interview with *The Hill*. "He said: 'If you send it over, certainly we're going to try to [bring] it up.'"[837]

Reid also felt the pressure. He had indicated that he wanted to adjourn the Senate at the close of business on Friday, December 17, and crucial votes still had to be cast on a long list of Obama's priorities—New START, the defense authorization bill, and the DREAM Act.

Republican Jim DeMint threatened to read the 2,000-page NDAA to get "Don't ask, don't tell" repeal off the table for good. "We need to take care of the nation's business and go home for Christmas," he said.[838] Lindsey Graham threatened to withdraw his support for New START if Reid tried to advance a vote on "Don't ask, don't tell" and the DREAM Act.[839] Another Republican, Bob Corker, also predicted the treaty's failure if the chamber moved onto what he called "partisan political issues brought forth to basically accommodate activist groups around this country."[840]

The groundwork had been laid for a Hail Mary.[841] On December 9, within minutes of the second failure to invoke cloture, Lieberman and Collins hastily arranged a press conference and announced they were taking the repeal language out of the NDAA and reintroducing it as a stand-alone bill.

The next day, braving the cold, about 150 veterans organized by SLDN rallied outside the Senate side of the Capitol.[842] "The Senate wants ... to go home to their families and not do their duties and sit by warm fireplaces comfortably in their homes for Christmas while the work remains unfinished," Mike Almy told them. "If I can serve overseas in harm's way for four Christmases defending our nation, the Senate can certainly do the same."[843]

At the other end of Pennsylvania Avenue, "Obama apparently was about cutting his losses," NPR reported. "He had other priorities—namely, getting the Senate to ratify the New START nuclear arms control pact with Russia."[844]

Barney Frank told *The Hill* that Hoyer "was under a lot of pressure not to do this [the repeal bill] because it would endanger START. He refused to do that."[845] House Speaker Nancy Pelosi also refused to bow to pressure to give up on ending "Don't ask, don't tell," Frank said.

On December 13, Hoyer told Pelosi he was moving forward. The next day, he and Murphy introduced a stand-alone bill in the House, using the same language that Lieberman and Collins had put in their bill. It was unclear, *The Washington Post* reported, whether the Senate would have time to consider the Lieberman-Collins legislation; if the House passed a bill with identical language and sent it to the Senate, that "could increase the pressure on the Senate to act before the lame-duck session ends."[846]

On December 15, the House of Representatives voted on the repeal bill. Howard "Buck" McKeon, the top Republican on the House Armed Services Committee, urged his colleagues to "do nothing at this time to threaten the readiness of our soldiers, sailors, airmen and marines, who are at the tip of the spear fighting America's two wars."[847]

Hoyer said, "It is never too late to do the right thing."[848]

The legislation passed, 250-175. It was sent to the Senate as a privileged resolution, a status requiring fewer hours of debate.[849] The Pentagon immediately urged senators to pass it.[850]

McCain was again threatening a filibuster. Lieberman and Collins were working to get Republican support, and Reid was skeptical about scheduling a cloture vote. "Are you sure you have those three Republicans?" he asked Lieberman.[851]

Having failed on the two cloture votes to end McCain's filibuster of the NDAA, the majority leader was right to be concerned. Lieberman assured Reid that he did have that Republican support. Reid had one other request: "Joe, please go back and tell them I can't allow amendments on this."[852] Amendments would disrupt the legislative calendar and could lead to further delay.

Publicly, Reid was still hedging his bets. Asked on December 16 about his plans for the bill, he told reporters, "I don't know if I'll bring it up before Christmas,"[853] since the legislative session technically didn't expire until January 3.

What was not known at the time is that for all of Reid's public timidity and miscalculated efforts to overcome McCain's filibuster, he was determined to see "Don't ask, don't tell" repealed, despite significant White House pressure to ensure that other bills moved forward first.

On December 4, Obama had summoned congressional leaders to the White House to outline his priorities for the rest of the legislative session—ones that didn't include "Don't ask, don't tell." In his book *We've Got People*, Ryan Grim described what happened after the meeting ended: "Reid stayed behind to talk to the president, one on one. ... 'Reid put the screws on him. ... Reid in so many words made it clear to the president that he wouldn't get his START treaty ratified if he didn't get on board with repealing "Don't ask, don't tell,"' said the person who'd previously been in the room and was told about it afterward. 'Let's put it this way: "don't ask, don't tell" became a priority for him.'

"On the night of December 16, Reid called President Obama in the Oval Office to tell him he planned to put repeal on the floor. Obama made a strong case against it, convinced it would fail and derail the remainder of the lame-duck agenda. ... Reid heard him out before delivering his response. 'Well, Mr. President, sometimes you just gotta roll the dice,' Reid said, and then he hung up."[854]

To be clear, Obama supported repeal; he just wanted to ensure that it would not derail other important legislation. His less than muscular support for it, though, is reflected in the scant four pages given to it in his 700-page memoir.[855]

"I had to make sure that I could pass both of them and I wasn't sure I could," Reid told Ryan Grim and Kelly Eleveld in 2019. "So I decided what I was going to do is get what I thought was going to be the hardest out of the way first, and that was 'Don't ask, don't tell.' I got that done, knew I had the votes for that, then I did the [START] thing, that's how it worked."[856]

Reid scheduled a vote to end McCain's filibuster and then a vote to repeal "Don't ask, don't tell" on December 18—my birthday. Lieberman, an Orthodox Jew, walked two hours from his synagogue in Georgetown to Capitol Hill in the bitter cold with a police escort.[857] He wasn't supposed to work on the Sabbath, but that day was different.

"Allowing people to serve our military regardless of sexual orientation is not a liberal or conservative idea, not a Republican or Democratic idea," he told his Senate colleagues before the vote. "It is an American idea consistent with American values."[858]

McCain's filibuster failed, 63-33. The Senate passed the Don't Ask, Don't Tell Repeal Act of 2010 by a vote of 65-31. David Axelrod, a senior White House advisor, would later say that repeal happened "to our mild surprise and great relief."[859]

The president called Patrick Murphy, who was at a Philadelphia Flyers game. "Is this Murph? This is Barack."[860]

As John McCain had predicted,[861] the salons of Georgetown cheered on the best birthday I've ever had.

Over the next few days, I wrote hundreds of notes, thanking friends, supporters, donors, colleagues, and allies for their actions that led to repeal and received hundreds in reply. "Without you, this does not happen," wrote Bridget Wilson, the pioneering gay-rights lawyer in San Diego. "I really did not think I would see this in my lifetime."

"Thank you for being there even before the beginning," said Margarethe Cammermeyer.

"Without everything you have done—we would not be where we are today," wrote Keith Meinhold, calling it "a watershed moment in our movement."

Despite any differences we had on strategy, Aaron Belkin responded to my congratulatory note to him and said, "I think history will record that it was all because of you and the rest of the SLDN team, past and current, who made this day happen."

One of my favorite notes was from a former client, Arabic linguist Bleu Copas: "The only thing I noticed is my head was held a little bit higher on the drive in [to work]. ... weird feeling."

EPILOGUE

CHAPTER 39

MISCHIEF

While the law repealed "Don't ask, don't tell," it remained in effect until the secretary of defense, the chairman of the Joint Chiefs, and the president certified to the House and Senate Armed Services and Appropriations Committees that repeal could be accomplished with no adverse effect on military readiness, effectiveness, unit cohesion, and recruiting and retention.[862]

Clifford Stanley, the under secretary of defense for personnel and readiness, was put in charge of the repeal implementation process. As a major general in the Marine Corps, he had relieved an officer for making derisive comments about gays after the murder of Barry Winchell. Members of the Repeal Implementation Team included its chairwoman, Virginia "Vee" Penrod, deputy assistant secretary for military personnel policy; Marine Major General Steven Hummer, the team's chief of staff;

and Doug Wilson, the assistant secretary of defense for public affairs (and an openly gay man[863]).

Two concerns remained. One was that the repeal of "Don't ask, don't tell" did not mandate non-discrimination. As President Obama and Vice President Biden made clear at the signing ceremony, and as those voting for repeal understood, non-discrimination was the clear intent. Nevertheless, SLDN pushed for an additional executive order clarifying the regulations on discrimination and harassment.[864]

"Signing legislation that allows for repeal of 'Don't ask, don't tell' was necessary, but it is not sufficient for ensuring equality in the military," Aubrey Sarvis said in a statement. "It's critical that gay and lesbian service members have the same avenues for recourse as their straight counterparts when it comes to harassment and discrimination."[865] Rarely does one get a do-over with respect to legislation. This was no exception, but would the administration issue an executive order or directive that established a principle of non-discrimination?

The second concern was that the delay in implementation created room for shenanigans by critics. The day that Obama signed the repeal legislation into law, Sarvis noted that as long as certification was outstanding, there was "room for mischief." Opponents of repeal could continue to propose legislation that would meddle with the process. "No one should be mistaken that opponents will try to undo this before it gets off the ground," he said.[866]

As an example, three days after the Senate voted to repeal "Don't ask, don't tell," Mitch McConnell tried to attach an amendment to the NDAA that would require the Army and Air Force chiefs, the chief of naval operations, and the commandant of the Marine

Corps to sign off on certification.[867] Since some of those service chiefs had previously expressed opposition to gays serving openly, such a measure could have delayed implementation indefinitely, if not outright killed it. Joe Lieberman blocked the amendment.[868]

On January 19, 16 days after Republicans took control of the House of Representatives, Duncan D. Hunter—the first Marine Corps combat veteran of the wars in Afghanistan and Iraq to serve in Congress—introduced a bill that would add the service chiefs to the certification process.[869] The new chairman of the House Armed Services Committee, "Buck" McKeon, supported the legislation,[870] and his committee added that language to the House version of the National Defense Authorization Act for fiscal year 2012.[871] But that is as far as it went—the Senate didn't consider the 2012 defense authorization bill until after certification was completed.

On June 16, Hunter sent a letter, signed by 23 Republicans, to Obama, requesting that he "refrain from transmitting certification until Congress has had sufficient time to review pending legislative matters of policy and law."[872] The White House did not delay the certification.

The service chiefs, even those who had previously noted some unease, expressed full confidence that their concerns would be properly accounted for by the secretary of defense and the chairman of the Joint Chiefs of Staff.[873] Shortly before final certification, McKeon tried one more maneuver, asking Gates's successor as secretary of defense, Leon Panetta, to delay final repeal until Congress had an opportunity to review the implementation regulations.[874] The tactic failed.

On July 22, at a ceremony at the White House, Obama, Mullen, and Panetta certified that repeal could be implemented with no deleterious impact on the armed forces. It would take effect 60 days later.

In a written statement, Panetta said, "All men and women who serve this nation in uniform—no matter their race, color, creed, religion, or sexual orientation—do so with great dignity, bravery, and dedication. ... They put their lives on the line for America, and that's what really matters."

In his statement, Mullen said, "My confidence in our ability to accomplish this work rests primarily on the fact that our people are capable, well-led, and thoroughly professional."[875]

At a Pentagon press briefing later that day, Stanley said that the Pentagon had already trained 1.9 million service members, both active-duty and Reserve, on the effects of repeal and that training would continue into September.[876]

"Don't ask, don't tell" was officially repealed on September 20. Stanley issued a memorandum banning discrimination on the basis of sexual orientation: "Sexual orientation may not be a factor in accession, promotion, separation, or other personnel decision-making."[877]

It also included this language: "The Department of Defense is committed to promoting an environment free from personal, social, or institutional barriers that prevent Service members from rising to the highest levels of responsibility possible regardless of sexual orientation." Non-discrimination was now the regulatory standard.

In a statement, Obama celebrated this achievement: "Today, the discriminatory law known as 'Don't ask, don't tell' is finally and formally repealed. As of today, patriotic Americans in uniform will no longer have to lie about who they are in order to serve the country they love. As of today, our armed forces will no longer lose the extraordinary skills and combat experience of so many gay and lesbian service members. And today, as Commander in Chief, I want those who were discharged under this law to know that your country deeply values your service."[878]

Mullen said that "with implementation of the new law fully in place, we are a stronger joint force, a more tolerant force, a force of more character and more honor, more in keeping with our own values."[879]

I said on that day, "Today is about a celebration of an extraordinary moment in our history. Today is an exclamation mark that we can achieve equality."

CHAPTER 40

CEREMONIES

On December 21, Jeremy and I attended the ceremony at the Capitol Visitor Center where Speaker of the House Nancy Pelosi formally signed the copy of the repeal bill that would be sent to the White House for the signature that would make it law.

"We are here to affirm a core American principle: that anyone who wishes to serve, secure, and defend this country should be welcomed, judged by their abilities, and honored for their sacrifice," Pelosi said. "We will strengthen our national security and recognize the contributions of all Americans, the contributions that they have made to our nation's defense."[880]

Flanking Pelosi were gay veterans Zoe Dunning, Eric Alva, Stacey Vasquez, Mike Almy, and Victor Fehrenbach. The legislation's chief sponsor in the House, Patrick Murphy, and Admiral Mike Mullen, chairman of the Joint Chiefs of Staff, also were there.

The next day, many of the same guests, and the heroes who helped pave the way for "Don't ask, don't tell" repeal, gathered at the Interior Department for the presidential signing ceremony. It was 20 degrees outside, but the atmosphere was warm as we lined up at 6:30 a.m. to get into the building.

Alva and Dunning stood next to Obama, along with the lawmakers from both chambers who had worked assiduously to pass the legislation, including Murphy, Pelosi, Joe Lieberman, Harry Reid, and Susan Collins. Mullen stood behind the president.[881] Lieberman described the atmosphere as "pulsating."[882] *The Atlantic* called it "a signing ceremony for the ages."[883]

Zoe Dunning captured the moment well in a post for a Democratic club in San Francisco:

> "Because of my personal story and my continued activism on 'Don't ask, don't tell,' I was honored to be invited to stand next to President Obama as he signed the bill. The most precious gift I received from that opportunity on stage was the perspective to look out at a room of brave heroes like Grethe Cammermeyer, Justin Elzie, Dan Choi, Miriam Ben-Shalom, and countless others who helped make this day happen. I witnessed jubilant smiles, tears of pain, tears of joy, and moments of healing. It was a magical place and time."[884]

I sat front row center, directly in front of the president. To my left sat Stacy Vasquez, a former SLDN staff member and *Cook* plaintiff. To my right was Michelle Benecke, who co-founded SLDN with me. It was old home week, as many of SLDN's most important supporters and clients were there:

Pat and Wally Kutteles, World War II veterans John Cook and Frank Kameny, Colonel Margarethe Cammermeyer, Captain Joan Darrah, Rear Admiral Alan Steinman, David Mixner, Andy Tobias, Colonel Stewart Bornhoft, Paul Boskind, Sergeant Justin Elzie, Sergeant Brian Fricke, Sergeant Mike Almy, Lieutenant Colonel Victor Fehrenbach, and Sergeant Jose Zuniga, who was named Sixth Army Soldier of the Year for 1992 and was discharged in 1993 after he came out in support of Clinton's pledge to end the ban.[885]

There were many others, like Petty Officer Keith Meinhold, who were not there; I wished that the White House had asked me for my Rolodex. Some were unable to join us because of holiday commitments or travel costs.

Prior to the signing, Biden told the audience, "This fulfills an important campaign promise the president and I made, and many here on this stage made, and many of you have fought for, for a long time, in repealing a policy that actually weakens our national security, diminished our ability to have military readiness, and violates the fundamental American principle of fairness and equality—that exact same set of principles that brave gay men and women will now be able to openly defend around the world."[886]

Then it was Obama's turn to speak: "No longer will our country be denied the service of thousands of patriotic Americans who are forced to leave the military, regardless of their skills, no matter their bravery or their zeal, no matter their years of exemplary performance because they happen to be gay."[887]

As he was signing his name, Zoe Dunning, whom I earlier described as "funny as hell," blurted out, "Make sure you spell it right."[888]

When Obama acknowledged Mullen, there was rapturous applause. "You would have thought it was for Lady Gaga," said Jeff Cleghorn, a former SLDN staff attorney. Mullen later recounted that Lieberman turned to him and said, "Gee, Mike, I guess you didn't think you'd see the day when you were the most popular guy in gay America."[889]

In an editorial prior to the signing, the *Milwaukee Journal Sentinel* captured the significance of the moment: "When Obama signs a bill repealing the military's 'Don't ask, don't tell' rule, it will be an event as significant for gay rights as President Harry Truman's order integrating the United States military was for black Americans. Obama's signature will mark historic progress for a nation that has for too long denigrated gay Americans. Our hope is that it is the death knell for one of the last frontiers of bigotry."[890]

Tears streamed down my face all day. When asked what that day meant to me, I told the *Washington Blade*, "I think when you reduce it down to its essential—the young gay man and lesbian is not going to have to call SLDN hiding, quivering, wondering if they're going to jail or if their career is going to be over the next day. ... America is now going to be with them for the first time, and they can serve with honor and integrity. Multiply that by a million, and that's the significant change that we have today."[891]

◆◆◆

One of the best celebrations of "Don't ask, don't tell" repeal occurred on September 18, 2012—one year after repeal. It was a sold-out gala aboard the USS *Intrepid* Sea, Air & Space Museum in New York City, reminiscent of the parties SLDN had hosted aboard the USS *Midway* in San Diego but decidedly more posh. The emcee was Barbara Walters; the honoree was Mike Mullen, who had retired from the Navy two months after repeal was certified.

"It's pretty easy to stand up and represent the values you have held close for your entire life and be fortunate enough to be in a leadership position where that value actually crosses over in a time and a place and in a way where you as a leader can really make a difference," Mullen told the crowd.[892] He also had the best one-liner of the evening: "Gay hero was never part of my career plan."[893]

The Pentagon held LGBT Pride celebrations following repeal, showing once again that when the military decides to do something, it goes all in. At the Pride event on June 25, 2013, Valerie Jarrett, one of Obama's closest advisors, talked about what repeal meant.

"Change is being able to put your family photo on your desk, just like everyone else," she said. "Change is being able to share with your co-workers about your weekend or vacation plans. ... Change is knowing that you're free to be who you are and love whomever you want without fear of harassment or losing your job. It's being able to openly embrace your partner in front of all the other families when he or she returns from a tour of duty, just like everyone else."[894]

What I loved about that moment was that Valerie was using the words I had said so often over 17 years. Deep gratitude welled up as the language of the framework that Michelle and I had constructed years before flowed easily off her lips.

CHAPTER 41

MEMORIAL DAY

On the Saturday before Memorial Day in 2011, I retrieved a voicemail from Michelle. I was in Rehoboth Beach with Jeremy. We had just returned from the beach and were resting before heading to Aqua, a sandy outdoor cocktail bar that would be rocking at the start of the summer season. I was draped across a lounge chair, my legs dangling off the armrest.

"Dixon, I got a disturbing call from Kevin Blaesing saying that Rich Richenberg may have harmed himself," Michelle said. "I haven't been able to get through to him."

Rich was one of the first who challenged the constitutionality of "Don't ask, don't tell." He later joined SLDN's staff and was a mentor to many service members dealing with coming out and the discrimination imposed by the law. Kevin Blaesing, who was discharged simply for asking the base counselor how someone might determine if he was gay, was one of his mentees.

"No, no, no, no, no!" I exclaimed. Jeremy asked, "What's wrong?"

I dialed Rich's cellphone. The call went directly to voicemail. I called his partner, Rob Parker, and got his voicemail, too. I looked on Rich's Facebook page; there was no information. Nothing had been reported in the press.

The day after the Senate voted to repeal "Don't ask, don't tell," I emailed hundreds of friends and colleagues, thanking them for their heroic efforts, and received hundreds of ecstatic responses. Rich's reply was more muted: "I don't think I ever realized how much of me was lost in that struggle back then. Thanks for being there to help me survive it with something of myself still intact." He was remorseful.

"You played a big role in this moment," I told him. "You stood up and put your life on the line. It is not easy to bear the scrutiny of the media and the courts. Your integrity, humility, humor, and wisdom educated so many. Thank you!" I believed that time would heal.

Rich took his own life six months later.[895] Kevin Blaesing did the same in April 2013.[896] His last words were reportedly "Rich, I'm coming to see you."

Despite the celebrations around "Don't ask, don't tell" repeal, Rich and Kevin remind us of what so many had lost. While they claimed their identity as gay men, they lost their identity as an Air Force officer and a marine. That loss of identity wounds deeply.

I traveled to San Diego for Rich's funeral, where I was honored to deliver his eulogy. I was surprised that no one else from the SLDN universe was present. Few in attendance knew of Rich's heroism. I told them his story.

Rich was stoic and understated—a reminder to all of us that we don't know the stories of those sitting next to us on the bus, or someone with whom we might start up a casual conversation at a bar. Histories remain hidden until told. I hugged Rich's partner, his sister, Linda, and his best friend, Lucia.

The deaths of Rich and Kevin left a hole in my heart, and I hope that their stories here honor their memories as I write them on Memorial Day.

CHAPTER 42

IMPACT

The sky did not fall, as supporters of the gay ban had expected. "None of the dire predictions of opponents, including warnings of a mass exodus of active-duty troops, have occurred," *The New York Times* reported.[897]

Even those who had wanted to keep the ban in place acknowledged that repeal was a non-issue. Six months after it took effect, "Buck" McKeon, the outspoken chairman of the House Armed Services Committee, said that allowing gay men and women to serve openly in the military was a settled issue.[898] Two months later, the Marine Corps' commandant, General James Amos, who had strongly opposed repeal, said in remarks at the National Press Club, "I get in front of the marines often, as often as I can, so often I get away from Washington. And I'll be honest with you, I don't even get a question. I don't hear anything. I don't see anything at all. I'm very pleased with how it's turned out."[899]

In a 2013 interview with *The New Republic*, even John McCain—who had repeatedly filibustered repeal legislation—conceded, "I think it has worked out."[900] He would later be a leading proponent of ending the ban on transgender service in the military.

Supporters of repeal were also pleased by the lack of controversy. "I have not found any negative effect on good order and discipline," Army General Martin Dempsey, who succeeded Mullen as chairman of the Joint Chiefs of Staff, said during a joint Pentagon briefing with Defense Secretary Panetta in May 2012.[901] At the Aspen Security Forum two months later, Admiral William McRaven, who led the Special Operations team that targeted Osama bin Laden, said, "We only care if you can't carry your rucksack. I am aware of no problems."[902] At the one-year celebration of repeal on the USS *Intrepid*, Mullen said, "I am delighted to report that, in all the feedback I get, from the fleet, from the field, and in the air, is it's a non-issue out there."[903]

In a commentary posted on the one-year anniversary of repeal, Bernard Rostker of the RAND Corporation, which conducted studies on gays in the military in 1993 and 2010, asked, "What has happened since DADT was repealed? Despite the fears of some, but in line with the experience of every other institution, both in the U.S. and abroad, that has experienced such a transition, there have been no significant problems."[904]

The Palm Center published a study co-authored by professors from the military academies and the Marine Corps War College. It concluded that not only had repeal produced no broad negative impact, it had created a positive impact.[905]

Perhaps most telling is this: Nine months after repeal took effect, the Pentagon celebrated LGBT Pride month for the first time. Pentagon general counsel Jeh Johnson, co-leader of the nine-month study that examined the impact of repealing "Don't ask, don't tell," led a panel discussion on the repeal process. In July, a military contingent marched in the San Diego Gay Pride parade. As David Crary of The Associated Press reported, "Soldiers and sailors [are] returning from deployment and, in time-honored tradition, embracing their beloved—this time with same-sex kisses."[906]

Six years later, at the Halifax International Security Forum, Army Colonel Katherine Graef, the logistics director for U.S. Special Operations Command Africa, came up to me. "I want to show you something," she said, pulling a photo out of her wallet. "This is my wife." She put her arms around me, tears in her eyes. "Thank you."

At a Pride event in June 2019 at the Defense Language Institute—the site of witch hunts in the 1990s and discharges of Arabic linguists after 9/11—Army Colonel Gary Hausman, the institute's commandant, "told the crowd at Weckerling Center that he believes LGBT troops have always served in the United States military, citing a belief amongst some historians that Revolutionary War hero and father of the Army's Non-commissioned Officer corps, Baron von Steuben, was a gay man."[907] In 2020, individual services and bases, installations, and ships marked Pride month with graphics and videos celebrating their service members, including the Marine Corps Recruit Depot at Parris Island[908] and RAF Mildenhall, the United Kingdom base that is home to a large U.S. Air Force contingent.[909]

Repeal may have also paved the way for other advancements, producing a profound shift in momentum on gay, transgender, and perhaps other issues in Washington.[910] Joe Lieberman said that repeal reflected a "coming of age of the LGBT community as a political force."[911]

In January 2013, the Pentagon lifted the ban on women in combat, though the steady advance of gender equality can stand on its own merits.[912] In December 2013, Congress repealed Article 125 of the Uniform Code of Military Justice as it pertained to consensual sex, ending the military's sodomy ban and bringing military law in line with the Supreme Court's decision in *Lawrence v. Texas* and the ruling by the Court of Appeals for the Armed Forces in *United States v. Marcum*.[913] In June 2016, the military ended its ban on transgender service members[914]—though just over a year later, President Donald Trump ordered in a tweet that the ban be reinstated.[915] After significant blowback from top military officers who argued against reinstating the ban, and litigation challenging the reversal, the Pentagon issued new directives prohibiting transgender individuals from enlisting and preventing currently serving service members who had not already been formally diagnosed with gender dysphoria from obtaining hormone treatments and transition surgery.[916] On January 25, 2021, in one of his first executive orders, President Joe Biden overturned those directives, enabling transgender patriots to serve our nation once again.[917]

"We should avail ourselves of the best possible talent regardless of gender identity," Defense Secretary Lloyd Austin, a retired Army general, said after Biden's executive order was announced. "It is the right thing to do. It is also the smart thing to do."[918] This time, the nondiscrimination rules should stick.

It is also possible that "Don't ask, don't tell" repeal paved the way for marriage equality. As *HuffPost*'s Ryan Grim and Kerry

Eleveld wrote in 2019, "In early 2009, no one imagined the Supreme Court's marriage decision in *Obergefell v. Hodges* was just over a handful of years away. But with the benefit of hindsight, it's difficult to imagine the high court delivering that decision without at least some demonstration of pro-gay political will serving as a down payment on those freedoms."[919]

Indeed, five weeks after "Don't ask, don't tell" was repealed, SLDN filed a lawsuit challenging the lack of marriage equality for lesbian and gay service members.[920] In videos co-produced by SLDN and Freedom to Marry, Major Shannon McLaughlin, a member of the Army National Guard and a longtime SLDN supporter, and her wife, Casey, explained that because of the Defense of Marriage Act, the 1996 law that denied federal benefits to legally married same-sex couples, Casey could not be added to Shannon's military health insurance.[921] In another video, Army Captain Steve Hill described how he wouldn't have been able to secure an emergency leave from Iraq if his husband died because the military didn't consider his husband as "immediate family"[922]—exactly what the soldier stationed in Afghanistan after 9/11 confronted when his partner was killed by a car while walking across a street in San Diego.

Michelle and I believed that repeal of "Don't ask, don't tell" and support of marriage equality were the linchpins for LGBT equality, and that repeal of the military's gay ban would open significant new opportunities for lesbian, gay, bisexual, and transgender Americans. Evan Wolfson, who founded Freedom to Marry and brilliantly conceived of and executed the plan for marriage equality, agreed. Andrew Sullivan, the provocative libertarian editor of *The New Republic*, was one of the few who got our theory of change early on.

He wrote in his book *Virtually Normal,* "If the military ban deals with the heart of what it is to be a citizen, the marriage ban deals with the core of what it is to be a member of civil society."[923]

"The most powerful industrial military complex in the history of the world has said 'yes,'" said Elizabeth Birch, former executive director of the Human Rights Campaign. "That makes everything else inevitable."[924]

◆◆◆

There is another way to measure impact—the stories that emerged post-repeal. Three stand out.

The first is the story of Eric Fanning, the bright-eyed Dartmouth College student with whom Michelle and I worked in 1994 to reverse attempts by the military services from recouping ROTC and graduate school scholarships from gay students. Eric joked that he learned more about the inner workings of the Pentagon just by trying to figure out who had decisional authority to reverse recoupment actions.

He clearly earned respect, because he was tapped by President Obama to serve as deputy under secretary of the Navy in 2009, under secretary of the Air Force in 2012, acting secretary of the Air Force in 2013, and secretary of the Army in 2015. He is the only openly gay person to hold any of those positions. The change in attitudes resulting from repeal created an environment where uniformed personnel could—and did—deeply respect his leadership.

At an LGBT Pride celebration at the Pentagon in June 2013, Eric reflected on working at the Defense Department in 1993. "I was working for an institution that discriminated against people just like me," he said. "It was a deeply conflicting time for me."[925] He acknowledged that had it not been for repeal, he might not have been in the leadership position he held.

The second story is that of Tammy Smith, an Army Reserve officer, who delivered the eulogy for Darren Manzella. On September 10, 2012, almost a year after the repeal of "Don't ask, don't tell," she became the first openly lesbian officer to be promoted to brigadier general. Her wife, Tracey Hepner, pinned the star on her uniform during a ceremony at the Women in Military Service for America Memorial in Arlington National Cemetery.[926] In an interview with NPR, Smith described what it meant to have Hepner there:

> "Part of our Army culture is just the importance of military family. And the fact that I was able to have my military family in the front row, there with me, supporting me in the role, following the tradition of participating with my dad promoting me was—it was just absolutely fantastic. I felt full, authentic and complete performing that ceremony with my family."[927]

In an interview with *The Advocate*, she reflected on what repeal meant to her. It "changed my life and my ability to be comfortable at work and just with who I was," she said. "For the first time in my entire career, I was able to live on a military post in one of those regular neighborhoods with all of the other military families, and it was just regular. It was so extraordinarily ordinary."[928] Smith retired as a major general on April 30, 2021.

The third story perhaps made possible in part by the repeal of "Don't ask, don't tell" is the incredible journey of Pete Buttigieg.

In 2020, Buttigieg, the mayor of South Bend, Indiana, and a candidate for the Democratic presidential nomination, became the first openly gay person to win one of the contests—the Iowa caucuses—in the nomination process, demonstrating an extraordinary change in public attitudes and acceptance of gay Americans. His story is punctuated, of course, by the fact that he is also a veteran. He was an intelligence officer in the Navy Reserve from 2009 to 2017 and served in Afghanistan for seven months.[929] I enthusiastically joined his campaign as a volunteer foreign policy advisor, happy to help advance the American story.

In a column for *Medium*, Buttigieg reflected on his service in a story he frequently told on the campaign trail—one that underscores both the pain of living under "Don't ask, don't tell" and the opportunities that repeal made possible:

> "On the day before my deployment to Afghanistan, I wrote a letter. It was for my family in the event that I didn't come home, a 32-year-old man's attempt to make sense of a short but very full life. Writing it had required as much of me as the hardest day of training. What I didn't put in the letter was that the act of writing it forced me to reflect on the possibility that I could die without ever having known what it felt like to be in love. ...

> "Gently setting the letter to my family in a desk drawer made it clear to me: You only get to live one life. And if you return home safe from a dangerous place, you owe it to yourself to build a life that is worthy of your own good fortune. So I came out. I met and married Chasten. I became whole."[930]

Five years after that deployment he was running for the Democratic presidential nomination. After Joe Biden was elected, Buttigieg became the first openly gay man to be confirmed by the Senate to a Cabinet position—secretary of transportation.

CHAPTER 43

REFLECTIONS

was asked more than once whether I ever lost hope during the 17-year battle to repeal "Don't ask, don't tell." I never did. I always saw tangible results from our work: how the pillars of discrimination propping up "Don't ask, don't tell" were crumbling, slowly but surely.

I found hope in every case we won, every person we kept safe, every policy we secured, every tick upward in public opinion we achieved, every report we published, every news story we broke, every Pride Day we attended, every speech we gave at a military academy, and every general and admiral who called for repeal. I found hope in every meeting at the Pentagon, every member of Congress who signed on to repeal, and every ally who joined the cause. As *Detroit News* columnist Deb Price wrote when I left

SLDN in 2007, "Big satisfaction ... has come from 'getting giants to dance'—getting the Pentagon brass to respond to his teensy group's investigations."[931]

I found the greatest hope in the brave men and women in uniform who told their truths, and I was honored to serve them. It was a privilege to work with, lobby for, and march alongside countless courageous veterans. Truth gives us hope. Each victory energized me to keep fighting.

There were long hours, threats, setbacks, lonely hours away from home—but that is true for anyone who is fighting for equality. Resilience, patience, humor, thick skin, grit, and humility joined with that deep well of hope to keep me pushing forward.

I compare developing the strategy to repeal "Don't ask, don't tell" to solving a Rubik's cube. I would twist and turn the cube this way and that to get the colors aligned. To end "Don't ask, don't tell," we had to align the public, elected officials, and the military.

SLDN set the stage for the legislative opening that was presented in 2009, and then marched through that opening. The road to repealing the ban on lesbian, gay, and bisexual service members did not start with SLDN, and was not solely due to SLDN—but from 1993 to 2010, SLDN played the most significant role.

"Policy windows ... have a 'use them or lose them' quality," Richard Valelly of Swarthmore College wrote in a review of the legislative process that led to repeal. Quoting political scientist John Kingdon, he noted: "'These policy windows, the opportunities for action on given initiatives, present themselves and stay open for only short periods.... If the window passes without action, it may not open again for a long time.' The 111th Congress was just that sort of policy window. If DADT repeal did not happen then, DADT might today still be in effect."[932]

Mike Mullen would agree with that analysis. He said that repeal came when it did because he, Robert Gates, and Barack Obama held the positions they did. Repeal also would not have happened without Senators Levin, Lieberman, and Collins, and Representatives Pelosi, Hoyer, and Murphy, and so many others who loudly or quietly lit the path for repeal. Repeal is ultimately a tribute to all the service members who told their truth.

Mullen was correct, and it is what SLDN said from the outset: Without integrity, readiness degrades. This was the struggle to achieve the freedom to serve.

ACKNOWLEDGMENTS

"The sky would be awfully dark with only one star."
— Anonymous

Our victory is shared by many. With the deepest gratitude and humility, I am thankful for all of the stars in equality's firmament. It was an extraordinary privilege and honor to be a part of the battle. In particular, I would like to thank:

- All of the LGBT service members who served on the front lines of "Don't ask, don't tell" and its prior incarnations, as well as those who are serving our nation today. Your service with dignity and courage honors us all.
- The gay service members who lost their lives in battle against the military's gay ban—Petty Officer Third Class Allen Schindler and Private First Class Barry Winchell—as

well as those who died in battle, notably Alan Rogers, the first openly gay soldier to be killed in the Iraq War.

- The LGBT service members who stood up in court, baring your lives to the world.
- The LGBT service members who shared your stories and changed people's minds.
- The retired generals and admirals, colonels and captains, and senior enlisted who came out as gay and showed that you served with distinction at the highest ranks and grades.
- Our straight allies in the military and Congress, and President Barack Obama, who defended our right to be ourselves.
- Michelle Benecke, who had a new vision of hope for gays in the military after the enactment of "Don't ask, don't tell."
- The extraordinary SLDN staff who led the charge against "Don't ask, don't tell" with skill and tireless resolve.
- The volunteers who pitched tents, hauled kegs, carved pumpkins, hosted wine tastings, threw pool parties, staffed Pride days, joined us in investigations at Lackland Air Force Base and Fort Campbell, and served on our boards.
- Our donors, whether you gave $5 or $500,000—I was always humbled and deeply moved by the generosity of spirit and time and wisdom and wealth that fueled the fight for equality.
- The LGBT veterans from World War II who helped build thriving LGBT communities in New York City and San Francisco.
- The pioneers who fought for equality in the armed forces before "Don't ask, don't tell."
- The allies who amplified SLDN's voice, both in collaboration with us and independently.
- All who have shared their truth in support of equality.

ENDNOTES

Chapter 1: My Birthday

1   Whenever "gay" is used throughout this book, it is used as an all-inclusive term for lesbian, gay, and bisexual. "Don't ask, don't tell," and its prior incarnations, was a sexual orientation–specific policy. Gender identity policies were addressed under separate regulations, though commanders too frequently conflated sexual orientation and gender identity. All individuals deserve the respect of self-identification. SLDN assisted LGBT and HIV+ service members seeking our help.

2   Ed O'Keefe and Felicia Sonmez, "'Don't ask, don't tell' repeal will clear Senate, Lieberman says," *The Washington Post*, December 17, 2010.

3   Chris Johnson, "Amos: Gays in military 'could cost Marines' lives,'" *Washington Blade*, December 14, 2010.

4   *Congressional Record*, Vol. 156, No. 169 (December 18, 2010), page S10652 (statement of Senator Webb).

5   O'Keefe and Sonmez, "'Don't ask, don't tell' repeal will clear Senate, Lieberman says."

6   Gail Russell Chaddock, "Why Susan Collins is blocking vote on 'Don't ask, don't tell,'" *The Christian Science Monitor*, September 21, 2010.

7   Kirk took office during the lame-duck session. He was elected in November 2010 to succeed Richard Burris, a Democrat who was

appointed to fill the seat left vacant when Barack Obama was elected president in 2008 and who chose not to run in 2010.

8   O'Keefe and Sonmez, "'Don't ask, don't tell' repeal will clear Senate, Lieberman says."

9   Liz Halloran, "Senate Defeat of 'Don't Ask, Don't Tell' Repeal Highlights Partisan Distrust," NPR, December 9, 2010.

10   O'Keefe and Sonmez, "'Don't ask, don't tell' repeal will clear Senate, Lieberman says."

11   Scott Wong, "'Don't ask' passes handily in House," *Politico*, December 15, 2010.

12   Chris Johnson, "Will time run out for 'Don't Ask' repeal?," *Washington Blade*, November 23, 2010.

13   Burr Statement on Repeal of Don't Ask Don't Tell, Office of Senator Richard Burr, December 28, 2010.

14   Chris Johnson, "HISTORIC: Senate approves 'Don't Ask' repeal," *Washington Blade*, December 18, 2010.

Chapter 2: If These Walls Could Weep

15   Karen Ocamb, "David Mixner on how DADT happened," *Los Angeles Blade*, December 20, 2018.

16   Jeffrey Schmalz, "Gay Groups Regrouping for War on Military Ban," *The New York Times*, February 7, 1993.

17   David W. Dunlap, "Thomas Stoddard, 48, Dies; An Advocate of Gay Rights," *The New York Times*, February 14, 1997.

18   Adam Liptak, "Civil Rights Law Protects Gay and Transgender Workers, Supreme Court Rules," *The New York Times*, June 15, 2020.

19   Art Pine, "Issue Explodes Into an All-Out Lobbying War," *Los Angeles Times*, January 28, 1993.

20   "Clinton: Policy on Gays in Military Is 'Sensible Balance,'" *The Washington Post*, July 20, 1993.

21   Department of Defense Directive 1332.14, *Enlisted Administrative Separations* at E3.A4.1.4.3 [hereinafter DODD 1332.14]; Department of Defense Instruction 1332.40, *Separation Procedures for Regular and Reserve Commissioned* [hereinafter DODI 1332.40].

22   *Policy Concerning Homosexuality in the Armed Forces: Hearings Before the Senate Committee on Armed Services*, 103rd Congress, page 786 (July 21, 1993).

23   *Policy Concerning Homosexuality in the Armed Forces: Hearings Before the Senate Committee on Armed Services*, 103rd Congress, page 709 (July 20, 1993) (statement of General Powell).

24   Michelle Benecke and C. Dixon Osburn, *Conduct Unbecoming: The Fourth Annual Report on "Don't Ask, Don't Tell, Don't Pursue, Don't Harass* [hereinafter, "SLDN Fourth Annual Report"].

25   Diane H. Mazur, "Sex and Lies: Rules of Ethics, Rules of Evidence, and Our Conflicted Views on the Significance of Honesty," *Notre Dame Journal of Law, Ethics and Public Policy*, 14:2, January 1, 2012.

Chapter 3: The Phoenix Rises

26   Lily Rothman, "How a Closeted Air Force Sergeant Became the Face of Gay Rights," *Time*, September 8, 2015.

27   C. Dixon Osburn, "Gay Life During Wartime," *The Advocate*, November 20, 2001.

28   Chris Bull, "Benecke, At Ease," *The Advocate*, February 27, 2001.

29   "Harvard Law School Second Annual Gay and Lesbian Legal Advocacy Conference: 'Don't Ask, Don't Tell,'" *Duke Journal of Gender Law & Policy*, 14:1173 (2007).

Chapter 4: 911 for Service Members

30   Michelle Benecke, "Turning Points: Challenges and Successes in Ending Don't Ask, Don't Tell," *William & Mary Journal of Women and the Law: 2011 Special Issue: The Repeal of "Don't Ask, Don't Tell,"* 18:1 (2011-2012) [hereafter "Benecke, 'Turning Points'"].

31   1995 First Quarter Report, Servicemembers Legal Defense Network.

32   1995 Third Quarter Report, Servicemembers Legal Defense Network.

33   1995 Third Quarter Report, Servicemembers Legal Defense Network.

34   1995 Third Quarter Report, Servicemembers Legal Defense Network.

35   1996 Third Quarter Report, Servicemembers Legal Defense Network.

36   1997 First Quarter Report, Servicemembers Legal Defense Network.

37   1997 Second Quarter Report, Servicemembers Legal Defense Network.

38   1997 Second Quarter Report, Servicemembers Legal Defense Network.

39   1998 First Quarter Report, Servicemembers Legal Defense Network.

40   1998 First Quarter Report, Servicemembers Legal Defense Network.

41   1998 First Quarter Report, Servicemembers Legal Defense Network.

42   1998 First Quarter Report, Servicemembers Legal Defense Network.

43   1998 First Quarter Report, Servicemembers Legal Defense Network.

44   1999 Second Quarter Report, Servicemembers Legal Defense Network.

45   1999 Third Quarter Report, Servicemembers Legal Defense Network.

46   1999 Fourth Quarter Report, Servicemembers Legal Defense Network.

47   2002 Third Quarter Report, Servicemembers Legal Defense Network.

48   2000 Fourth Quarter Report, Servicemembers Legal Defense Network.

49   *Frontlines*, Servicemembers Legal Defense Network, 2004 Third Quarter.

50   1996 Third Quarter Report, Servicemembers Legal Defense Network.

51   1997 Second Quarter Report, Servicemembers Legal Defense Network.

52   2002 Second Quarter Report, Servicemembers Legal Defense Network.

53   Tom Oliphant, "Military's War on Gays," *The Boston Globe*, March 19, 2002.

54   Andrew Sullivan, "Undone by 'Don't Ask, Don't Tell,'" *The New York Times*, April 9, 1998.

55   Bradley Graham, "Military Reviews Allegations of Harassment Against Gays," *The Washington Post*, May 14, 1997.

56   Norman Kempster, "Discharges Up After 'Don't Ask, Don't Tell,'" *Los Angeles Times*, February 27, 1997.

57   Matt Cover, "Kagan Called 'Don't Ask, Don't Tell' A 'Moral Injustice of the First Order,'" CNSNews, May 11, 2010.

58   Peter Baker, "McCurry Alters Statement on Military Policy on Gays," *The Washington Post*, July 22, 1997.

59   Baker, "McCurry Alters Statement on Military Policy on Gays."

60   Doug Ireland, "Search and Destroy," *The Nation*, June 22, 2000.

Chapter 5: Reporting for Duty

61   *Thomasson v. Perry*, 80 F.3d 915 (4th Cir. 1996).

62   Eric Schmitt, "The New Rules on Gay Soldiers: A Year Later, No Clear Results," *The New York Times,* March 13, 1995.

63   Schmitt, "The New Rules on Gay Soldiers: A Year Later, No Clear Results."

64   *Steffan v. Aspin,* 8 F.3d 57 (D.C. Cir. 1993).

65   *Cammermeyer v. Aspin,* 850 F.Supp. 910 (W.D. Wash. 1994).

66   *Meinhold v. United States Department of Defense,* 34 F.3d 1469 (9th Cir. 1994).

67   *Steffan v. Perry,* 41 F.3d 677 (D.C. Cir. 1994).

68   *Thomasson v. Perry,* 895 F.Supp. 820 (E.D. Va. 1995).

69   *Thomasson v. Perry* (1995).

70   *Thomasson v. Perry* (1995).

71   *Thomasson v. Perry,* 80 F.3d 915 (4th Cir. 1996)

72   Edward Feisenthal, "Supreme Court Won't Review Gays-in-the-Military Policy," *The Wall Street Journal,* October 22, 1996.

Chapter 6: Just Good Folk

73   Offutt AFB Officer Board – Google Groups, December 3, 1993 (post includes this article: Jason Gertzen, "Gay Captain at Offutt Faces Ouster," *Omaha World-Herald,* December 2, 1993).

74   Richard F. Richenberg Jr. death notice, Legacy.com/ *The Desert Sun,* June 19, 2011.

75   Offutt AFB Officer Board – Google Groups.

76   Offutt AFB Officer Board – Google Groups.

77   Offutt AFB Officer Board – Google Groups.

78   "Results Mixed on Military's Gay Policy," *Tampa Bay Times,* March 13, 1995.

79   *Wikipedia: The Free Encyclopedia,* "Blue Discharge" (accessed July 21, 2021).

80   *Richenberg v. Perry,* 909 F. Supp. 1303 (D. Neb. 1995).

81   *Richenberg v. Perry.*

82 *Richenberg v. Perry.*

83 *Richenberg. v. Perry,* 97 F.3d 256 (8th Cir. 1996).

84 *Able v. United States,* 968 F. Supp. 850 (E.D.N.Y. 1997).

Chapter 7: Policy Chops

85 Tamar Lewin, "Navy Drops Efforts to Seek Repayment From 2 Gay Students," *The New York Times,* May 9, 1990.

86 Randy Shilts, *Conduct Unbecoming: Lesbians and Gays in the U.S. Military* (New York: St. Martin's Press, 1993) [hereinafter "Shilts, *Conduct Unbecoming*"].

87 Bernard D. Rostker *et al., Sexual Orientation and U.S. Military Personnel Policy* (Santa Monica: RAND Corporation, 2010).

88 "West Point Gives Up Dunning Gay Graduate for His Tuition," *Chicago Tribune,* March 26, 1997.

89 Tammye Nash, "Discharged Gay Officer Fights Army's Duns," *Dallas Voice,* March 28, 1997.

90 "West Point Gives Up Dunning Gay Graduate for His Tuition."

91 "West Point Gives Up Dunning Gay Graduate for His Tuition."

92 1999 Second Quarter Report, Servicemembers Legal Defense Network.

93 Marlene Cimons, "Clinton Ends Prohibition of Security Clearances for Gays," *Los Angeles Times,* August 5, 1995.

94 The Crittenden Report: *Report of the Board Appointed to Prepare and Submit Recommendations to the Secretary of the Navy for the Revision of Policies, Procedures and Directives Dealing with Homosexuals* (1956–57).

95 Key Dates in U.S. Military LGBT Policy, Naval History Blog, U.S. Naval Institute.

96 "DADT, R.I.P.," *Armed Forces Journal,* September 1, 2012.

97 Warren E. Leary, "Government Agency Ferreted Out Names of Its Gay Workers," *The New York Times,* May 14, 1992.

98 "Clinton Bans Sexual Orientation Discrimination in Security Clearances," The Associated Press, August 5, 1995.

99 Eric Cervini, *The Deviant's War: The Homosexual vs. the United States of America* (New York: Farrar, Straus and Giroux, 2020).

100 Cimons, "Clinton Ends Prohibition of Security Clearances for Gays."

101 William Claiborne, "'B-1 Bob' Dornan Is on the Attack Again," *The Washington Post*, May 1, 1998.

102 Valerie Heithusen and Brendan W. McGarry, "Defense Primer: The NDAA Process," Congressional Research Service, February 16, 2021.

103 Philip Shenon, "Reluctantly, Clinton Signs Defense Bill," *The New York Times*, February 11, 1996.

104 *Conduct Unbecoming: Second Annual Report on "Don't Ask, Don't Tell, Don't Pursue,"* Servicemembers Legal Defense Network (1996) [hereinafter "SLDN Second Annual Report].

105 SLDN Second Annual Report.

106 Alison Mitchell, "President Finds a Way to Fight Mandate to Oust H.I.V. Troops," *The New York Times*, February 10, 1996.

107 Kirk Childress, "HIV Positive Servicemembers" (letter to the editor), *Los Angeles Times*, March 15, 1996.

108 Gebe Martinez, "Dornan HIV Law on Way Out," *Los Angeles Times*, April 25, 1996.

109 2000 Fourth Quarter Report, Servicemembers Legal Defense Network.

Chapter 8: "Lieutenant Stunning"

110 Zoe Dunning, "A Witness to History," Alice B. Toklas Democratic Club, January 20, 2011.

111 Zoe Dunning, "My Unexpected Journey," TEDxAmador Valley High, October 19, 2015.

112 National Defense Research Institute, "The History of 'Don't Ask, Don't Tell,'" *Sexual Orientation and U.S. Military Personnel Policy: An Update of RAND's 1993 Study* (Santa Monica: RAND Corporation, 2010).

113 SLDN Second Annual Report.

114 "Bruce A. Lehman," United States Patent and Trademark Office.

115 SLDN Fourth Annual Report.

116 SLDN Fourth Annual Report.

117 Nathaniel Frank, *Unfriendly Fire: How the Gay Ban Undermines the Military and Weakens America* (New York: Thomas Dunne Books, 2009).

Chapter 9: The Doctor Is In

118   Michelle Benecke and C. Dixon Osburn, *Conduct Unbecoming Continues: The First Year Under "Don't Ask, Don't Tell, Don't Pursue"* (1995) [hereinafter "SLDN First Annual Report"].

119   Department of the Navy, NAVMED P-85134, General Medical Officer Manual (May 1996).

120   Michelle Benecke, C. Dixon Osburn et al., *Conduct Unbecoming: The Sixth Annual Report on "Don't Ask, Don't Tell, Don't Pursue, Don't Harass"* (2000) [hereinafter "SLDN Sixth Annual Report"].

121   C. Dixon Osburn et al., *Conduct Unbecoming: The Seventh Annual Report on "Don't Ask, Don't Tell, Don't Pursue, Don't Harass"* (2001) [hereinafter "SLDN Seventh Annual Report"].

122   U.S. Department of Defense, Office of the Assistant Secretary of Defense (Personnel and Readiness), *Review of the Effectiveness of the Application and Enforcement of the Department's Policy on Homosexual Conduct in the Military* (April 1998). [Hereinafter: April 1998 Review of application and enforcement of "Don't Ask, don't tell."]

123   SLDN Fourth Annual Report.

124   Chris Bull, "His Public Domain, His Private Pain," *The Washington Post*, July 11, 1999.

125   Dr. Martin Chin, "Being Discharged Under 'Don't Ask, Don't Tell'" in *Gay Mental Healthcare Providers and Patients in the Military: Personal Experiences and Clinical Care* (Cameron Elspeth Ritchie, Joseph E. Wise, Bryan Pyle eds.)(Cham, Switzerland: Springer International Publishing, 2017).

Chapter 10: You've Got Mail

126   SLDN Fourth Annual Report.

127   *McVeigh v. Cohen*, 983 F. Supp. 217 (D.D.C. 1998).

128   Rajiv Chandrasekaran, "AOL Admits Violating Its Own Disclosure Policy," *The Washington Post*, January 22, 1998.

129   *McVeigh v. Cohen*.

130   *McVeigh v. Cohen*.

Chapter 11: A Walking Talking Contradiction

131 James Sterngold, "An Unlikely 'Don't Tell' Target: Lawmaker May Face Discharge," *The New York Times*, August 26, 1999.

132 Sterngold, "An Unlikely 'Don't Tell' Target: Lawmaker May Face Discharge."

133 Amy Silverman, "Confessions of a Gay, Right-Wing Mormon," *Phoenix New Times*, April 12, 1999.

134 Sterngold, "An Unlikely 'Don't Tell' Target: Lawmaker May Face Discharge."

135 SLDN Seventh Annual Report.

Chapter 12: Papa Don't Preach

136 SLDN Third Annual Report.

137 Amy Goodman, "Gay and Lesbian Service Members," *Democracy Now*, February 27, 1997.

138 SLDN Third Annual Report.

139 1996 Second Quarter Report, Servicemembers Legal Defense Network.

140 Michelle Benecke, C. Dixon Osburn *et al.*, *Conduct Unbecoming: The Fifth Annual Report on "Don't Ask, Don't Tell, Don't Pursue"* (1999) [hereinafter "SLDN Fifth Annual Report"].

141 C. Dixon Osburn *et al.*, *Conduct Unbecoming: The Ninth Annual Report on "Don't Ask, Don't Tell, Don't Pursue, Don't Harass"* (2003) [hereinafter "SLDN Ninth Annual Report"].

142 SLDN Seventh Annual Report.

143 C. Dixon Osburn *et al.*, *Conduct Unbecoming: The Tenth Annual Report on "Don't Ask, Don't Tell, Don't Pursue, Don't Harass"* (2004) [hereinafter "SLDN Tenth Annual Report"].

144 "Navy Discharging Lesbian for Attending Gay Marriage Rally," *The Dallas Voice*, July 20, 2006.

Chapter 13: Lackland

145 David Burrelli and Jody Feder, "Homosexuals and U.S. Military: Current Issues," Congressional Research Service, July 22, 2009.

146   Shilts, *Conduct Unbecoming*.

147   *Wikipedia: The Free Encyclopedia*, "Don't ask, don't tell" (accessed July 22, 2021).

148   Eric Rosenberg, "Group to Look Into AF Rules," *Fort Lauderdale Sun-Sentinel*, January 29, 1999.

149   Rosenberg, "Group to Look Into AF Rules."

150   1999 Fourth Quarter Report, Servicemembers Legal Defense Network.

Chapter 14: The Homosexual Questionnaires

151   SLDN First Annual Report.

152   SLDN Third Annual Report.

153   SLDN Fourth Annual Report.

154   SLDN Ninth Annual Report.

155   SLDN Third Annual Report.

156   SLDN First Annual Report.

157   SLDN Third Annual Report.

158   SLDN Second Annual Report.

159   SLDN Second Annual Report.

160   SLDN Second Annual Report.

161   SLDN Fourth Annual Report.

162   SLDN Tenth Annual Report.

163   SLDN Third Annual Report.

164   SLDN Third Annual Report.

165   Ireland, "Search and Destroy."

166   Fiona Morgan, "Inside a Lesbian 'Witch Hunt,'" *Salon*, June 8, 2000.

167   Robert Suro, "Navy Sends Agents Into Gay Bars," *The Washington Post*, June 17, 2000.

168   Stacey Sobel, letter to David L. Brant, GLAA Archives, June 2, 2000.

Chapter 15: Platform Shoes

169   U.S. Congress, Senate Committee on Naval Affairs, "Alleged Immoral Conditions at Newport (R.I.) Naval Training Station" (1921). "Lay Navy

Scandal to F.D. Roosevelt: Senate Naval Sub-Committee Accuses Him and Daniels in Newport Inquiry. DETAILS ARE UNPRINTABLE. Minority Report Asserts Charges of Immorally Employing Men Do Officials Injustice," *The New York Times*, July 20, 1921.

170   Shilts, *Conduct Unbecoming.*

171   Steve Rothaus, "Trail Blazer, Still Vigilant and Telling All," *The Miami Herald*, March 14, 2010.

Chapter 16: Ciao

172   J. Jennings Moss, "Lesbian Baiting in the Barracks," *The Advocate*, February 4, 1997.

173   SLDN Third Annual Report.

174   SLDN Third Annual Report.

175   Benecke, "Turning Points."

176   *Barnes v. Perry*, Defendant's Opposition to Plaintiff's Motion for Preliminary Injunction, Civil Action No. 96-591-ES (1996).

177   *Barnes v. Perry*, Defendant's Opposition to Plaintiff's Motion for Preliminary Injunction.

178   *Report of the Advisory Board on the Investigative Capability of the Department of Defense, Volume I* (Washington: U.S. Government Printing Office, 1995).

179   Charles F.C. Ruff *et. al.*, "Report of the Advisory Board on the Investigative Committee of the Department of Defense," October 4, 1995.

180   Moss, "Lesbian Baiting in the Barracks."

181   SLDN Second Annual Report.

182   Benecke, "Turning Points."

Chapter 17: Come to Jesus

183   *Cook v. Gates*, No. 06-2313 (1st Cir. argued March 7, 2007), Brief of Constitutional Law Professors as Amici Curiae Supporting Appellants.

184   1997 First Quarter Report, Servicemembers Legal Defense Network.

185   Air Force Inspector General Report of Investigation, September 11, 1996.

186   Gregg K. Kakesako, "NCO accuses Air Force of gay 'witch hunt,'" *Honolulu Star-Bulletin*, February 14, 1997.

187 "Witch hunt did happen — and it was very spooky" (letter to the editor), *Honolulu Star-Bulletin*, February 22, 1997.

188 April 1998 Review of application and enforcement of "Don't Ask, don't tell."

189 Jonathan S. Landay, "Congress jumps into military social fray," *Las Vegas Sun*, July 18, 1996.

Chapter 18: DLI

190 SLDN Sixth Annual Report.

191 SLDN Sixth Annual Report.

192 SLDN Sixth Annual Report.

193 Morgan, "Inside a Lesbian Witch Hunt."

194 Morgan, "Inside a Lesbian Witch Hunt."

195 Morgan, "Inside a Lesbian Witch Hunt."

196 Morgan, "Inside a Lesbian Witch Hunt."

197 SLDN Sixth Annual Report.

198 SLDN Sixth Annual Report.

199 SLDN Sixth Annual Report.

200 SLDN Sixth Annual Report.

201 SLDN Sixth Annual Report.

202 SLDN Sixth Annual Report.

203 SLDN Sixth Annual Report.

204 SLDN Sixth Annual Report.

205 SLDN Sixth Annual Report.

206 SLDN Sixth Annual Report.

207 SLDN Seventh Annual Report.

208 SLDN Seventh Annual Report.

209 SLDN Seventh Annual Report.

210 SLDN Seventh Annual Report.

211 Morgan, "Inside a Lesbian Witch Hunt."

Chapter 19: Mustang

212 "Homosexuals in the Military," C-SPAN, December 22, 1993.

213   SLDN Third Annual Report.

214   SLDN Third Annual Report.

215   SLDN Fourth Annual Report.

216   SLDN Fourth Annual Report.

217   SLDN Third Annual Report.

218   "Homosexuals in the Military."

219   Benecke, "Turning Points."

220   "Jury Acquits Air Force Major Accused of Lesbian Affair," *The New York Times*, August 17, 1996.

221   "Jury Acquits Air Force Major Accused of Lesbian Affair."

222   Margaret Hartmann, "Where the Gay Rights Movement Stands," *Intelligencer/New York Magazine*, June 30, 2014.

223   SLDN Fifth Annual Report.

Chapter 20: Bullseye

224   "Perspectives," *Newsweek*, April 3, 2000.

225   Susan Stevens, "Mother Continues Fight for Justice," *The Times* (Munster, Indiana), September 28, 1997.

226   Ranny Green, "'Any Mother's Son' Captures Many Emotions," *The Seattle Times*, August 10, 1997.

227   Stevens, "Mother Continues Fight for Justice."

228   Stevens, "Mother Continues Fight for Justice."

229   SLDN Third Annual Report.

230   SLDN Third Annual Report.

231   SLDN Fourth Annual Report.

232   E.A. Barrera, "Battles Loom as to When Gays Will Serve Openly in Military," *East County Magazine*, May 2009.

233   SLDN Seventh Annual Report.

234   "Removal of Gay Officer from Army Challenged," *Tampa Bay Times*, July 26, 1997.

235   Bradley Graham, "Gay Officer's Removal Fuels Charges of Bias," *The Washington Post*, July 26, 1997.

236   Graham, "Gay Officer's Removal Fuels Charges of Bias."

237 SLDN Seventh Annual Report.

238 SLDN Seventh Annual Report.

239 SLDN Seventh Annual Report.

240 SLDN Seventh Annual Report.

241 SLDN Seventh Annual Report.

242 SLDN Seventh Annual Report.

243 C. Dixon Osburn *et al.*, *Conduct Unbecoming: SLDN's Eighth Annual Report on "Don't Ask, Don't Tell, Don't Pursue, Don't Harass* (2002) [hereinafter "SLDN Eighth Annual Report"].

244 SLDN Eighth Annual Report.

245 Letter from Rear Admiral S.R. Pietropaoli, Chief of Navy Information, to Elizabeth Birch, executive director, Human Rights Campaign (October 17, 2001).

246 Allen White, "Defense Department Labels Gay Kiss-In Credible Threat to Terrorism," *Beyond Chron*, December 2, 2005.

247 White, "Defense Department Labels Gay Kiss-In Credible Threat to Terrorism."

248 Statement from SLDN in John Aravosis, "Pentagon anti-terror investigators labeled gay law school groups a 'credible threat' of terrorism," AMERICAblog, December 20, 2005.

249 Ireland, "Search and Destroy."

250 Ireland, "Search and Destroy."

251 Ireland, "Search and Destroy."

252 Ireland, "Search and Destroy."

Chapter 21: Lesbian-Baiting

253 Michelle M. Benecke and Kirstin S. Dodge, "Military Women in Nontraditional Job Fields: Casualties of the Armed Forces' War on Homosexuals," *Harvard Women's Law Journal* (1990).

254 Adrienne Rich, "Compulsory Heterosexuality and Lesbian Existence," *Signs: Journal of Women in Culture and Society*, University of Chicago Press Journals (1980).

255 SLDN Tenth Annual Report.

256 Kim Barker, "Woman Wins Emotional War With Military Will Stay in Service, But Says Justice Denied," *The Spokesman-Review* (Spokane, Washington), August 6, 1995.

257 SLDN Second Annual Report.

258 Barker, "Woman Wins Emotional War With Military."

259 Barker, "Woman Wins Emotional War With Military."

260 Nathaniel Frank, "Don't Ask, Don't Tell: Detailing the Damage," Palm Center/University of California, Santa Barbara, August 2010.

261 1997 Fourth Quarter Report, Servicemembers Legal Defense Network.

262 Ireland, "Search and Destroy."

263 Ireland, "Search and Destroy."

264 SLDN Sixth Annual Report.

265 SLDN Sixth Annual Report.

266 SLDN Sixth Annual Report.

267 SLDN Sixth Annual Report.

268 Kasper Zeuthen, "Accuser's Story Disputed in Army Sex Case," *Los Angeles Times*, July 30, 1997.

269 Elaine Sciolino, "From a Love Affair to a Court-Martial," *The New York Times*, May 11, 1997.

Chapter 22: Louisville Slugger

270 Buzz Bissinger, "Don't Ask, Don't Kill," *Vanity Fair*, May 2005.

271 Francis X. Clines, "Mother Sees No End to Ordeal in Slaying," *The New York Times*, January 10, 2000.

272 Bissinger, "Don't Ask, Don't Kill."

273 Thomas Hackett, "The Execution of Private Barry Winchell," *Rolling Stone*, March 2, 2000.

274 Hackett, "The Execution of Private Barry Winchell."

275 Calpernia Addams, *"Soldier's Girl — The Reality,"* Calpernia.com.

276 David France, "An Inconvenient Woman," *The New York Times*, May 28, 2000.

277 The Army's Criminal Investigation Division, or CID, was formally established in 1918 by General John J. Pershing. In 1971,

its responsibilities were expanded and its name was changed to the Criminal Investigation Command, but it is still known as "CID" as a link to the division's history. See "History of CID," U.S. Army Criminal Investigation Command.

278 James Sterngold, "The Gay Troop Issue," *The New York Times*, January 31, 1993.

279 Hackett, "The Execution of Private Barry Winchell."

280 Hackett, "The Execution of Private Barry Winchell."

281 Francis X. Clines, "For Gay Soldier a Daily Barrage of Threats and Slurs," *The New York Times*, December 12, 1999.

282 Hackett, "The Execution of Private Barry Winchell."

283 Hackett, "The Execution of Private Barry Winchell."

284 Bissinger, "Don't Ask, Don't Kill."

285 Hackett, "The Execution of Private Barry Winchell."

286 SLDN Sixth Annual Report (2000).

287 Bissinger, "Don't Ask, Don't Kill."

288 Bissinger, "Don't Ask, Don't Kill."

289 Bissinger, "Don't Ask, Don't Kill."

290 France, "An Inconvenient Woman."

291 Bissinger, "Don't Ask, Don't Kill."

292 Bissinger, "Don't Ask, Don't Kill."

293 SLDN Sixth Annual Report.

294 Bissinger, "Don't Ask, Don't Kill."

295 Bissinger, "Don't Ask, Don't Kill."

296 Bissinger, "Don't Ask, Don't Kill."

297 Bissinger, "Don't Ask, Don't Kill."

298 Bissinger, "Don't Ask, Don't Kill."

299 Hackett, "The Execution of Private Barry Winchell."

300 Bissinger, "Don't Ask, Don't Kill."

301 Bissinger, "Don't Ask, Don't Kill."

302 Hackett, "The Execution of Private Barry Winchell."

303 Bissinger, "Don't Ask, Don't Kill."

304   Bissinger, "Don't Ask, Don't Kill."

305   Bissinger, "Don't Ask, Don't Kill."

306   Bissinger, "Don't Ask, Don't Kill."

307   Bissinger, "Don't Ask, Don't Kill."

308   Bissinger, "Don't Ask, Don't Kill."

309   Bissinger, "Don't Ask, Don't Kill."

310   Bissinger, "Don't Ask, Don't Kill."

311   Bissinger, "Don't Ask, Don't Kill."

312   Bissinger, "Don't Ask, Don't Kill."

313   Bissinger, "Don't Ask, Don't Kill."

314   Hackett, "The Execution of Private Barry Winchell."

315   Bissinger, "Don't Ask, Don't Kill."

316   SLDN Sixth Annual Report.

317   SLDN Sixth Annual Report.

318   SLDN Sixth Annual Report.

319   SLDN Sixth Annual Report.

320   Michael Radutzky (producer), "The War At Home," *60 Minutes*, January 17, 1999.

321   SLDN Ninth Annual Report.

322   SLDN Ninth Annual Report.

323   SLDN Ninth Annual Report.

324   SLDN Seventh Annual Report.

325   SLDN Sixth Annual Report.

326   SLDN Sixth Annual Report.

327   SLDN Sixth Annual Report.

328   SLDN Sixth Annual Report.

329   SLDN Sixth Annual Report.

330   SLDN Sixth Annual Report.

331   Doug Ireland, "Search and Destroy," *The Nation*, June 22, 2000.

332   SLDN Sixth Annual Report.

333   Ireland, "Search and Destroy."

334 Peter Cassels, "Retired General Speaks Out About Winchell Murder, EDGE Media Network, January 11, 2007.

335 Mary D. Ferguson, "Cody Takes Command of 101st, Fort Campbell," *Kentucky New Era*, June 10, 2000.

336 SLDN Seventh Annual Report.

337 SLDN Eighth Annual Report.

338 SLDN Ninth Annual Report.

339 SLDN Ninth Annual Report.

340 SLDN Seventh Annual Report.

341 Aaron Belkin, *How We Won: Progressive Lessons from the Repeal of "Don't Ask, Don't Tell"* (Huffington Post Media Group, 2011).

342 Clines, "Mother Sees No End to Ordeal in Slaying."

343 Nancy Zuckerbrod, "Army Denies Claim of Soldier's Mom," The Associated Press, September 29, 2000.

344 Carla Marinucci, "End 'Don't Ask, Don't Tell,' Gore Insists," *San Francisco Chronicle*, December 14, 1999.

345 Marinucci, "End 'Don't Ask, Don't Tell,' Gore Insists."

346 William J. Clinton interview with Mark Knoller and Peter Maer of CBS News, December 11, 1999.

347 Robin Givhan, "Clearing the Decks at Gore Headquarters," *The Washington Post*, November 16, 1999.

348 Veronica Wells, "'Who Says I Just Like Men?' Donna Brazile Opens Up About Her Sexuality With Wendy Williams," Madamenoire, December 3, 2018.

Chapter 23: Shin-Kicker

349 Memorandum of Under Secretary of Defense Edwin Dorn, "Guidelines for Investigating Threats Against Service Members Based on Alleged Homosexuality," March 24, 1997.

350 Ireland, "Search and Destroy."

351 SLDN Fourth Annual Report.

352 SLDN Fourth Annual Report.

353 SLDN Fourth Annual Report.

354   SLDN Fourth Annual Report.

355   SLDN Fourth Annual Report.

356   SLDN Fourth Annual Report.

357   U.S. Department of Defense, Office of the Assistant Secretary of Defense (Personnel and Readiness), *Review of the Effectiveness of the Application and Enforcement of the Department's Policy on Homosexual Conduct in the Military*, April 1998.

358   SLDN Sixth Annual Report (2000).

359   Philip Shenon, "Pentagon Moving to End Abuses of 'Don't Ask, Don't Tell' Policy," *The New York Times*, August 13, 1999.

360   SLDN Sixth Annual Report.

361   SLDN Sixth Annual Report.

362   SLDN Sixth Annual Report.

363   Roberto Suro, "Military's Different Lesson Plans Reflect Unease on Gay Policy," *The Washington Post*, March 4, 2000.

364   2000 Fourth Quarter Report, Servicemembers Legal Defense Network.

365   SLDN Sixth Annual Report.

366   Suro, "Military's Different Lesson Plans Reflect Unease on Gay Policy."

367   Suro, "Military's Different Lesson Plans Reflect Unease on Gay Policy."

368   Suro, "Military's Different Lesson Plans Reflect Unease on Gay Policy."

369   Suro, "Military's Different Lesson Plans Reflect Unease on Gay Policy."

370   SLDN Sixth Annual Report.

371   SLDN Sixth Annual Report.

372   SLDN Sixth Annual Report.

373   SLDN Seventh Annual Report.

374   SLDN Seventh Annual Report.

375   Suro, "Military's Different Lesson Plans Reflect Unease on Gay Policy."

376   Suro, "Military's Different Lesson Plans Reflect Unease on Gay Policy."

377   SLDN Sixth Annual Report.

378   SLDN Sixth Annual Report.

379   SLDN Sixth Annual Report.

380   SLDN Sixth Annual Report.

381   SLDN Sixth Annual Report.

Chapter 24: Hate Crimes

382   William J. Clinton, Statement on Signing the Executive Order Amending the Manual for Courts-Martial, October 7, 1999.

Chapter 25: Little Ears

383   Elizabeth Becker and Katharine Q. Seelye, "The Military Orders Spot Checks of Bases On Gay Harassment," *The New York Times,* December 14, 1999.

384   Defense Department Daily Briefing, C-SPAN, December 9, 1999.

385   Paul Richter, "Armed Forces Find 'Disturbing' Level of Gay Harassment," *Los Angeles Times,* March 25, 2000.

386   "Homosexuals in the Military," C-SPAN, March 24, 2000.

387   Office of Inspector General, Department of Defense, *Evaluation Report: Military Environment with Respect to the Homosexual Conduct Policy* (Report No. D-2000-101), March 16, 2000.

388   Ireland, "Search and Destroy."

389   Steven Lee Meyers, "Transfer of General at Site of Anti-Gay Killing Protested," *New York Times,* June 9, 2000.

390   Ireland, "Search and Destroy."

391   Letter from Lawrence J. Korb to The Honorable Carol A. DiBattiste, Undersecretary of the Air Force (May 8, 2000), SLDN Seventh Annual Report (2001).

392   Letter from Edwin Dorn to The Honorable Carol DiBattiste, Under Secretary of the Air Force (May 1, 2000), SLDN Seventh Annual Report.

393   SLDN Tenth Annual Report.

394   Department of Defense Working Group, Anti-Harassment Action Plan (July 21, 2000).

395   Jason Linkins, "'Don't Ask Don't Tell' Policy Explained By Comic Book," *HuffPost,* December 6, 2017.

396   *Dignity & Respect: A Training Guide on Homosexual Conduct Policy,* Department of Defense, April 29, 2016.

397 SLDN Sixth Annual Report.

398 SLDN Sixth Annual Report.

399 Stephen Green, "'Don't Ask, Don't Tell' Training to Be Set Up; Pentagon Will Stress 'Don't Harass' as Well," *San Diego Union-Tribune*, January 26, 2000.

400 SLDN Seventh Annual Report.

401 "Slain Gay Soldier's Case Slows a General's Rise," *The New York Times*, May 18, 2003.

402 John Files, "Committee Approves Promoting General in Gay-Bashing Case," *The New York Times*, October 24, 2003.

403 Tom Brokaw, "Mother Tries to Prevent Promotion of General Who Commanded a Base Where Her Son Was Killed for Being Gay," *NBC Nightly News*, June 17, 2003.

404 *Congressional Record*, Vol. 149, No. 167 (November 18, 2003), page S15030 (statement of Senator Kennedy).

405 *Congressional Record*, Vol. 149, No. 167 (November 18, 2003), page S15040 (statement of Senator Dayton).

406 SLDN Tenth Annual Report.

407 Thomas Oliphant, "General Rises Despite a Tainted Command," *The Boston Globe*, October 16, 2002.

408 Ireland, "Search and Destroy."

409 Deb Price, "Gays refuse to retreat from war with Pentagon," *The Detroit News*, April 25, 1998.

Chapter 26: Reframing the Debate

410 Anna Quindlen, "President's Policy on Gays in the Military Remains a Muddle," *Chicago Tribune*, December 5, 1994.

411 "An assault on gays on the military" (editorial), *The Boston Globe*, March 8, 1997.

412 Andrew Sullivan, "Undone by 'Don't Ask, Don't Tell,'" *The New York Times*, April 9, 1998.

413 Specialist Edgar Rosa, Delta Co., 2nd/502nd, Article 32 Hearing for Specialist Justin Fisher, September 1, 1999.

414 SLDN Third Annual Report.

415 SLDN Fifth Annual Report.

416 SLDN Sixth Annual Report.

417 Bootie Cosgrove-Mather, "Debating 'Don't Ask, Don't Tell,'" CBS News, March 25, 2003.

418 2002 First Quarter Report, Servicemembers Legal Defense Network.

419 2002 First Quarter Report, Servicemembers Legal Defense Network.

420 2002 First Quarter Report, Servicemembers Legal Defense Network.

421 2002 First Quarter Report, Servicemembers Legal Defense Network.

422 "No Gays Except ..." (editorial), *The Washington Post*, March 26, 2003.

423 Tom Oliphant, "Gays in Military See an Easing of Discrimination," *The Boston Globe*, April 8, 2003.

424 Benecke, "Turning Points."

425 Elizabeth Kier, "Homosexuals in the U.S. Military: Open Integration and Combat Effectiveness," *International Security*, Volume 23, No. 2 (Fall 1998).

426 *Policy Implications of Lifting the Ban on Homosexuals in the Military: Hearings Before the Committee on Armed Services, House of Representatives*, 103rd Congress, page 181 (May 4, 1993) (statement of Chaplain James M. Hutchens).

427 Frank, *Unfriendly Fire.*

428 Neel Burton, "When Homosexuality Stopped Being a Mental Disorder," *Psychology Today*, September 18, 2015.

429 Burton, "When Homosexuality Stopped Being a Mental Disorder."

430 Marlene Cimons, "Clinton Ends Prohibition of Security Clearances for Gays," *Los Angeles Times*, August 5, 1995.

431 SLDN Eighth Annual Report (2002).

432 Lauren Collins, "Don't Ask, Don't Ink," *The New Yorker*, February 5, 2010.

433 Bob Roehr, "As he departs Dixon Osburn reflects on SLDN," *Between The Lines*, May 17, 2007.

434 Ireland, "Search and Destroy."

435 Ireland, "Search and Destroy."

436 Ireland, "Search and Destroy."

437 Rothaus, "Trail blazer still vigilant, and telling all."

438 Lauren Hough, *Leaving Isn't the Hardest Thing* (New York: Vintage Books, 2021).

439 "Report: Support Growing for Openly Gay Soldiers," *The Advocate*, October 27, 2004.

440 Mark Thompson, "Aspin Mutes Gay Polling in Military," *Daily Press*, April 30, 1993.

441 G. Dean Sinclair, "Homosexuality and the Military: A Review of the Literature," *Journal of Homosexuality*, 56:6 (2009).

442 Daryl Lindsey, "Round 2: Should Gays Serve?" *Salon*, June 13, 2000.

443 "Report: Support Growing for Openly Gay Soldiers," *The Advocate*, October 27, 2004.

444 Brian McCabe, "Public Opinion on 'Don't Ask, Don't Tell,'" FiveThirtyEight, November 30, 2010.

445 Letter from Ken Lynch, *Navy Times*, February 3, 2003.

446 McCabe, "Public Opinion on 'Don't Ask, Don't Tell.'"

447 McCabe, "Public Opinion on 'Don't Ask, Don't Tell.'"

448 McCabe, "Public Opinion on 'Don't Ask, Don't Tell.'"

449 McCabe, "Public Opinion on 'Don't Ask, Don't Tell.'"

450 Singer, "How *The Real World* Ended 'Don't Ask, Don't Tell,'" Foreign Policy at Brookings, Policy Paper Number 6, August 2008.

451 Jon Barrett, "Danny's new real world," *Advocate*, November 7, 2006.

452 "Gay 'married' couple Reichen & Chip Amazing Race 4 in 2003" (video), YouTube, posted July 7, 2011.

453 *The Amazing Race*, Emmy Awards, National Academy of Television Arts and Sciences.

454 Johnny Diaz, "Out of Synch," *The Boston Globe*, December 6, 2006.

455 Randy Shulman, "Reichen's Reality," *Metro Weekly*, October 1, 2003.

456 Diaz, "Out of Synch."

457 Diaz, "Out of Synch."

458 "Soldier's Girl," The Peabody Awards.

459 "'Soldier's Girl' Named to AFI Top 10 List" (press release), Showtime, December 17, 2003.

460 "Why Peabody Matters," The Peabody Awards.

461 Calpernia Addams, "Soldier's Girl — The Reality," Calpernia.com.

462 Lynne Heffley, "Homophobia at Heart of 'Any Mother's Son,'" *Los Angeles Times*, August 11, 1997.

463 Ranny Green, "'Any Mother's Son' Captures Many Emotions," *Seattle Times*, August 10, 1997.

464 Randy Shulman, "Cybill Rights," *Metro Weekly*, March 21, 2007.

465 Pam Spaulding, "Welcome to SLDN's 15th Annual National Dinner Live Blogging Event," *Shadowproof*, March 24, 2007.

466 Shulman, "Cybill Rights."

467 Singer, "How *The Real World* Ended 'Don't Ask, Don't Tell.'"

468 Lacey Rose, "Ellen DeGeneres to End Talk Show: 'I Need Something New to Challenge Me' (Exclusive)," *The Hollywood Reporter*, May 12, 2021.

469 Meghan Werft, "Obama Honors Ellen DeGeneres and LGBT Rights With Medal of Freedom," Global Citizen, November 23, 2016.

470 David Eldridge, "Biden 'comfortable' with gay marriage, cites 'Will & Grace,'" *The Washington Times*, May 6, 2012.

471 Justice Antonin Scalia (dissent), *Romer, Governor of Colorado, et al. v. Evans et al.* (94-1039), 517 U.S. 620 (1996).

Chapter 27: How Many and How Much

472 Gary Gates, "Gay Veterans Top One Million," Urban Institute, July 9, 2003.

473 Will O'Bryan, "Gay Is Good: How Frank Kameny Changed the Face of America," *Metro Weekly*, October 5, 2006.

474 2002 Third Quarter Report, Servicemembers Legal Defense Network.

475 John R. Cook (death notice), *Richmond Times-Dispatch*, December 28, 2013.

476 Waverly Manson Cole (death notice), Legacy.com, August 30, 2009.

477 Military units: Army, U.S. Department of Defense.

478 Hope Hodge Seck, "Active Ships in the U.S. Navy," Military.com.

479 Saphora Smith and Lauren Egan, "'It is time to end America's longest war': Biden announces full withdrawal of troops from Afghanistan," NBC News, April 14, 2021.

480 "Why Doesn't Uncle Sam Want These Troops," ABC News, November 1, 2005.

481 *Ask Not* (trailer for 2009 PBS documentary), Johnny Symons (producer/director), Vimeo, uploaded February 6, 2014.

482 Jason Horowitz, "Rudy on Gays in the Military: Not Now," *The New York Observer*, March 13, 2007.

483 SLDN First Annual Report.

484 *Defense Force Management: DOD's Policy on Homosexuality*, U.S. General Accounting Office, June 12, 1992.

485 SLDN Tenth Annual Report.

486 George Cahlink, "Army May Temporarily Boost Troop Size," *Government Executive*, January 28, 2004.

487 Lisa Burgess, "Shipment of Body Armor Vests on its Way to Kuwait, Iraq-bound Troops," *Stars and Stripes*, January 13, 2004.

488 Christopher L. Neff and Luke R. Edgell, "The Rise of Repeal: Policy Entrepreneurship and Don't Ask, Don't Tell," *Journal of Homosexuality*, 60:2-3 (2013).

489 *Military Personnel: Financial Cost and Loss of Critical Skills Due to DOD's Homosexual Conduct Policy Cannot Be Completely Estimated*, U.S. Government Accountability Office, February 23, 2005.

490 *Financial Analysis of 'Don't Ask, Don't Tell': How much does the gay ban cost?*, University of California Blue Ribbon Commission, February 14, 2006.

491 Nathaniel Frank, "'Don't Ask, Don't Tell': Detailing the Damage," Palm Center, University of California, Santa Barbara, August 2010.

Chapter 28: Arabic Linguists

492 2001 Third Quarter Report, Servicemembers Legal Defense Network.

493 "Excerpts from the Debate Among GOP Candidates," *The New York Times*, January 7, 2000.

494 "Cheney Questions Fairness of Military Ban on Homosexuals," *Orlando Sentinel*, August 1, 1991.

495 SLDN Eighth Annual Report.

496 Anne Hull, "How 'Don't Tell' Translates," *The Washington Post*, December 3, 2003.

497 Hull, "How 'Don't Tell' Translates."

498 Cathleen Glover, "Coming Out in a World of Hatred," *The Monterey Herald*, November 10, 2002.

499 Hull, "How 'Don't Tell' Translates."

500 John Johnson, "9 Gay Linguists Discharged From the Army," *Los Angeles Times*, November 16, 2002.

501 Nathaniel Frank, "Perverse," *The New Republic*, November 15, 2002.

502 Nathaniel Frank, "Perverse."

503 2002 Third Quarter Report, Servicemembers Legal Defense Network.

504 Associated Press, "Gay Policy in Military Is Called Tool of Vengeance," *The New York Times*, July 28, 2006.

505 Associated Press, "Gay Policy in Military Is Called Tool of Vengeance."

506 Jason Jones, "Tangled Up In Bleu," *The Daily Show*, September 18, 2006.

507 *All Things Considered*, National Public Radio, April 19, 1993.

508 *All Things Considered*, National Public Radio, April 19, 1993.

509 SLDN Ninth Annual Report (2003).

510 Hull, "How 'Don't Tell' Translates."

511 *Foreign Languages: Human Capital Approach Needed to Correct Staffing and Proficiency Shortfalls*, U.S. General Accounting Office, January 31, 2002.

512 Johnson, "9 Gay Linguists Discharged From the Army."

513 "No Gay Help Wanted" (editorial), *The Washington Post*, November 20, 2002.

514 "The Democrats' Second 2008 Presidential Debate" (transcript), *The New York Times*, June 3, 2007.

515 2005 Second Quarter Report, Servicemembers Legal Defense Network.

516 Deirdre Fulton, "Getting the Boot," *Boston Phoenix*, March 11, 2005.

Chapter 29: Poppycock

517 John Files, "Gay Officers Say 'Don't Ask' Doesn't Work," *The New York Times*, December 10, 2003.

518 *People*, January 12, 2004.

519 Mubarak Dahir, "Coming Out on Top," *The Advocate*, February 3, 2004.

Chapter 30: The Magnificent Seven

520 Steve Weinstein, "Back in Action," *The Advocate*, April 9, 2007.

521 Aamer Madhani, "Drop 'Don't Ask, Don't Tell,' Pace Says," *Chicago Tribune*, May 13, 2007.

522 *Don't Ask Don't Tell Review: Hearing Before the Military Personnel Subcommittee of the Committee on Armed Services, House of Representatives*, 110th Congress, page 6 (July 23, 2008) (statement of Captain Joan E. Darrah).

523 Joan E. Darrah, "My secret life under 'don't ask, don't tell,'" CNN, February 4, 2010.

524 President John F. Kennedy, "Radio and Television Report to the American People on Civil Rights, June 11, 1963," John F. Kennedy Presidential Library and Museum.

525 United States Holocaust Memorial Museum, "King Christian X of Denmark."

526 Joe Rosato Jr., "SF Gay Vets Celebrate End of DADT," NBC Bay Area, September 20, 2011.

527 Pam Spaulding, "Executive Director of SLDN Steps Down," Pam's House Blend/Shadowproof, April 21, 2007.

Chapter 31: General Powell Called

528 *Policy Concerning Homosexuality in the Armed Forces: Hearings Before the Senate Committee on Armed Services* (statement of General Powell).

529 U.S. Department of Defense Directive 1304.26, *Qualification Standards for Enlistment, Appointment and Induction*, December 21, 1993.

530 *Policy Concerning Homosexuality in the Armed Forces: Hearings Before the Senate Committee on Armed Services* (statement of General Powell).

531 Cosgrove-Mather, "Debating 'Don't Ask, Don't Tell.'"

532 John M. Shalikashvili, "Second Thoughts on Gays in the Military," *The New York Times*, January 2, 2007.

533 Nathaniel Frank, "The President's Pleasant Surprise: How LGBT Advocates Ended Don't Ask, Don't Tell," *Journal of Homosexuality*, 60:2-3 (2013).

534 Elisabeth Bumiller, "Admiral's Opposition to Gay Policy Was Years in the Making," *The New York Times*, February 3, 2010.

535 Eric Schmitt, "Joint Chiefs Fighting Clinton Plan to Allow Homosexuals in the Military," *The New York Times*, January 23, 1993.

536 Adam K. Raymond, "Colin Powell Supports Ending 'Don't Ask, Don't Tell,'" *New York*, February 4, 2010.

Chapter 32: Reinforcements

537 "Retired Lieutenant General Claudia J. Kennedy to Keynote SLDN National Dinner," *Gay Pride*, April 15, 2016.

538 2006 Second Quarter Report, Servicemembers Legal Defense Network.

539 Paul Johnson, "General Wesley Clark Would 'Welcome' Gays to Military," 365gay.com, June 17, 2003.

540 "Westboro Baptist Church," Southern Poverty Law Center.

541 Alan K. Simpson, "Bigotry That Hurts Our Military," *The Washington Post*, March 14, 2007.

542 Thom Shanker, "Chairman of Joint Chiefs Will Not Be Reappointed," *The New York Times*, June 9, 2007.

543 John Ydstye, "Barr Shifts Stance on Gays in Military," National Public Radio, June 16, 2007.

544 "ACLU announces collaboration with Rep. Bob Barr; says conservative congressman will consult on privacy issues," American Civil Liberties Union, November 25, 2002.

545 *Defense of Marriage Act: Hearing Before the Subcommittee on the Constitution of the Committee on the Judiciary, House of Representatives*, 108th Congress, pages 14-20 (March 30, 2004) (statement of the Honorable Bob Barr).

546 Bob Barr, "No Defending Defense of Marriage Act," *Los Angeles Times*, January 5, 2009.

547 Bob Barr, "Don't Ask, Who Cares," *The Wall Street Journal*, June 13, 2007.

548 Andy Towle, "Former President Jimmy Carter: Repeal 'Don't Ask, Don't Tell,'" Towleroad, May 15, 2007.

549 Thom Shanker and Patrick Healy, "A New Push to Roll Back 'Don't Ask, Don't Tell,'" *The New York Times*, November 30, 2007.

550 "52 Military Leaders Say Gays Should Serve," Palm Center, July 8, 2008.

551   Associated Press, "Admirals, generals: Let gays serve openly," November 18, 2008.

Chapter 33: Lawrence

552   *Lawrence v. Texas,* 539 U.S. 558 (2003).

553   *United States v. Fagg,* 34 M.J. 179 (1992).

554   *Lawrence v. Texas.*

555   *Able v. United States,* 88 F.3d 1280 (2nd Cir. 1996).

556   *Thomasson v. Perry,* 80 F.3d 915 (4th Cir. 1996).

557   *Richenberg v. Perry,* 97 F.3d 256 (8th Cir. 1996).

558   *Holmes v. California Army National Guard,* 124 F.3d 1126 (9th Cir. 1997).

559   *Richenberg v. Perry,* 909 F. Supp. 1303 (D.C. Ne. 1995).

560   Hastings Wyman, "Pentagon Redux: Gay Issues Get Hot Again," CAMP Rehoboth Community Center, July 13, 2001.

561   Craig Malisow, "Don't Ask, Don't Be," *Houston Press,* January 5, 2006.

562   Patty Reinert, "12 ousted troops sue over 'don't ask, don't tell,'" *Houston Chronicle,* February 6, 2005.

563   SLDN Ninth Annual Report.

564   Julia O'Malley, "Discharged in Anchorage, gay airman finds his way to the White House," *Anchorage Daily News,* January 23, 2013.

565   Julia O'Malley, "Gay airman discharged under 'don't ask, don't tell' recounts White House visit," *Anchorage Daily News,* January 24, 2013.

566   *Cook v. Rumsfeld* (complaint), December 6, 2004.

567   Lornet Turnbull, "Seattle man forced from Navy fights 'don't ask, don't tell,'" *Seattle Times,* August 19, 2005.

568   Turnbull, "Seattle man forced from Navy fights 'don't ask, don't tell.'"

569   "Stuart Delery, Third-Ranking DOJ Official, Joins Gibson Dunn in Washington, DC," Gibson Dunn & Crutcher, September 16, 2016.

570   Dan Abrams, *The Abrams Report,* MSNBC, December 7, 2004.

571   *Cook v. Rumsfeld,* 429 F. Supp. 2d 385 (D. Mass. 2006).

572   *Cook v. Gates,* 528 F.3d 42 (1st Cir. 2008).

573   *Witt v. Department of the Air Force,* 527 F.3d 806 (9th Cir. 2008).

574 "Witt v. United States Department of the Air Force," National Legal Foundation.

575 *Witt v. Department of the Air Force.*

576 *Witt v. Department of the Air Force,* 739 F. Supp. 2d 1308 (W.D. Wash. 2010).

577 *Log Cabin Republicans v. United States,* 716 F. Supp. 2d 884 (C.D. Cal. 2010).

578 *Log Cabin Republicans v. United States.*

579 Robert J. Lopez. "Jury awards no damages to injured judge," *Los Angeles Times,* February 26, 2008.

580 *Log Cabin Republicans v. United States,* Filing 71: Status Report and Request for Status Conference, December 11, 2008.

581 *Log Cabin Republicans v. United States,* 716 F. Supp. 2d 884 (C.D. Cal. 2010).

582 Lizette Alvarez, "Unexpected Turns for Suit Over Don't Ask Rule," *The New York Times,* October 13, 2010.

583 *Fehrenbach v. U.S. Air Force* (complaint), August 11, 2010.

584 James Dao, "Officer Sues to Block His Discharge Under Gay Ban," *The New York Times,* August 11, 2010.

585 *Fehrenbach v. U.S. Air Force.*

586 Dao, "Officer Sues to Block His Discharge Under Gay Ban."

Chapter 34: Storming the Hill

587 Darren K. Carlson, "Public OK with Gays, Women in the Military," Gallup, December 23, 2003.

588 Lydia Saad, "Gallup Vault: Issue of Gays in Military Split Americans in 1993," Gallup, July 28, 2017.

589 SLDN Tenth Annual Report.

590 Eleven allied countries with troops in Operation Iraqi Freedom allowed open service: Australia, Czech Republic, Denmark, Italy, Lithuania, Netherlands, New Zealand, Norway, Slovenia, Spain, and Great Britain. Twelve coalition partners in Operation Enduring Freedom allowed lesbian, gay, and bisexual troops to serve openly: Australia, Belgium, Canada, Czech Republic, Denmark, France, Germany, Great Britain, Italy, Netherlands, Norway and Spain.

591 Aaron Belkin and Jason Nichol, *Effects of the 1992 Lifting of Restrictions on Gay and Lesbian Service in the Canadian Forces: Appraising the Evidence*, Center for Study of Sexual Minorities in the Military, University of California, Santa Barbara, April 2000.

592 Aaron Belkin and Jason Nichol, *Effects of Lifting of Restrictions on Gay and Lesbian Service in the Australian Defence Forces: Appraising the Evidence*, Center for Study of Sexual Minorities in the Military, University of California, Santa Barbara, September 19, 2000.

593 Aaron Belkin and R.L. Evans, *Effects of Lifting of Restrictions on Gay and Lesbian Service in the British Armed Forces: Appraising the Evidence,* Center for Study of Sexual Minorities in the Military, University of California, Santa Barbara, November 2000.

594 Cosgrove-Mather, "Debating 'Don't ask, don't tell.'"

595 "Servicemembers Legal Defense Network 15th Annual Dinner," *Band of Thebes*, March 26, 2007.

596 *Wikipedia, the Free Encyclopedia*, "Military Readiness Enhancement Act" (accessed July 14, 2021).

597 Greg Hernandez, "Patrick Murphy honored for leading repeal of Don't Ask Don't Tell," *Gay Star News*, February 17, 2012.

598 "How Don't Ask, Don't Tell has affected LGBTQ service members, 10 years after repeal," Ali Rogin, *PBS NewsHour*, December 22, 2020.

599 Steve Benen, "Taking on 'Don't ask, don't tell' — the politically smart way," *The Carpetbagger Report*, March 3, 2005.

600 Benen, "Taking on 'Don't ask, don't tell' — the politically smart way."

601 Spaulding, "SLDN Executive Director Steps Down."

602 2005 First Quarter Report, Servicemembers Legal Defense Network.

603 2004 First Quarter Report, Servicemembers Legal Defense Network.

604 Jeff Zeleny, "Obama Signs Hate Crimes Bill," *The New York Times*, October 28, 2009.

605 *Bostock v. Clayton County*, 590 U.S.__ (2020).

606 Michael Kinsley, "The Quiet Gay Revolution," *Time*, June 14, 2007.

607 Josh Richman, "Tauscher tackles "Don't Ask, Don't Tell,'" *East Bay Times*, June 14, 2007.

608 House Armed Services Committee, Military Personnel Subcommittee, *Don't Ask, Don't Tell Review*, July 23, 2008.

609   Dana Milbank, "Sorry We Asked, Sorry You Told," *The Washington Post*, July 24, 2008.

Chapter 35: Stop Lost

610   Bryan Bender, "Military Retaining More Gays," *The Boston Globe*, March 19, 2006.

611   Lindsey McPherson, "Military takes no action on gay medic from Chautauqua County," *The Buffalo News*, February 4, 2008.

612   Pelin Sidki, "Discharged under 'don't ask, don't tell,'" CNN, November 10, 2009.

613   Lesley Stahl, "Military Soft on Don't Ask, Don't Tell?," *60 Minutes*, December 13, 2007.

614   Steve Ralls interview with C. Dixon Osburn, February 2, 2021.

615   Admiral Mike Mullen interview with C. Dixon Osburn, February 3, 2021.

616   Nathaniel Frank, "Obama's False 'Don't Ask, Don't Tell' Narrative," *The New Republic*, February 19, 2013.

617   Leo Shane III, "'Don't ask, don't tell' in limbo for now," *Stars and Stripes*, June 22, 2009.

618   Frank, "Obama's False 'Don't Ask, Don't Tell' Narrative."

619   Bryan Bender, "Obama Seeks Assessment on Gays in Military," *The Boston Globe,* February 1, 2009.

620   Bender, "Obama Seeks Assessment on Gays in Military."

621   Frank, "The President's Pleasant Surprise: How LGBT Advocates Ended Don't Ask, Don't Tell."

622   Chris Johnson, "Obama 'blindsided' Gates over 'Don't Ask' repeal," *Washington Blade*, January 9, 2014.

623   David A. Graham, "Robert Gates, America's Unlikely Gay-Rights Hero," *The Atlantic*, July 28, 2015.

624   Jeh Johnson interview with C. Dixon Osburn, March 1, 2021.

625   Johnson interview.

626   Johnson interview.

627   Johnson interview.

628   Johnson interview.

629   Johnson interview.

630   Johnson interview.

631   Eric Milzarski, "7 regulations from Von Steuben's 'Blue Book' that troops still follow," *We Are the Mighty,* January 28, 2019.

632   Erin Blakemore, "The Revolutionary War Hero Who Was Openly Gay," History.com.

633   Richard Socarides, "A Chance for Barack Obama to Take Bold Action on Behalf of Gay Americans," *The Washington Post,* May 2, 2009.

634   "Jason Bellini: Has the HRC Delayed Pushing to Repeal Don't Ask Don't Tell?" (video), *The Daily Beast,* June 11, 2009.

635   Sheryl Gay Stolberg, "As Gay Issues Arise, Obama Is Pressed to Engage," *The New York Times,* May 7, 2009.

636   Stolberg, "As Gay Issues Arise, Obama Is Pressed to Engage."

637   Stolberg, "As Gay Issues Arise, Obama Is Pressed to Engage."

638   Stolberg, "As Gay Issues Arise, Obama Is Pressed to Engage."

639   Aaron Belkin, Nathaniel Frank, Gregory M. Herek *et al., How to End "Don't Ask, Don't Tell": A Roadmap of Political, Legal, Regulatory, and Organizational Steps to Equal Treatment,* Palm Center, May 11, 2009.

640   Frank, "The President's Pleasant Surprise: How LGBT Advocates Ended Don't Ask, Don't Tell."

641   Anna Quindlen, "End the Ban on Gays in the Military," *Newsweek,* April 3, 2009.

642   Lawrence J. Korb, Sean E. Duggan, and Laura Conley, *Ending 'Don't Ask, Don't Tell': Practical Steps to Repeal the Ban on Openly Gay Men and Women in the U.S. Military,* Center for American Progress, June 2009.

643   William Gibson, "Hastings: End Limits on Gays in the Military," *South Florida Sun-Sentinel,* June 22, 2009.

644   2001 Fourth Quarter Report, Servicemembers Legal Defense Network.

645   David Kirby, "Think Before You Tell," *The Advocate,* December 4, 2001.

646   Frank, "Obama's False 'Don't Ask, Don't Tell' Narrative."

647   Nathaniel Frank, "Battle Plans," *The New Republic,* May 12, 2009.

648   Sean Bugg, "Marching Forward," *Metro Weekly,* May 20, 2004.

649   Korb *et al., Ending 'Don't Ask, Don't Tell': Practical Steps to Repeal the Ban on Openly Gay Men and Women in the U.S. Military.*

650 "President Obama Should Let Gay Men and Lesbians Serve in the Military" (editorial), *Washington Post*, June 27, 2009.

651 Nathaniel Frank and Diane H. Mazur, "Palm Center View on Don't Ask Policy," Palm Center, July 23, 2009.

652 *The Rachel Maddow Show* (transcript), June 8, 2009.

653 Ben Smith and Josh Gerstein, "Obama Fails to Quell Gay Uproar," *Politico*, June 18, 2009.

654 Frank, "The President's Pleasant Surprise: How LGBT Advocates Ended Don't Ask, Don't Tell."

655 Liz Halloran, "With Repeal of 'Don't Ask, Don't Tell,' An Era Ends," NPR, September 20, 2011.

656 Linda Hirshman, "'Don't Ask, Don't Tell': How It Was Repealed," *The Daily Beast*, December 18, 2010.

657 Philip Elliott, "Promises, Promises: Obama Slow on Pledge to Gays," The Associated Press, June 25, 2009.

658 Carlos Santoscoy, "Gay Politicos Shaken but Plan to Attend Dinner," *On Top Magazine*, June 25, 2009.

659 Andy Towle, "Despite Protests, DNC LGBT Fundraiser Takes In More Than Last Year," Towleroad, June 26, 2009.

660 Elliott, "Promises, Promises: Obama Slow on Pledge to Gays."

661 Patrick Murphy interview with C. Dixon Osburn, January 23, 2021.

662 Bryan Bender, "Continued discharges anger 'don't ask, don't tell' critics," *The Boston Globe*, May 20, 2009.

663 Jennifer Millman, "Gillibrand Forces Action on 'Don't Ask, Don't Tell,'" NBC New York, July 27, 2009.

664 Jason Bellini, "Finally, Action on Gay Soldiers," *The Daily Beast*, July 26, 2009.

665 Kirsten Gillibrand, "I Stand with Lt. Dan Choi, It's Time To Repeal DADT," *The Huffington Post*, July 19, 2009.

666 "Senator Kirsten Gillibrand Discusses Don't Ask Don't Tell with Jason Bellini" (video), *The Daily Beast*, July 27, 2009.

667 E.A. Barrera, "Battles Loom As To When Gays Will Serve Openly In Military," *East County Magazine*, May 2009.

668 Aaron Belkin, "Self-Inflicted Wound: How and Why Gays Give the White House a Free Pass on 'Don't Ask, Don't Tell'" Palm Center, July 27, 2009.

669   Belkin, "Self-Inflicted Wound."

670   Belkin, "Self-Inflicted Wound."

671   Ben Smith, "Friendly Fire on 'Don't Ask,'" *Politico*, July 28, 2009.

672   Smith, "Friendly Fire on 'Don't Ask.'"

673   Ryan Grim, "Reid Appeals Directly To Obama: Help Us Repeal Don't Ask, Don't Tell," *The Huffington Post*, December 1, 2009.

674   "Obama aide: Ending 'don't ask, don't tell' must wait," CNN, January 15, 2009.

675   Briefing by White House press secretary Robert Gibbs, June 17, 2009.

676   Elisabeth Bumiller, "Rare Source of Attack on 'Don't Ask, Don't Tell,'" *The New York Times*, October 1, 2009.

677   Peter Singer, "How *The Real World* Ended 'Don't Ask, Don't Tell,'" Foreign Policy at Brookings, Policy Paper Number 6, August 2008.

678   Om Prakash, "The Efficacy of 'Don't Ask, Don't Tell,'" *Joint Force Quarterly*, Issue 55, 4th Quarter 2009.

679   Bumiller, "Rare Source of Attack on 'Don't Ask, Don't Tell.'"

680   Prakash, "The Efficacy of 'Don't Ask, Don't Tell.'"

681   Frank, "The President's Pleasant Surprise: How LGBT Advocates Ended Don't Ask, Don't Tell."

682   Brian Bond, "Ending Don't Ask Don't Tell," The White House (Obama archives), December 18, 2010.

Chapter 36: Murphy Amendment

683   Carol E. Lee, "Obama Pushes for Repeal of DADT," *Politico*, January 27, 2010.

684   Mullen interview.

685   Mullen interview.

686   Elisabeth Bumiller, "Forces Pushing Obama on Don't Ask, Don't Tell," *New York Times*, January 31, 2010.

687   Frank, "The President's Pleasant Surprise: How LGBT Advocates Ended Don't Ask, Don't Tell."

688   Frank, "The President's Pleasant Surprise: How LGBT Advocates Ended Don't Ask, Don't Tell."

689　Ari Berman, "Jim Messina: Obama's Enforcer," *The Nation*, March 30, 2011.

690　Kevin Naff, "HRC, Joe Solmonese in the hot seat," *Washington Blade*, April 23, 2010.

691　Andy Towle, "Take Action on DADT," Towleroad, February 16, 2010.

692　Federal News Service, Hearing of the Senate Armed Services Committee (transcript), February 2, 2010.

693　Jen Dimascio and Josh Gerstein, "'Don't ask' on slow road to repeal?," *Politico*, February 2, 2010.

694　Deb Price, "House of Cards Collapsing on Opponents of Gay Soldiers," Creators.com, February 9, 2010.

695　Mullen interview.

696　Dimascio and Gerstein, "'Don't ask' on slow road to repeal?"

697　Federal News Service, Hearing of the Senate Armed Services Committee (transcript).

698　Johnson interview.

699　Ryan Grim and Kerry Eleveld, "Barack Obama, Harry Reid, and the Secret History of 'Don't ask, don't tell' Repeal," *HuffPost*, May 28, 2019.

700　"Gates Issues Terms for 'Don't Ask, Don't Tell' Review," Office of the Secretary of Defense Public Affairs, March 2, 2010.

701　Stephanie Condon, "Colin Powell Favors Repealing 'Don't Ask, Don't Tell,'" CBS News, February 3, 2010.

702　"Rep. Patrick Murphy on Repealing Don't Ask, Don't Tell," *The Rachel Maddow Show*, February 3, 2010.

703　*Meet the Press* transcript for February 21, 2010, NBC News.

704　*The Situation Room* transcript for February 22, 2010, CNN.

705　*This Week* transcript: Former Vice President Dick Cheney, ABC News, February 14, 2010.

706　James Kirchick, "On 'Ask,' Lieberman Answers the Call," *New York Daily News*, February 21, 2010.

707　Chris Johnson, "Chairmen Sending Mixed Signals on Don't Ask," *Washington Blade*, January 20, 2010.

708　Richard Sisk, "Sen. Joe Lieberman Backs Bill Repealing Don't Ask, Don't Tell," *New York Daily News*, February 21, 2010.

709   Julie Bolcer, "Lieberman To Introduce DADT Repeal Bill," *The Advocate*, February 22, 2010.

710   2008 Democratic Party Platform, The American Presidency Project, University of California, Santa Barbara. "We will … put national security above divisive politics. More than 12,500 service men and women have been discharged on the basis of sexual orientation since the 'Don't ask, don't tell' policy was implemented, at a cost of over $360 million. Many of those forced out had special skills in high demand, such as translators, engineers, and pilots. At a time when the military is having a tough time recruiting and retaining troops, it is wrong to deny our country the service of brave, qualified people. We support the repeal of 'Don't Ask Don't Tell' and the implementation of policies to allow qualified men and women to serve openly regardless of sexual orientation."

711   Chris Johnson, "General Says Open Service Would Be Problematic," *Washington Blade*, March 22, 2010

712   "Marine officer: Gays, straights shouldn't share housing," CNN, March 26, 2010.

713   Rowan Scarborough, "Veteran groups resist 'don't ask' repeal," *The Washington Times*, February 4, 2010.

714   Chris Johnson, "General says open service would be problematic," *Washington Blade*, March 22, 2010.

715   Chris Johnson, "Moderate senators back Pentagon's 'Don't Ask' review," *Washington Blade*, February 10, 2010.

716   "SLDN HRC Launch 2010 Grassroots Campaign, Human Rights Campaign, July 29, 2010.

717   Johnson, "Moderate senators back Pentagon's 'Don't Ask' review."

718   Chris Johnson, "Questions surround Lieberman's 'Don't Ask' repeal bill," *Washington Blade*, February 23, 2010.

719   Johnson, "Questions surround Lieberman's 'Don't Ask' repeal bill."

720   Chris Johnson, "Kathy Griffin to headline 'Don't Ask' rally in D.C. on Thursday," *Washington Blade*, March 15, 2010.

721   Chris Johnson, "General says open service would be problematic," *Washington Blade*, March 22, 2010.

722   Nathaniel Frank, "Obama's False 'Don't Ask, Don't Tell' Narrative," *The New Republic*, February 19, 2013.

723 *Wikipedia, the Free Encyclopedia,* Dan Choi (accessed July 16, 2021).

724 *The Rachel Maddow Show* for March 20, 2009 (transcript), MSNBC.

725 Kevin Douglas Grant, "The Making of Dan Choi," *Global Post,* September 20, 2011.

726 Nathaniel Frank, "Obama's False 'Don't Ask, Don't Tell" Narrative," *The New Republic,* February 19, 2013.

727 Brian Montopoli, "Lt. Dan Choi Arrested at White House During Gay Rights Rally," CBS News, March 18, 2010.

728 Brian Montopoli, "Dan Choi, Other Gay Rights Protestors Arrested After Chaining Selves to White House Fence," CBS News, April 20, 2010.

729 Suzanne Malveaux, "Gay rights protestors demand Obama help end 'don't ask, don't tell,'" CNN, November 15, 2010.

730 Eve Conant, "Dan Choi's Hunger Strike Starts After Congress Votes on Don't Ask, Don't Tell Amendment," *Newsweek,* May 27, 2010.

731 Ben Smith, "White House delaying 'Don't Ask' repeal," *Politico,* April 18, 2010.

732 Chris Johnson, "Panelists hammer White House on 'Don't Ask' position," *Washington Blade,* May 2, 2010.

733 Johnson, "Panelists hammer White House on 'Don't Ask' position."

734 Chris Johnson, "'Don't Ask' repeal faces delay, uncertainty," *Washington Blade,* May 6, 2010.

735 Johnson, "'Don't Ask' repeal faces delay, uncertainty."

736 Eric Etheridge, "Is 'Don't Ask, Don't Tell' Done For?," *The New York Times,* October 1, 2009.

737 David A. Graham, "Robert Gates, America's Unlikely Gay-Rights Hero," *The Atlantic,* July 28, 2015.

738 Defense Secretary Robert Gates and Joint Chiefs Chairman Mike Mullen, "'Don't Ask, Don't Tell' Policy" (video), C-SPAN, March 25, 2020.

739 Johnson, "'Don't Ask' repeal faces delay, uncertainty."

740 Jonathan Capehart, "Justified anger over Sec. Gates' letter on don't ask don't tell," *The Washington Post,* May 4, 2010.

741 Roxana Tiron, "Pelosi push on 'Don't ask, don't tell' puts panel chairman in a tough spot," *The Hill,* May 21, 2010.

742 Michael Riley, "Dems in Congress unwilling to wait on military repeal of 'don't ask, don't tell,'" *The Denver Post*, April 20, 2010.

743 Johnson, "'Don't Ask' repeal faces delay, uncertainty."

744 Johnson, "'Don't Ask' repeal faces delay, uncertainty."

745 Chris Johnson, "Repeal groups disagree on 'Don't Ask' strategy," *Washington Blade*, May 4, 2010.

746 Winnie Stachelberg interview with C. Dixon Osburn, March 17, 2021.

747 Johnson, "Repeal groups disagree on 'Don't Ask' strategy."

748 C. Dixon Osburn, "A Bad Prescription for Don't Ask, Don't Tell," *The Bilerico Project*, July 10, 2008.

749 Stachelberg interview.

750 Stachelberg interview.

751 Russell Berman, "Gay Rights Advocates Say Dem Leader Hoyer Saved Don't Ask Repeal," *The Hill*, December 22, 2010.

752 Chris Johnson, "Mission accomplished or another setback?," *Washington Blade*, May 26, 2010.

753 John M. Shalikashvili, "Congress should repeal 'don't ask, don't tell' and let the Pentagon do the rest," *Washington Post*, May 22, 2010.

754 Johnson, "Mission accomplished or another setback?"

755 Johnson, "Mission accomplished or another setback?"

756 Johnson, "Mission accomplished or another setback?"

757 Frank, "The President's Pleasant Surprise: How LGBT Advocates Ended Don't Ask, Don't Tell."

758 Ed O'Keefe, "Obama's letters supporting 'don't ask, don't tell' repeal," *The Washington Post*, May 24, 2010.

759 Roxana Tiron, "Congress and White House reach deal on 'Don't ask, don't tell' policy repeal," *The Hill*, May 25, 2010.

760 Ben Smith, "Gates 'can accept' 'Don't Ask' repeal' plan," *Politico*, May 25, 2010.

761 Patrick J. Murphy, "The Political Battle for Repeal: Personal Reflections from the Frontlines," *Journal of Homosexuality*, Volume 60:2-3, 2013.

762 Winnie Stachelberg and Rudy deLeon, "Joe Biden's LGBTQ+ Legacy 10 Years After DADT Repeal," *The Advocate*, June 9, 2020.

763 Jonathan Lee interview with C. Dixon Osburn, May 29, 2020.

764 Michael Riley, "Pentagon's "Don't Ask, Don't Tell' Study Draws Fire from Advocates, Gay Soldiers," *Denver Post*, June 8, 2010.

765 David Badash, "Stories from the Frontlines: Letters to Barack Obama," *New Civil Rights Movement*, April 26, 2010.

766 "Stories from the Frontlines: Major General Vance Coleman," *The Advocate*, May 27, 2010.

767 David Badash, "Stories from the Frontline: Letters to Barack Obama: A Military Chaplain," New Civil Rights Movement, April 29, 2010.

768 "SLDN, HRC Launch 'Countdown 2010' Grassroots Campaign," Human Rights Campaign, July 29, 2010.

769 "SLDN, HRC Launch 'Countdown 2010' Grassroots Campaign."

770 "Repealing Don't Ask, Don't Tell," Human Rights Campaign.

771 "Human Rights Campaign Announces Comprehensive Campaign to End Failed 'Don't Ask, Don't Tell,'" Human Rights Campaign, January 27, 2010.

772 *Ask Not* (trailer for 2009 PBS documentary).

773 Bob Roehr, "Murphy to Lead Repeal of Don't Ask, Don't Tell; National Tour Launched for Repeal," *Windy City Times*, July 8, 2009.

774 "Repealing Don't Ask, Don't Tell," Human Rights Campaign.

775 Lady Gaga, "A Message from Lady Gaga to the Senate" (video), YouTube, September 16, 2010.

776 "Don't Ask, Don't Tell," *Gagapedia*.

777 Lady Gaga's Portland Speech (video), WMTW-TV, September 20, 2010.

778 Gil Kaufman, "Did Lady Gaga Have Any Impact on Don't Ask Don't Tell Vote?," MTV News, September 21, 2010.

779 Robert Reich, "How McConnell Is Killing the Senate," *The American Prospect*, April 16, 2019.

780 Richard Valelly, "Making a Rainbow Military: Parliamentary Skill and the Repeal of 'Don't Ask, Don't Tell,'" *Congress and Policy Making in the 21st Century* (Cambridge: Cambridge University Press, 2016).

781 Geoffrey W. Bateman and Claude J. Summers, "Don't Ask, Don't Tell," GLBTQ Archive, 2015.

782 Meena Hartenstein, "Bill Clinton Regrets Don't Ask, Don't Tell," *New York Daily News*, September 21, 2010.

783 Elisabeth Bumiller, "Top Defense Officials Seek to End Don't Ask, Don't Tell," *The New York Times*, February 3, 2010.

784 Frank James, "John McCain Contradicts John McCain on 'Don't Ask, Don't Tell,'" NPR, February 2, 2010.

785 2008 Republican Party platform, The American Presidency Project, University of California, Santa Barbara. "To protect our servicemen and women and ensure that America's Armed Forces remain the best in the world, we affirm the timelessness of those values, the benefits of traditional military culture, and the incompatibility of homosexuality with military service."

786 Andy Towle, "McCain Restates Support for 'Don't Ask, Don't Tell,'" Towleroad, May 4, 2007.

787 Bateman and Summers, "Don't Ask, Don't Tell."

788 Bateman and Summers, "Don't Ask, Don't Tell."

789 Aamani Lyle, "Hagel, Obama Advisor Salute Gay, Lesbian Military Community," American Forces Press Service, U.S. Department of Defense, June 25, 2013.

790 Laura Meckler, "Drive to Repeal Don't Ask Policy All But Lost for Now," *The Wall Street Journal*, November 8, 2010.

791 Jeffrey A. Jenkins and Eric Patashnik, "Lame Duck Outlook: Many Issues, Little Resolution," *CQ Weekly*, November 15, 2010.

792 John Stanton and Kathleen Hunter, "Road Map: Still No Agenda for Lame Duck," *Roll Call*, November 29, 2010.

793 Jessica Brady, "Lieberman Predicts DADT Repeal in Lame Duck," *Roll Call*, November 18, 2010.

794 Brady, "Lieberman Predicts DADT Repeal in Lame Duck."

795 Ed O'Keefe, "'Don't ask, don't tell' splitting gay rights groups," *The Washington Post*, November 15, 2010.

796 Josh Rogin, "Levin: We may have to separate DADT from defense bill," *Foreign Policy*, November 16, 2010.

797 Lisa Keen, "Levin ready to strip DADT repeal from defense bill," *Windy City Times*, November 24, 2010.

798 Will Kohler, *Back2Stonewall*, November 16, 2010.

799 O'Keefe, "'Don't ask, don't tell' splitting gay rights groups."

800 Ed O'Keefe and Greg Jaffe, "Sources: Pentagon group finds there is minimal risk to lifting gay ban during war," *The Washington Post*, November 11, 2010.

801 Chris Johnson, "Pentagon leaks are aiding repeal effort," *Washington Blade*, November 13, 2010.

802 Roxana Tiron, "Gay rights groups: Obama, Reid to push ahead on 'Don't ask, don't tell' repeal," *The Hill*, November 18, 2010.

Chapter 37: The Pentagon Study

803 Jeh Charles Johnson and General Carter F. Ham (co-chairs), *Report of the Comprehensive Review of the Issues Associated with a Repeal of "Don't Ask, Don't Tell,"* Department of Defense, November 30, 2010.

804 Chris Johnson, "A personal victory for gay Pentagon official," *Washington Blade*, July 27, 2011.

805 Geoffrey W. Bateman and Claude J. Summers, "Don't Ask, Don't Tell," GLBTQ Archive, 2015.

806 Johnson and Ham, *Report of the Comprehensive Review of the Issues Associated with a Repeal of "Don't Ask, Don't Tell."*

807 Johnson and Ham, *Report of the Comprehensive Review of the Issues Associated with a Repeal of "Don't Ask, Don't Tell."*

808 Elisabeth Bumiller, "Pentagon Sees Little Risk in Allowing Gay Men and Women to Serve Openly," *The New York Times*, December 1, 2010.

809 Statement of Admiral Michael G. Mullen, Senate Armed Services Committee, December 2, 2010.

810 Johnson and Ham, *Report of the Comprehensive Review of the Issues Associated with a Repeal of "Don't Ask, Don't Tell."*

811 Johnson interview.

812 Johnson interview.

813 Bumiller, "Pentagon Sees Little Risk in Allowing Gay Men and Women to Serve Openly."

814 Statement of Secretary of Defense Robert Gates, Senate Armed Services Committee, December 2, 2010.

815 Statement of Admiral Michael G. Mullen.

816 Bernard D. Rostker, Susan Hosek, John D. Winkler *et al.*, *Sexual*

Orientation and U.S. Military Personnel Policy: An Update of RAND's 1993 Study (Santa Monica: RAND Corporation, 2010).

817　David Gardner, "Divided We Stand: America's Military Leaders Split Over Don't Ask, Don't Tell," *The Daily Mail*, December 3, 2010.

818　Bateman and Summers, "Don't Ask, Don't Tell."

819　Ed O'Keefe, "'Don't ask, don't tell' report authors speak out," *The Washington Post*, November 30, 2010.

820　O'Keefe, "'Don't ask, don't tell' report authors speak out."

821　Chris Johnson, "Will time run out for 'Don't Ask' repeal?," *Washington Blade*, November 23, 2012.

822　Josh Gerstein, "Scott Brown backs 'don't ask' repeal measure," *Politico*, December 3, 2010.

823　Joel Connelly, "GOP Sen. Murkowski: Repeal 'Don't Ask-Don't Tell,'" *Seattle Post-Intelligencer*, December 8, 2010.

824　Liz Halloran, "Senate Defeat Of 'Don't Ask, Don't Tell' Repeal Highlights Partisan Distrust," NPR, December 9, 2010.

825　Grim and Eleveld, "Barack Obama, Harry Reid and the Secret History of 'Don't Ask, Don't Tell' Repeal."

826　Valelly, "Making a Rainbow Military."

827　Associated Press, "Collins says no, and 'don't ask' stalls in Senate," *Bangor Daily News*, September 21, 2010.

828　Leo Shane III, "'Don't ask, don't tell' repeal effort dies in Senate," *Stars and Stripes*, December 9, 2010.

829　Alexander Nicholson, *Fighting to Serve: Behind the Scenes in the War to Repeal "Don't Ask, Don't Tell"* (Chicago: Chicago Review Press, 2012).

830　Jennifer Steinhauer, "Senate Stalls Bill to Repeal Gay Policy in Military," *The New York Times*, December 9, 2010.

831　Ed O'Keefe and Fred Whitlock, "New bill introduced to end 'don't ask, don't tell,'" *The Washington Post*, December 11, 2010.

832　Susan Donaldson James, "Gay Activist Dan Choi Hospitalized for Breakdown," ABC News, December 16, 2010.

833　Autumn Sandeen, "Dan Choi Hospitalized; A Discussion About Our Community's Multi-Faceted Sacrifices," *Pam's House Blend*, December 14, 2010.

Chapter 38: Hail Mary

834 Russell Berman, "Gay-rights advocates say Dem leader Hoyer saved 'Don't ask' repeal," *The Hill*, December 22, 2010.

835 Stachelberg interview.

836 Berman, "Gay-rights advocates say Dem leader Hoyer saved 'Don't ask' repeal."

837 Berman, "Gay-rights advocates say Dem leader Hoyer saved 'Don't ask' repeal."

838 Scott Wong, "Don't Ask Passes Handily in House," *Politico*, December 15, 2010.

839 Chris Johnson, "GOP in last ditch effort to block 'Don't Ask' repeal?," *Washington Blade*, December 17, 2010.

840 Johnson, "GOP in last ditch effort to block 'Don't Ask' repeal?"

841 O'Keefe and Whitlock, "Senators introduce new bill to repeal 'don't ask, don't tell.'"

842 "DADT Repeal Rally" (video), *Metro Weekly*, December 10, 2010.

843 Chris Johnson, "'Don't Go Home!' until 'Don't Ask' is done," *Washington Blade*, December 10, 2010.

844 Frank James, "Saving Don't Ask Repeal Took Wily Band of Lawmakers," NPR, December 22, 2010.

845 Berman, "Gay-rights advocates say Dem leader Hoyer saved 'Don't ask' repeal."

846 Greg Sargent: "Breaking: House Dems will introduce stand-alone DADT bill," *The Washington Post*, December 14, 2010.

847 Kitty Felde, "House debates whether to drop 'don't ask, don't tell' policy," KPCC, December 15, 2010.

848 Jennifer Steinhauer, "House Votes to Repeal 'Don't Ask, Don't Tell,'" *The New York Times*, December 15, 2010.

849 Ed O'Keefe, "House votes again to repeal 'don't ask, don't tell,'" *The Washington Post*, December 15, 2010.

850 Valelly, "Making a Rainbow Military."

851 Howard Kurtz, "Joe Lieberman: Liberal Hero for Role in Repealing Don't Ask, Don't Tell," *The Daily Beast*, December 19, 2010.

852 Kurtz, "Joe Lieberman: Liberal Hero for Role in Repealing Don't Ask, Don't Tell."

853 Greg Sargent, "Good news and bad news on DADT," *The Washington Post*, December 16, 2010.

854 Ryan Grim, *We've Got People: From Jesse Jackson to Alexandria Ocasio-Cortez, the End of Big Money and the Rise of a Movement* (Washington: Strong Arm Press, 2019).

855 Barack Obama, *A Promised Land* (Crown: New York, 2020).

856 Grim and Eleveld, "Barack Obama, Harry Reid and the Secret History of 'Don't Ask, Don't Tell' Repeal."

857 Joseph I. Lieberman, interview with C. Dixon Osburn, February 4, 2021.

858 Lisa Mascaro and James Oliphant, "Senate votes to repeal 'don't ask, don't tell,'" *Los Angeles Times*, December 18, 2010.

859 Grim and Eleveld, "Barack Obama, Harry Reid and the Secret History of 'Don't Ask, Don't Tell' Repeal."

860 Patrick J. Murphy, "The Political Battle for Repeal: Personal Reflections from the Frontlines," *Journal of Homosexuality*, 60:2-3, 2013.

861 Garance Franke-Ruta, "John McCain's 'Don't Ask, Don't Tell' Last Stand," *The Atlantic*, December 18, 2010.

Chapter 39: Mischief

862 Jim Garamone, "Pentagon Officials Explain Repeal Implementation," American Forces Press Service, July 25, 2011.

863 Chris Johnson, "Personal victory for gay Pentagon official," *Washington Blade*, July 27, 2011.

864 Chris Johnson, "SLDN to Obama: Ban LGBT military bias with executive order," *Washington Blade*, July 26, 2011.

865 Chris Johnson, "BREAKING: Obama, Pentagon certify 'Don't Ask, Don't Tell' repeal," *Washington Blade*, July 22, 2011.

866 Johnson, "HISTORIC: Obama signs 'Don't Ask' repeal."

867 Johnson, "HISTORIC: Obama signs 'Don't Ask' repeal."

868 Johnson, "HISTORIC: Obama signs 'Don't Ask' repeal."

869 Gloria Penner and Megan Burke, "SD Congressman Challenges Don't Ask Don't Tell Repeal," KPBS, January 21, 2011.

870 Chris Johnson, "McKeon backs legislation to disrupt 'Don't Ask' repeal," *Washington Blade*, April 19, 2011.

871 H.R. 1540 – National Defense Authorization Act for Fiscal Year 2012, Section 533: Additional condition on repeal of Don't Ask Don't Tell policy.

872 Chris Johnson, "House GOP urges delay in 'Don't Ask' repeal certification," *Washington Blade*, June 16, 2011.

873 Johnson, "McKeon backs legislation to disrupt 'Don't Ask' repeal."

874 Hillary Stemple, "House GOP members attempting to delay 'Don't ask, don't tell' repeal," *Jurist*, September 16, 2011.

875 Jim Garamone, "'Don't Ask, Don't Tell' Repeal Certified by President Obama," American Forces Press Service, July 26, 2011.

876 Garamone, "Pentagon Officials Explain Repeal Implementation."

877 Office of Under Secretary of Defense for Personnel and Readiness, September 20, 2011.

878 Statement by the President on the Repeal of Don't Ask, Don't Tell, The White House, September 20, 2011.

879 "'Don't Ask, Don't Tell' Is Repealed" (archived material), U.S. Department of Defense.

Chapter 40: Ceremonies

880 Pelosi Remarks at Enrollment Ceremony for Legislation Repealing "Don't Ask, Don't Tell," Office of Congresswoman Nancy Pelosi, December 21, 2010.

881 Johnson, "HISTORIC: Obama signs 'Don't Ask' repeal."

882 Lieberman interview.

883 Garance Franke-Ruta, "A Signing Ceremony for the Ages," *The Atlantic*, December 22, 2010.

884 Zoe Dunning, "A Witness to History," Alice B. Toklas Democratic Club, January 20, 2011.

885 Jenifer Warren, "Gay Sergeant Told He's Not Welcome in Army, for Now," *Los Angeles Times*, April 30, 1993.

886 Remarks by the President and Vice President at Signing of the Don't Ask, Don't Tell Repeal Act of 2010, The White House, December 22, 2010.

887 Remarks by the President and Vice President at Signing of the Don't Ask, Don't Tell Repeal Act of 2010.

888 Dunning, "My Unexpected Journey."

889 Evan Mulvihill, "That Time Joe Lieberman Called Admiral Mike Mullen 'The Most Popular Guy in Gay America,'" *The Huffington Post*, September 19, 2012.

890 "Making Good History," *Milwaukee Journal Sentinel*, December 20, 2010.

891 Johnson, "HISTORIC: Obama signs 'Don't Ask' repeal."

892 Chuck Colbert, "Seaside Celebration," *Metro Weekly*, September 19, 2012.

893 Mulvihill, "That Time Joe Lieberman Called Admiral Mike Mullen the Most Popular Guy in Gay America."

894 Lyle, "Hagel, Obama Advisor Salute Gay, Lesbian Military Community."

Chapter 41: Memorial Day

895 "Richard F. Richenberg Jr.," *The Desert Sun*/Legacy.com, June 19, 2011.

896 "Kevin Michael Blaesing," *Savannah Morning News*/Legacy.com, April 28, 2013.

Chapter 42: Impact

897 Elisabeth Bumiller, "One Year Later, Military Says Gay Policy Is Working," *The New York Times*, September 20, 2012.

898 Donna Cassata, "McKeon Says Gays in Military Issue Is Settled," The Associated Press, June 21, 2012.

899 National Press Club luncheon with General James Amos (transcript), August 28, 2012.

900 Isaac Chotiner, "John McCain, Undecided 2016 Voter," *The New Republic*, July 30, 2013.

901 Anna Mulrine, "Panetta: No hitches in military's repeal of 'don't ask, don't tell,'" *The Christian Science Monitor*, May 10, 2012.

902   CNN, "Adm. William McRaven Talks About Gays in the Military" (video), YouTube, July 26, 2012.

903   Mulvihill, "That Time Joe Lieberman Called Admiral Mike Mullen 'The Most Popular Guy in Gay America.'"

904   Bernard D. Rostker, "A Year After Repeal of Don't Ask, Don't Tell," The RAND Blog, September 20, 2012.

905   Aaron Belkin *et al.*, *One Year Out: An Assessment of DADT's Repeal on Military Readiness*, The Palm Center, University of California, Los Angeles, September 10, 2012.

906   David Crary, "Military still standing after end of don't ask, don't tell," The Associated Press, September 17, 2012.

907   Marcus Fichtl, "Presidio celebrates LGBT pride with story, acceptance," Presidio of Monterey Public Affairs, June 28, 2019.

908   Facebook page for Marine Corps Recruit Depot, Parris Island, June 22, 2020.

909   Facebook Watch (video) for RAF Mildenhall, June 23, 2020.

910   Grim and Eleveld, "Barack Obama, Harry Reid and the Secret History of 'Don't Ask, Don't Tell' Repeal."

911   Lieberman interview.

912   Elisabeth Bumiller and Thom Shanker, "Pentagon Says It Is Lifting Ban on Women in Combat," *The New York Times*, January 24, 2013.

913   Margaret Hartmann, "Where the Gay Rights Movement Stands, 1 Year After the Repeal of DOMA" *New York*, June 30, 2014.

914   Jennifer Rizzo and Zachary Cohen, "Pentagon ends transgender ban," CNN, June 30, 2016.

915   Jeremy Diamond, "Trump to reinstate US military ban on transgender people," CNN, July 26, 2017.

916   Lolita C. Baldor, "New Pentagon transgender rules sets limits for troops," The Associated Press, March 12, 2019.

917   Dave Philipps, "As Biden Lifts a Ban, Transgender People Get a Long-Sought Chance to Enlist," *The New York Times*, January 25, 2021.

918   Alex Horton, "Pentagon sets policies for transgender troops to openly serve again, reversing Trump-era ban," *The Washington Post*, March 31, 2021.

919 Grim and Eleveld, "Barack Obama, Harry Reid And The Secret History Of 'Don't Ask, Don't Tell' Repeal."

920 Ed O'Keefe, "Gay troops to file suit challenging Defense of Marriage Act," *The Washington Post*, October 27, 2011.

921 Freedom to Marry, *Meet the McLaughlins* (video), YouTube, October 23, 2012.

922 Freedom to Marry, *Booed Soldier and Husband Boo the Defense of Marriage Act* (video), YouTube, June 11, 2012.

923 Andrew Sullivan, *Virtually Normal* (New York: Alfred A. Knopf, 1995).

924 Chuck Colbert, "Seaside Celebration," *Metro Weekly*, September 19, 2012.

925 Paul D. Shinkman, "First Openly Gay Military Secretary Describes Continued Harassment," *U.S. News & World Report*, June 25, 2013.

926 Thomas Frank, "All That You Can Be," *Oregon Quarterly*, April 13, 2013.

927 Lynn Neary, "Tammy Smith First Openly Gay US General," NPR, August 14, 2012.

928 "Lesbian General Tammy Smith on Being Out in the Military," *The Advocate*, May 7, 2018.

929 Thomas Beaumont, "Pete Buttigieg touts his military service on campaign trail, but is careful to not overstate his role," The Associated Press, November 18, 2019.

930 Pete Buttigieg, "I served in the reserves during the end of 'Don't ask, don't tell.' The fight for equality continues," *Medium*, September 20, 2019.

Chapter 43: Reflections

931 Deb Price, "Gay Troop Proponent Serves America Honorably," *Detroit News*, May 7, 2007.

932 Valelly, "Making a Rainbow Military: Parliamentary Skill and the Repeal of 'Don't Ask, Don't Tell.'"

CPSIA information can be obtained
at www.ICGtesting.com
Printed in the USA
LVHW022234020921
696837LV00004B/10/J

9 781737 482406